# Engineering AutoCAD

# Engineering AutoCAD

**A.P. Gautam**
*Assistant Professor*
*Designer (CAD/CAM)*
Department of Mechanical Engineering
Hi-tech Institute of Engineering & Technology, Ghaziabad

**Pradeep Jain**
*Associate Professor*
Department of Mechanical Engineering
Ajay Kumar Garg Engineering College, Ghaziabad

**KHANNA BOOK PUBLISHING CO. (P) LTD.**
Publisher of Engineering and Computer Books
4C/4344, Ansari Road, Darya Ganj, New Delhi-110002
**Phone** : 011-23244447-48 **Mobile:** +91-9910909320
**E-mail** : contact@khannabooks.com
**Website** : www.khannabooks.com

Dear Readers,

To prevent the piracy, this book is secured with HIGH SECURITY HOLOGRAM on the front title cover. In case you don't find the hologram on the front cover title, please write us to at contact@khannabooks.com or whatsapp us at +91-99109 09320 and avail special gift voucher for yourself.

Specimen of Hologram on front Cover title:

Moreover, there is a SPECIAL DISCOUNT COUPON for you with EVERY HOLOGRAM.

How to avail this SPECIAL DISCOUNT:

Step 1: Scratch the hologram
Step 2: Under the scratch area, your "coupon code" is available
Step 3: Logon to www.khannabooks.com
Step 4: Use your "coupon code" in the shopping cart and get your copy at a special discount
Step 5: Enjoy your reading!

**ISBN:** 978-93-81068-94-6

**Engineering AutoCAD** *by*
Pradeep Jain, A.P. Gautam

First Edition: 2013
**Reprint: 2026**

To view complete list of books, Please scan the QR Code:

KPH

*Published by:*
**Khanna Book Publishing Co. (P) Ltd.**
*CIN: U22110DL1998PTC095547*

Visit us at: **www.khannabooks.com**
Write us at: **contact@khannabooks.com**

Printed in Bharat.

# ✍ *Preface*

The aim of writing this book on the "AutoCAD" is to introducing the AutoCAD software to each and every technical student. The text material of this book is simple to understand inducing example and exercises.

The book consists of 12 chapters. All chapters of the book consist of simple and self explanatory figures. At the end of the book objective type question are given and very helpful clearing interviews based on AutoCAD.

Book has sufficient material arranged in a systematically and easy to understand. Once, student works with this book sincerely no doubt he or she can have commendable knowledge of AutoCAD subject. All the latest techniques, practices and commands which are used in industries are used in this book to bring the students at par

The authors got inspired from the challenges while teaching this subject to the students from different books. This book is comprehensive and single hand guide to the students.

We have taken all the precaution to eliminate errors in text material, example and diagrams, but if you are finding any irrelevant material we will be so happy to know it. We look forward for your valuable feedback

***A. P. Gautam***
***Pardeep Jain***

# Acknowledgement

I am grateful to hon'ble Vice-Chairman Mr. Vihang Garg (HIET), Director General Dr. S.N. Gupta (HIET), Director Dr. Vijay Kumar (HIET) and Dr R. K. Agarwal (Director AKGEC) for their valuable suggestion.

I am also Grateful Prof. P.C. Sharma (HOD, ME Deptt. HIET), Prof. I.P. Sharma (HOD Mech. AKGEC), Prof. M.K. Goel, Prof. P.S. Sandhu, Prof. T.K. Mukharjee and my colleague Mr. B. D. Kaushik, Mr. S.K. Gupta, Mr. R.K. Mohanty, Mr. Ansar Ali, Mr. Neeraj Kumar, Mr. Abhishek Saxena, Mr, Ashwani Prakash. Mrs. Lucky Agarwal, Mr. Rahul Jain (RKGEC), Mr. Dharmendra Singh (RKGEC), Mr. Sachine Thakur (AKGEC), Mr. J.S. Shirohi (AKGEC) for their suggestion

I am special thanks to some industrial person Mr. S.K. Dixit (Director, Creative Robotics Pvt. Ltd), Mr. Danish Faraz (Unitech Technologies Corporation, Meerut) Dr. Deepak Bhalla (Director, Acme Engineering college) and Mr. Gajendra Sharma (Director, Insy Labs) for their support and valuable suggestions for publishing this book.

*A. P. Gautam*
*Pardeep Jain*

## Foreword

I am very glad to introduce a very good book on "AutoCAD" written by Prof. A.P. Gautam and Prof. Pradeep Jain for mechanical and civil engineering students.

Prof. Gautam and Prof. Jain are well versed in industrial application of the AutoCAD, they have fully utilized their knowledge and experience in monument a role for himself by authoring this book, I have gone through this book and in my opinion it is a remarkable piece of work and I am sure that students of mechanical/ civil Engineering will benefitted from this simple and effective book.

I strongly recommend this book for the Mechanical and Civil Engineering Students of any standard.

***Dr. S. N. Gupta***
*Ex Professor and Head*
Mechanical Engineering
I.T. BHU, Varanasi
Director General
HIET, Ghaziabad

# Foreword

I am pleased to introduce a good book on "AutoCAD" written by Prof. A.P. Gautam and Prof. Pradeep Jain for technical student those who want to learn AutoCAD.

Authors have constantly kept in mind the requirement of all the engineering student of Mechanical/civil Branch.

They have taken care to make the book as self explanatory as possible and within the graphical ability of average students.

***Dr. Vijay Kumar***
*Director*
*Ph.D ME*
HIET, Ghaziabad

# Contents

CHAPTER 1

# Concept of Engineering Drawings

## 1. AN ENGINEERING DRAWING

Anengineering drawing, a type oftechnical drawing, is used to fully and clearly define requirements for engineered items.

Engineering drawing (the activity) produces engineering drawings (the documents). More than just the drawing of pictures, it is also a language—a graphical language that communicates ideas and information from one mind to another.

## 2. ENGINEERING DRAWING: COMMAND FEATURE

**Drawings convey the following critical information:**

- Geometry the shape of the object; represented as views; how the object will look when it is viewed from various angles, such as front, top, side, etc.
- Dimensions the size of the object is captured in accepted units.
- Tolerances the allowable variations for each dimension.
- Material represents what the item is made of
- Finish specifies the surface quality of the item, functional or cosmetic. For example, a mass-marketed product usually requires a much higher surface quality than, say, a component that goes inside industrial machinery.

## 3. LINE STYLES AND TYPES

**1.1 Visible lines:** Visible lines represent visible edges and boundaries. The line type is **continuous** and the line weight is **thick** (0.5 - 0.6 mm).

**1.2 Hidden lines:** Hidden lines represent edges and boundaries that cannot be seen. The line type is **dashed** and the line weight is **medium thick** (0.35 - 0.45 mm).

**1.3 Center lines:** Center lines represent axes of symmetry and are important for interpreting cylindrical shapes. Crossed center lines should be drawn at the centers of circles. They are also used to indicate circle of centers and paths of motion. The line type is **long dash – short dash** and the line weight is **thin** (0.3 mm).

**1.4 Phantom lines:** Phantom lines are used to indicate imaginary features. For example, they are used to indicate the alternate positions of moving parts, and adjacent positions of related parts. The line type is **long dash – short dash – short dash** and the line weight is usually **thin** (0.3 mm).

**1.5 Dimension and Extension lines:** Dimension and extension lines are used to show the size of an object. In general, a dimension line is placed between two extension lines and is terminated by arrowheads, which indicates the direction and extent of the dimension. The line type is **continuous** and the line weight is **thin** (0.3 mm).

**1.6 Cutting plane lines:** Cutting plane lines are used to show where an imaginary cut has been made through the object in order to view interior features. The line type is **phantom** and the line weight is **very thick** (0.6 to 0.8 mm). Arrows are placed at both ends of the cutting plane line to indicate the direction of sight.

**1.7 Section lines:** Section lines are used to show areas that have been cut by the cutting plane. Section lines are grouped in parallel line patterns and usually drawn at a 45° angle. The line type is usually **continuous** and the line weight is **thin** (0.3 mm).

**1.8. Break lines:** Break lines are used to show imaginary breaks in objects. A break line is usually made up of a series of connecting arcs. The line type is **continuous** and the line weight is usually **thick** (0.5 – 0.6 mm).

## 4. RULES FOR LINE CREATION AND USE

The rules and guide lines for line creation should be followed in order to create lines that are effective in communicating the drawing information. However, due to computer automation, some of the rules may be hard to follow.

### 4.1 Hidden Lines

Hidden lines represent edges and boundaries that cannot be seen.

**Rule-1.** The length of the hidden line dashes may vary slightly as the size of the drawing changes. For example, a very small part may require smaller dashes in order for the hidden line to be recognized.

**Rule-2.** Hidden lines should always begin and end with a dash, except when the hidden line begins or ends at a parallel visible line.

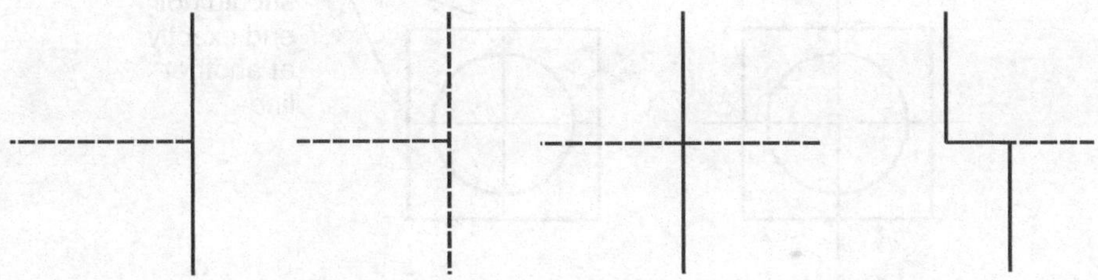

**Rule-3** Dashes should join at corners

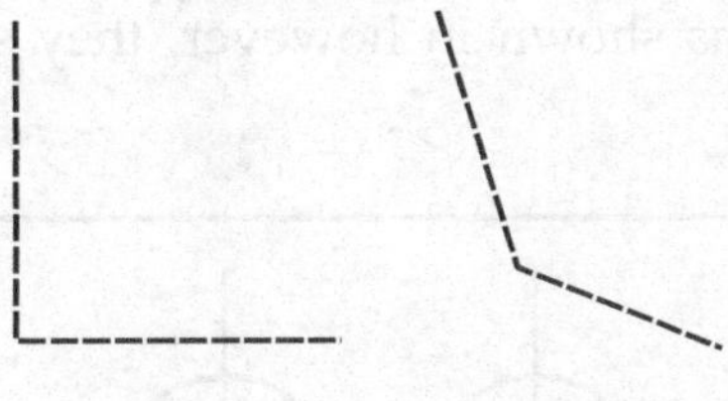

### 4.2 Center Lines

Center lines represent axes of symmetry and are important for interpreting cylindrical Shapes. They are also used to indicate circle of centers and paths of motion

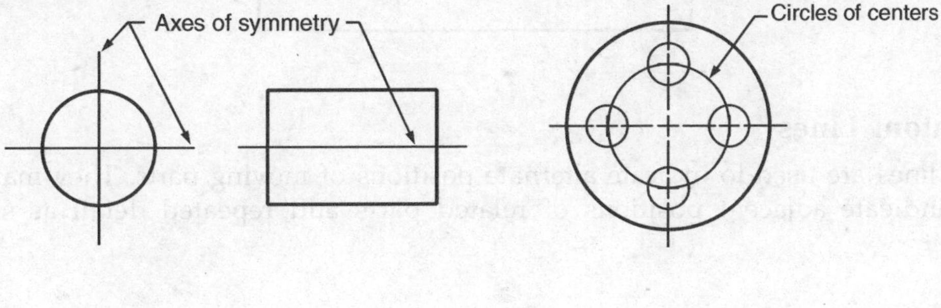

**Rule-1** Center lines should start and end with long dashes

**Rule-2** Center lines should intersect by crossing either the long dashes or the short dashes

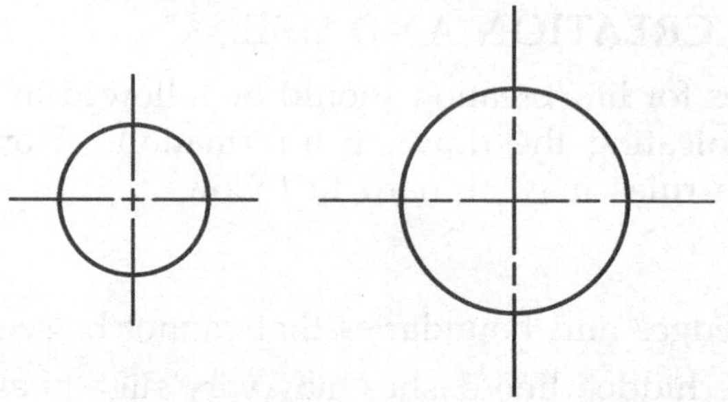

**Rule-3** Center lines should extend a short distance beyond the object or feature. They should not terminate at other lines of the drawing

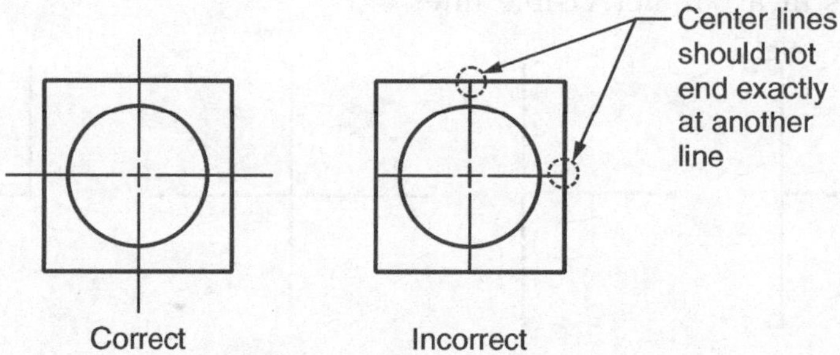


**Rule-4** Center lines may be connected within a single view to show that two or more features lie in the same plane as shown in however, they should not extend through the space between views

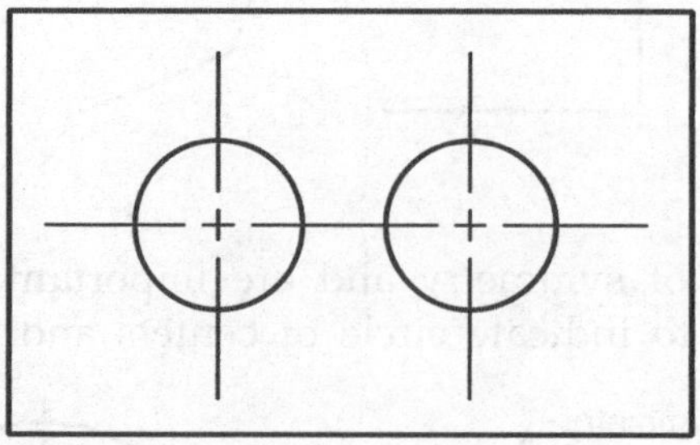

## 4.3 Phantom Lines

Phantom lines are used to indicate alternate positions of moving parts. They may also be used to indicate adjacent positions of related parts and repeated detail as shown in

Figures and rounds in the view that does not show the radius. In this case, the phantom lines are used to show a change in surface direction

**Rule-1** Phantom lines should start and end with a long dash.

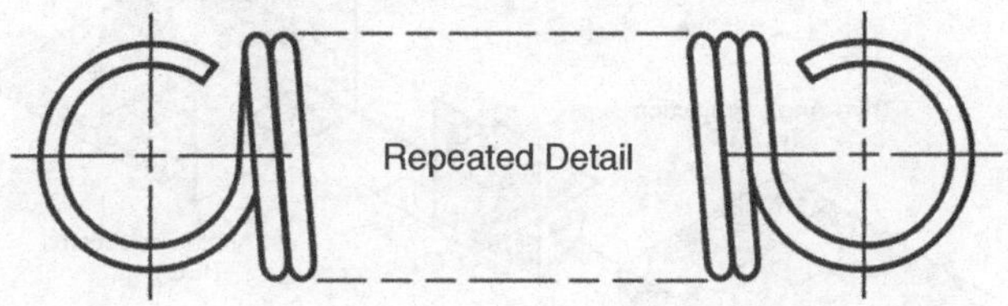


## 4.4 Break Lines

Break lines are used to show imaginary breaks in an object. For example, when drawing a long rod, it may be broken and drawn at a shorter length

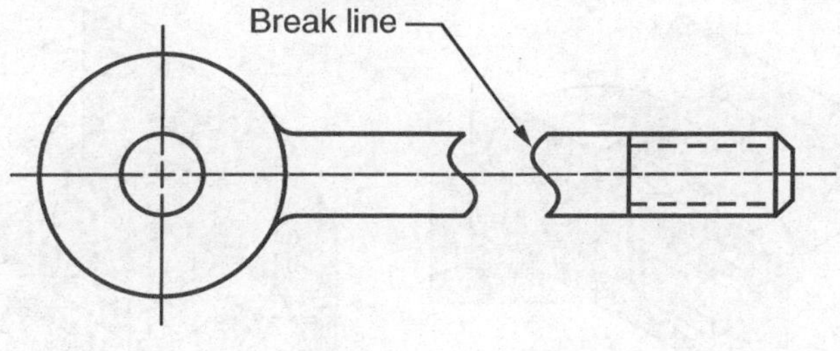


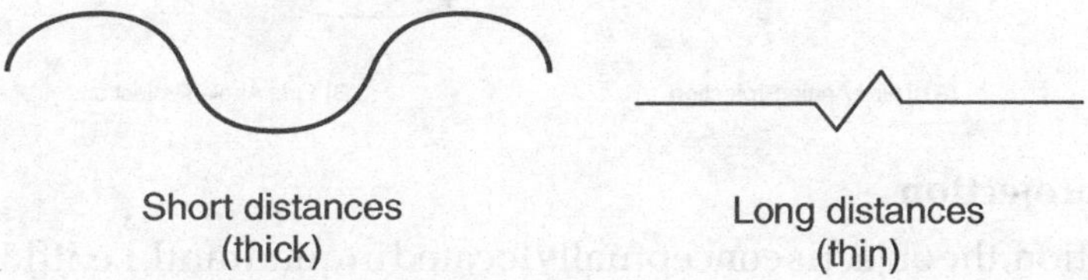


# 5. MULTIPLE VIEWS AND PROJECTIONS

In most cases, a single view is not sufficient to show all necessary features, and several views are used. Types of views include the following:

## 5.1 Orthographic projection

Theorthographic projectionshows the object as it looks from the front, right, left, top, bottom, or back, and are typically positioned relative to each other according to the rules of either first-angle or third-angle projection. The origin and vector direction of the projectors (also called projection lines) differs, as explained below.

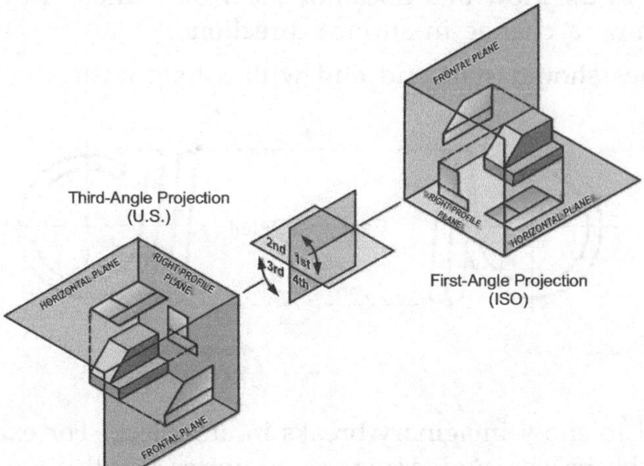


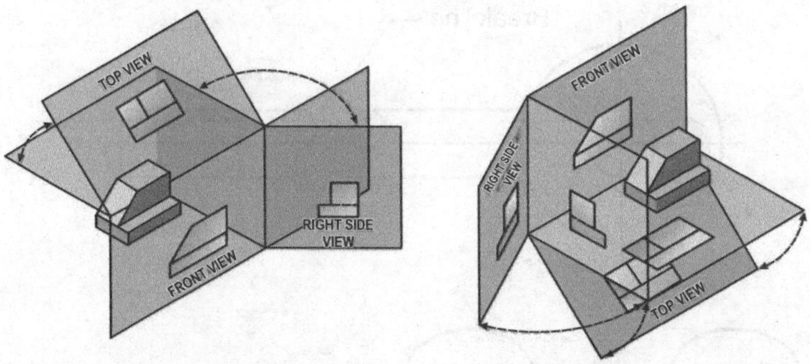


(A) Third-Angle Projection (B) First Angle Projection

### 5.1.1 First-angle projection

In first-angle projection, the object is conceptually located in quadrant I, i.e. it floats above and before the viewing planes, the planes are opaque, and each view is pushed through the object onto the plane furthest from it. (Mnemonic: an "actor on a stage".) Extending to the 6-sided box, each view of the object is projected in the direction (sense) of sight of the object, onto the (opaque) interior walls of the box; that is, each view of the object is drawn on the opposite side of the box. A two-dimensional representation of the object is then created by "unfolding" the box, to view all of the interior walls. This produces two plans and four elevations. A simpler way to visualize this is to place the object on top of an upside-down bowl. Sliding the object down the right edge of the bowl reveals the right side view.

### 5.1.2 Third-angle projection

In third-angle projection, the object is conceptually located in quadrant III, i.e. it is positioned below and behind the viewing planes, the planes are transparent, and each view is pulled onto the plane closest to it. (Mnemonic: a "shark in a tank", esp. that is sunken into the floor.) Using the 6-sided viewing box, each view of the object is projected opposite to the direction (sense) of sight, onto the (transparent) exterior walls of the box; that is, each view of the object is drawn on the same side of the box. The box is then unfolded to view all of its exterior walls. A simpler way to visualize this is to place the object in the bottom of a bowl. Sliding the object up the right edge of the bowl reveals the right side view.

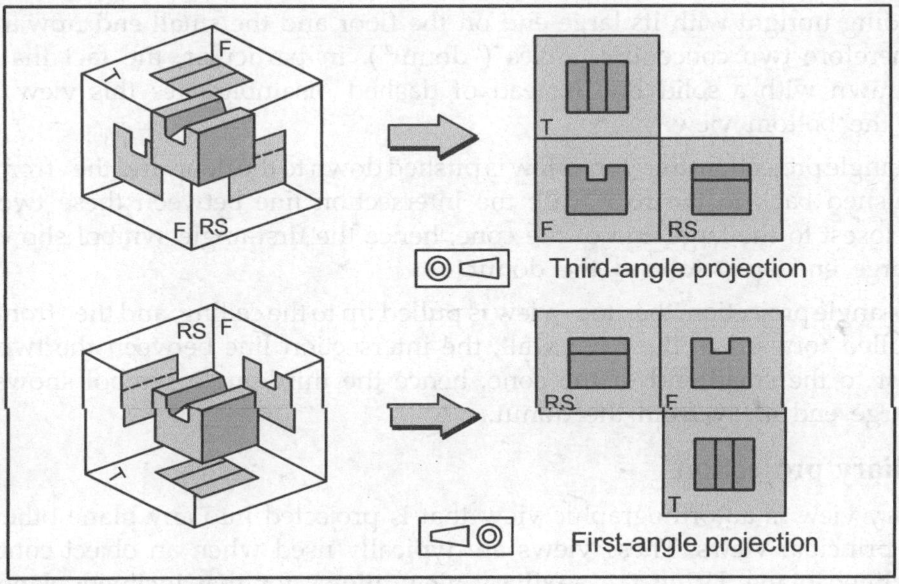


### 5.1.3 Additional information

First-angle projection is as if the object were sitting on the paper and, from the "face" (front) view, it is rolled to the right to show the left side or rolled up to show its bottom. It is standard throughout Europe (excluding the UK) and Asia. First-angle projection used to be common in the UK, and may still be seen on historical design drawings, but has now fallen into disuse in favor of third-angle projection.

Third-angle is as if the object were a box to be unfolded. If we unfold the box so that the front view is in the center of the two arms, then the top view is above it, the bottom view is below it, the left view is to the left, and the right view is to the right. It is standard in the United Kingdom (BS 8888:2006 specifies it as the default projection system), USA (ASME Y14.3-2003 specifies it as the default projection system), Canada, and Australia.

Both first-angle and third-angle projections result in the same 6 views; the difference between them is the arrangement of these views around the box.

A great deal of confusion has ensued in drafting rooms and engineering departments when drawings are transferred from one convention to another. On engineering drawings, the projection angle is denoted by an international symbol consisting of a truncatedcone, respectively for first-angle (FR) and third-angle (US):

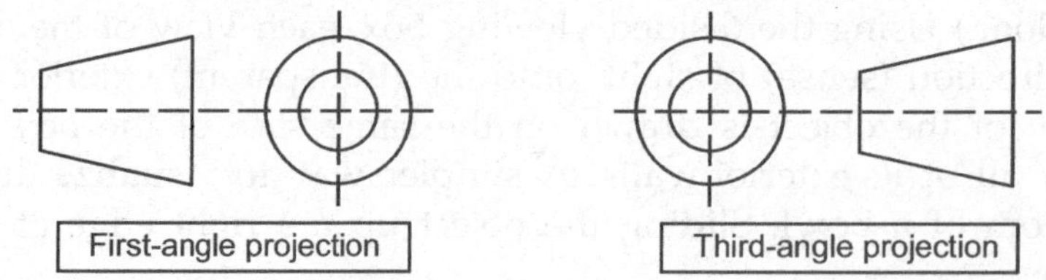


The 3D interpretation of the symbol can be deduced by envisioning a solid truncated cone, standing upright with its large end on the floor and the small end upward. The top view is therefore two concentric circles ("donut"). In particular, the fact that the inner circle is drawn with a solid line instead of dashed disambiguates this view as the top view, not the bottom view.

Infirst-angleprojection,the top view is pushed down to the floor, and the front view is pushed back to the rear wall; the intersection line between these two planes is therefore closest to the large end of the cone, hence the first-angle symbol shows the cone with its large end open toward the donut.

Inthird-angle projection,the top view is pulled up to the ceiling, and the *front* view is pulled forward to the front wall; the intersection line between the two planes is thus closest to the small end of the cone, hence the third-angle symbol shows the cone with its large end away from the donut.

## 5.2 Auxiliary projection

An auxiliary view is an orthographic view that is projected into any plane other than one of the six principal views. These views are typically used when an object contains some sort of inclined plane. Using the auxiliary view allows for that inclined plane (and any other significant features) to be projected in their true size and shape. The true size and shape of any feature in an engineering drawing can only be known when the Line of Sight (LOS) is perpendicular to the plane being referenced. It is shown like a 3 dimensional object.

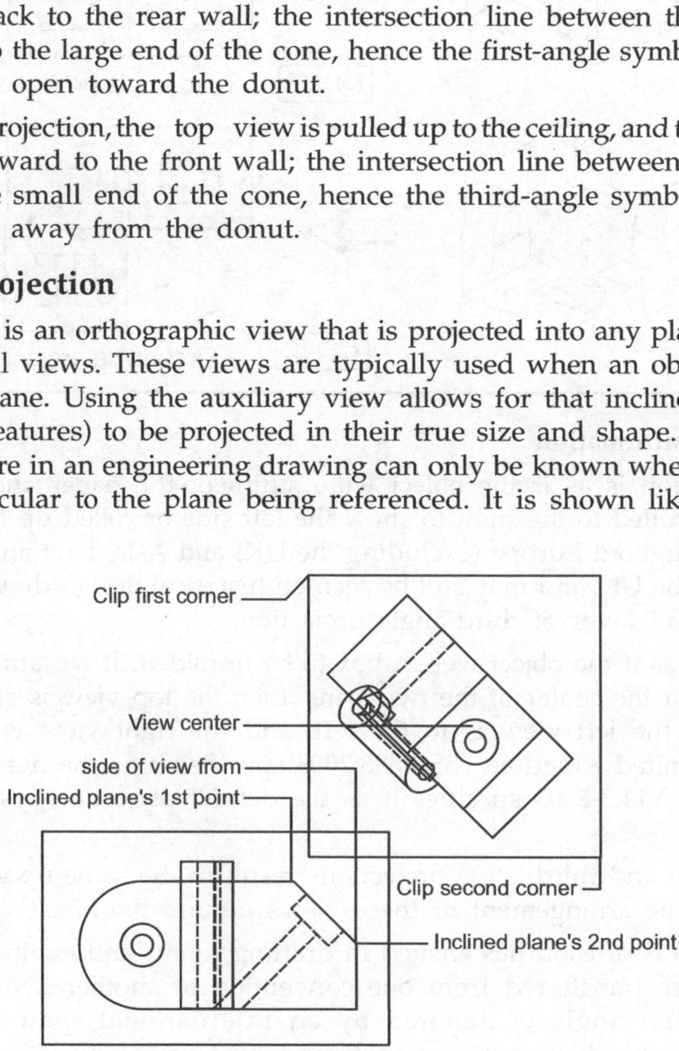

## 5.3 Isometric projection

Theisometric projectionshow the object from angles in which the scales along each axis of the object are equal. Isometric projection corresponds to rotation of the object by ± 45° about the vertical axis, followed by rotation of approximately ± 35.264° [= arcsin(tan(30°))] about the horizontal axis starting from an orthographic projection view. "Isometric" comes from the Greek for "same measure". One of the things that make isometric drawings so attractive is the ease with which 60 degree angles can be constructed with only acompassand straightedge.

Isometric projection is a type of axonometric projection. The other two types of axonometric projection are:

- Diametric projection
- Trimetric projection

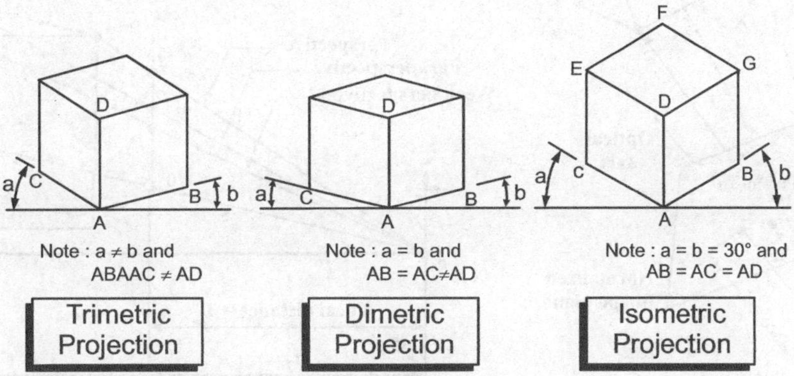


## 5.4 Oblique projection

Anobliqueprojectionisasimpletypeofgraphicalprojectionusedforproducingpictorial, two-dimensionalimagesof three-dimensional objects:

- it projects an image by intersecting parallel rays (projectors)
- From the three-dimensional source object with the drawing surface (projection plan).

In both oblique projection and orthographic projection, parallel lines of the source object produce parallel lines in the projected image.

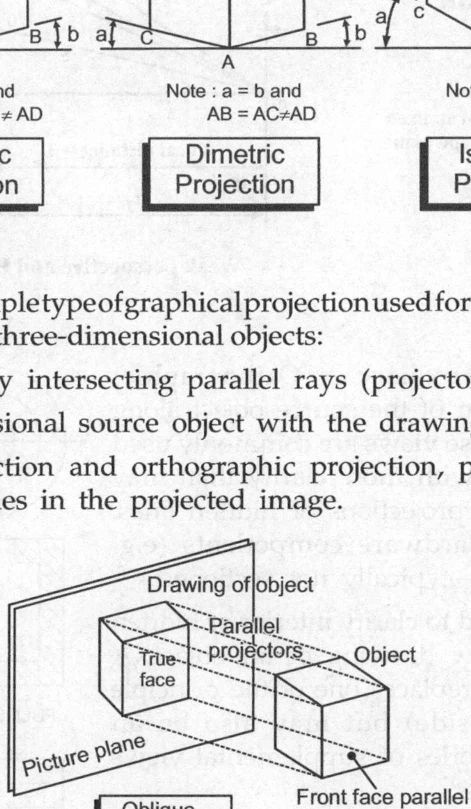

## 5.5 Perspective

Perspectiveis an approximate representation on a flat surface, of an image as it is perceived by the eye. The two most characteristic features of perspective are that objects are drawn:

- Smaller as their distance from the observer increases
- Foreshortened: the size of an object's dimensions along the line of sight is relatively shorter than dimensions across the line of sight.

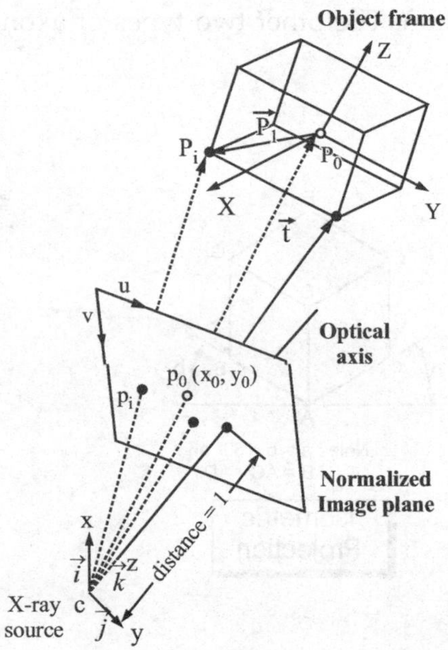


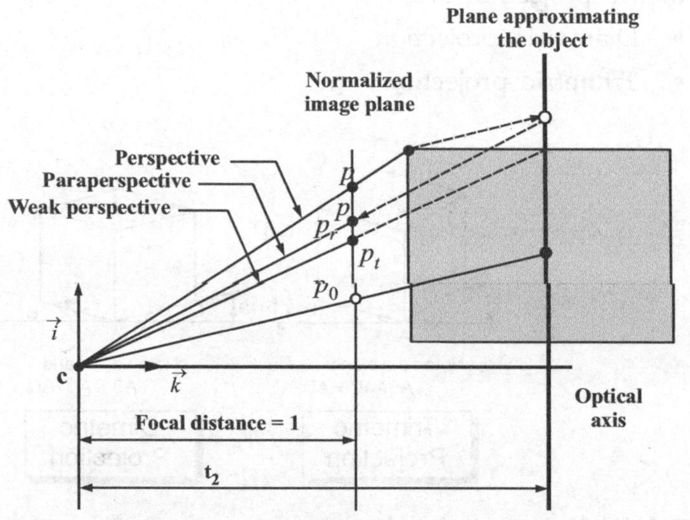


Weak perspective and Perspective projection

## 5.6 Section Views

Projected views (either Auxiliary or Orthographic) which show a cross section of the source object along the specified cut plane. These views are commonly used to show internal features with more clarity than may be available using regular projections or hidden lines. In assembly drawings, hardware components (e.g. nuts, screws, washers) are typically not sectioned.

- Sectional views are used to clarify interior or hidden details on a multi-view drawing of an object. A sectional view usually replaces one of the principle views (top, front or side) but may also be an additional view or a series of supplemental views depending on the type.

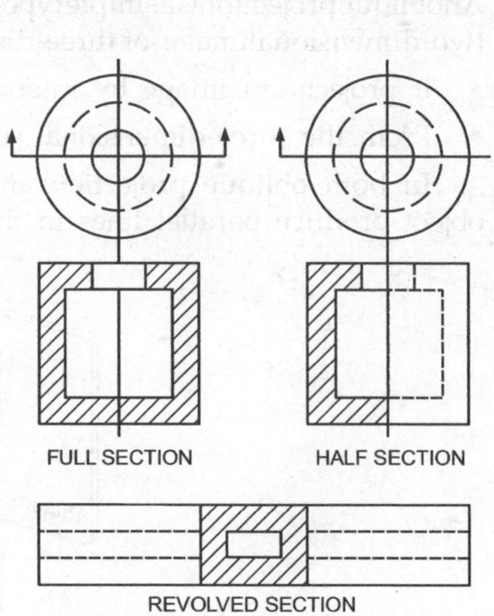

- There are many types of sectional views: Full, Half, Removed, Revolved (Rotated), Aligned, Offset, Broken-out, Partial, Assembly and Pictorial.
- A Full Section view is used to show the object as if one half of the object was removed.
- A Half Section view is used to show the object as if one quarter of the object was removed.
- A Removed Section view is used to show the variable shape of the object from end to end.
- A Revolved (Rotated) Section view is used to show the uniform shape of the object from end to end.
- An Aligned Section view is used to show the shape of features that do not align with the vertical and horizontal center lines of the object.
- A Broken-out Section view is used to show the material thickness of a hollow object.
- A Partial Section view is similar to a Broken-out but usually covers a larger area but less than a Half Section.
- An Assembly Section is used to show the arrangement and relationship of parts that makeup an object.
- A Pictorial Section is used to show the arrangement and relationship of parts that makeup an object in a three dimensional view with a quarter to a half of the object removed.
- Sectional views are located by creating a Cutting Plane Line in one view. The Cutting Plane Line is a thick, dark line composed of a long dash, two short dashes and a long dash. An optional Cutting Plane Line consisting of thick, dark, long dashes may also be used. Short perpendicular lines with arrowheads pointing away from the line are added to each end to indicate the viewing direction or line of sight. The arrows should also point away from the view that is sectioned. Identification "Letters" (A-A, B-B, C-C, etc.) should be placed above the arrows when more than one section view is needed on a drawing.

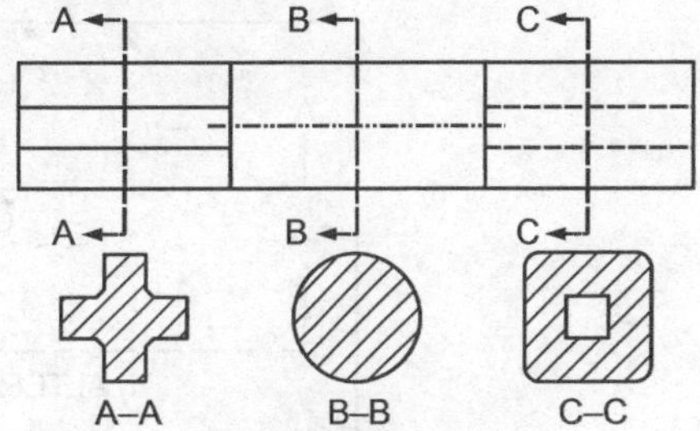


REMOVED SECTIONS

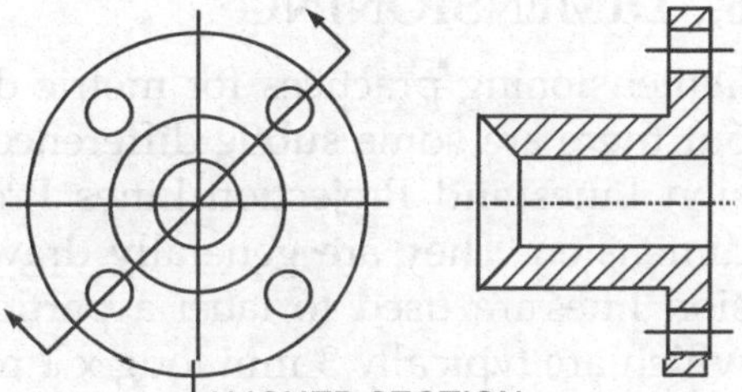

ALIGNED SECTION

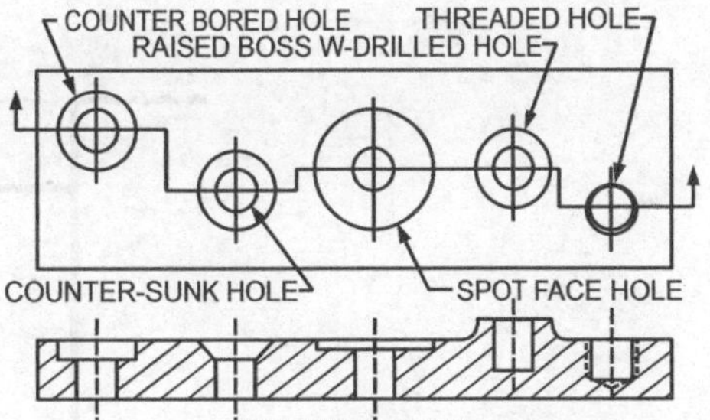


OFFSET SECTION

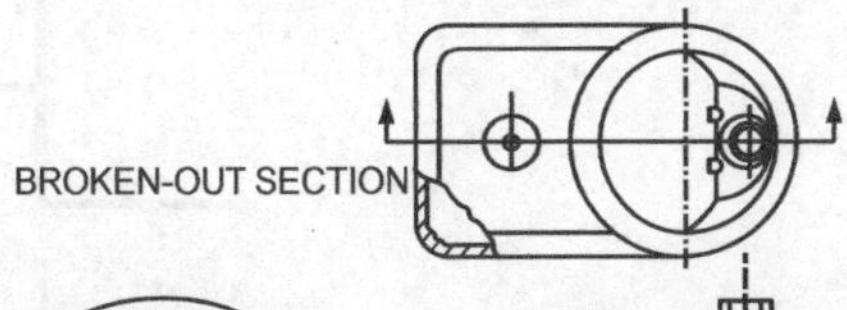


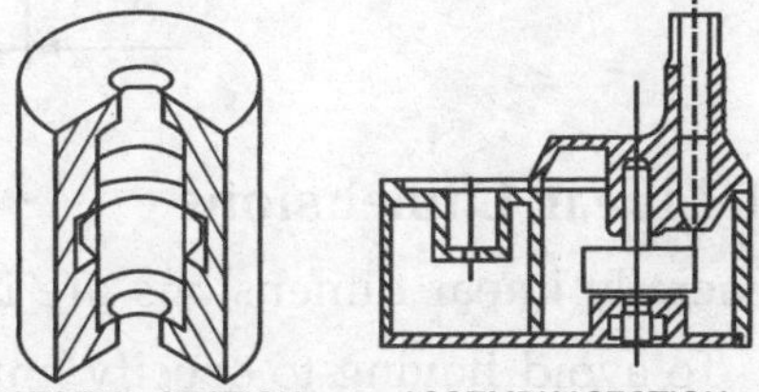

PICTORIAL SECTION ASSEMBLY SECTION

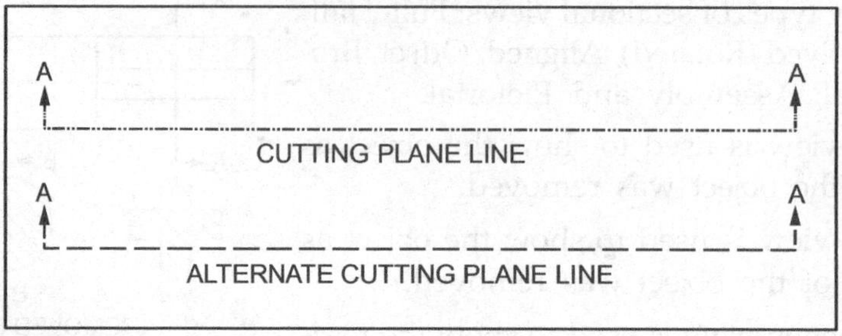


## 6. DIMENSIONING

Dimensioning practices for metric drawings are similar to those for non-metric drawings, but there are some subtle differences. This material outlines the current practices. Dimension Lines and Projection Lines Projection lines are used to indicate the extremities of a dimension. They are generally drawn up to 1 mm from the outline of the object. Dimension lines are used to label a particular dimension. They have one or more arrowheads, which are typically 3 mm long x 1 mm wide. Thin type B lines are used for both projection lines and dimension lines.

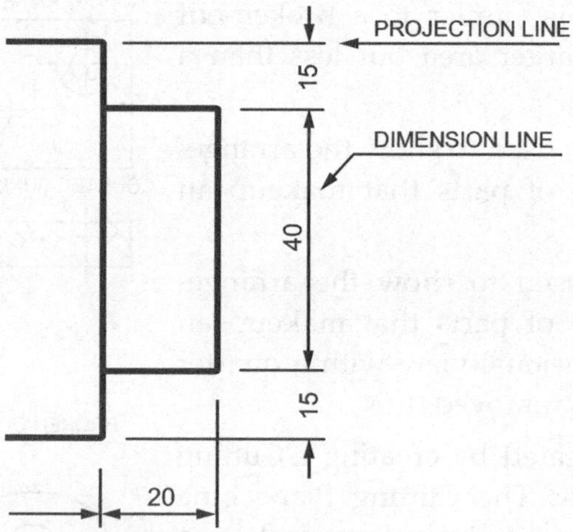


### 6.1 Linear Dimensions

Generally linear dimensions are in millimeters (millimeter).

To avoid having to specify 'mm' after every dimension, a label such as 'all dimensions in mm' or 'unless otherwise stated all dimensions are in mm' is usually contained in the title block.

If the dimension is less than one a leading zero should be used before the decimal point. After reduction to microfilm and subsequent re-enlargement, the decimal point may sometimes become unreadable. To avoid possible misreading of the dimension a comma is often used instead of a decimal point.

## 6.2 Angular Dimensions

Angular dimensions are usually specified in decimal degrees, degrees and minutes, or degrees minutes and seconds.

eg.27.5 27 30′27 30 16"

If the angle is less than one degree a leading zero should be used.

eg.0.5 0 30′

## 6.3 Dimensioning Methods

Two methods of dimensioning are in common use.

- **Unidirectional-** The dimensions are written horizontally.
- **Aligned-** The dimensions are written parallel to their dimension line. Aligned dimensions should always be readable from the bottom or the right of the drawing.

Unidirectional Dimensioning Aligned Dimensioning

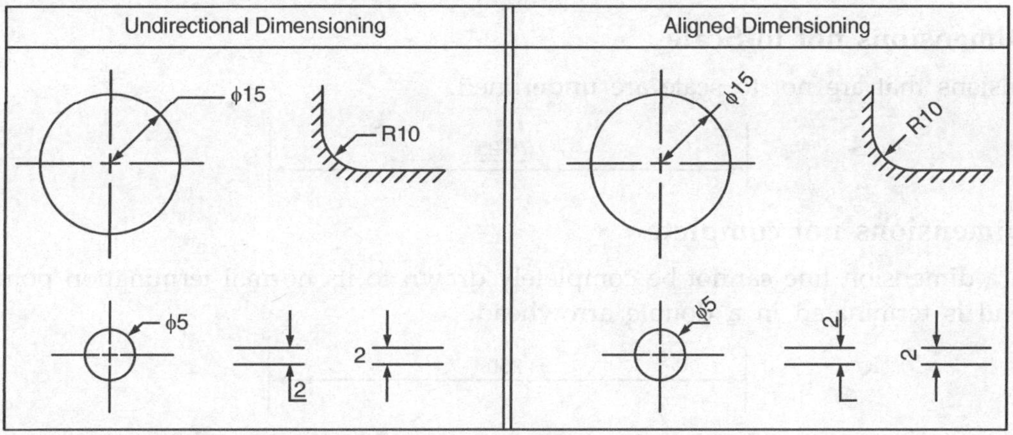


## 6.4 OVERALL DIMENSIONS

When several dimensions make up an overall length, the overall dimension can be shown outside these component dimensions.

When specifying an overall dimension, one or more non-critical component dimensions must be omitted.

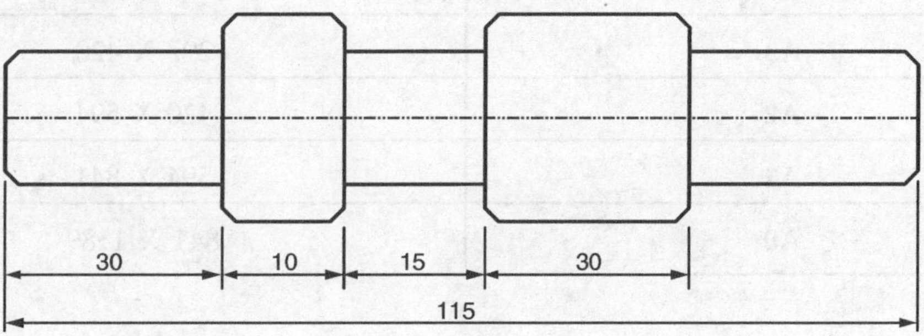

## 6.5 Auxiliary Dimensions

When all of the component dimensions must be specified, an overall length may still be specified as an auxiliary dimension.

Auxiliary dimensions are never tolerance, and are shown in brackets.

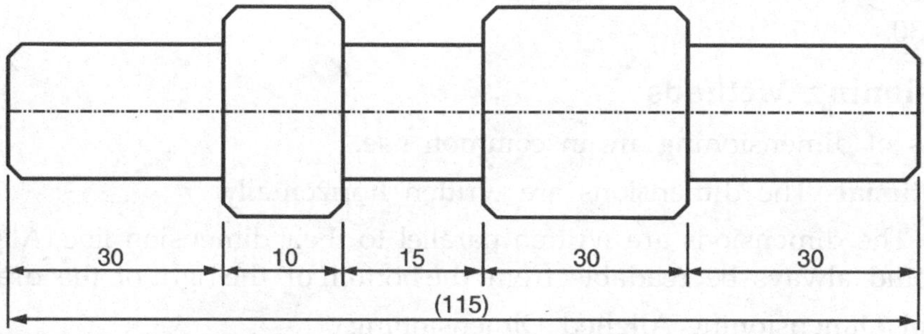


## 6.6 Dimensions not to Scale

Dimensions that are not to scale are underlined.

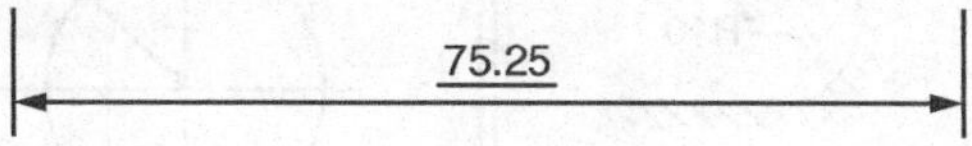


## 6.7 Dimensions not complete

When a dimension line cannot be completely drawn to its normal termination point, the free end is terminated in a double arrowhead.

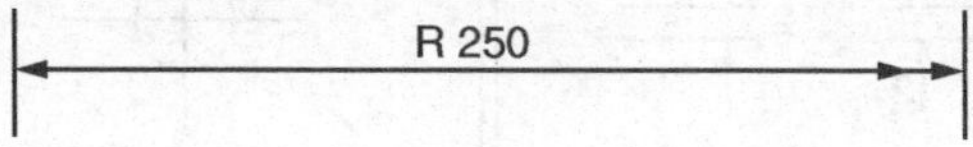


## 7. SIZES OF DRAWINGS

Sizes of drawings typically comply with either of two different standards, ISO (World Standard) or ANSI/ASME Y14 (American), according to the following tables:

| ISO | |
|---|---|
| **A4** | 210 X 297 |
| **A3** | 297 X 420 |
| **A2** | 420 X 594 |
| **A1** | 594 X 841 |
| **A0** | 841 X 1189 |

| ANSI/ASME Drawing Sizes (inches) | |
|---|---|
| **A** | 8.5" X 11" |
| **B** | 11" X 17" |
| **C** | 17" X 22" |
| **D** | 22" X 34" |
| **E** | 34" X 44" |

| Other U.S. Drawing Sizes | |
|---|---|
| **D1** | 24" X 36" |
| **E1** | 30" X 42" |
| **H** | largerstill[intercompanystandards] |
| **I** | largerstill[intercompanystandards] |
| **J** | largerstill[intercompanystandards] |

The metric drawing sizes correspond to international paper sizes. These developed further refinements in the second half of the twentieth century, when photocopying became cheap. Engineering drawings could be readily doubled (or halved) in size and put on the next larger (or, respectively, smaller) size of paper with no waste of space. And the metrictechnicalpenswerechoseninsizessothatonecouldadddetailordraftingchanges with a pen width changing by approximately a factor of the square root of 2. A full set of pens would have the following nib sizes: 0.13, 0.18, 0.25, 0.35, 0.5, 0.7, 1.0, 1.5, and 2.0mm.However,theInternationalOrganizationforStandardization(ISO)calledforfour pen widths and set a colour code for each: 0.25 (white), 0.35 (yellow), 0.5 (brown), 0.7 (blue); these nibs produced lines that related to various text character heights and the ISO paper sizes.

All ISO paper sizes have the same aspect ratio, one to the square root of 2, meaning that a document designed for any given size can be enlarged or reduced to any other size and will fit perfectly. Given this ease of changing sizes, it is of course common to copy or print a given document on different sizes of paper, especially within a series, e.g. a drawing on A3 may be enlarged to A2 or reduced to A4.

The U.S. customary "A-size" corresponds to "letter" size, and "B-size" corresponds to "ledger" or "tabloid" size. There were also once British paper sizes, which went by names rather than alphanumeric designations.

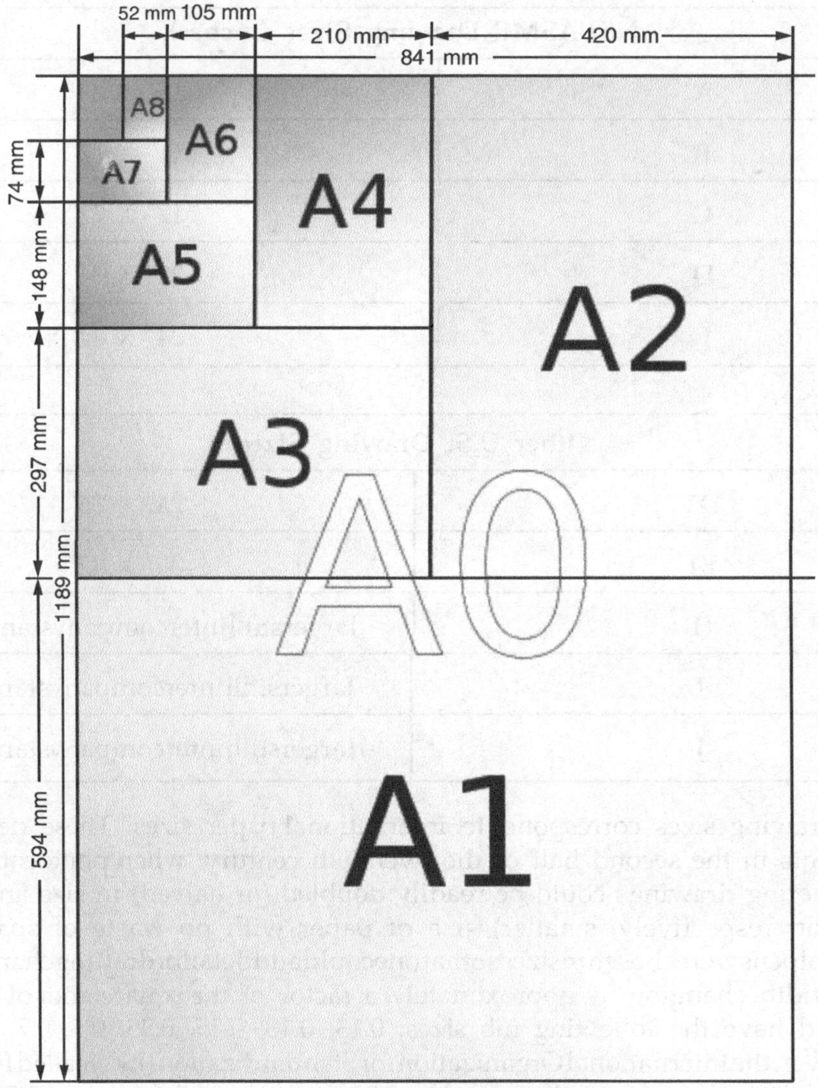
52 mm
105 mm
210 mm
420 mm
841 mm
74 mm
148 mm
297 mm
1189 mm
594 mm
A8
A7
A6
A5
A4
A3
A2
A1
A0

CHAPTER
2

# An Introduction of AutoCAD

## 1. WHAT IS AUTOCAD?

AutoCAD is a software package used for drafting and designing almost anything you wish. The software has evolved massively over the years and now offers various 'themed' versions catering for the specific requirements of different engineering disciplines, such as mechanical engineering, civil engineering and architecture.

Basically AutoCAD provides a 3D space (model space) in which you construct or draw your design. It provides drawing layout tools which enable you to prepare and plot conventional 2D drawings of your model. More recent versions also include advanced rendering tools, enabling you to create photo-realistic images of your design.

## 2. THE INTERFACE

Standard Windows type command buttons, pull down menus etc. are provided to use AutoCAD. One strong feature of AutoCAD is the continued support of its **command line.** Any function or command you can give AutoCAD can be given by typing in the appropriate command on the screen. AutoCAD supports legacy commands, from previous versions, so learning to use AutoCAD through the command line means you should be able to use any subsequent or previous releases of the software without getting lost in the menu systems.

This manual will encourage you to use the command line but may also involve use of tool bars and pull down menus.

## 3. AUTOCAD DISPLAY SCREEN

### 3.1 AutoCAD classic mode

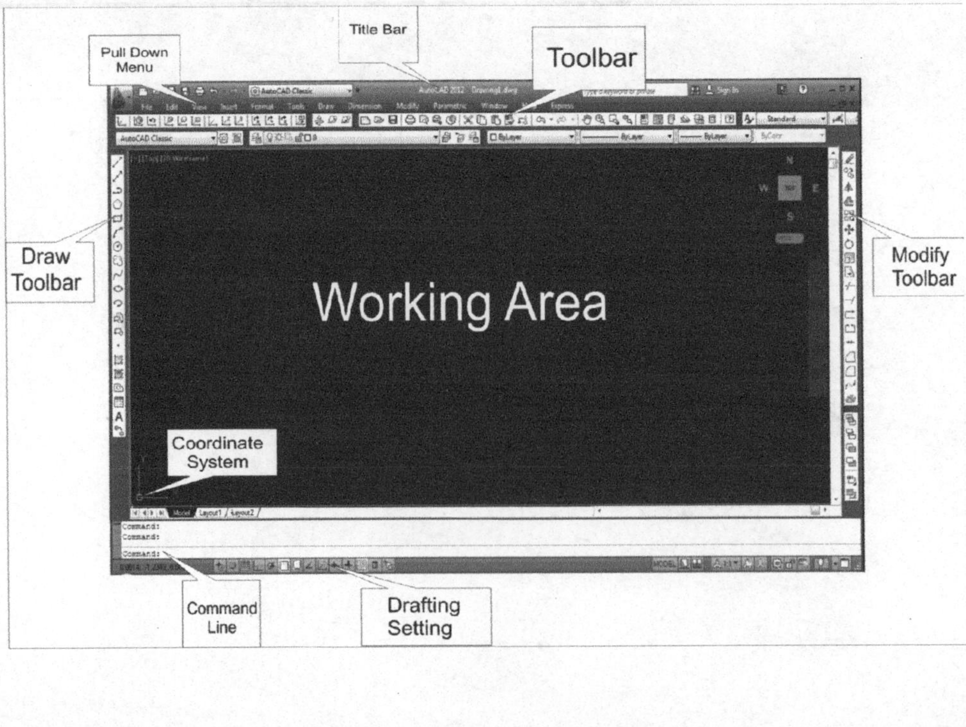

## 3.2 3D Modeling Mode

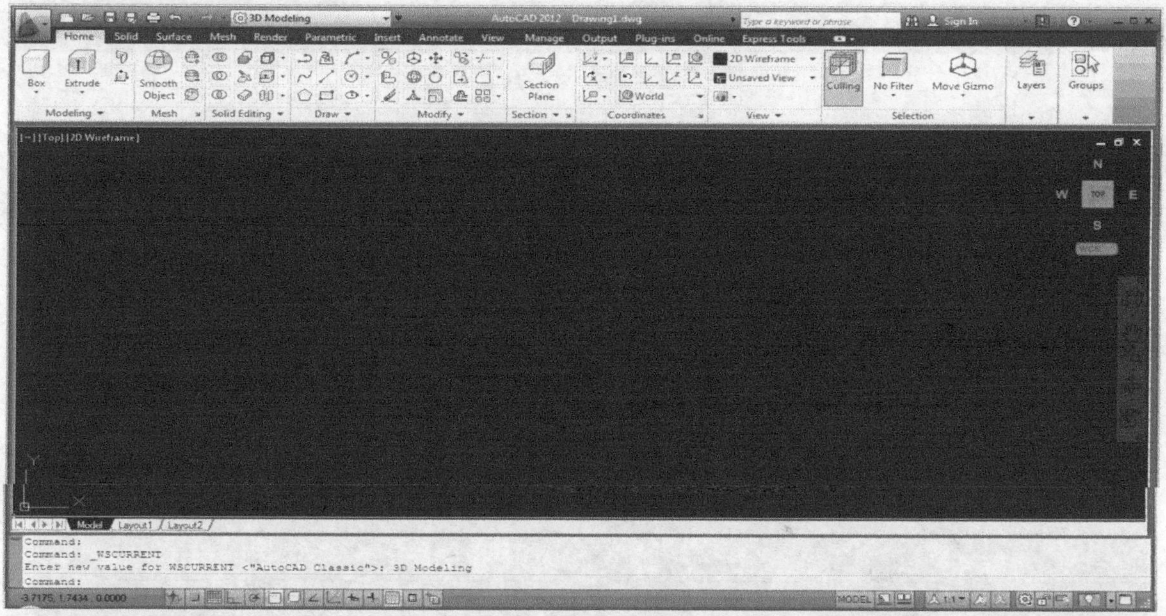

## 3.3 3D Basics Mode

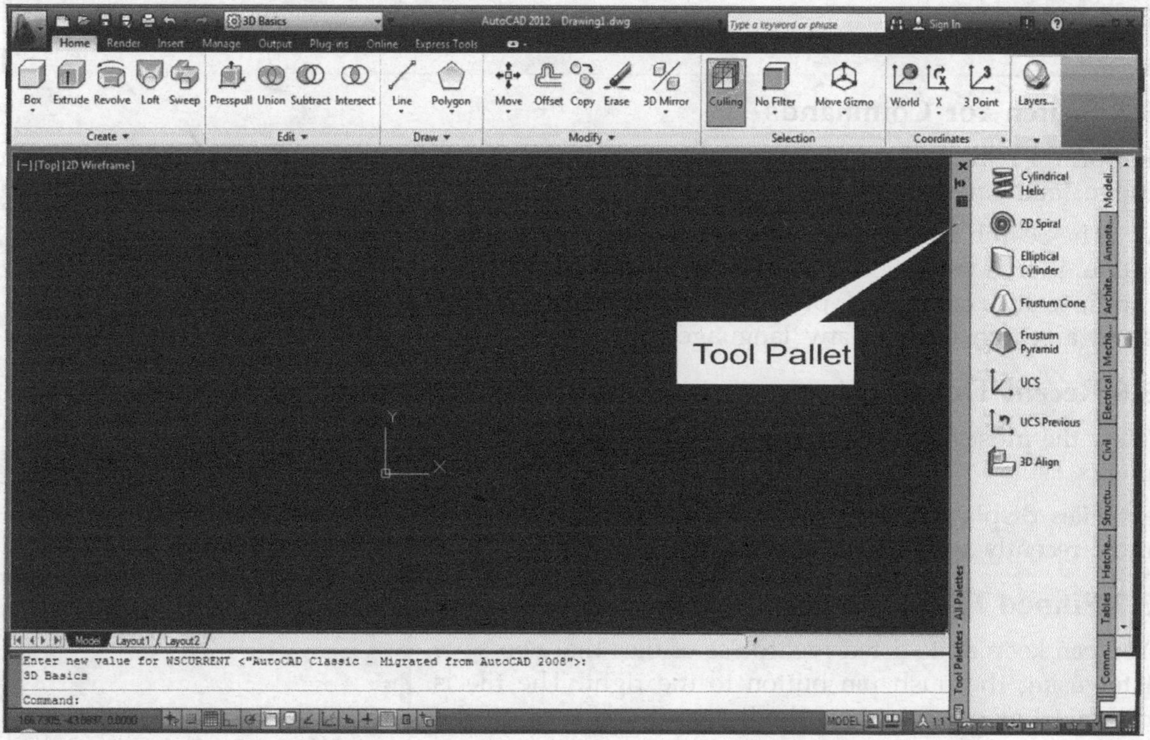

## 3.4 Drafting Annotation Mode

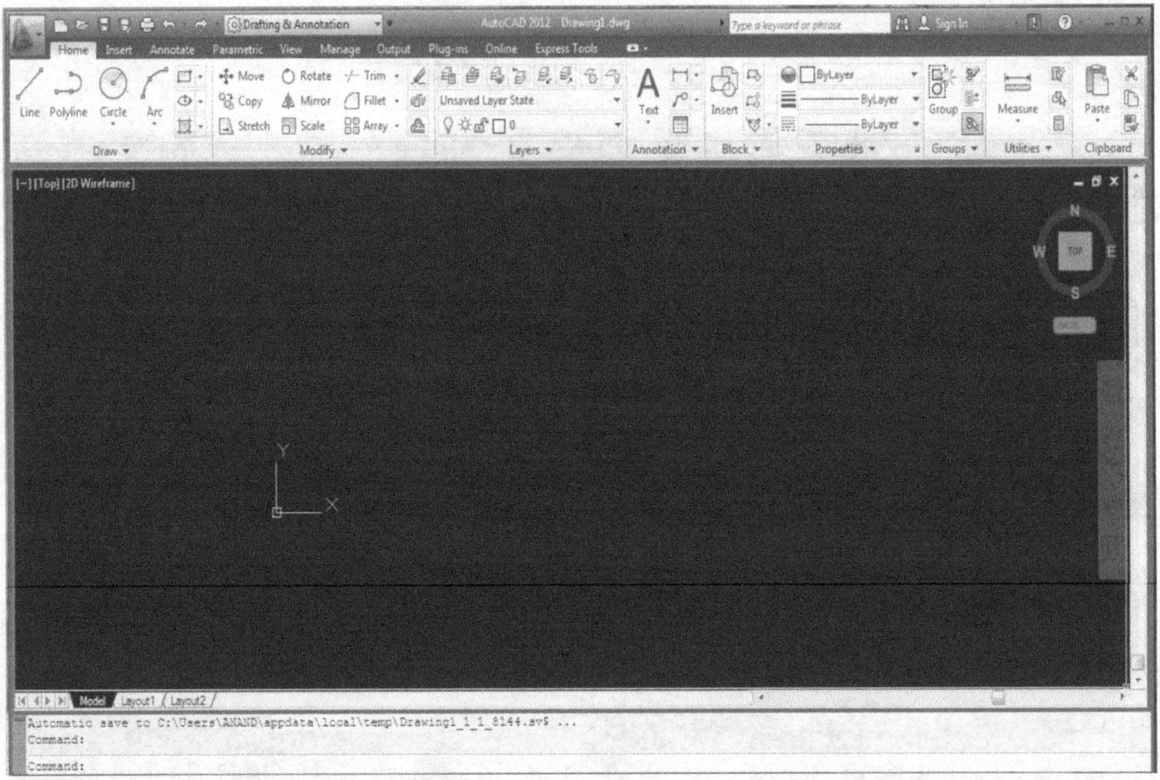

## 3.5 Search for Commands

Perform a real-time search for commands on the Quick Access toolbar, in the application menu, and on the ribbon.

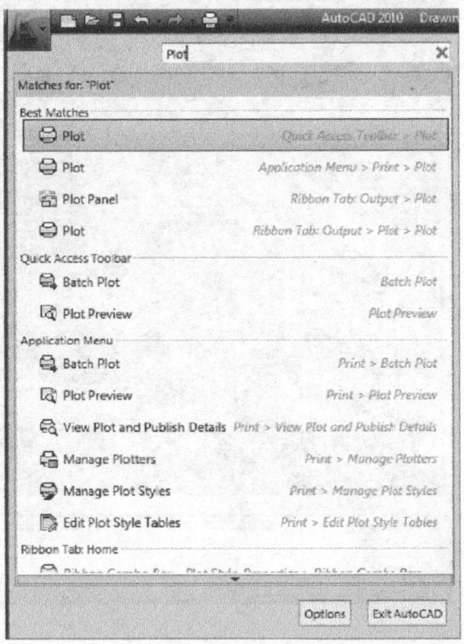

The Search field displays at the top of the application menu. Search results can include menu commands, basic tooltips, and command prompt text strings. You can enter a search term in any language.

## 3.6 Recent Documents

View the most recently used files with the Recent Documents list.

Files display in the Recent Documents list with the most recently used file at the top by default.

## 3.7 Pinned Files

You can keep a file listed regardless of files that you save later using the push pin button to the right. The file is displayed at the bottom of the list until you turn off the push pin button.

## Sort and Group Options

Use the drop-down list at the top of the Recent Documents list to sort or group files by

- File name
- File size
- File type
- Date the files were last modified

## To change the preview display options for recent documents

1. Click the Application menu and then, click Recent Documents.
2. Under the Search text box, click the Display Options menu.
3. Select a display option.

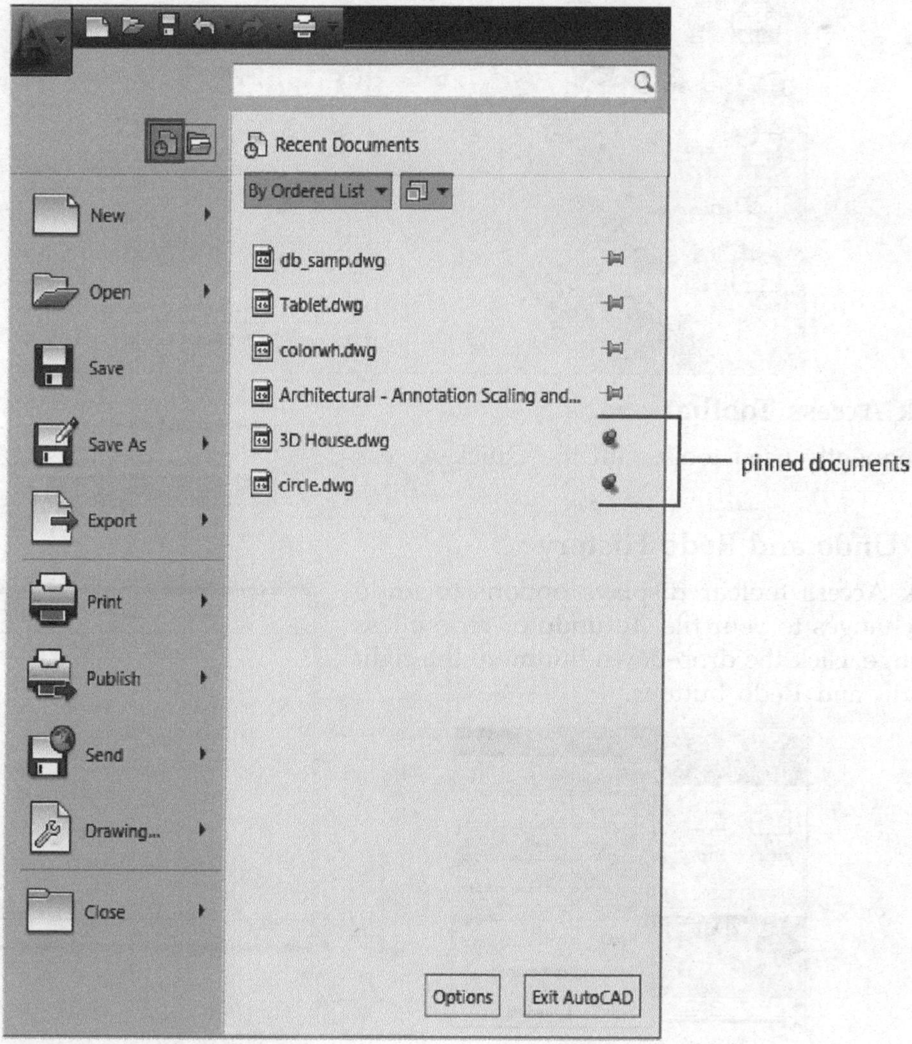

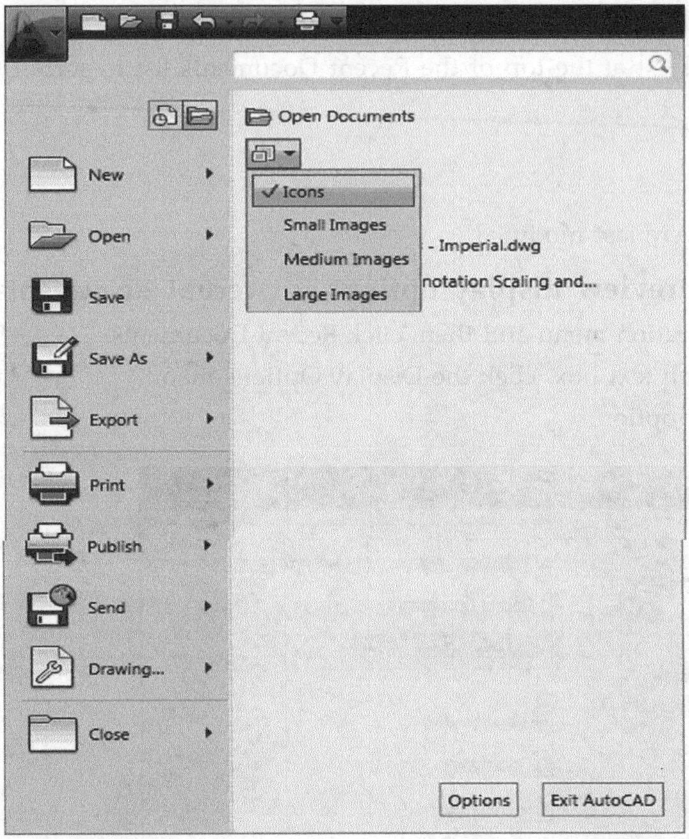


## 3.8 Quick Access Toolbar

Display frequently used tools with the Quick Access toolbar.

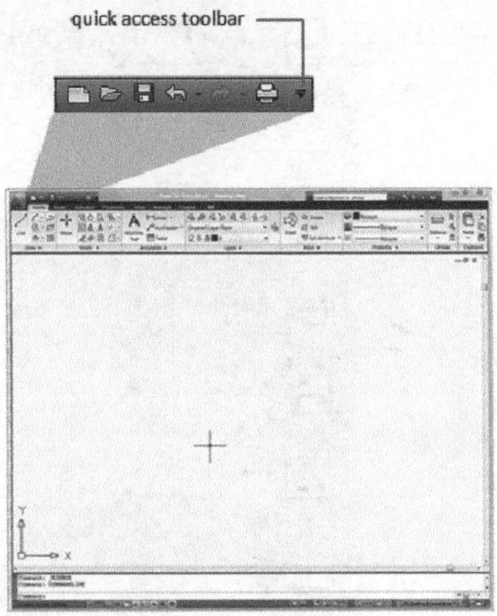


## 3.9 View Undo and Redo History

The Quick Access toolbar displays options to undo and redo changes to your file. To undo or redo a less recent change, click the drop-down button to the right of the Undo and Redo buttons.

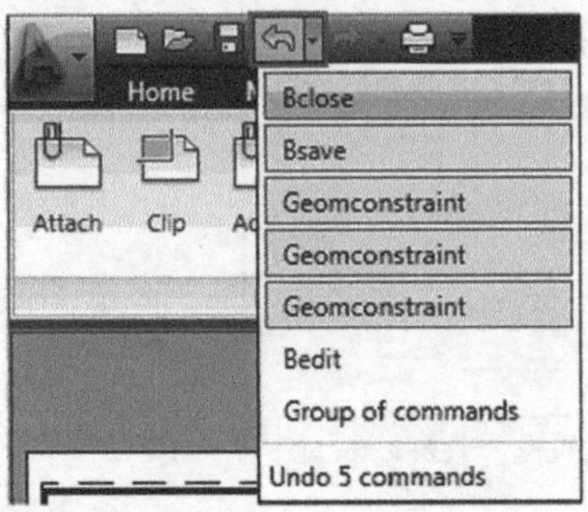

## 3.10 Add Commands and Controls

Add unlimited tools to the Quick Access toolbar. Tools that extend past the maximum length of the toolbar are displayed in a flyout button.

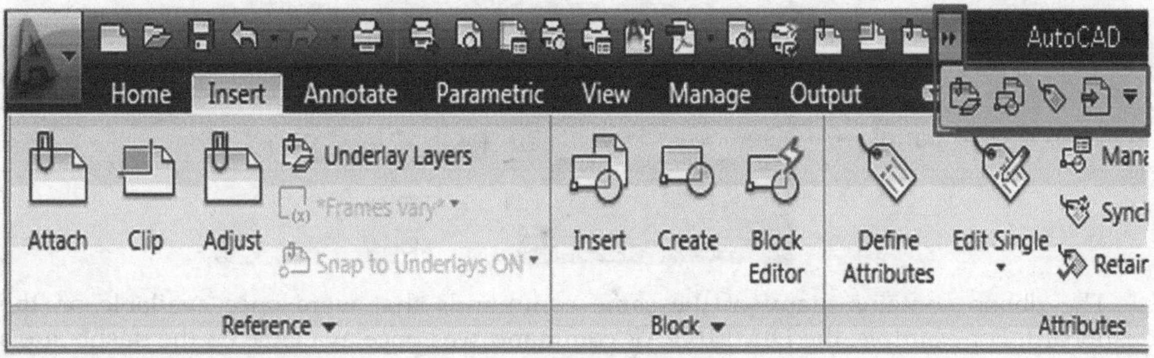


To add a ribbon button to the Quick Access toolbar, right-click the button on the ribbon and click Add to Quick Access toolbar. Buttons are added to the right of the default commands on the Quick Access toolbar.

## 3.11 Move the Quick Access Toolbar

Place the Quick Access toolbar either above or below the ribbon using the Customization button.

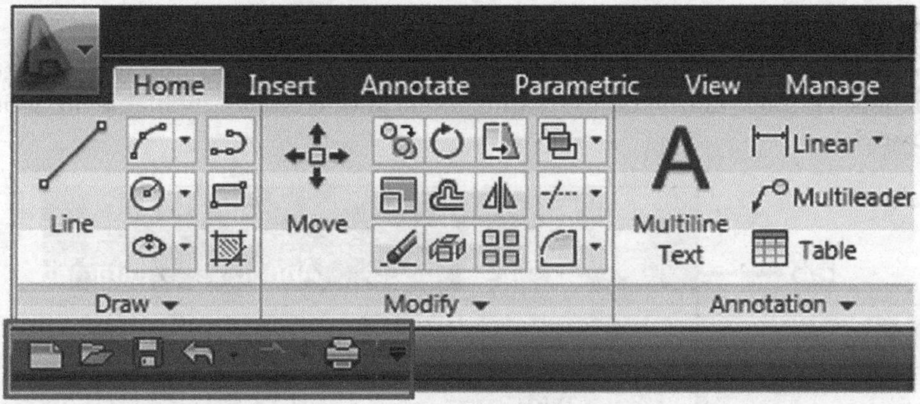


## 3.12 Overview of the Ribbon

The ribbon is displayed automatically when you create or open a file, providing a compact palette of all of the tools necessary to create your file.

The ribbon contains many of the same commands that were once available on the dashboard. For example, the DIMLINEAR command was once available on the dashboard's Dimensions control panel. On the ribbon, DIMLINEAR *is located on the Annotation tab*, in the Dimensions panel.

## 3.13 Display and Organize the Ribbon

The ribbon is displayed horizontally or vertically.

The horizontal ribbon is displayed across the top of the file window. You can dock the vertical ribbon to the left or right of the application window.

The vertical ribbon can also float in the file window or on a second monitor.

## 3.14 Ribbon Tabs and Panels

The ribbon is composed of a series of panels, which are organized into tabs labeled by task. Ribbon panels contain many of the same tools and controls available in toolbars and dialog boxes.

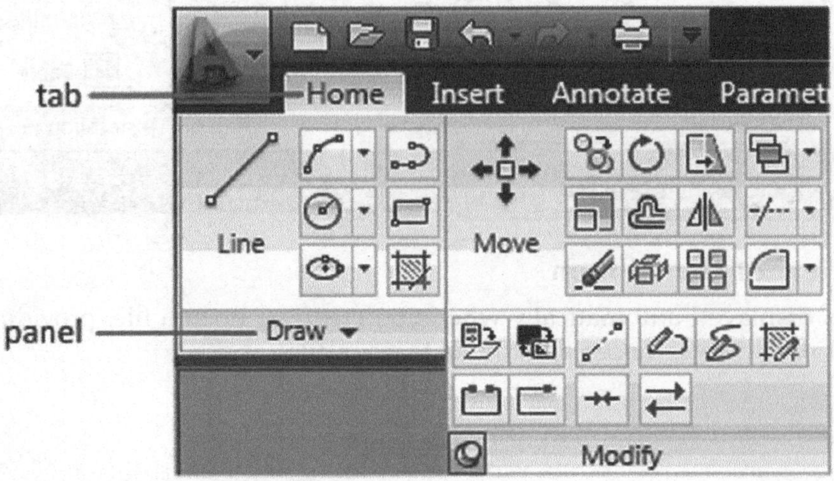

Some ribbon panels display a dialog box related to that panel. An icon in the lower-right corner of the panel indicates that you can display a related dialog box. Click the icon to display the associated dialog box.

To specify which ribbon tabs and panels are displayed, right-click the ribbon and, on the shortcut menu, click or clear the names of tabs or panels.

### 3.15 Floating Panels

If you pull a panel off of a ribbon tab and into the drawing area or onto another monitor, that panel floats where you placed it. The floating panel remains open until you return it to the ribbon, even if you switch ribbon tabs.

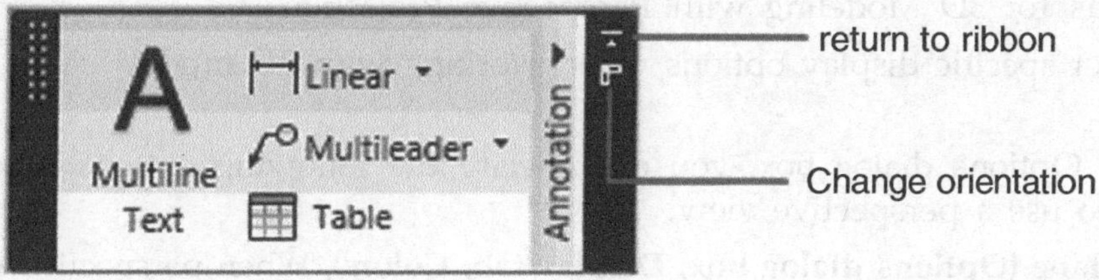


### 3.16 Expanded Panels

An arrow to the right of a panel title indicates that you can expand the panel to display additional tools and controls. By default, an expanded panel closes automatically when you click another panel. To keep a panel expanded, click the push pin icon in the bottom-left corner of the expanded panel.

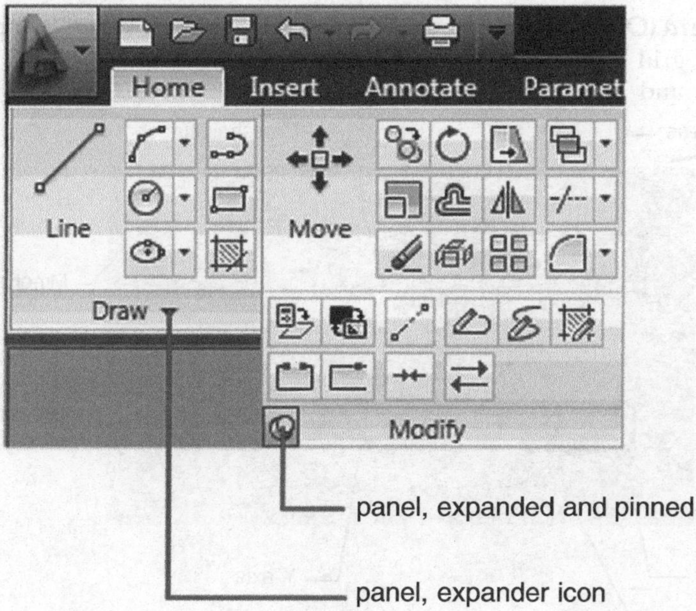

## 3.17 Contextual Ribbon Tabs

When you execute some commands, a special contextual ribbon tab is displayed instead of a toolbar or dialog box. The contextual tab is closed when you end the command.

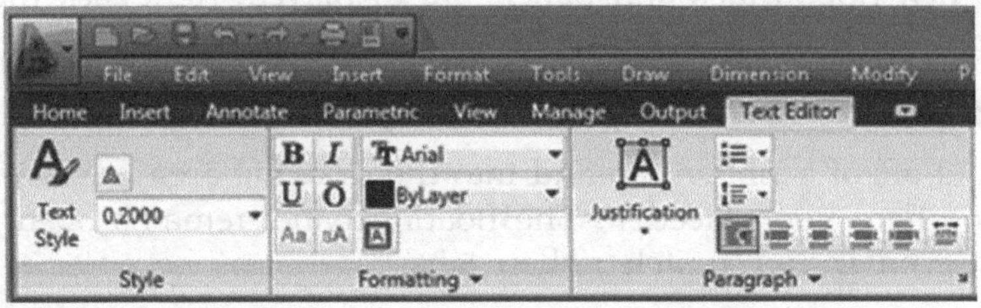


Set Options for 3D Modeling with Perspective Projection

You can set specific display options when working with 3D models using perspective projection.

Using the Options dialog box, you can specify the following options when your 3D model is set to use a perspective view:

- **Ground Plane (Options dialog box, Display tab, Colors).** When perspective projection is turned on, the XY plane of the UCS displays as a ground plane with a gradient color. The ground plane displays a gradient from the ground horizon to the ground origin.
- **Sky (Options dialog box, Display tab, Colors).** The area not covered by the ground plane is the *sky,* which displays a gradient color from the sky horizon to the sky zenith.
- **Underground (Options dialog box, Display tab, Colors).** If the ground plane is viewed from below ground, the ground plane displays a gradient from the earth horizon to the earth azimuth.
- **Ground Plane Grid (Options dialog box, Display tab, Colors).** When perspective projection is turned on, the grid displays as a ground plane grid. Colors are set for major grid lines, minor grid lines, and axis lines.

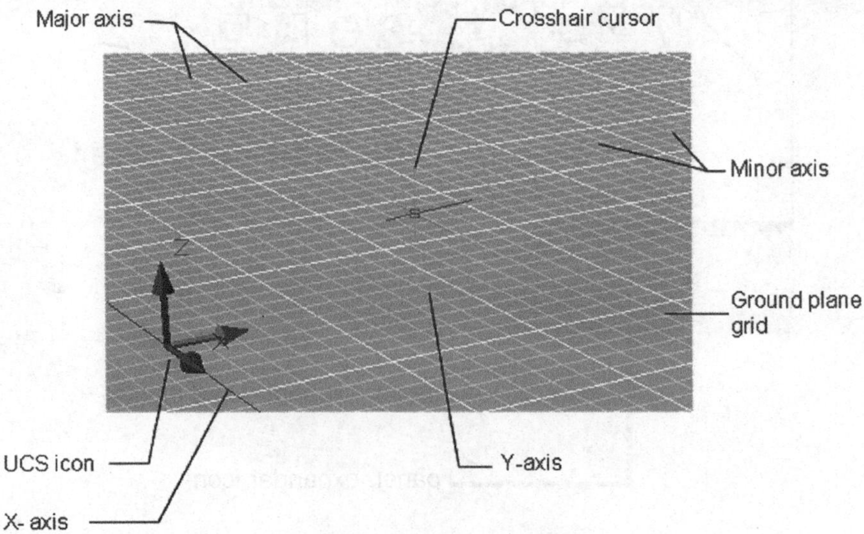

## 4. SAVING YOUR AUTOCAD WORK:

You are responsible for the safe keeping of your work with AutoCAD. Work saved on your network U:\ drive is safe, but the drive is limited in storage capacity. You may wish to use other removable media such as a USB flash stick (pen drive). Get into the habit of creating a folder for each project. When you save work, AutoCAD will create a *.dwg file and a *.bak file of your work. The *.bak file is a backup copy of the *.dwg file.

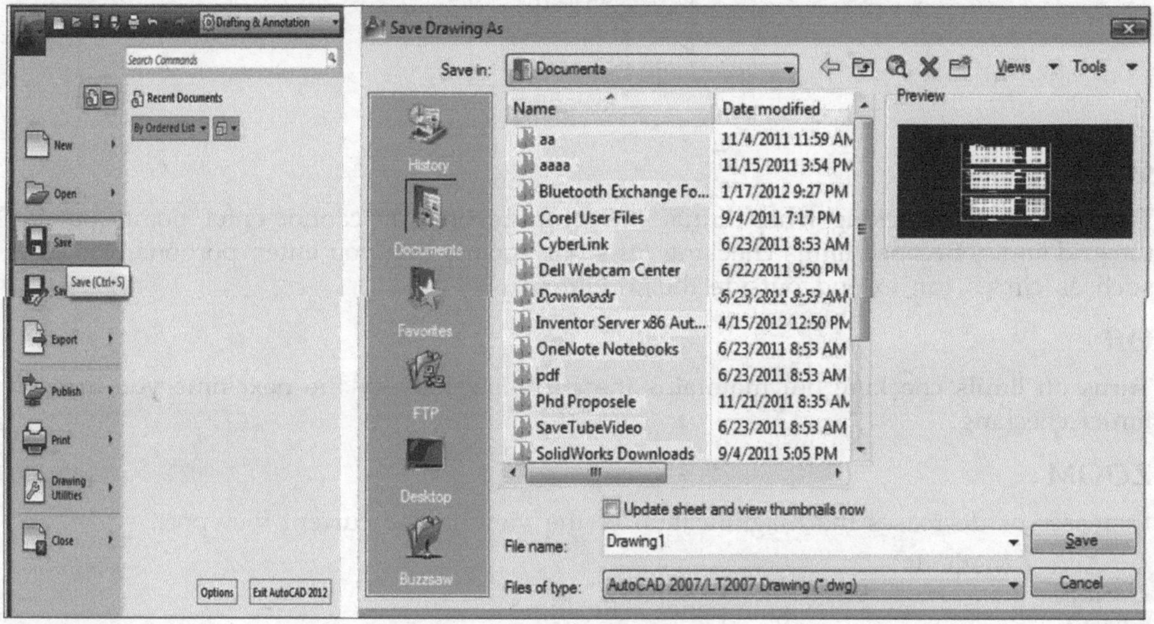


## 5. AUTOCAD - CREATING A NEW DRAWING:

In this section you will use AutoCAD to create and set up a new drawing file. You will also become familiar with the toolbars, menus and command line.

## 6. ACTIVATING AUTOCAD:

Only certain rooms contain computers with access to AutoCAD. You will find a shortcut installed under the University Software list, under A for AutoDesk. Click the appropriate shortcut and wait for the program to load. Video clips will require use of headphones.

## 7. LIMITS

Sets and controls the limits of the grid display in the current Model or layout tab.

Menu: Format ➤ Drawing Limits

Command entry: ***limits*** (or ***'limits*** for transparent use)

**Specify lower left corner or [ ON/ OFF] <current>:** Specify a point, enter **on** or **off**, or press ENTER

Lower-Left Corner

Specifies the lower-left corner for the grid limits

**Specify upper right corner** *<current>: Specify a point or press* ENTER

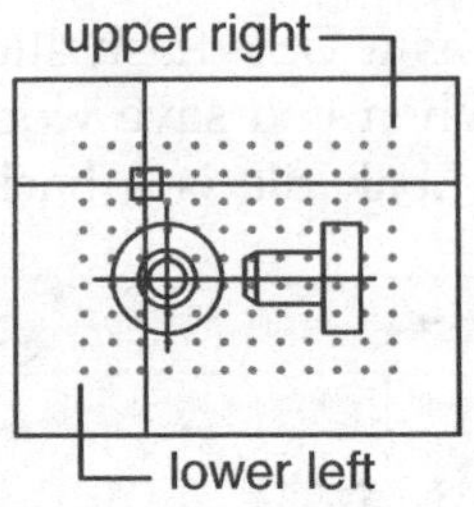


## On

Turns on limits checking when limits checking are on, you cannot enter points outside the grid limits. Because limits checking tests only points that you enter, portions of objects such as circles can extend outside the grid limits.

## Off

Turns off limits checking but maintains the current values for the next time you turn on limits checking.

# ZOOM

Increases or decreases the magnification of the view in the current viewport.

Access Methods

Ribbon: View tab ➤ Navigate panel ➤ Realtime

Menu: View ➤ Zoom ➤ Realtime

**Toolbar: Standard** 

Shortcut menu: With no objects selected right-click in the drawing area and choose Zoom to zoom in real time.

Command entry: ***zoom*** (or ***'zoom*** for transparent use)

You can change the magnification of a view by zooming in and out, which is similar to zooming in and out with a camera. Using ZOOM does not change the absolute size of objects in the drawing. It changes only the magnification of the view.

In a perspective view, ZOOM displays the 3DZOOM prompts.

**Specify corner of window, enter a scale factor (nX or nXP),** or

**[ All/ Center/ Dynamic/ Extents/ Previous/ Scale/ Window/ Object]** < real time>:

## All

Zooms to display the entire drawing in the current viewport in a plan view, All zooms to the grid limits or current extents, whichever is greater. In a 3D view, ZOOM all is equivalent to ZOOM Extents. The display shows all objects even if the drawing extends outside the grid limits.

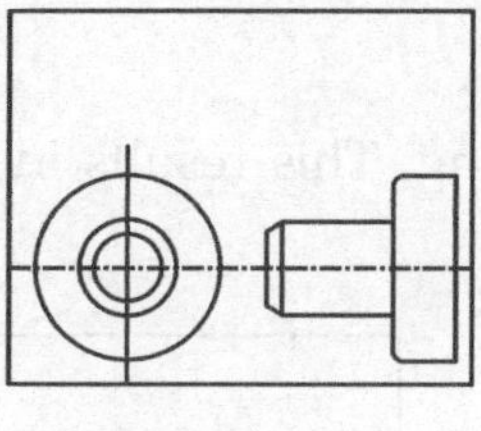

before ZOOM All

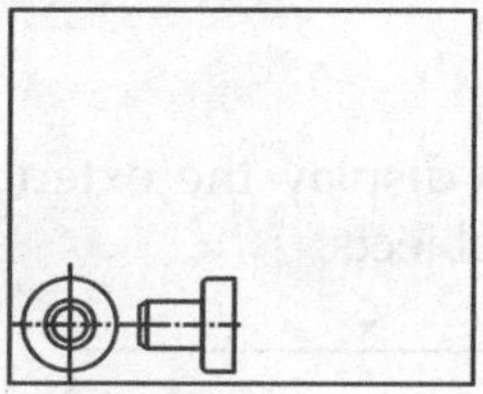

after ZOOM All

In the illustration, LIMITS is greater than the extents of the drawing.

Because it always regenerates the drawing, you cannot use ZOOM all transparently.

**Center**

Zooms to display a view defined by a center point and a magnification value or a height a smaller value for the height increases the magnification. A larger value decreases the magnification.

Specify center point: *Specify a point (1)*

Enter magnification or height *<current>: Enter a value or press* ENTER

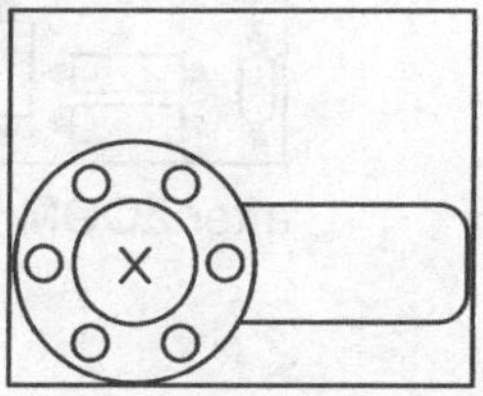

before ZOOM center

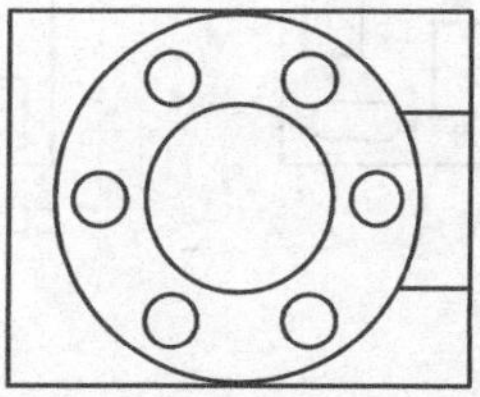

after ZOOM center, magnification increased

**Dynamic**

Pans and zooms using a rectangular view box. The view box represents your view, which you can shrink or enlarge and move around the drawing. Positioning and sizing the view box pans or zooms to fill the viewport with the view inside the view box.

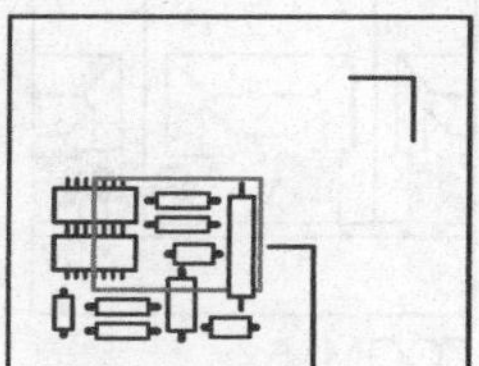

view box

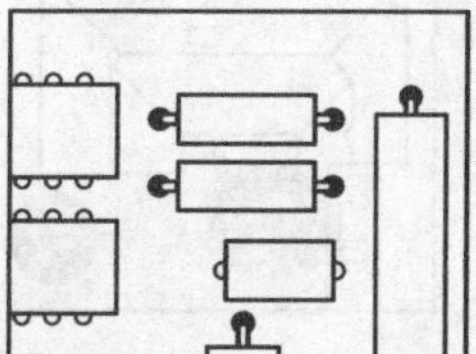

new view

- To change the size of the view box, click, resize it, and click again to accept the new size of the view box.
- To pan with the view box, drag it to the location you want and press ENTER.

## Extents

Zooms in or out to display the extents of the drawing. This results in the largest possible display of all the objects.

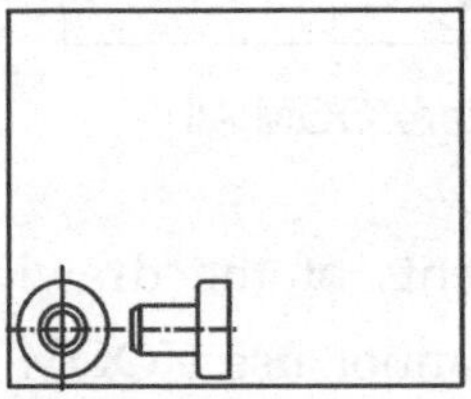

before ZOOM Extents

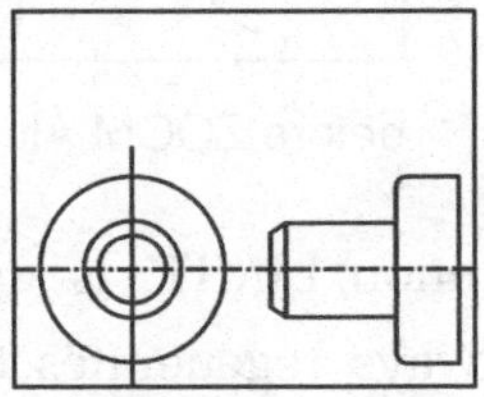

after ZOOM Extents

## Previous

Zooms to display the previous view. You can restore up to 10 previous views.

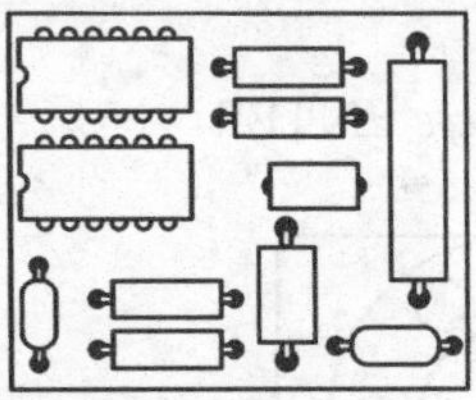

original view

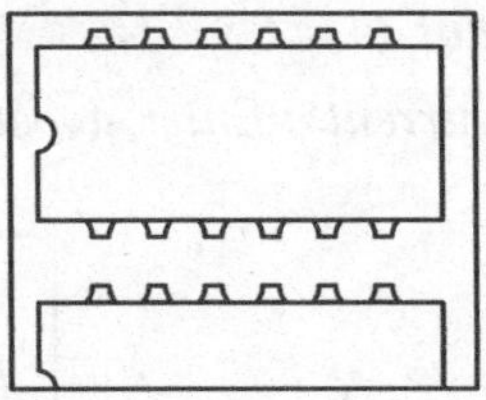

current view

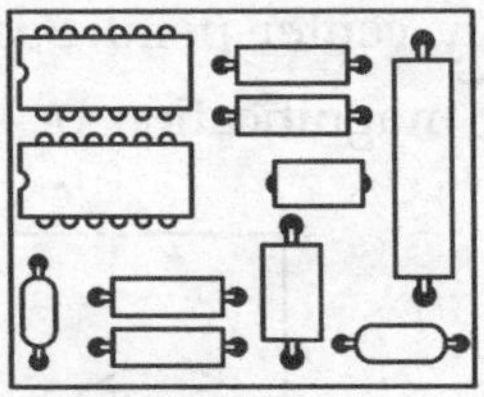

after ZOOM Previous

## Scale

Zooms to change the magnification of a view using a scale factor

Enter a scale factor (nX or nXP): *Specify a value*

- Enter a value followed by ***x*** to specify the scale relative to the current view.
- Enter a value followed by ***xp*** to specify the scale relative to paper space units.

For example, entering ***.5x*** causes each object to be displayed at half its current size on the screen.

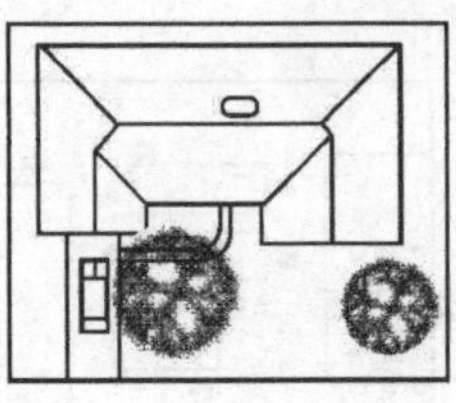

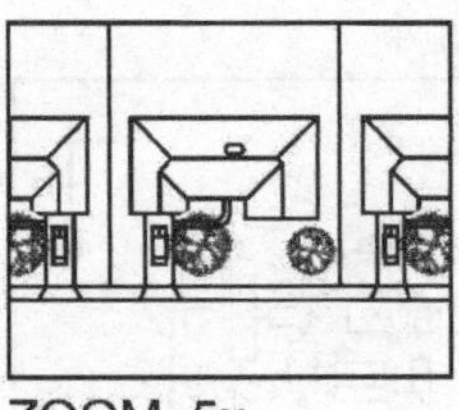

ZOOM .5x

Entering *.5xp* displays model space at half the scale of paper space units. You can create a layout with each viewport displaying objects at a different scale.

Enter a value to specify the scale relative to the grid limits of the drawing. (This option is rarely used.) For example, entering **2** displays objects at twice the size they would appear if you were zoomed to the limits of the drawing.

ZOOM 2

## Window

Zooms to display an area specified by two opposite corners of a rectangular window

**Specify first corner:** *Specify a point (1)*

**Specify opposite corner:** *Specify a point (2)*

before ZOOM Window after ZOOM Window

## Object

Zooms to display one or more selected objects as large as possible and in the center of the view. You can select objects before or after you start the ZOOM command.

## Real Time

Zooms interactively to change the magnification of the view

Press ESC or ENTER to exit, or right-click to display the shortcut menu

The cursor changes to a magnifying glass with plus (+) and minus (-) signs. See Zoom Shortcut Menu for a description of the options that are available while zooming in real time.

Holding down the pick button at the midpoint of the window and moving vertically to the top of the window zooms in to 100%. Conversely, holding the pick button down at the midpoint of the window and moving vertically to the bottom of the window zooms out by 100%.

When you reach the zoom-in limit, the plus sign in the cursor disappears, indicating that you can no longer zoom in. When you reach the zoom-out limit, the minus sign in the cursor disappears, indicating that you can no longer zoom out.

When you release the pick button, zooming stops You can release the pick button, move the cursor to another location in the drawing, and then press the pick button again and continue to zoom the display from that location. To exit zooming, press ENTER or ESC

## 8. MVSETUP

When the TILEMODE system variable is on (the default), the following prompt is displayed:

**Enable paper space? [No/Yes] <Y>:** Enter n or press *Enter*

Pressing Enter turns off TILEMODE and proceeds as described in the following section, MVSETUP on a Layout Tab

Entering ***n*** displays the following prompt:

**Enter units type [Scientific/Decimal/Engineering/Architectural/Metric]:** *Enter an option*

A list of available units and prompts for the scale factor and paper size are displayed.

Enter the scale factor: *Enter a value*

Enter the paper width: *Enter a value*

**Enter the paper height: *Enter a value***

A bounding box is drawn and the command ends.

## 9. DRAFTING SETTINGS

**Menu:** Tools ➤ Drafting Settings

**Shortcut menu:** Right-click Snap, Grid, Polar, Osnap, Otrack, Dyn or Quick Properties on the status bar and click Settings.

**Command entry: dsettings** (or **'dsettings** for transparent use)

Specifies drafting settings organized for drawing aids in the following categories: Snap and Grid, Polar Tracking, Object Snap, Dynamic Input and Quick Properties.

## Options

Displays the Drafting tab in the Options dialog box You cannot access the Options dialog box from the Drafting Settings dialog box if you are running DSETTINGS transparently.

Snap and Grid Tab (Drafting Settings Dialog Box)

Specifies Snap and Grid settings

## Snap On

Turns Snap mode on or off. You can also turn Snap mode on or off by clicking Snap on the status bar, by pressing F9, or by using the SNAPMODE system variable.

## Snap Spacing

Controls an invisible, rectangular grid of snap locations that restricts cursor movement to specified *X* and *Y* intervals.

## Snap X Spacing

Specifies the snap spacing in the *X* direction The value must be a positive real number. (SNAPUNIT system variable)

## Snap Y Spacing

Specifies the snap spacing in the *Y* direction The value must be a positive real number. (SNAPUNIT system variable)

## Equal X and Y Spacing

Forces the X and Y spacing to the same values for snap spacing and for grid spacing. The snap spacing intervals can be different from the grid spacing intervals.

## Polar Spacing

Controls the PolarSnap increment distance

## Polar Distance

Sets the snap increment distance when PolarSnap is selected under Snap Type & Style If this value is 0, the PolarSnap distance assumes the value for Snap X Spacing. The Polar Distance setting is used in conjunction with polar tracking and/or object snap tracking. If neither tracking feature is enabled, the Polar Distance setting has no effect. (POLARDIST system variable) Snap Type Sets the snap style and snap type.

## Grid Snap

Sets the snap type to Grid When you specify points, the cursor snaps along vertical or horizontal grid points. (SNAPTYPE system variable)

**Rectangular Snap:** Sets the snap style to standard Rectangular snap mode. When the snap type is set to Grid snap and Snap mode is on, the cursor snaps to a rectangular snap grid. (SNAPSTYL system variable)

**Isometric Snap:** Sets the snap style to Isometric snap mode. When the snap type is set to Grid snap and Snap mode is on, the cursor snaps to an isometric snap grid. (SNAPSTYL system variable)

## PolarSnap

Sets the snap type to Polar When Snap mode is on and you specify points with polar tracking turned on, the cursor snaps along polar alignment angles set on the Polar Tracking tab relative to the starting polar tracking point. (SNAPTYPE system variable)

## Grid On

Turns the grid on or off You can also turn grid mode on or off by clicking Grid on the status bar, by pressing F7, or by using the GRIDMODE system variable.

## Grid Spacing

Controls the display of a grid that helps you visualize distances.

## Grid X Spacing

Specifies the grid spacing in the X direction If this value is 0, the grid assumes the value set for Snap X Spacing. (GRIDUNIT system variable)

## Grid Y Spacing

Specifies the grid spacing in the Y direction If this value is 0, the grid assumes the value set for Snap Y Spacing. (GRIDUNIT system variable)

## Major Line Every

Specifies the frequency of major grid lines compared to minor grid lines Grid lines rather than grid dots are displayed when the VSCURRENT is set to any visual style except 2D Wireframe.

(GRIDMAJOR system variable)

## Grid Behavior

Controls the appearance of the grid lines that are displayed when VSCURRENT is set to any visual style except 2D Wireframe

## Adaptive Grid

Limits the density of the grid when zoomed out (GRIDDISPLAY system variable)

Allow Subdivision Below Grid Spacing:

Generates additional, more closely spaced grid lines when zoomed in the frequency of these grid lines is determined by the frequency of the major grid lines. (GRIDDISPLAY and GRIDMAJOR system variables)

## Display Grid beyond Limits

Displays the grid beyond the area specified by the LIMITS command (GRIDDISPLAY system variable)

## Follow Dynamic UCS

Changes the grid plane to follow the XY plane of the dynamic UCS (GRIDDISPLAY system variable)

## Polar Tracking Tab (Drafting Settings Dialog Box)

Controls the AutoTrack settings

## Polar Tracking On

Turns polar tracking on and off you can also turn polar tracking on or off by pressing F10 or by using the AUTOSNAP system variable.

## Polar Angle Settings

Sets the alignment angles for polar tracking (POLARANG system variable)

## Increment Angle

Sets the polar increment angle used to display polar tracking alignment paths you can enter any angle, or select a common angle of 90, 45, 30, 22.5, 18, 15, 10, or 5 degrees from the list. (POLARANG system variable)

## Additional Angles

Makes any additional angles in the list available for polar tracking the Additional Angles check box is also controlled by the POLARMODE system variable, and the list of additional angles is also controlled by the POLARADDANG system variable.

**Note:** Additional angles are absolute, not incremental.

## List of Angles

If Additional Angles is selected, lists the additional angles that are available. To add new angles, click New. To remove existing angles, click Delete. (POLARADDANG system variable)

## New

Adds up to 10 additional polar tracking alignment angles

## Delete

Deletes selected additional angles. Object Snap Tracking Settings Sets options for object snap tracking.

## Track Orthogonally Only

Displays only orthogonal (horizontal/vertical) object snap tracking paths for acquired object snap points when object snap tracking is on. (POLARMODE system variable)

## Track Using All Polar Angle Settings

Applies polar tracking settings to object snap tracking when you use object snap tracking, the cursor tracks along polar alignment angles from acquired object snap points (POLARMODE system variable) Polar Angle Measurement sets the basis by which polar tracking alignment angles are measured.

### Absolute

Bases polar tracking angles on the current user coordinate system (UCS)

### Relative to Last Segment

Bases polar tracking angles on the last segment drawn.

### Object Snap Tab (Drafting Settings Dialog Box)

Controls running object snap settings. With running object snap settings, also called Osnap, you can specify a snap point at an exact location on an object. When more than one option is selected, the selected snap modes are applied to return a point closest to the center of the aperture box. Press TAB to cycle through the options.

### Object Snap On

Turns running object snaps on and off. The object snaps selected under Object Snap Modes are active while object snap is on. (OSMODE system variable)

### Object Snap Tracking On

Turns object snap tracking on and off. With object snap tracking, the cursor can track along alignment paths based on other object snap points when specifying points in a command. To use object snap tracking, you must turn on one or more object snaps. (AUTOSNAP system variable)

### Object Snap Modes

Lists object snaps that you can turn on as running object snaps.

### Endpoint

Snaps to the closest endpoint of an arc, elliptical arc, line, multiline, polyline segment, spline, region, or ray, or to the closest corner of a trace, solid, or 3D face

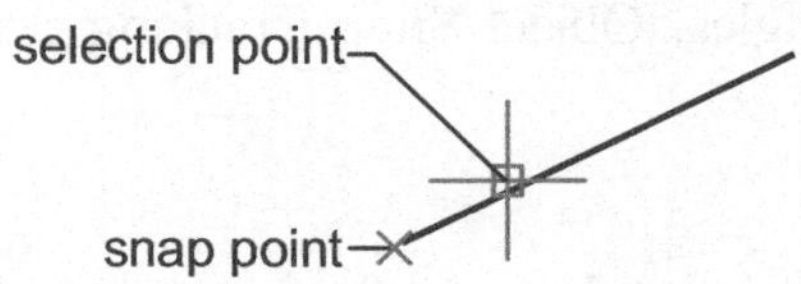


### Midpoint

Snaps to the midpoint of an arc, ellipse, elliptical arc, line, multiline, polyline segment, region, solid, spline, or xline

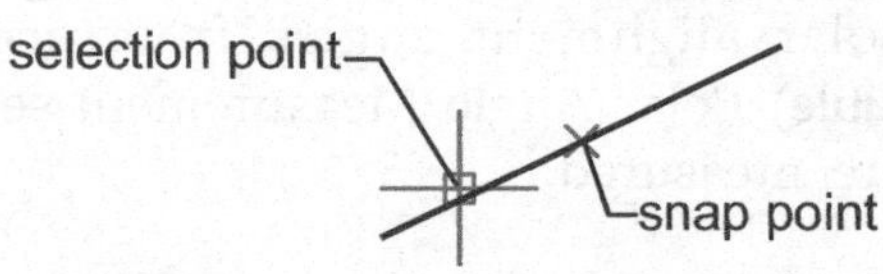

## Center

Snaps to the center of an arc, circle, ellipse, or elliptical arc

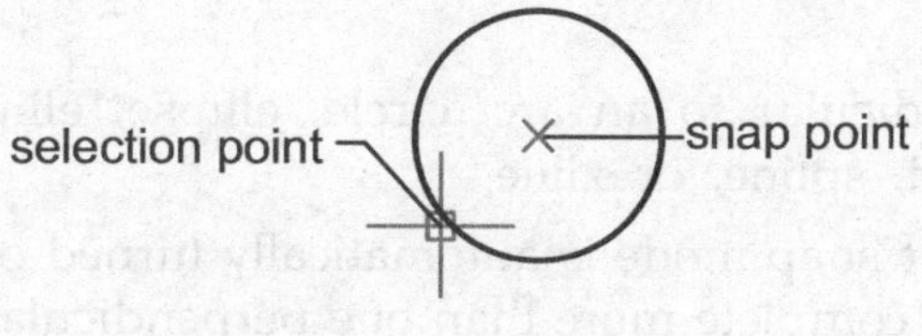


## Node

Snaps to a point object, dimension definition point, or dimension text origin.

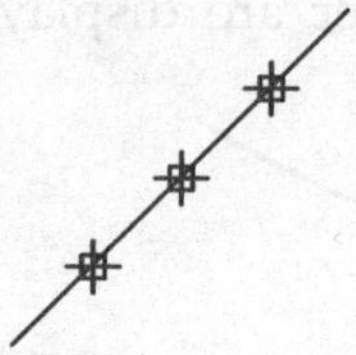

## Quadrant

Snaps to a quadrant point of an arc, circle, ellipse, or elliptical arc.

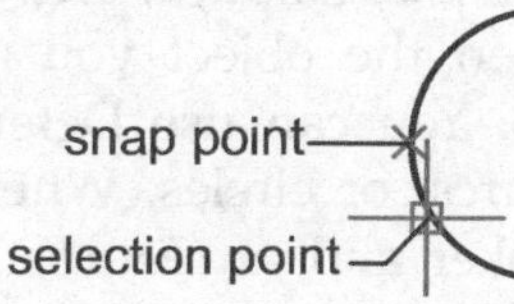


## Intersection

Snaps to the intersection of an arc, circle, ellipse, elliptical arc, line, multiline, polyline, ray, region, spline, or xline Extended Intersection is not available as a running object snap

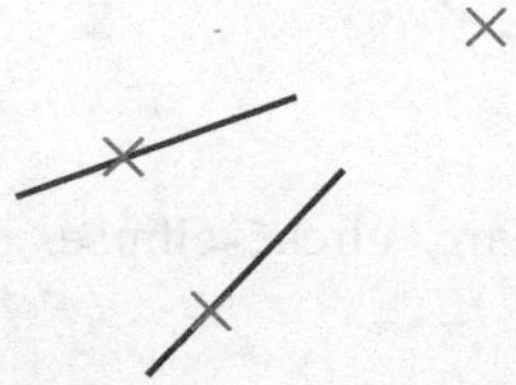

Intersection and Extended Intersection do not work with edges or corners of 3D solids.

## Extension

Causes a temporary extension line or arc to be displayed when you pass the cursor over the endpoint of objects, so you can specify points on the extension

**Note:** When working in perspective view, you cannot track along the extension line of an arc or elliptical arc.

## Insertion

Snaps to the insertion point of an attribute, a block, a shape, or text

## Perpendicular

Snaps to a point perpendicular to an arc, circle, ellipse, elliptical arc, line, multiline, polyline, ray, region, solid, spline, or xline

Deferred Perpendicular snap mode is automatically turned on when the object you are drawing requires that you complete more than one perpendicular snap. You can use a line, arc, circle, polyline, ray, xline, multiline, or 3D solid edge as an object from which to draw a perpendicular line. You can use Deferred Perpendicular to draw perpendicular lines between such objects. When the aperture box passes over a Deferred Perpendicular snap point, an AutoSnap tooltip and marker are displayed.

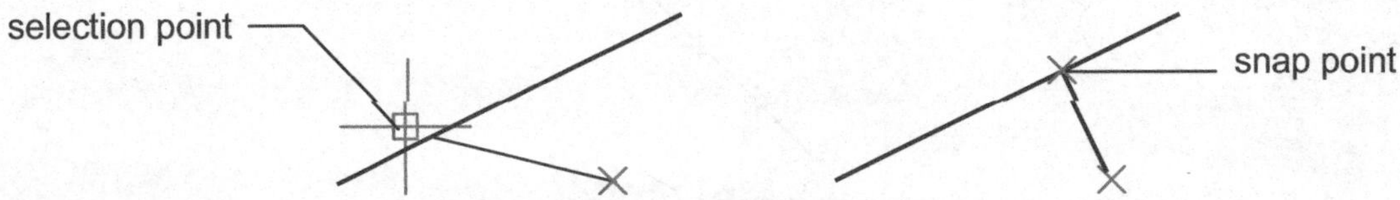


## Tangent

Snaps to the tangent of an arc, circle, ellipse, elliptical arc, or spline deferred Tangent snap mode is automatically turned on when the object you are drawing requires that you complete more than one tangent snap. You can use Deferred Tangent to draw a line or xline that is tangent to arcs, polyline arcs, or circles. When the aperture box passes over a Deferred Tangent snap point, a marker and an AutoSnap tooltip are displayed.

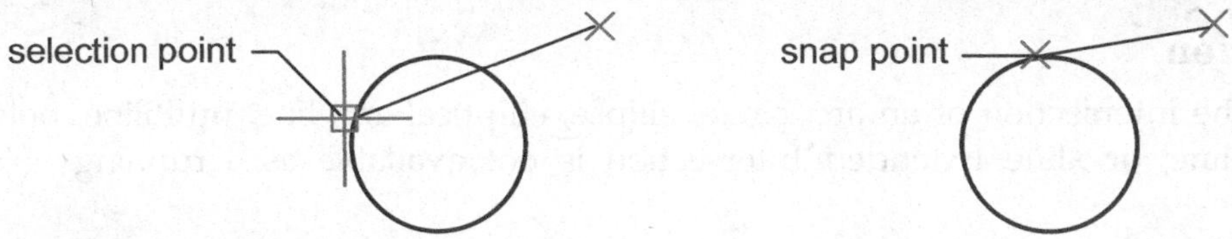


## Nearest

Snaps to the nearest point on an arc, circle, ellipse, elliptical arc, line, multiline, point, polyline, ray, spline, or xline

## Apparent Intersection

Snaps to the visual intersection of two objects that are not in the same plane but may appear to intersect in the current view

Extended Apparent Intersection is not available as a running object snap. Apparent and Extended Apparent Intersection do not work with edges or corners of 3D solids.

## Parallel

Constrains a line segment, polyline segment, ray or xline to be parallel to another linear object after you specify the first point of a linear object, specify the parallel object snap. Unlike other object snap modes, you move the cursor and *hover* over another linear object until the angle is acquired. Then, move the cursor back toward the object that you are creating. When the path of the object is parallel to the previous linear object, an alignment path is displayed, which you can use to create the parallel object.

## Select All

Turns on all object snap modes

## Clear All

Turns off all object snap modes

## Dynamic Input Tab (Drafting Settings Dialog Box)

Controls pointer input, dimension input, dynamic prompting, and the appearance of drafting tooltips

Enable Pointer Input

Turns on pointer input

When pointer input and dimensional input are both turned on, dimensional input supersedes pointer input when it is available. (DYNMODE system variable)

Pointer Input

Displays the location of the crosshairs as coordinate values in a tooltip near the cursor

When a command prompts you for a point, you can enter coordinate values in the tooltip instead of in the Command window.

## Preview Area

Shows an example of pointer input

## Settings

Displays the Pointer Input Settings dialog box. Enable Dimension Input

Turns on dimensional input Dimensional input is not available for some commands that prompt for a second point. (DYNMODE system variable)

Dimension Input

Displays a dimension with tooltips for distance value and angle value when a command prompts you for a second point or a distance the values in the dimension tooltips change as you move the cursor. You can enter values in the tooltip instead of on the command line.

### Preview Area

Shows an example of dimensional input

### Settings

Displays the Dimension Input Settings dialog box.

Dynamic Prompts

Displays prompts in a tooltip near the cursor when necessary in order to complete the command. You can enter values in the tooltip instead of on the command line.

### Preview Area

Shows an example of dynamic prompts

### Show Command Prompting and Command Input near the Crosshairs

Displays prompts in Dynamic Input tooltips. (DYNPROMPT system variable) Drafting Tooltip Appearance

Displays the Tooltip Appearance dialog box

### Quick Properties Tab (Drafting Settings Dialog Box)

Specifies the settings for displaying the Quick Properties palette

### Enable Quick Properties Palette

Depending on the object type, you can enable or disable Quick Properties palette. Quick Properties palette can also be turned on or off by clicking Quick Properties on the status bar or by using the QPMODE system variable.

### Palette Display

Sets the display settings of the Quick Properties palette

### All Objects

Sets the Quick Properties palette to display for any selection of objects

### Only Objects with Specified Properties

Sets the Quick Properties palette to display only for objects that are defined in the Customize User Interface (CUI) editor to display properties

### Palette Location

Sets the display position of the Quick Properties palette

### Cursor-Dependent

Sets the Palette Location mode to Cursor-dependent in cursor-dependent mode, the Quick Properties palette displays in a location relative to where you selected the object. (QPLOCATION system variable)

Quadrant: Specifies the relative location to display the Quick Properties palette. You can select one of the four quadrants top-right, top-left, bottom-right, or bottom-left.

Distance in Pixels: Sets the distance in pixels when Cursor is selected under the Palette Location modes. You can specify values in the range of 0 to 400 (only integer values).

## Static

Sets the location mode to Static (QPLOCATION system variable)

## Palette Behavior

Sets the behavior of Quick Properties palette

## Collapse Palette Automatically

Enables the Quick Properties palette to display only a specified number of properties in the idle state

**Minimum Number of Rows:** Sets the minimum number of rows for the Quick Properties palette to display in the collapsed idle state. You can specify values in the range of 1 to 30 (only integer value.

CHAPTER

3

# AutoCAD Command Shortcuts

# 1. COMMON COMMANDS

| SHORTCUT | COMMAND | COMMENT |
|---|---|---|
| A | ARC | Draw an arc |
| AL | ALIGN | Align an object with another |
| AP | APPLOAD | Opens application load dialogue box |
| AR | ARRAY | Opens array dialogue box |
| AUDIT | AUDIT | Audit drawing for errors |
| AV | DSVIEW ER | Opens ariel view of drawing |
| B | BLOCK | Opens block dialogue box |
| C | CIRCLE | Draw a circle |
| *CO* | *COPY* | *Copy an object* |
| CHA | CHAMFER | Chamfer between 2 non-parallel lines |
| COL | COLOR | Opens select color dialogue box |
| CUI | | Opens customise user interface dialogue |
| D | DIMSTYLE | Opens dimstyle manager |
| DC | ADCENTER | Opens designcenter |
| DI | DIST | Check a distance |
| DIV | DIVIDE | Inserts point node a set division |
| DO | DONUT | Draw a solid donut shape |
| DV | DVIEW | Perspective view |
| E | ERASE | Erase a selection |
| EX | EXTEND | Extend a selection |
| F | FILLET | Draw an arc between 2 intersecting lines |
| FI | FILTER | Opens filter dialogue box |
| FLATTEN | FLATTEN | Converts 3D to 2D |
| G | GROUP | Launches the group dialogue box |
| H | HATCH | Opens hatch and gradient dialogue box |
| I | INSERT | Insert a block |
| IM | IMAGE | Launches image manager |

| | | |
|---|---|---|
| J | JOIN | Joins 2 objects to form single object |
| JPGOUT | JPGOUT | Creates a JPEG file of current drawing |
| L | LINE | Draw a line |
| LA | LAYER | Opens layer manager |
| LE | QLEADER | Draw a leader line (may need to adjust settings) |
| LEAD | LEADER | Leader line with annotation |
| LI or LS | LIST | Display information about objects in a text window |
| LO | -LAYOUT | Creates a new layout tab |
| LTS | LTScale | Change the linetype scale |
| M | MOVE | Move a selection |
| MA | MATCHPROPERTIES | Match properties of an object |
| ME | MEASURE | Inserts point node at input distance |
| O | OFFSET | Offset a selection |
| OP | OPTIONS | Launches options dialogue box |
| P | PAN | Pan in drawing |
| PE | POLYEDIT | Edit a polyline |
| PL | PLINE | Draw a polyline |
| PLOT | PLOT | Opens plot/print dialogue box |
| PO | POINT | Point marker or node - DDPTYPE to change point style |
| PR | PROPERTIES | Opens properties dialogue box |
| PRE | PREVIEW | Preview a plot |
| PU | PURGE | Opens purge dialogue box to remove unused elements |
| RE | REGEN | Regenerate the display |
| REC | RECTANG | Draw a rectangle |
| REN | RENAME | Opens rename dialogue box to rename blocks, layers, etc |

| | | |
|---|---|---|
| RO | ROTATE | Rotate a selection |
| SP | SPELL | Spell check a selection - ALL to check entire drawing |
| T | MTEXT | Insert multiline text |
| TB | TABLE | Opens insert a table dialogue box |
| TP | TOOLPALETTES | Displays toolpalette |
| TR | TRIM | Trim a selection |
| U | UNDO | Undo last command |
| UN | UNITS | Opens units dialogue box |
| V | VIEW | Opens view dialogue box |
| W | WBLOCK | Write a block |
| WHOHAS | WHOHAS | Displays who has a drawing open |
| X | EXPLODE | Explode a selection |
| XR | XREF | Opens x-reference manager |
| Z | ZOOM | Zoom in display - A=All, E=EXTENTS, W=WINDOW |

## 2. DRAWING OBJECTS

| SHORTCUT | COMMAND | COMMENT |
|---|---|---|
| A | ARC | Draw an arc with 3 points |
| B | BLOCK | Opens block dialogue box in order to make a block |
| BO | BOUNDARY | Draw a boundary |
| C | CIRCLE | Draw a circle |
| DO | DONUT | Draw a solid donut shape |
| DT | TEXT | Single line text |
| DIV | DIVIDE | Inserts point node a set division |
| EL | ELLIPSE | Draw an ellipse |
| F | FILLET | Draw an arc between 2 intersecting lines |
| G | GROUP | Opens object grouping dialogue |

| | | |
|---|---|---|
| H | HATCH | Opens hatch and gradient dialogue box |
| L | LINE | Draw a line |
| LE | QLEADER | Draw a leader line (may need to adjust settings) |
| LEAD | LEADER | Leader line with annotation |
| ML | MLINE | Draw multilines |
| O | OFFSET | Offset an object by distance |
| PL | PLINE | Draw a polyline - a complex line |
| PO | POINT | Point marker or node - DDPTYPE to change pointstyle |
| POL | POLYGON | Draw a regular polygon 3 to 1024 sides |
| RAY | RAY | Construction line in one direction |
| REC | RECTANG | Draw a rectangle |
| REG | REGION | Region - for shading for example |
| REVCLOUD | REVCLOUD | Revision cloud - note can select a polyline |
| SPL | SPLINE | Spline or smooth curve along points |
| T | MTEXT | Multi-line text |
| WIPEOUT | WIPEOUT | Masks part of drawing for clarity |
| XL | XLINE | Construction line of infinite length |

## 3. BLOCK

| SHORTCUT | COMMAND | COMMENT |
|---|---|---|
| ATT | ATTDEF | Opens attribute definition dialogue box |
| ATTEDIT | ATTEDIT | Edit attribute values for a specific block |
| B | BLOCK | Opens block dialogue box in order to make a block |
| BATTMAN | BATTMAN | Opens block attribute manager |
| BATTORDER | BATTORDER | Displays attribute order dialogue box |
| BC | BCLOSE | Closes the block editor |
| BCOUNT | BCOUNT | Counts the blocks in a drawing |

| BE | BEDIT | Opens the edit block definition dialogue box |
|---|---|---|
| EATTEXT | EATTEXT | Enhanced attribute extraction wizard to count blocks |
| GATTE | GATTE | Global attribute edit of multiple blocks |
| I | INSERT | Opens insert dialogue to insert a block |
| -I | INSERT | Insert a block by name |
| MINSERT | MINSERT | Insert block in rectangular array |
| REFEDIT | REFEDIT | Edit a block reference in place |
| REN | RENAME | Opens rename dialogue box to rename blocks, layers, etc |
| W | WBLOCK | Write a block - for use in other drawings |
| XLIST | XLIST | Lists type/block name/layer name/color/linetype of a nested object in a block or an xref |

## 4. DIMENSIONING

| SHORTCUT | COMMAND | COMMENT |
|---|---|---|
| CTRL+8 | QUICKCALC | Displays the calculator |
| D | DIMSTYLE | Opens dimension style manager dialogue box |
| DAL | DIMALIGNED | Aligned linear dimension line |
| DAN | DIMANGULAR | Angular dimension line |
| DAR | DIMARC | Arc length dimension |
| DBA | DIMBASELINE | Ordinate dimension from baseline of previous dimension |
| DCO | DIMCONTINUE | Ordinate dimension from 2nd extension line of previous dimension |
| DDI | DIMDIAMETER | Diameter dimension for circles and arcs |
| DED | DIMEDIT | Edit dimension text on dimension objects |
| DI | DIST | Check a distance |
| DIMCENTER | DIMCENTER | Creates center mark |
| DLI | DIMLINEAR | Linear dimension |
| DOR | DIMORDINATE | Ordinate point dimension |

| DOV | DIMOVERRIDE | Override dimension style |
|---|---|---|
| DRA | DIMRADIUS | Radial dimension for circles and arcs |
| ID | ID | Display the co-ordinate values of a point |
| UN | UNITS | Opens drawing units dialogue box |

## 5. FORMATTING

| SHORTCUT | COMMAND | COMMENT |
|---|---|---|
| AP | APPLOAD | Opens application load dialogue box |
| BE | BEDIT | Opens the edit block definition dialogue box |
| BH | BHATCH | Opens hatch and gradient dialogue box |
| CUI | | Opens customise user interface dialogue |
| D | DIMSTYLE | Opens dimension style manager dialogue box |
| DC | ADCENTER | Opens designcenter |
| DDPTYPE | DDPTYPE | Opens point style dialogue box |
| LA | LAYER | Opens layer manager |
| LT | DDLTYPE | Opens line type manager |
| LTS | LTSCALE | Change the linetype scale |
| LW | LWEIGHT | Opens line weight settings dialogue box |
| MA | MATCH PROPERTIES | Match properties of an object |
| OP | OPTIONS | Launches options dialogue box |
| OS | DDOSNAP | Opens drafting settings object snap dialogue |
| PR | DDCHPROP | Opens properties dialogue box |
| SSM | SHEETSET | Opens sheet set manager palette |
| ST | DDSTYLE | Opens text style dialogue box |
| TP | TOOLPALETTES | Displays toolpalette |
| TS | TABLESTYLE | Opens table style dialogue box |

## 6. FUNCTION KEYS

| SHORTCUT | COMMAND | COMMENT |
|---|---|---|
| F1 | HELP | Opens Autocad help |
| F2 | TEXTSCR<br>GRAPHSCR | Switches between text screen and graphic area |
| F3 | OSNAP | Switches osnap on/off |
| F5 or CTRL+E | ISOPLANE | Cycles through isoplanes |
| F6 or CTRL+D | COORDS | Turns coordinate display on/off |
| F7 or CTRL+G | GRID | Turns grid on/off |
| F8 or CTRL+L | ORTHO | Turns ortho on/off |
| F9 or CTRL+B | SNAP | Turns snap on/off |
| F10 or CTRL+U | POLAR | Turns polar on/off |
| F11 or CTRL+W | OSNAP TRACK | Turns object snap tracking on/off |
| F12 | DYNMODE | Turns dynamic input on/off |

## 7. CONTROL KEY

| | | |
|---|---|---|
| CTRL+0 | CLEANSCREEN | Turns user interface elements on/off |
| CTRL+1 | PROPERTIES | Turns properties on/off |
| CTRL+2 | ADCENTER | Turns design center on/off |
| CTRL+3 | TOOLPALETTES | Turns tool palettes window on/off |
| CTRL+8 | QUICKCALC | Launches calculator window |
| CTRL+A | | Select all |
| CTRL+C | COPYCLIP | Copies objects to clipboard |
| CTRL+H | | Turns a group on or off |
| CTRL+J | | Repeats last command |
| CTRL+N | NEW | Opens create new drawing dialogue box |
| CTRL+O | OPEN | Opens the select file dialogue box |
| CTRL+P | PLOT | Opens the plot dialogue box |
| CTRL+R | CVPORT | Switches between viewports |

| CTRL+S | QSAVE | Opens the save drawing as dialogue box |
|---|---|---|
| CTRL+SHIFT+S | | Save as |
| CTRL+V | PASTECLIP | Pastes data from clipboard to drawing |
| CTRL+X | CUTCLIP | Removes select object from drawing to clipboard |
| CTRL+Y | REDO | Performs the operation cancelled by UNDO |
| CTRL+Z | UNDO | Undoes the last operation |
| CTRL+TAB | | Switches between open drawings |
| CTRL+PAGE UP | | Switch up between layout tabs |
| CTRL+PAGE DOWN | | Switch down between layout tabs |
| ARROW UP/Down | | Recall last command |

## 8. COORDINATE ENTRY

| #X,Y | Location measured by distance from 0,0 in current UCS |
|---|---|
| @X,Y | Location measured by distance from last point |
| #distance<angle | Location measured by distance and angle from 0,0 in current UCS |
| @distance<angl e | Location measured by distance and angle from last point |
| .x or.y or .xy etc | Location by extracting and combining coordinate values from 2 or 3 points |
| distance | Location direct from current position in direction of movement |
| <angle | An angle override from current point |

## 9. INQUIRY

| SHORTCUT | COMMAND | COMMENT |
|---|---|---|
| AA | AREA | Calculate the area |
| DI | DIST | Calculate a distance and angle |

| | | |
|---|---|---|
| DDPTYPE | DDPTYPE | Opens point style dialogue box |
| ID | ID | Display the co-ordinate values of a point |
| LI or LS | LIST | Display information about objects in a text window |
| MASSPROP | MASSPROP | Calculate the region/mass properties of a solid |
| PR | PROPERTIES | Opens properties dialogue box |
| WHOHAS | WHOHAS | Displays who has a drawing open |
| XLIST | XLIST | Lists type/block name/layer/name/color/linetype of a nested object in a block or an xref |

## 10. LAYERS

| SHORTCUT | COMMAND | COMMENT |
|---|---|---|
| LA | LAYER | Opens layer manager |
| LAYCUR | LAYERCURRENT | Change objects to current layer |
| LAYDEL | LAYERDELETE | Delete a layer by selecting object |
| LAYFRZ | LAYERFREEZE | Freeze a layer by selecting object |
| LAYISO | LAYERISOLATE | Isolates a layer by selecting object |
| LAYLCK | LAYERLOCK | Lock a layer by selecting object |
| LAYMCH | LAYERMATCH | Match properties of a layer |
| LAYMRG | LAYERMERGE | Moves objects from first layer to second and deletes first |
| LAYOFF | LAYEROFF | Switches a layer off |
| LAYON | LAYERON | Switches all layers on except frozen layers |
| LAYERP | LAYERPREVIOUS | Restores previous layer state |
| LAYTHW | LAYTHW | Thaws all layers |
| LAYWALK | LAYERWALK | Walk through layers |
| LMAN | LMAN | Access Layer manager to save and restore layer states |

## 11. MODIFYING OBJECTS

| SHORTCUT | COMMAND | COMMENT |
|---|---|---|
| AL | ALIGN | Align an object with another |
| AR | ARRAY | Make multiple copies of an object |
| BR | BREAK | Break a line by defining 2 points |
| CO or CP | COPY | Copy object |
| COPYTOLAYER | COPYTOLAYER | Copy object from one layer to another |
| CHA | CHAMFER | Chamfer between 2 non-parallel lines |
| E | ERASE | Erase selection |
| EX | EXTEND | Extend a line to meet another |
| F | FILLET | Draw an arc between 2 intersecting lines |
| G | GROUP | Opens object grouping dialogue - use to copy or move |
| LEN | LENGTHEN | Lengthen or shorten a line |
| M | MOVE | Move an object |
| MI | MIRROR | Mirror an object |
| MOCORO | MOVE/COPY/ ROTATE | Copy move and rotate an object with one command |
| O | OFFSET | Offset an object by distance |
| RO | ROTATE | Rotate an object |
| S | STRETCH | Stretch an object |
| SC | SCALE | Scale an object |
| TR | TRIM | Trim objects |
| X | EXPLODE | Explode single entity to component parts |

## 12. OBJECT SELECTION

| SHORTCUT | COMMAND | COMMENT |
|---|---|---|
| A | ADD | Adds each successive object, switches from remove |

| ALL | ALL | All objects on thawed layers |
|---|---|---|
| CP | CPOLYGON | Objects touching or enclosed by selection polygon |
| C | CROSSING | Objects touched or enclosed by window - Move right to left |
| F | FENCE | Objects touch by single selection fence |
| G | GROUP | Opens object grouping dialogue - use with copy/move/etc |
| L | LAST | Most recently created visible object |
| P | PREVIOUS | Most recent selection set |
| R | REMOVE | Objects to remove from selection set |
| SNAPANG | SNAPANGLE | Change the snap angle from default 0° |
| W | WINDOW | Objects enclosed by window - Move left to right |
| WP | WPOLYGON | Objects within a window polygon |

## 13. OBJECT SNAP - OSNAP

| SHORTCUT | COMMAND | COMMENT |
|---|---|---|
| F3 | OSNAP | Switches osnap on/off |
| F9 or CTRL+B | SNAP | Turns snap on/off |
| F11 or CTRL+W | OSNAP TRACK | Turns object snap tracking on/off |
| APP | APPARENT INT | Apparent intersection of 2 objects |
| CEN | CENof | Snap to centre point |
| DS | DDOSNAP | Opens drafting settings/object snap dialogue |
| END | ENDPOINT | Snap to end of line etc |
| EXT | EXTENSION | Extends lines beyond endpoint |
| FRO | FROM | Snap to an offset distance from an object snap |
| INS | INSERTION | Snap to insertion point of text or block |
| INT | INTERSECTION | Snap to intersection of lines, circles, arcs |

| MID | MIDPOINT | Snap to midpoint of line etc |
|---|---|---|
| MTP | | Snap midpoint between two points |
| NEA | NEAREST | Snap near to an object |
| NOD | NODE | Snap to point node |
| NON | NONE | Turns off object snap modes |
| PAR | PARALLEL | Continues a line parallel to existing |
| PER | PERPENDICULAR | Snap to perpendicular of line etc |
| QUA | QUADRANT | Snap to quadrant of circle, arc, ellipse |
| TAN | TANGENT | Snap to tangent of circle, arc, ellipse |
| TK | TRACK | Locate points without drawing lines |
| TT | TT | Temporary tracking point |

## 14. TEXT

| SHORTCUT | COMMAND | COMMENT |
|---|---|---|
| %%C | Ø | Diameter dimensioning symbol |
| %%D | ° | Degrees symbol |
| %%O | OVERSCORE | Toggles overscore mode on/off |
| %%P | ± | Plus/minus symbol |
| %%U | UNDERSCORE | Toggles underscore on/off |
| DT | DTEXT | Single line dynamic text - Justify/Align to fit within text line |
| ED | DDEDIT | Edit text |
| FIND | FIND | Opens find and replace dialogue box |
| JUSTIFYTEXT | JUSTIFYTEXT | Change the justification point without moving text |
| MIRRTEXT | MIRRTEXT | Mirrtext 0 to turn off |
| SCALETEXT | SCALETEXT | Scales text without moving the text insertion point |
| SPELL | SPELLCHECK | Performs spellcheck - ALL checks all text in drawing |

| | | |
|---|---|---|
| ST | STYLE | Opens text style dialogue box |
| T or MT | MTEXT | Multiline/paragraph text |
| TCIRCLE | TCIRCLE | Places circle, slot, or rectangle around each selected text object |
| TEXT | DTEXT | Single line dynamic text |
| TEXTFIT | TEXTFIT | Stretches/shrinks text by selecting new start and/or end points |
| TORIENT | TORIENT | Rotates text, mtext, and attribute definition objects |
| TXT2MTXT | TXT2MTXT | Converts DTEXT to MTEXT |
| WIPEOUT | WIPEOUT | Masks part of drawing for clarity |

## 15. THREE DIMENTIONAL

| SHORTCUT | COMMAND | COMMENT |
|---|---|---|
| 3D | 3D | Command line 3D solid options |
| BOX | BOX | Draw a cube |
| CYLINDER | CYLINDER | Draw a cylinder |
| DDUCS | DDUCS | Opens ucs dialogue |
| DDUCSP | DDUCSP | Opens ucs dialogue at orthographic tab |
| EXT | EXTRUDE | Extrude a face |
| IN | INTERSECT | Intersect an object |
| REV | REVOLVE | Revolves an object about an axis |
| RR | RENDER | Open render dialogue box |
| SE | SECTION | Section |
| SL | SLICE | Slice a solid |
| SU | SUBTRACT | Subtract selection from solid |
| TOR | TORUS | Draw torus shape |
| UC | DDUCS | Displays UCS manager dialogue box |
| UCS | UCS | UCS command line options |
| UNI | UNION | Union solids |

| | | |
|---|---|---|
| VPORTS | VPORTS | Opens viewport dialogue box |
| WE | WEDGE | Draw a wedge |

## 16. UCS

| SHORTCUT | COMMAND | COMMENT |
|---|---|---|
| OB | OBJECT | Align UCS with an object, first select UCS |
| UC | DDUCS | Display UCS manager dialogue box |
| UCS | UCS | Universal co-ordinate system options |
| UCSICON | UCSICON | Change the UCS icon appearance |
| W | WORLD | Return to the WCS |

## 17. VIEWPORT

| SHORTCUT | COMMAND | COMMENT |
|---|---|---|
| CTRL+R | | Cycle through viewports |
| CTRL+PAGE UP | | Switch up between layout tabs |
| CTRL+PAGE DOWN | | Switch down between layout tabs |
| DV | DVIEW | Perspective view. |
| MS | MSPACE | Switch to modelspace in a viewport |
| MV | MVIEW | Make a viewport in paperspace |
| PS | PSPACE | Switch to paperspace from viewport |
| VPORTS | VPORTS | Opens viewports dialogue box |
| -VPORTS | -VPORTS | Create a viewport using command line |

CHAPTER

4

# Draw Toolbar

## DRAW TOOLBAR OUTLINE

Draw commands are the main and basic AutoCAD commands that most AutoCAD drawings are composed of. Therefore a good understanding of the Draw commands is needed to have an efficient use of AutoCAD. The most frequently used Draw commands will be covered by the following sections. Three different ways can be used to access all the AutoCAD drawings, command names (short cut) entered at the command window by keyboard, Draw toolbar, and the Draw drop down menu shown below. Choosing the method to use is dependent upon the type of work you are doing and how familiar you are with AutoCAD. In the mean time, you don't have to worry too much about which way is easiest or most convenient to use. With experience your drawing skills will improve over time, so it is not a problem if you are not working very quickly at the beginning.

### Draw Toolbar AUTOCAD New Version

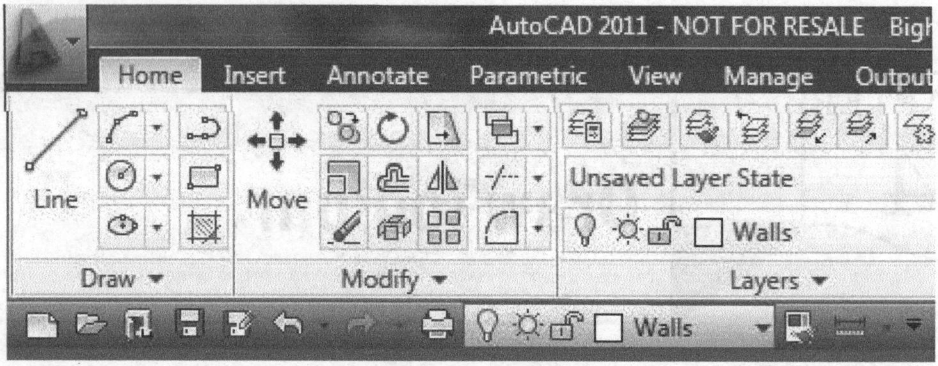


### Draw Toolbar AUTOCAD old Version

Draw toolbar command explain in this chapter like line, xline, rectangle, circle etc.

## 1. INTRODUCTION

This tutorial is designed to show you how all of the AutoCAD Draw commands work. If you just need information quickly, use the Quick find toolbar below to go straight to the command you want or select a topic from the contents list above. Not the entire Draw commands that appear on the Draw toolbar are covered in this tutorial. Blocks, Hatch and Text for example are all tutorial topics in their own right!

The Draw commands can be used to create new objects such as lines and circles. Most AutoCAD drawings are composed purely and simply from these basic components. A good understanding of the

Draw commands is fundamental to the efficient use of AutoCAD.

The sections below cover the most frequently used Draw commands such as Line, Polyline and Circle as well as the more advanced commands like Multiline and Multiline Style. As a newcomer to AutoCAD, you may wish to skip the more advanced commands in order to properly master the basics. You can always return to this tutorial in the future *when you are more confident.*

In common with most AutoCAD commands, the Draw commands can be started in a number of ways. Command names or short-cuts can be entered at the keyboard; commands can be started from the Draw pull-down menu, shown on the right or from the Draw toolbar. The method you use is dependent upon the type of work you are doing and how experienced a user you are. Don't worry too much about this, just use whatever method feels easiest or most convenient at the time. Your drawing technique will improve over time and with experience so don't expect to be working very quickly at first.

If you are working with the pull-down menus, it is worth considering the visual syntax that is common to all pull-downs used in the Windows operating system. For example, a small arrow like so "▸" next to a menu item means that the item leads to a sub-menu that may contain other commands or command options. An ellipsis, "..." after a menu item means that the item displays a dialogue box. These little visual clues will help you to work more effectively with menus because they tell you what to expect and help to avoid surprises for the newcomer.

## 2. LINE

Lines are probably the most simple of AutoCAD objects. Using the Line command, a line can be drawn between any two points picked within the drawing area. Lines are usually the first objects you will want to draw when starting a new drawing because they can be used as "construction lines" upon which the rest of your drawing will be based. Never forget that creating drawings with AutoCAD is not so dissimilar from creating drawings on a drawing board. Many of the basic drawing methods are the same.

Anyone familiar with mathematics will know that lines drawn between points are often called vectors. This terminology is used to describe the type of drawings that AutoCAD creates. AutoCAD drawings are generically referred to as "vector drawings". Vector drawings are extremely useful where precision is the most important criterion because they retain their accuracy irrespective of scale.

## 1.1 The Line Command

| | | |
|---|---|---|
| Toolbar | Draw | |
| Pull-down | **Draw ▸ Line** | |
| Keyboard | **LINE** | short-cut **L** |

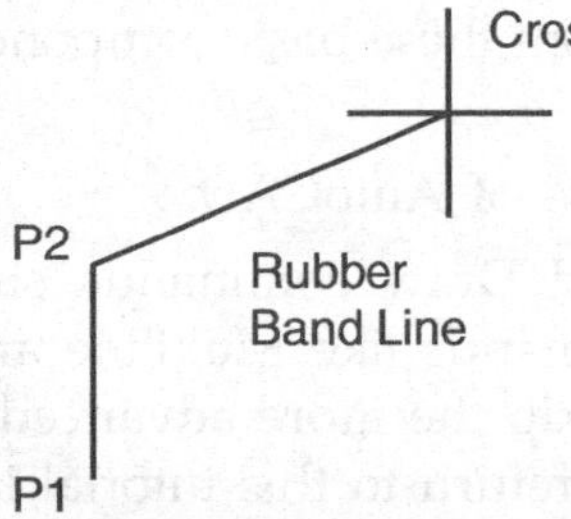


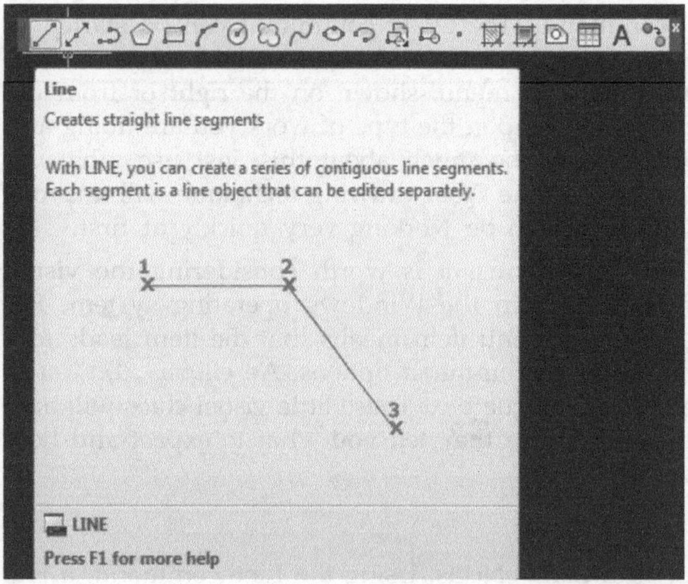


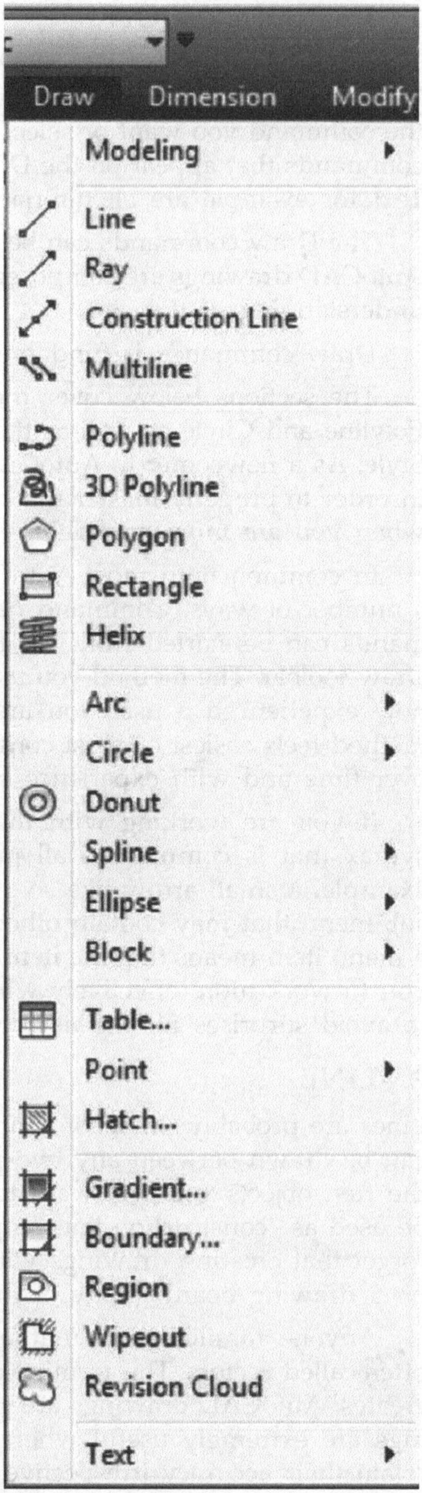


With the Line command you can draw a simple line from one point to another. When you pick the first point and move the cross-hairs to the location of the second point you will see a rubber band line which shows you where the line will be drawn when the second point is picked. Line objects have two ends (the first point and the last point). You can continue picking points and AutoCAD will draw a straight line between each picked point and the previous point.

Each line segment drawn is a separate object and can be moved or erased as required. To end this command, just hit the ↵ key on the keyboard.

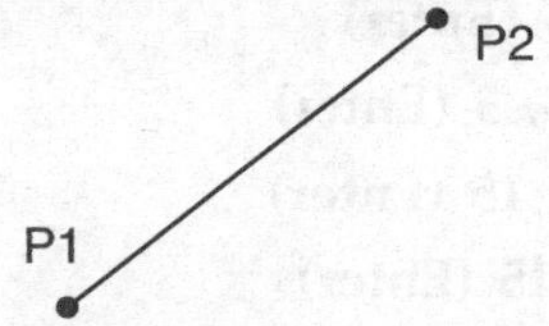


Command: **LINE**

Specify first point: (pick P1)

Specify next point or [Undo]: (pick P2)

Specify next point or [Undo]: ↵ (to end)

You can also draw lines by entering the co-ordinates of their end points at the command prompt rather than picking their position from the screen. This enables you to draw lines that are off screen, should you want to. You can also draw lines using something called direct distance entry.

## 1.2 Using co-ordinate system:

There are three type of co-ordinate system

(a) Absolute co-ordinate system

(b) Relative rectangular co-ordinate system

(c) Relative polar co-ordinate system

**(a) Absolute co-ordinate system:** In this type of coordinate system, the coordinate of all point taken from the origin.

**Syntax: x, y**

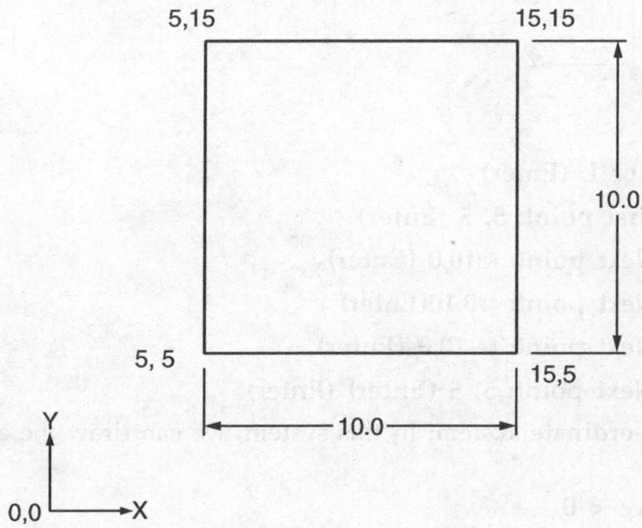

**For the figure:**

**Command: line or L (Enter)**

**Line specifies first point: 5, 5 (Enter)**

**Line specifies Next point: 1 5, 5 (Enter)**

**Line specifies Next point: 15, 15 (Enter)**

**Line specifies Next point: 5, 15 (Enter)**

**Line specifies Next point: 5, 5 (Enter) (Enter)**

(b) **Relative Rectangular coordinate system:** In this type of coordinate system, the coordinate of next point is taken from previous point.

**Syntax: @x, y**

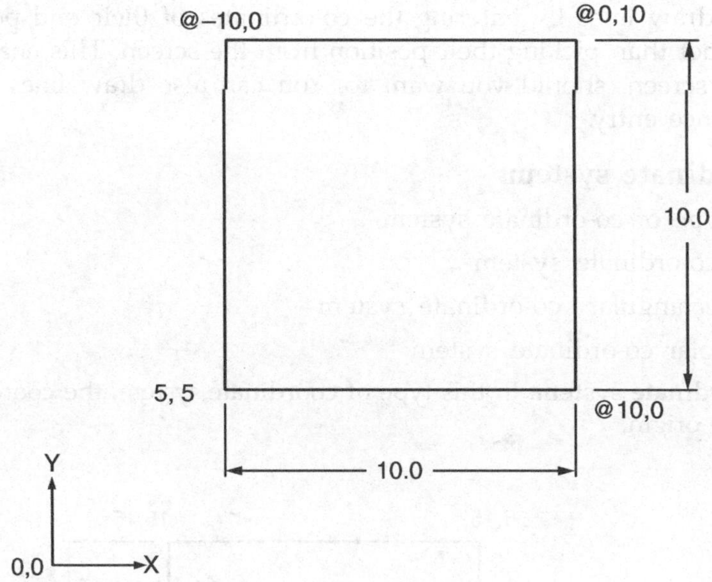


**For the figure:**

**Command: line or L (Enter)**

**Line specifies first point: 5, 5 (Enter)**

**Line specifies Next point: @10,0 (Enter)**

**Line specifies Next point: @0,10(Enter)**

**Line specifies Next point: @-10,0 (Enter)**

**Line specifies Next point: 5, 5 (Enter) (Enter)**

(c) **Relative polar co-ordinate system:** In this system, we can draw the angular line from the specific point.

**Syntax: @distance < θ**

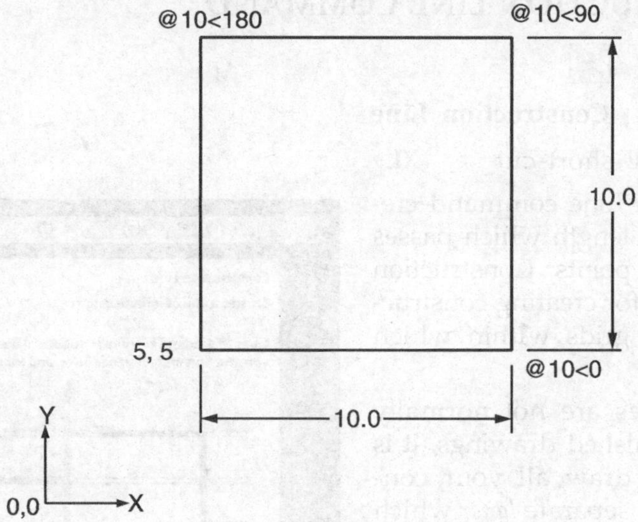


**For the figure:**

**Command: line or L (Enter)**

**Line specifies first point: 5, 5 (Enter)**

**Line specifies Next point: @10<0 (Enter)**

**Line specifies Next point: @10<90(Enter)**

**Line specifies Next point: @10<180 (Enter)**

**Line specifies Next point:@10<270 or 5, 5 (Enter) (Enter)**

**Angle direction:**

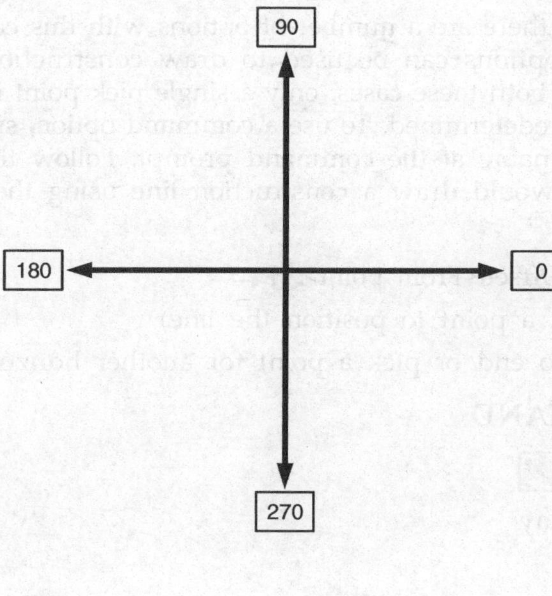

## 3 THE CONSTRUCTION LINE COMMAND

Toolbar Draw 

Pull-down **Draw ▸ Construction Line**

Keyboard **XLINE** short-cut **XL**

The Construction Line command creates a line of infinite length which passes through two picked points. Construction lines are very useful for creating construction frameworks or grids within which to design.

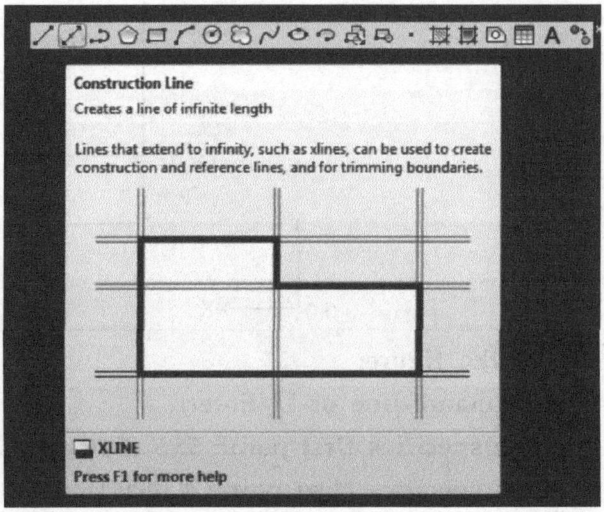


Construction lines are not normally used as objects in finished drawings, it is usual, therefore, to draw all your construction lines on a separate *layer* which will be turned off or frozen prior to printing. See the Object Properties tutorial to find out how to create new layers. Because of their nature, the Zoom Extents command option ignores construction lines.

Command: **XLINE**

Specify a point or [Hor/Ver/Ang/Bisect/Offset]: (pick a point)

Specify through point: (pick a second point)

Specify through point: ↵ (to end or pick another point)

You may notice that there are a number of options with this command. For example, the "Hor" and "Ver" options can be used to draw construction lines that are truly horizontal or vertical. In both these cases, only a single pick point is required because the direction of the line is predetermined. To use a command option, simply enter the capitalized part of the option name at the command prompt. Follow the command sequence below to see how you would draw a construction line using the Horizontal option.

Command: **XLINE**

Hor/Ver/Ang/Bisect/Offset/<From point>: **H** ↵

Through point: (pick a point to position the line)

through point: ↵ (to end or pick a point for another horizontal line)

## 4. THE RAY COMMAND

Toolbar custom 

Pull-down **Draw ▸ Ray**

Keyboard **RAY**

The Ray command creates a line similar to a construction line except that it extends infinitely in only one direction from the first pick point. The direction of the Ray is determined by the position of the second pick point.

Command: **RAY**

Specify start point: (pick the start point)

Specify through point: (pick a second point to determine direction)

Specify through point: ↵ (to end or pick another point)

## 5. THE POLYLINE FAMILY

Polylines differ from lines in that they are more complex objects. A single polyline can be composed of a number of straight-line or arc *segments*. Polylines can also be given line widths to make them appear solid. The illustration below shows a number of polylines to give you an idea of the flexibility of this type of line.

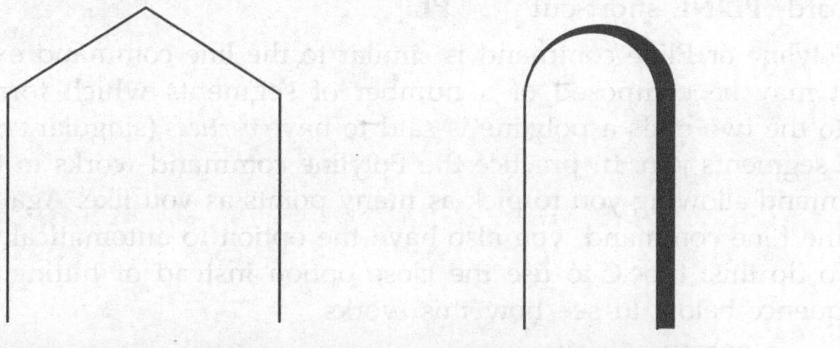

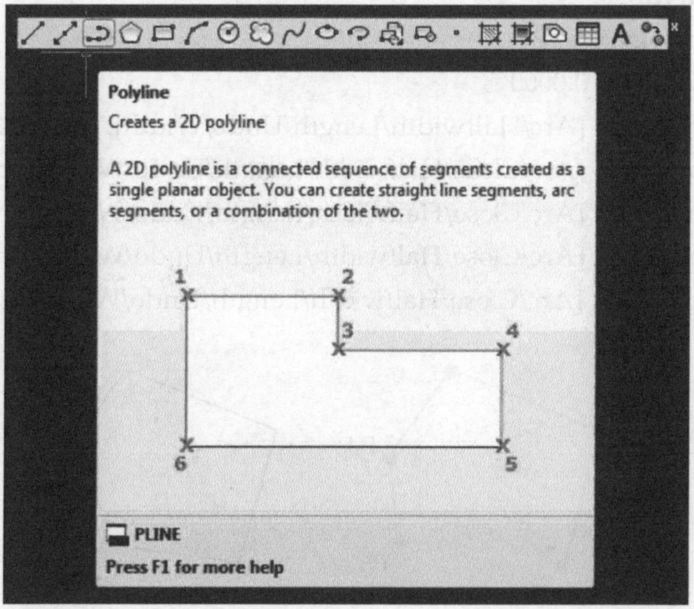

You may be wondering, if Polylines are so useful, why bother using ordinary lines at all? There are a number of answers to this question. The most frequently given answer is that because of their complexity, polylines use up more disk space than the equivalent line. As it is desirable to keep file sizes as small as possible, it is a good idea to use lines rather than polylines unless you have a particular requirement. You will also find, as you work with AutoCAD that lines and polylines are operationally different. Sometimes it is easier to work with polylines for certain tasks and at other times lines are best. You will quickly learn the pros and cons of these two sorts of line when you begin drawing with AutoCAD.

## 6. THE POLYLINE COMMAND

Toolbar Draw

Pull-down **Draw ▸ Polyline**

Keyboard **PLINE** short-cut **PL**

The Polyline or Pline command is similar to the line command except that the resulting object may be composed of a number of segments which form a single *object*. In addition to the two ends a polyline is said to have *vertices* (singular *vertex*) where intermediate line segments join. In practice the Polyline command works in the same way as the Line command allowing you to pick as many points as you like. Again, just hit ↵ to end. As with the Line command, you also have the option to automatically *close* a polyline end to end. To do this, type C to use the close option instead of hitting ↵. Follow the command sequence below to see how this works.

Command: **PLINE**

Specify start point: (pick P1)

Current line-width is 0.0000

Specify next point or [Arc/Halfwidth/Length/Undo/Width]: (pick P2)

Specify next point or [Arc/Close/Halfwidth/Length/Undo/Width]: (pick P3)

Specify next point or [Arc/Close/Halfwidth/Length/Undo/Width]: (pick P4)

Specify next point or [Arc/Close/Halfwidth/Length/Undo/Width]: (pick P5)

Specify next point or [Arc/Close/Halfwidth/Length/Undo/Width]: ↵ (or **C** to close)

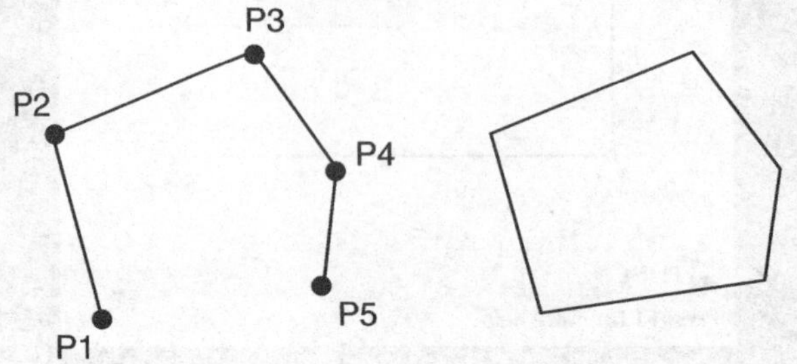


**Open Polyline** **Closed Polyline**

In the illustration on the right, the figure on the left was created by hitting the ↵ key after the fifth point was picked. The figure on the right demonstrates the effect of using the Close option.

It is worth while taking some time to familiarize yourself with the Polyline command as it is an extremely useful command to know. Try experimenting with options such as Arc and Width and see if you can create polylines like the ones in the illustration above. The Undo option is particularly useful. This allows you to unpick polyline vertices, one at a time so that you can easily correct mistakes.

Polylines can be edited after they are created to, for example, change their width. You can do this using the PEDIT command, **Modify ▸ Object ▸ Polyline** from the pull-down menu.

## 7. THE RECTANGLE COMMAND

Toolbar Draw

Pull-down **Draw ▸ Rectangle**

Keyboard **RECTANGLE** short-cuts **REC, RECTANG**

The Rectangle command is used to draw a rectangle whose sides are vertical and horizontal. The position and size of the rectangle are defined by picking two diagonal corners. The rectangle isn't really an AutoCAD object at all. It is, in fact, just a closed polyline which is automatically drawn for you.

Command: **RECTANG**

Specify first corner point or [Chamfer/Elevation/Fillet/Thickness/Width]:(pick P1)
Specify other corner point or [Dimensions]: (pick P2)

The Rectangle command also has a number of options. Width works in the same way as for the Polyline command. The Chamfer and Fillet options have the same effect as the Chamfer and Fillet commands; see the Modifying Objects tutorial for details. Elevation and Thickness are 3D options.

Command: **RECTANG**

Specify first corner point or [Chamfer/Elevation/Fillet/Thickness/Width]:(pick a point)

Specify other corner point or [Dimensions]: **D**

Specify length for rectangles <0.0000>: **20**

Specify width for rectangles <0.0000>: **10**

Specify other corner point or [Dimensions]: (pick a point to fix the orientation)

This method provides a good alternative to using relative Cartesian co-ordinates for determining length and width. See the Using Co-ordinates tutorial for more details.

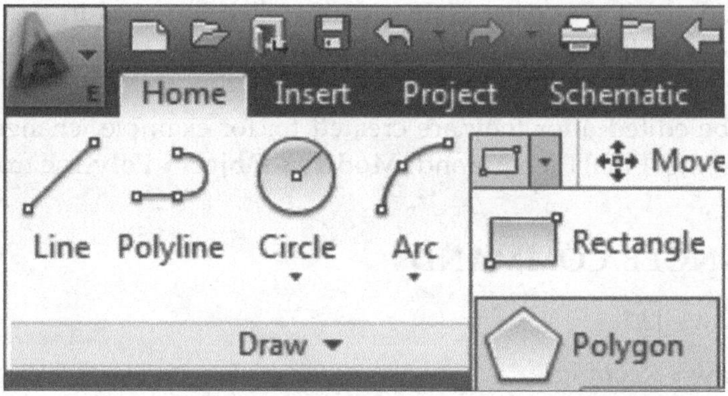


## 8. THE POLYGON COMMAND

Toolbar Draw 

Pull-down **Draw ▸ Polygon**

Keyboard **POLYGON** short-cut **POL**

The Polygon command can be used to draw any regular polygon from 3 sides up to 1024 sides. This command requires four inputs from the user, the number of sides, a pick point for the centre of the polygon, whether you want the polygon *inscribed* or *circumscribed* and then a pick point which determines both the radius of this imaginary circle and the orientation of the polygon. The polygon command creates a closed polyline in the shape of the required polygon.

This command also allows you to define the polygon by entering the length of a side using the Edge option. You can also control the size of the polygon by entering an exact radius for the circle. Follow the command sequence below to see how this command works.

Command: **POLYGON**

Enter number of sides <4>: **5** ↵

Specify center of polygon or [Edge]: (pick P1 or type **E** to define by edge length)

Enter an option [Inscribed in circle/Circumscribed about circle] <I>: ↵ (to accept the inscribed default or type **C** for circumscribed)

Specify radius of circle: (pick P2 or enter exact radius)

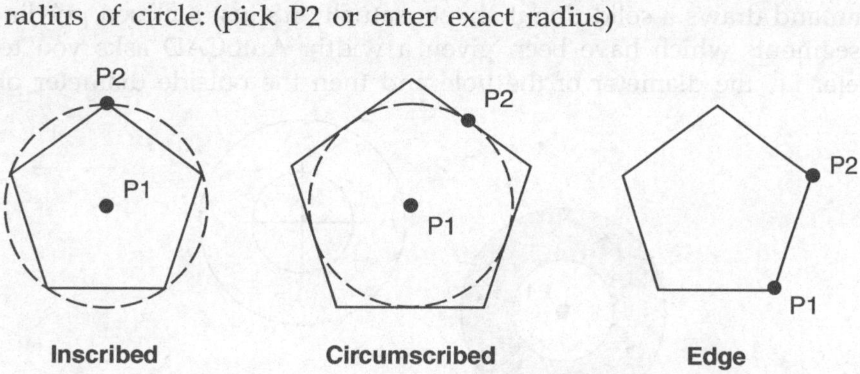


In the illustration above, the polygon on the left is inscribed (inside the circle with the polygon vertexes touching it), the one in the middle is circumscribed (outside the circle with the polyline edges tangential to it) and the one on the right is defined by the length of an edge.

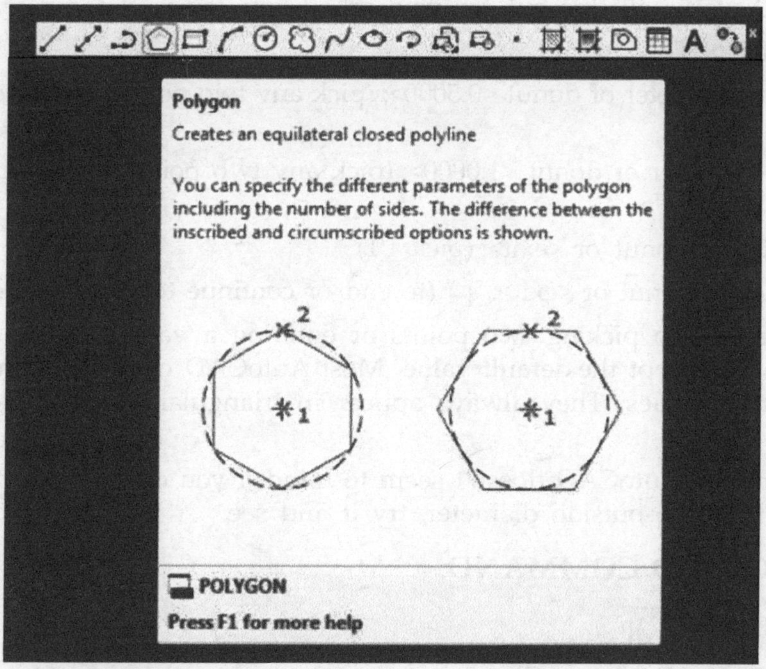


## 9. THE DONUT COMMAND

Toolbar custom

Pull-down **Draw ▸ Donut**

Keyboard **DONUT** short-cut **DO**

This command draws a solid donut shape, actually it's just a closed polyline consisting of two arc segments which have been given a width. AutoCAD asks you to define the inside diameter i.e. the diameter of the hole and then the outside diameter of the donut.

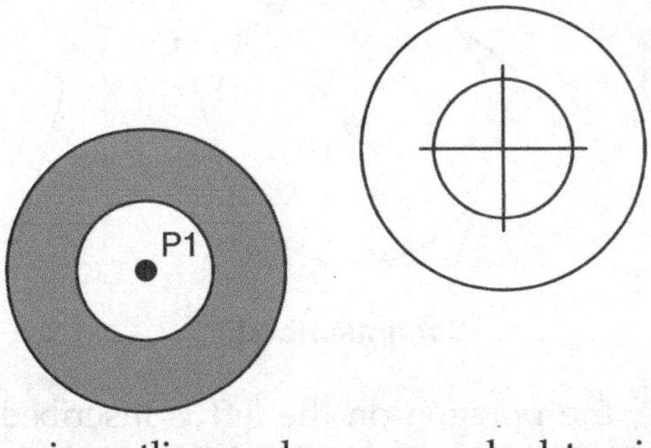


The donut is then drawn in outline and you are asked to pick the centre point in order to position the donut. You can continue picking centre points to draw more donuts or you can hit ↵ to end the command. Surprisingly, donuts are constructed from single closed polylines composed of two arc segments which have been given a width. Fortunately AutoCAD works all this out for you, so all you see is a donut.

Command: **DONUT**

Specify inside diameter of donut <0.5000>: (pick any two points to define a diameter or enter the exact length)

Specify outside diameter of donut <1.0000>: (pick any two points to define a diameter or enter the exact length)

Specify center of donut or <exit>: (pick P1)

Specify center of donut or <exit>: ↵ (to end or continue to pick for more doughnuts)

As an alternative to picking two points or entering a value for the diameters, you could just hit ↵ to accept the default value. Most AutoCAD commands that require user input have default values. They always appear in triangular brackets like this <default value>.

Curiously enough AutoCAD doesn't seem to mind if you make the inside diameter of a donut larger than the outside diameter, try it and see.

## 10. THE REVCLOUD COMMAND

Toolbar Draw

Pull-down **Draw ▸ Revision Cloud**

Keyboard **REVCLOUD**

The Revcloud command is used to draw a "freehand" revision cloud or to convert any closed shape into a revision cloud.

Command: **REVCLOUD**

Minimum arc length: 66.6377 Maximum arc length: 116.6159

Specify start point or [Arc length/Object] <Object>: (Pick P1)

Guide crosshairs along cloud path...

Move the mouse to form a closed shape; the command automatically ends when a closed shape is formed.

Revision cloud finished.

You can use the "Arc length" option to control the scale of the revision cloud. This is achieved by specifying the minimum and maximum arc length. The "Object" option is used to transform any closed shape, such as a polyline, spline or circle into a revision cloud.

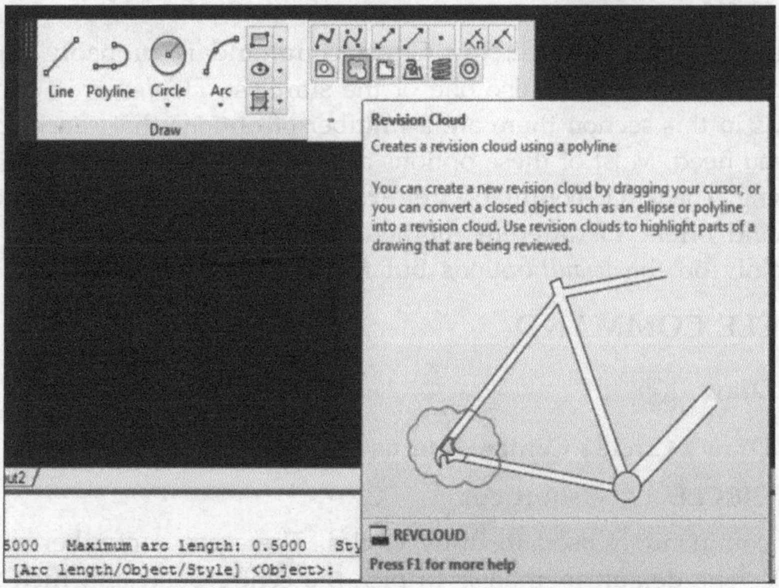


## 11. THE 3D POLYLINE COMMAND

Toolbar custom

Pull-down **Draw ▸ 3D Polyline**

Keyboard **3DPOLY**

The 3D Polyline command works in exactly the same way as the Polyline command. The main difference between a normal polyline and a 3D polyline is that each vertex (pick point) of a 3D polyline can have a different value for Z (height). In normal (2D) polylines, all vertexes must have the same Z value.

3D polyline objects are not as complex as their 2D cousins. For example, they cannot contain arc segments and they cannot be given widths. However, they can be very useful for 3D modeling.

Command: **3DPOLY**

Specify start point of polyline: (pick a point)

Specify endpoint of line or [Undo]: (pick another point)

Specify endpoint of line or [Undo]: (pick a third point)

Specify endpoint of line or [Close/Undo]: ↵ (to end, **C** to close or continue picking points)

Notice that you are not prompted for a Z value each time you pick a point. You must either use one of the Object Snaps to pick a point with the required Z value or use the "**.XY**" filter to force AutoCAD to prompt for a Z value.

**Circles, Arcs etc.**

Along with Line and Polyline, the Circle command is probably one of the most frequently used. Fortunately it is also one of the simplest. However, in common with the other commands in this section there are a number of options that can help you construct just the circle you need. Most of these options are self explanatory but in some cases it can be quite confusing. The Circle command, for example, offers 6 ways to create a circle, while the Arc command offers 10 different methods for drawing an arc. The sections below concentrate mainly on the *default* options but feel free to experiment.

## 12. THE CIRCLE COMMAND

Toolbar Draw 

Pull-down **Draw ▸ Circle ▸ Center, Radius**

Keyboard **CIRCLE** short-cut **C**

The Circle command is used to draw circles. There are a number of ways you can define the circle. The default method is to pick the centre point and then to either pick a second point on the circumference of the circle or enter the circle radius at the keyboard.

Command Sequence

Command: **CIRCLE**

Specify center point for circle or [3P/2P/Ttr (tan tan radius)]: (pick P1)

Specify radius of circle or [Diameter] <50.0195>: (pick P2 or enter the exact radius)

Center, Radius
Center, Diameter

2 Points
3 Points

Tan, Tan, Radius
Tan, Tan, Tan

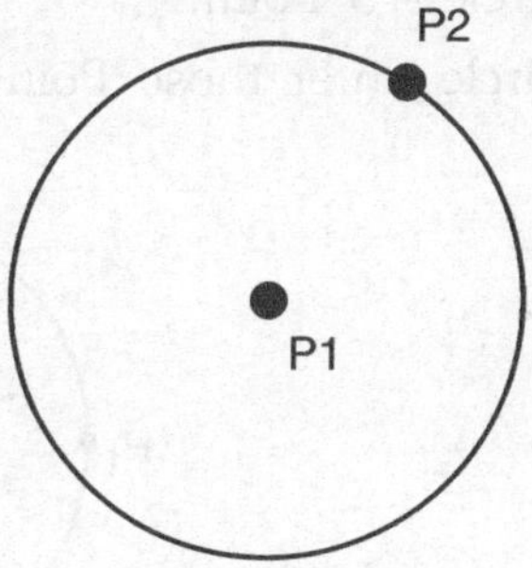


As you can see from the command prompt above the default options are always indicated in triangular brackets like so<Default> and command options appear within square brackets like so [Option]. Each *option* is separated by a forward slash like this /. You can choose to use the alternative options by typing them at the prompt. For example, the circle command gives you three extra options to define a circle. 3P which uses any three points on the circumference, 2P which uses two points on the circumference to form a diameter and Ttr which stands for Tangent Tangent Radius. Obviously to use this last option you need to have drawn two lines which you can use as tangents to the circle. Try these options out to see how they work. Note that to invoke a command option, you need only type the upper-case part of the option name. For example, if you want to use the Ttr option, you need only enter "T". There are two more circle options on the pull-down menu that enable you to draw a circle by defining the center and diameter or by using 3 tangents.

Following Method to Draw circle.

1. Centre, diameter
2. 2P
3. 3P
4. Tan, Tan, Radius
5. Tan, Tan, Tan

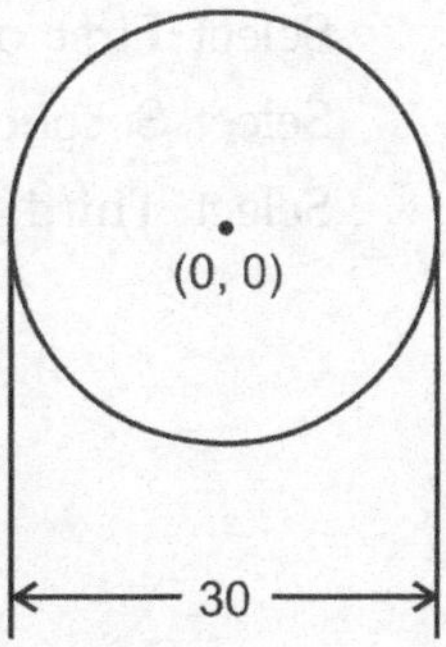


**1. Centre, Diameter:** Draw – circcle – centre, Radius/Diameter

Specity centre of circle - 0,0

Enter the Radius or [Diameter] – 15 (Radius)↵

For Diameter

Enter the Radius or [Diameter] – D↵

Enter the Diameter – 30↵

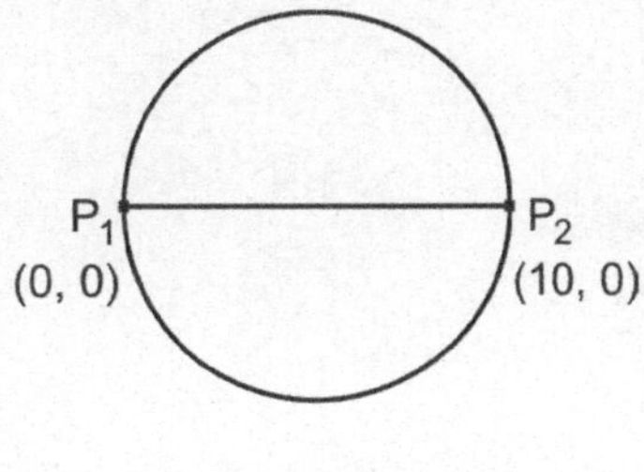


**2. 2P:** Draw - Circle - 2 point.

Enter the First Point = 0, 0↵ ($P_1$)

Enter the Second Point = 10,0↵ ($P_2$)

3. **3P:** Draw - circle - 3 Point.

For 3 Point circle Enter those Point from which circle Passed.

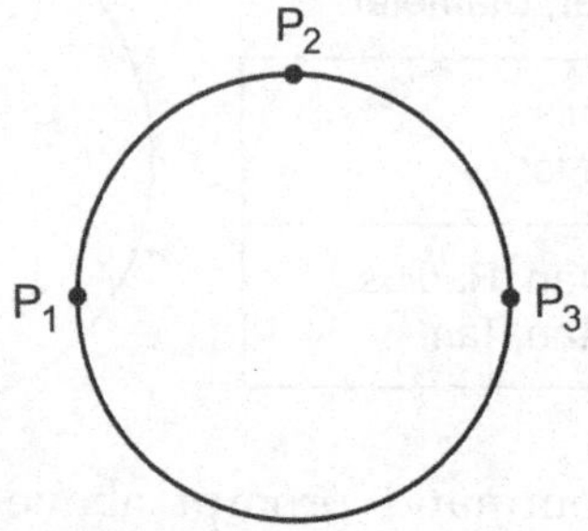


4. **Tan, Tan, Radius:** Select first object to Tangent

Select Second object to Tangent

Enter the Radius of circle - 10

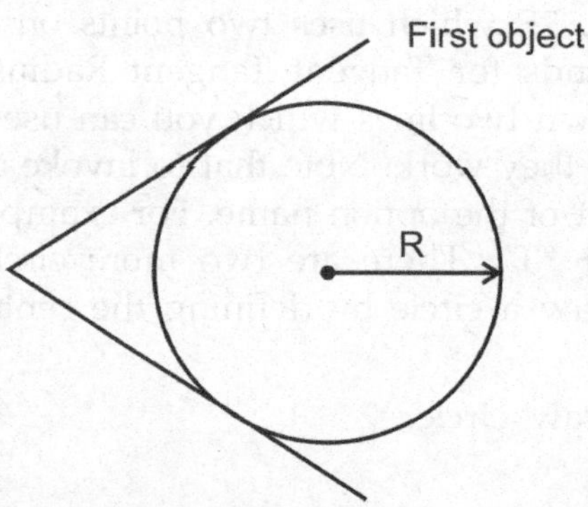


5. **Tan, Tan, Tan:** First Draw Any three object to which the circle is tangent

Select First object to Tangent

Select Second object to Tangent

Select Third object to Tangent

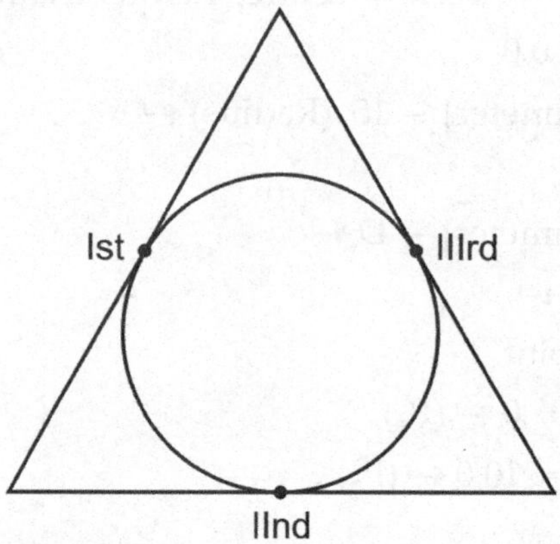

## 13. THE ARC COMMAND

Toolbar Draw

Pull-down **Draw ▸ Arc ▸ 3 Points**

Keyboard **ARC** short-cut **A**

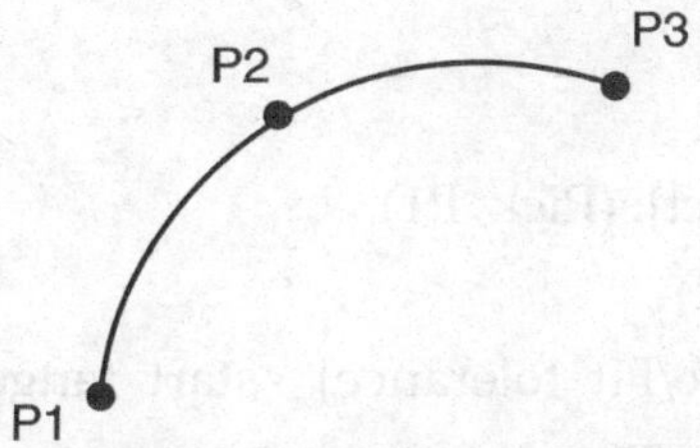


The Arc command allows you to draw an arc of a circle. There are numerous ways to define an arc, the default method uses three pick points, a start point, a second point and an end point. Using this method, the drawn arc will start at the first pick point, pass through the second point and end at the third point. Once you have mastered the default method try some of the others. You may, for example need to draw an arc with a specific radius. All of the Arc command options are available from the pull-down menu.

Command: **ARC**

Specify start point of arc or [Center]: (pick P1)

Specify second point of arc or [Center/End]: (pick P2)

Specify end point of arc: (pick P3)

It is also possible to create an arc by trimming a circle object. In practice, many arcs are actually created this way. See the Trim command on the Modifying Objects tutorial for details.

## 14. THE SPLINE COMMAND

Toolbar Draw

Pull-down **Draw ▸ Spline**

Keyboard **SPLINE** short-cut **SPL**

The Spline command creates a type of spline known as a nonuniform rational B-spline, NURBS for short. A spline is a smooth curve that is fitted along a number of control points. The Fit Tolerance option can be used to control how closely the spline conforms to the control points. A low tolerance value causes the spline to form close to the control points. A tolerance of 0 (zero) forces the spline to pass through the control points. The illustration on the right shows the effect of different tolerance values on a spline that is defined using the same four control points, P1, P2, P3 and P4.

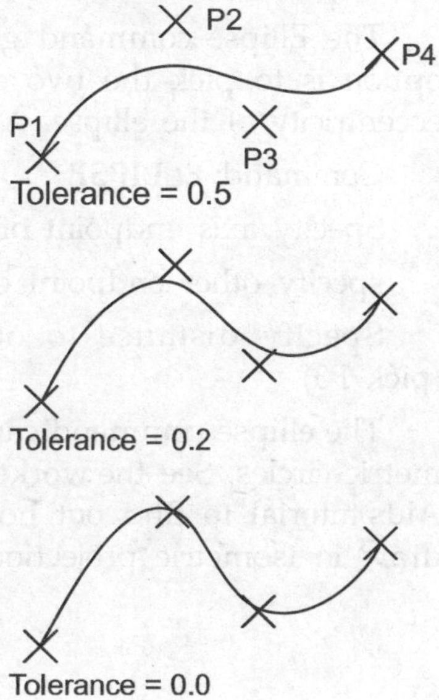

Splines can be edited after they have been created using the SPLINEDIT command, **Modify ▸ Object ▸ Spline** from the pull-down menu. Using this command, you can change the tolerance, add more control points move control points and close splines, amongst other things. However, if you just want to move spline control points, it is best to use grips. See the Stretching with Grips section of the Modifying Objects tutorial for details.

Command Sequence

Command: **SPLINE**

Specify first point or [Object]: (Pick P1)

Specify next point: (Pick P2)

Specify next point or [Close/Fit tolerance] <start tangent>: (Pick P3)

Specify next point or [Close/Fit tolerance] <start tangent>: (Pick P4)

Specify next point or [Close/Fit tolerance] <start tangent>: ↵

Specify start tangent: (pick a point)

Specify end tangent: (pick a point)

You can create linear approximations to splines by smoothing polylines with the PEDIT command, **Modify ▸ Polyline** from the pull-down menu. However, you can also turn polylines into true splines using the Object option of the Spline command.

## 15. THE ELLIPSE COMMAND

Toolbar Draw

Pull-down **Draw ▸ Ellipse ▸ Axis, End**

Keyboard **ELLIPSE** short-cut **EL**

The Ellipse command gives you a number of different creation options. The default option is to pick the two end points of an axis and then a third point to define the eccentricity of the ellipse. After you have mastered the default option, try out the others.

Command: **ELLIPSE**

Specify axis endpoint of ellipse or [Arc/Center]: (pick P1)

specify other endpoint of axis: (pick P2)

Specify distance to other axis or [Rotation]: (pick P3)

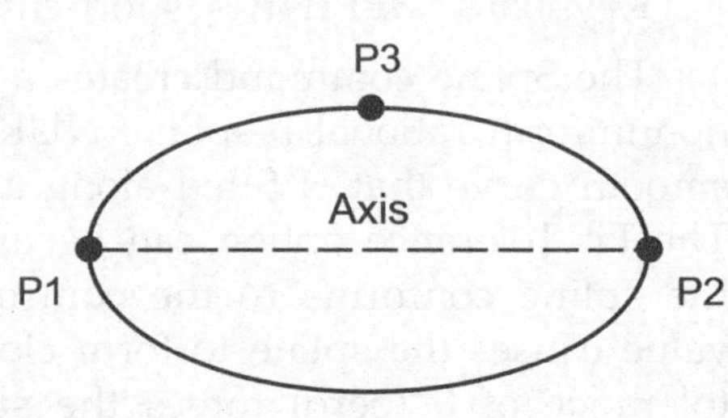


The ellipse command can also be used to draw isometric circles. See the worked example in the Drawing Aids tutorial to find out how to do this and how to draw in isometric projection with AutoCAD.

## 16. THE ELLIPSE ARC COMMAND

Toolbar Draw 

Pull-down **Draw ▸ Ellipse ▸ Arc**

Keyboard **ELLIPSE ↵ A** short-cut **EL ↵ A**

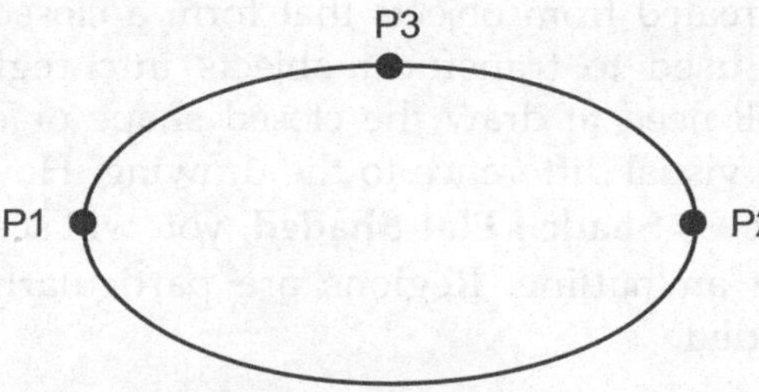


Start = 270 degrees
End = 90 degrees

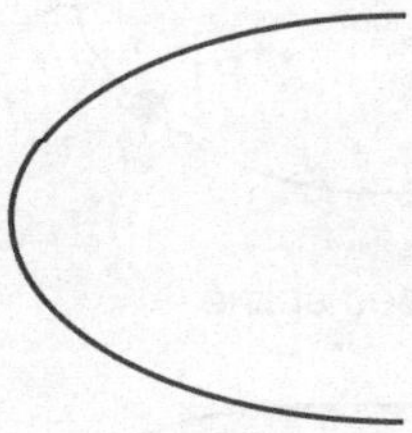

Result = half an ellipse

The Ellipse Arc command is very similar to the Ellipse command, described above. The only difference is that, in addition to specifying the two axis end points and the "distance to other axis" point, you are prompted for a start and end angle for the arc. You may specify angles by picking points or by entering values at the command prompt. Remember that angles are measured in an anti-clockwise direction, starting at the 3 o'clock position.

In truth, the Ellipse Arc command is not a new or separate command; it is just an option of the Ellipse command and it therefore has no unique command line name. It is curious why Autodesk considered this option important enough to give it it's own button on the Draw toolbar. Still, there it is.

Command: **ELLIPSE**

Specify axis endpoint of ellipse or [Arc/Center]: **A**

Specify axis endpoint of elliptical arc or [Center]: (pick P1)

Specify other endpoint of axis: (pick P2)

Specify distance to other axis or [Rotation]: (pick P3)

Specify start angle or [Parameter]: **270**

Specify end angle or [Parameter/Included angle]: **90**

## 17. THE REGION COMMAND

Toolbar Draw

Pull-down **Draw ▸ Region**

Keyboard **REGION** short-cut **REG**

A region is a surface created from objects that form a closed shape, known as a loop. The Region command is used to transform objects into regions rather than actually drawing them (i.e. you will need to draw the closed shape or *loop* first). Once a region is created, there may be little visual difference to the drawing. However, if you set the shade mode to "Flat Shaded", **View ▸ Shade ▸ Flat Shaded**, you will see that the region is, in fact, a surface and not simply an outline. Regions are particularly useful in 3D modeling because they can be extruded.

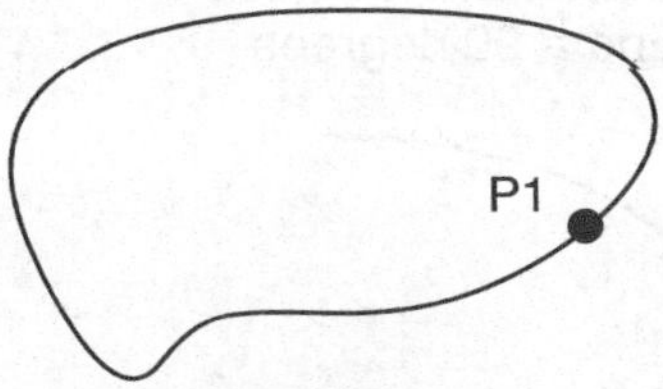


Source = closed spline

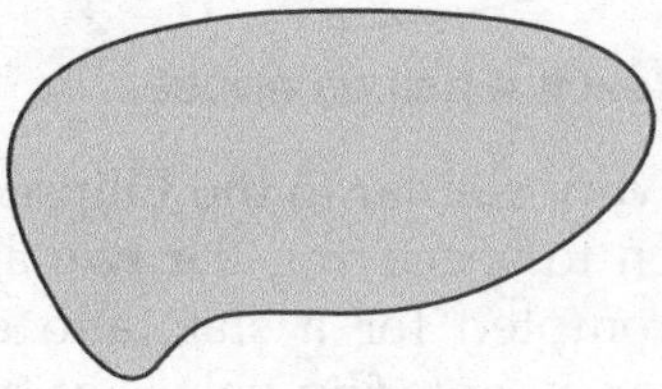

Result = region

Before starting the Region command, draw a closed shape such as a rectangle, circle or any closed polyline or spline.

**Command:** REGION

Select objects: (Pick P1)

Select objects: ↵

1 loop extracted.

1 Region created.

You can use the Boolean commands, Union, Subtract and Intersect to create complex regions.

## 18. POINTS AND POINT STYLES

Points are very simple objects and the process of creating them is also very simple. Points are rarely used as drawing components although there is no reason why they could not be. They are normally used just as drawing aids in a similar way that Construction Lines and Rays are used. For example, points are automatically created when you use the Measure and Divide commands to set out distances along a line.

When adding points to a drawing it is usually desirable to set the point style first because the default style can be difficult to see.

### 18.1 The Point Command

Toolbar Draw 

**Draw ▸ Point ▸ Single Point**

Keyboard **POINT**short-cut **PO**

The point command will insert a point marker in your drawing at a position which you pick in the drawing window or at any co-ordinate location which you enter at the keyboard. The default point style is a simple dot, which is often difficult to see but you can change the point style to something more easily visible or elaborate using the point style dialogue box. Points can be used for "setting out" a drawing in addition to construction lines. You can *snap* to points using the Node object snap. See the Object Snap tutorial for details.

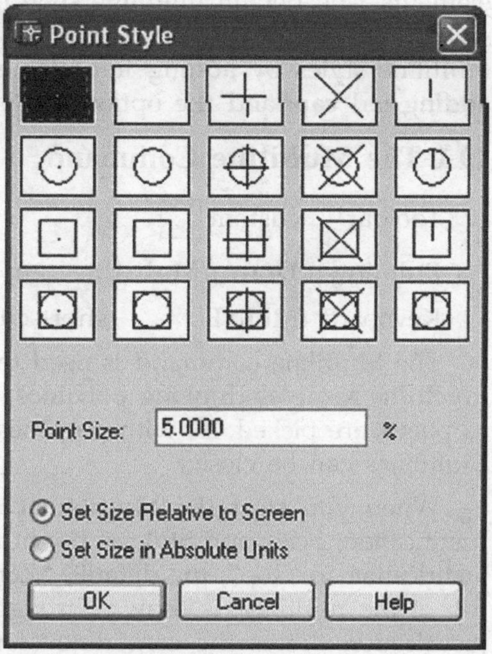


Command: **POINT**

Current point modes: PDMODE=0 PDSIZE=0.0000

specify a point: (pick any point)

Strangely, in Multiple Point mode (the default for the Point button on the Draw toolbar) you will need to use the escape key (Esc) on your keyboard to end the command. The usual right-click or enter doesn't work.

### 18.2 The Point Style

Toolbar

Pull-down **Format ▸ Point Style...**

Keyboard **DDPTYPE**

You can start the point style command from the keyboard by typing DDPTYPE or you can start it from the pull-down menu at **Format ▸ Point Style...** The command starts by displaying a dialogue box offering a number of options. To change the point style, just pick the picture of the style you want and then click the "OK" button. You will need to use the Regen command, REGEN at the keyboard or **View ▸ Regen** from the pull-down to force any existing points in your drawing to display in the new style. Any new points created after the style has been set will automatically display in the new style. One interesting aspect of points is that their size can be set to an absolute value or relative to the screen size, expressed as a percentage. The default is for points to display relative to the screen size, which is very useful because it means that points will remain the same size, irrespective of zoom factor. This is particularly convenient when drawings become complex and the drawing process requires a lot of zooming in and out.

## 19. MULTILINES

Multilines are complex lines that consist of between 1 and 16 parallel lines, known as elements. The default multiline style has just two elements but you can create additional styles of an almost endless variety. The Multiline Style command enables you to create new multiline styles by adding line elements, changing the colour and linetypes of elements, adding end caps and the option of displaying as a solid colour.

### 19.1 The Multiline Command

Toolbar custom

Pull-down **Draw ▸ Multiline**

Keyboard **MLINE** short-cut **ML**

The Multiline command is used to draw Multilines. This process of drawing is pretty much the same as drawing polylines, additional line segments are added to the multiline as points are picked. As with polylines, points can be unpicked with the Undo option and Multilines can be closed.

When you start the Multiline command you also have the option to specify the Justification, Scale and Style of the multiline. The Justification option allows you to set the justification to "Top", the default, "Zero" or "Bottom". When justification is set to top, the top of the multiline is drawn through the pick points, as in the illustration below. Zero justification draws the centerline of the multiline through the pick points and Bottom draws the bottom line through the pick points. Justification allows you to control how the multiline is drawn relative to your setting out information. For example, if you are drawing a new road with reference to its centre line, then Zero justification would be appropriate.

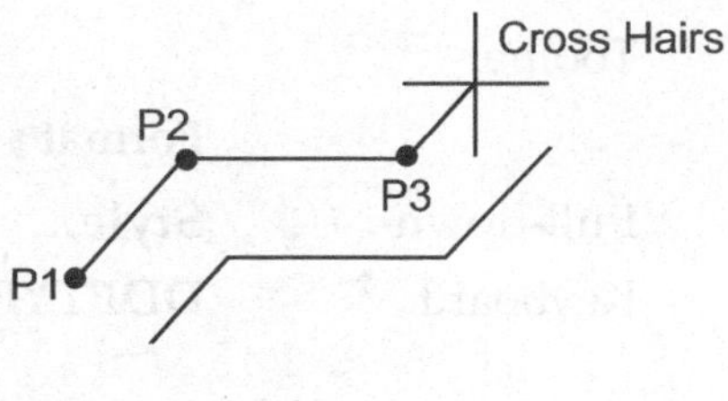


The Scale option allows you to set a scale factor, which effectively changes the width of the multiline. The default scale factor is set to 1.0 so to half the width of the multiline, a value of 0.5 would be entered. A value of 2.0 would double the width.

The Style option enables you to set the current multiline style. The default style is called "Standard". This is the only style available unless you have previously created a new style with the Multiline Style command. Follow the command sequence below to see how the Multiline command works and then try changing the Justification and Scale options.

Command: **MLINE**

Current settings: Justification = Top, Scale = 20.00, Style = STANDARD

Specify start point or [Justification/Scale/STyle]: (Pick P1)

Specify next point: (Pick P2)

Specify next point or [Undo]: (Pick P3)

Specify next point or [Close/Undo]: ↵ (to end or continue picking or **C** to close)

The Multiline Style Command

Toolbar none

Pull-down **Format ▸ Multiline Style...**

Keyboard **MLSTYLE**

The Multiline style command is used to create new multiline styles, which can then be used with the Multiline command. When you start the command for the first time, you will see the Multiline Styles dialogue box indicating that the Standard style is "Current". To create a new style, enter a new style name in the "Name" edit box by overwriting "STANDARD" and enter an optional description in the "Description" edit box. The dialogue box should now look something like the one on the right. When you are happy with the new name and description, simply click on the "Add" button. Your new style will now appear in the "Current" box. The new style you have created is simply a copy of the Standard style, so the next step is to change the style to suit your own purposes. Click on the "Element Properties..." button to proceed.

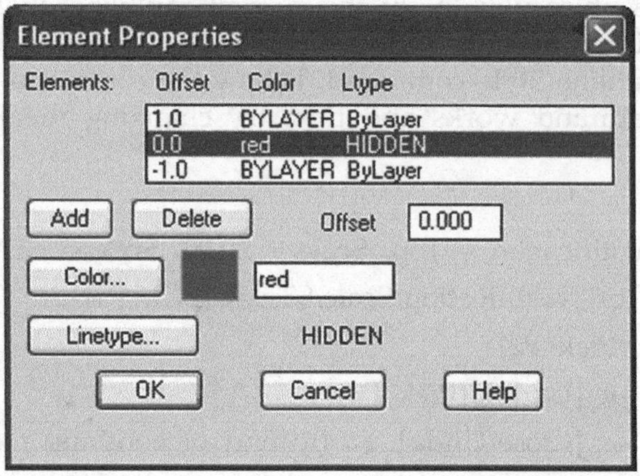


You will now see the Element Properties dialogue box appear. This dialogue box allows you to add new line elements or delete existing ones and to control the element offset, colour and linetype. Click the "Add" button to add a new element. A new line element now appears with an offset of 0.0, in other words, this is a centre line. Highlight the top element in the "Elements" list and change the offset to 1.0 by entering this value in the "Offset" edit box. Now do the same with the bottom element remembering to enter a value of -1.0 because this is a negative offset. You now have a multiline that is 2 drawing units wide with a centre line. Let's now change the colour and linetypes of the centre line.

Highlight the 0.0 offset elements by clicking it in the "Elements" list. To change the colour, simply click on the Colour... button and select an appropriate colour from the palette. When a colour has been selected, click the "OK" button on the palette to return to the Element Properties dialogue box.

Changing the linetypes is a little more complicated because we will need to load the required linetype first. However, click on the "Linetype..." button to proceed.

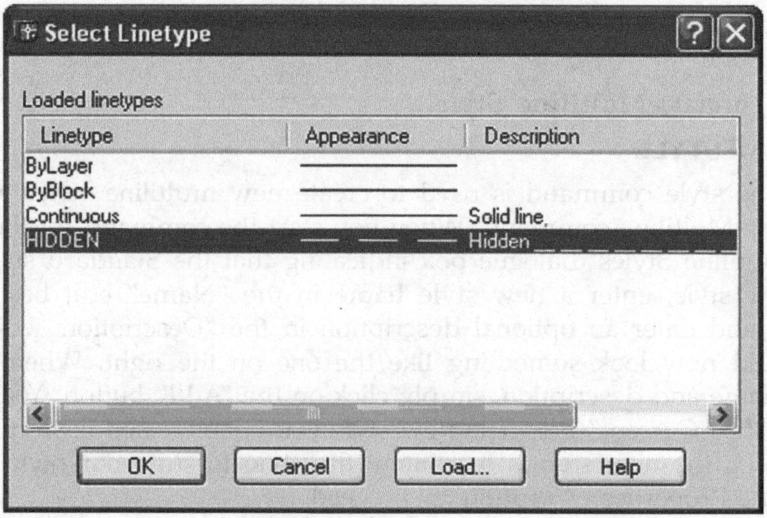

The Select Linetype dialogue box appears with just a few solid linetypes listed, ByLayer, ByBlock and Continuous. Click on the "Load..." button. The Load or Reload Linetypes dialogue box now appears. Scroll down the list of linetypes until you find one called "Hidden". Highlight Hidden and then click the "OK" button. You will now see the Hidden linetypes appear in the "Loaded linetypes" list in the Select Linetype dialogue box, which should now look similar to the one shown above. Finally, highlight Hidden and click the "OK" button. Your Element Properties dialogue box should now look similar to the one in the illustration above. To complete our new style, we will add some end caps and a solid fill. Click on the "Multiline Properties..." button to proceed.

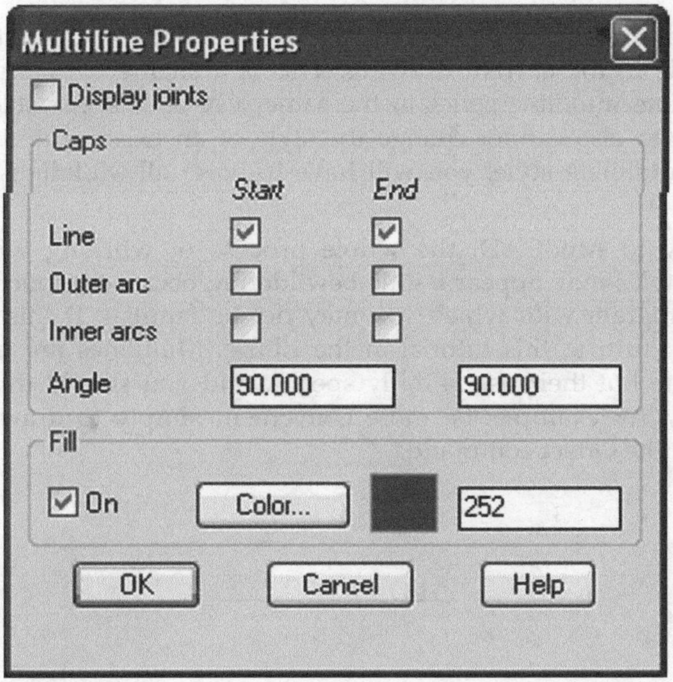


In the Multiline Properties dialogue box, click in the "Line" check boxes under "Start" and "End". This will have the effect of capping the ends of the multiline with a 90 degree line. As you can see from the dialogue box, you can change this angle if you wish to give a chamfered end. Next, click the "On" check box in the "Fill" section and then click on the Colour... button and select the fill colour from the palette. The Multiline Properties dialogue box should now look like the one in the illustration on the left. Finally, click the "OK" button in the Multiline Properties dialogue box and again in the Multiline Style dialogue box. You are now ready to draw with your new multiline.

Start the Multiline command, pick a number of points and admire your handiwork. If you have followed this tutorial closely, your new multiline should look something like the one in the illustration on the right. Notice the effect of the various changes you have made compared with the Standard multiline style.

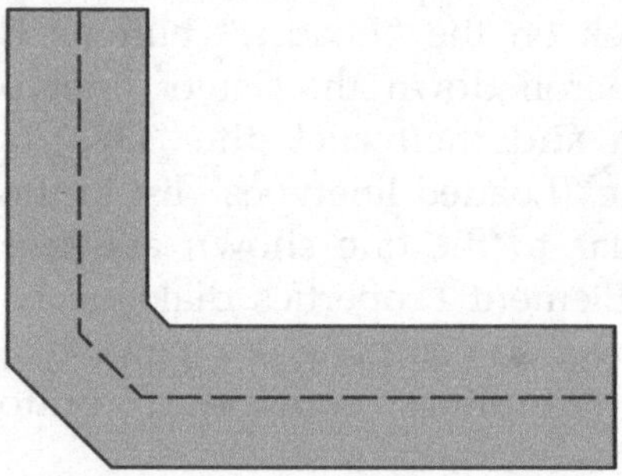

One limitation of multiline styles is that you cannot modify a style if there are Multilines referencing the style in the current drawing. This is a shame because it means that it is not possible to update multiline styles in the same way as it is possible to update text or dimension styles. You also cannot change the style of an existing multiline. If you really want to modify a multiline style, you will have to erase all Multilines that reference the style first.

If you are new to AutoCAD, the whole process of working with Multilines and creating multiline styles may appear a little bewildering because it touches upon a number of aspects of the program with which you may not be familiar. If this is the case, it may be a good idea to return to this tutorial in the future. Multilines are useful because they can save lots of time but their use is fairly specific and you should think carefully before using them. It may, for example, be more convenient simply to draw a polyline and to create offsets using the Offset command.

CHAPTER 5

# Modify Toolbar

## MODIFY TOOLBAR OUTLINE

### To modify a toolbar

1. From the View menu, choose Toolbars.
2. If the toolbar you want to modify is not displayed, select it in the Toolbars dialog box. Choose Customize.
3. While the Customize Toolbars dialog box is displayed, you can modify any displayed toolbar as follows:
   - Drag toolbar buttons right or left to reposition them.
   - Create spaces by dragging a button to the right or left edge of the button beside it, but not past the middle.
   - Remove toolbar buttons by dragging them off the toolbar.
   - Add buttons to toolbars by dragging them from the Customize Toolbars dialog box to the toolbar. Change the Categories selection to display the buttons you want to add.
   - Drag buttons from one toolbar to another, or press CTRL while you drag to copy the toolbar button to another toolbar.
   - Choose Close to exit the dialog boxes.

   Command line TOOLBAR

   Shortcut menu Right-click a toolbar and choose Customize.

### To rename a toolbar

1. From the View menu, choose Toolbars.
2. In the Toolbars dialog box, select the toolbar name, and then choose Properties.
3. In the Toolbar Properties dialog box, enter a new name.
4. To change the text displayed on the status line, enter new text at Help, and then choose Apply.
5. In the Toolbars dialog box, choose Close.

### Draw Toolbar AUTOCAD New Version

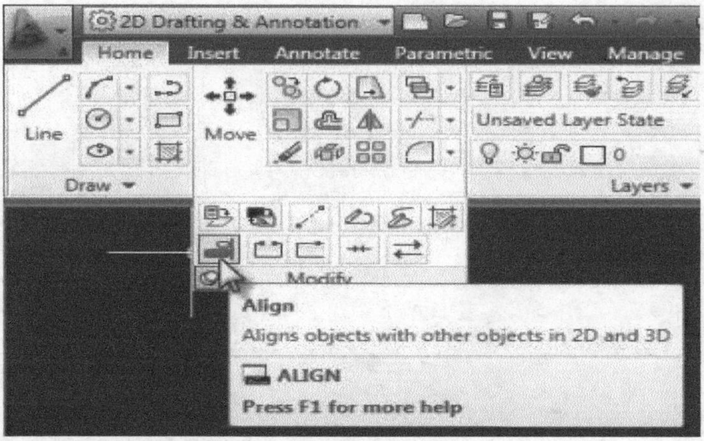

## Draw Toolbar AUTOCAD old Version

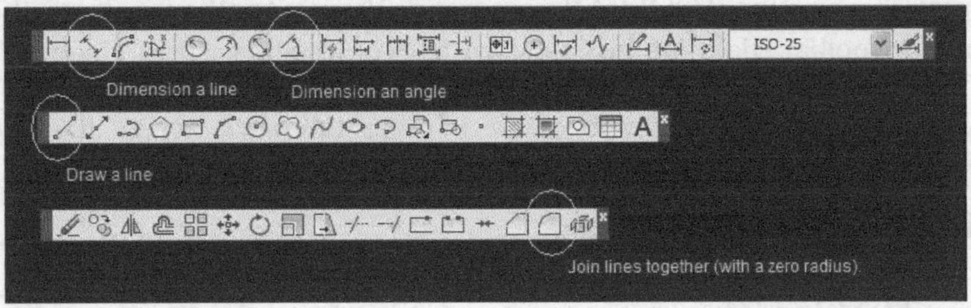


## 1. INTRODUCTION

AutoCAD drawings are rarely completed simply by drawing lines, circles etc. Most likely you will need to modify these basic drawing objects in some way in order to create the image you need. AutoCAD provides a whole range of modify tools such as Move, Copy, Rotate and Mirror. As you can see, the command names are easily understandable. However, the way these commands work is not always obvious. This tutorial is designed to show you how all of the Modify commands work. If you just need information quickly, use the Quick Find toolbar below to go straight to the information you need or select a topic from the contents list above.

As is usual with AutoCAD, the Modify tools can be accessed in one of three ways, from the keyboard, from the pull-down menu and from the toolbar. All of the Modify tools are available from the Modify pull-down and the Modify toolbar. In each section below, the toolbar, pull-down and keyboard options are given. The method you choose is entirely up to you. Ultimately you will use the method that you feel most comfortable with or the one you find most efficient. AutoCAD allows great flexibility and there aren't any right or wrong ways of working. That said, it should be pointed out that the use of toolbars in AutoCAD is almost always quicker than any other method.

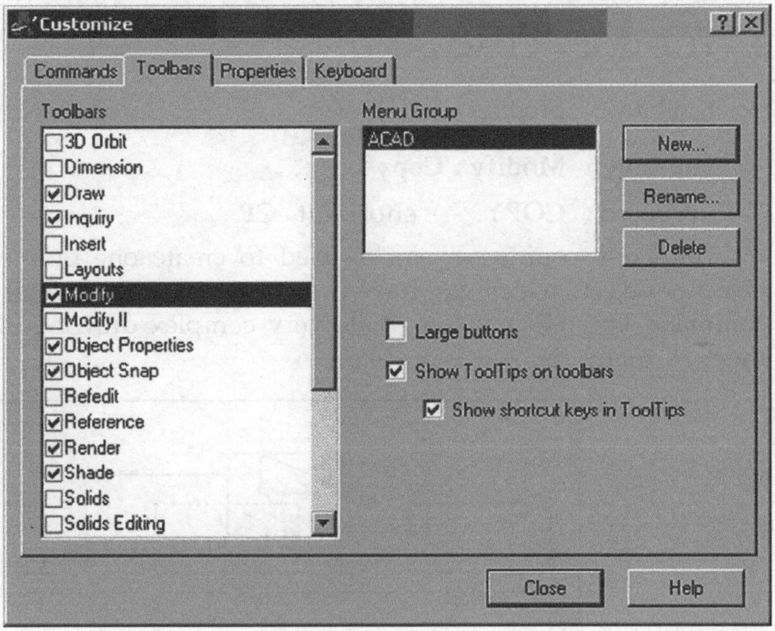

The Modify toolbar is usually displayed by default but if it is not already displayed, you can display it using the TOOLBAR command, **View ▸ Toolbars...** from the pull-down menu. When the Toolbar dialogue box (shown above) appears, simply check the box next to "Modify" in the toolbars list. Many AutoCAD users work with the Modify toolbar permanently docked on their screen because it gives one-click access to all of the commands, making the drawing process much more efficient.

## 2. THE ERASE COMMAND

Toolbar Modify 

Pull-down **Modify ▸ Erase**

Keyboard **ERASE** short-cut **E**

The Erase command is one of the simplest AutoCAD commands and is one of the most used. The command erases (deletes) any selected object(s) from the drawing. Remember you can always get deleted *objects back by typing* **U** *to undo,*  from the Standard toolbar or by using the OOPS command.

Command: **ERASE**

Select objects: (pick an object to erase)

Select objects: ↵ (to end the selection and erase the object)

If you simply want to erase the last object you created you can type **L** at the "Select objects" prompt. The last object will be highlighted and you can then select more objects or ↵ to end the command. See the "Object Selection" tutorial for more information on selecting objects.

## 3. THE COPY COMMAND

Toolbar Modify 

Pull-down **Modify ▸ Copy**

Keyboard **COPY** short-cut **CP**

The Copy command can be used to create one or more duplicates of any drawing object or objects which you have previously created. Copy is a very useful and time-saving command because you can create very complex drawing elements and then simply copy them as many times as you like.

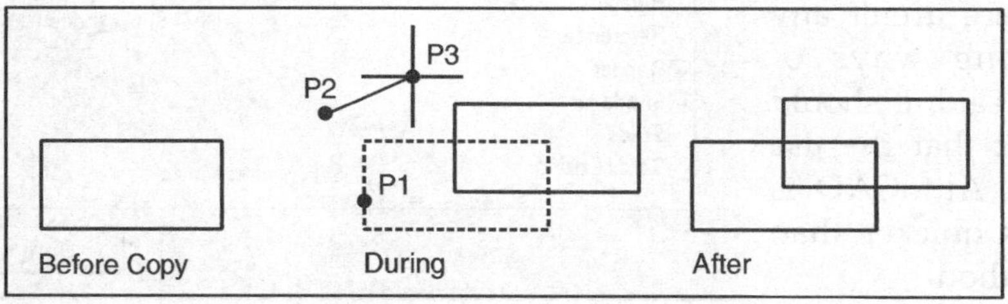

Command: **COPY**

Select objects: (pick object to copy, P1)

Select objects: ↵ (to end selection)

Specify base point or displacement, or [Multiple]: (pick P2 or M for multiple copies)

Specify second point of displacement or <use first point as displacement>:(pick P3)

The multiple option allows you to create additional copies of the selected object(s) by picking as many new points as you like. To end a multiple copy, just hit the ↵ key.

Notice that the "Base point", P2 and the "Second point", P3 do not have to be picked on or near the object. The two points are simply used to indicate the distance and direction of the copied object from the original object.

## 4. THE MIRROR COMMAND

Toolbar Modify

Pull-down **Modify ▸ Mirror**

Keyboard **MIRROR** short-cut **MI**

The Mirror command allows you to mirror selected objects in your drawing by picking them and then defining the position of an imaginary mirror line using two points.

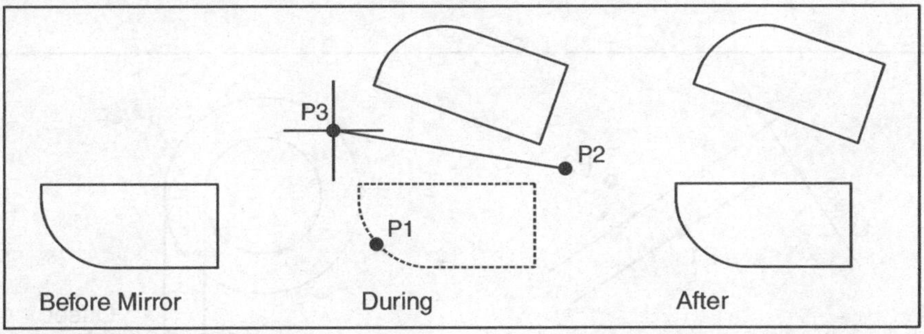


Command: **MIRROR**

Select objects: (pick object to mirror, P1)

Select objects: ↵ (to end selection)

Specify first point of mirror line: (pick P2)

Specify second point of mirror line: (pick P3)

Delete source objects? [Yes/No] <N>: ↵ (for No to keep the original object)

Notice that in the command sequence above, pressing the ↵ key when asked whether to "Delete source objects?" resulted in a "No" response. This is because "No" is the *default* option. AutoCAD always shows the default option within triangular brackets, in this case "<N>". Many AutoCAD commands offer default options. They are usually the most commonly used and you need only right-click and select "Enter" from the menu or press ↵ on the keyboard to accept them.

## 5. THE OFFSET COMMAND

Toolbar Modify

Pull-down **Modify ▸ Offset**

Keyboard **OFFSET** short-cut **O**

Offset is probably one of the most useful commands for constructing drawings. The Offset command creates a new object parallel to or concentric with a selected object. The new object is drawn at a user defined distance (the offset) from the original and in a direction chosen by the user with a pick point. You can offset lines, arcs, circles, ellipses, 2D polylines, xlines, rays and planar splines.

Command: **OFFSET**

Specify offset distance or [Through] <1.0000>: **10** (specify distance)

Select object to offset or <exit>: (select object, P1)

Specify point on side to offset: (pick direction, P2)

Select object to offset or <exit>: ↵ (to end or select another object to offset)

In the illustration below, a line (cyan) has been offset to the right through a distance "Offset" by picking a point to the right of the original line. The result is a new line (red) to the right of the original.

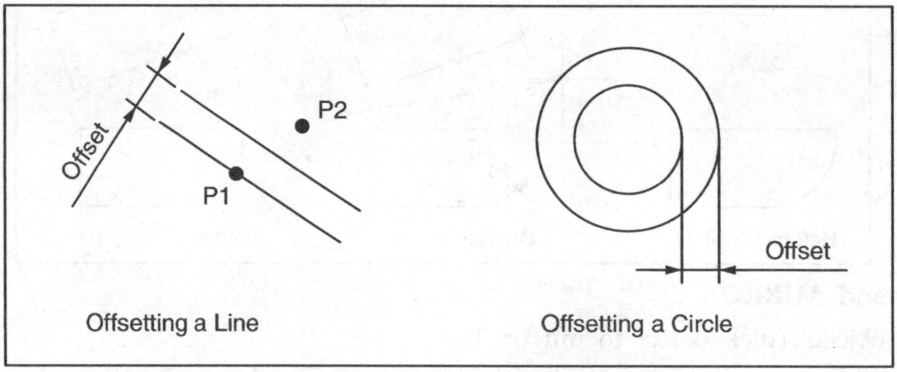


Offsetting a Line

Offsetting a Circle

Circles can be offset inside or outside of themselves to create a new circle which is concentric (has the same centre point) with the original circle. In the illustration, a new circle (red) has been created outside of the original by picking a point outside of the original circle. The radius of the new circle is the offset distance "Offset" plus the radius of the original circle.

In the illustration above, the new objects and original objects are shown in different colours for clarity. In reality, offset objects inherit their object properties from the original object. See the "Object Properties" tutorial for details.

## 6. THE ARRAY COMMAND

Toolbar Modify

Pull-down **Modify ▸ Array**

Keyboard **ARRAY** short-cut **AR**

The Array command makes multiple copies of selected objects in a rectangular matrix (columns and rows) or a polar (circular) pattern. This command has been completely transformed in AutoCAD 2000i. It is now completely dialogue box driven with the option to see a preview of the array before it is created. You can also now create rectangular arrays at a user specified angle. This constitutes a major improvement in usability.

### 6.1 The Rectangular Array

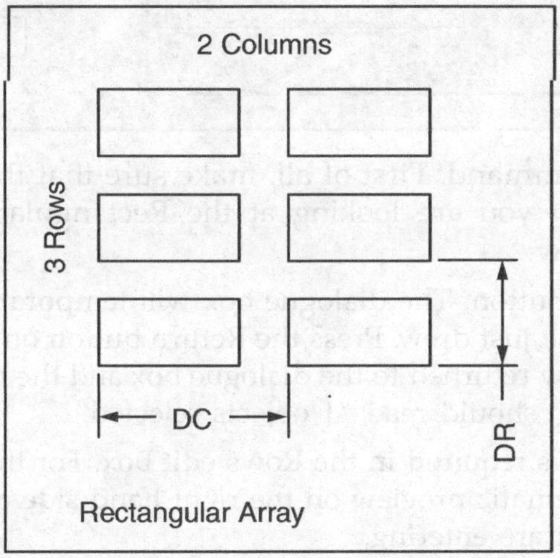


The illustration on the right shows the results of a rectangular array with two columns an three rows. The distance between rows is indicated with the dimension **DR** and between columns with **DC**. When creating rectangular arrays it is important to remember that new rows are created above the original object and new columns are created to the right of the original object. The resulting array is, therefore, always created with the original object in the bottom left hand position with respect to the current co-ordinate system. In the illustration, the original object is shown in cyan and the new objects in red. It is possible to create arrays which do not align with the World Co-ordinate System by setting a User Co-ordinate System first. Try creating this array yourself. First, draw a rectangle 20 drawing units wide and 10 drawing units tall. To do this, start the rectangle command **Draw ▸ Rectangle** from the pull-down menu. When you are prompted to pick a point, pick somewhere in the lower left quarter of the drawing area. Then, when you are prompted for a second point, enter the relative Cartesian co-ordinate **@20, 10**. You have now drawn a rectangle at the right size. See the Using Co-ordinates tutorial for more information on drawing with co-ordinates.

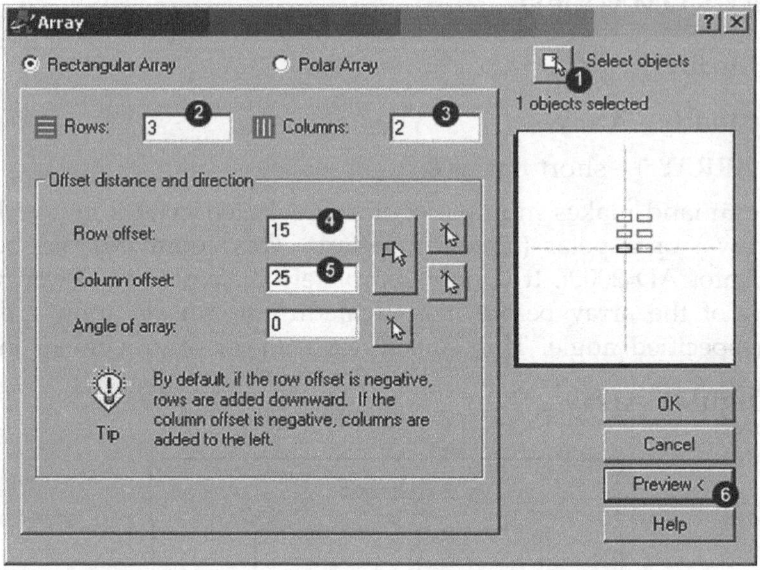


Now start the Array command. First of all, make sure that the Rectangular Array radio button is selected and that you are looking at the Rectangular Array dialogue box and now follow the steps below:

1. Click the Select objects button. The dialogue box will temporarily disappear enabling you to select the rectangle you just drew. Press the Return button on your keyboard to complete the selection. You are now returned to the dialogue box and the message immediately below the Select Objects button should read "1 objects selected".
2. Enter the number of rows required in the Rows edit box. For this example, enter the value "3". Notice that the schematic preview on the right hand side of the dialogue box updates to reflect the values you are entering.
3. Enter the number of columns required in the Columns edit box. Enter the value "2".
4. Enter the row offset in the Row Offset edit box. This is the distance DR in the illustration above. Note that tis is not the distance between rows. In this example, our rectangle is 10 units high and we will enter a row offset of 15. The result will be a 5 unit gap between rectangles.
5. Enter the column offset in the Column Offset edit box. The same parameters apply as for the row offset. Enter a value of 25 to give a 5 unit gap between our rectangles.

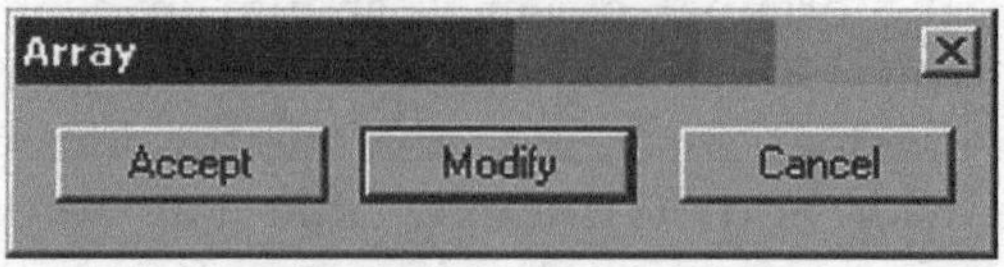


6. Click on the Preview button. Once again, the dialogue box disappears and the specified array is temporarily drawn so that we can preview it. We are now offered 3 choices. If the array isn't quite right, click the Modify button to return to the Array dialogue box. If you are happy with the array, click the Accept button, the array will be permanently drawn and the command is ended.

You should now have an array that looks similar to the one in the illustration above consisting of 6 rectangles arranged in 3 rows and 2 columns. As you can see, this command is very powerful and can save lots of time if used carefully.

## 6.2 The Polar Array

The polar array works in a similar way to the rectangular array. The main difference is that rather than specifying the number and offset for rows and columns, you must specify a center point and the total number of objects in the array (including the original object).

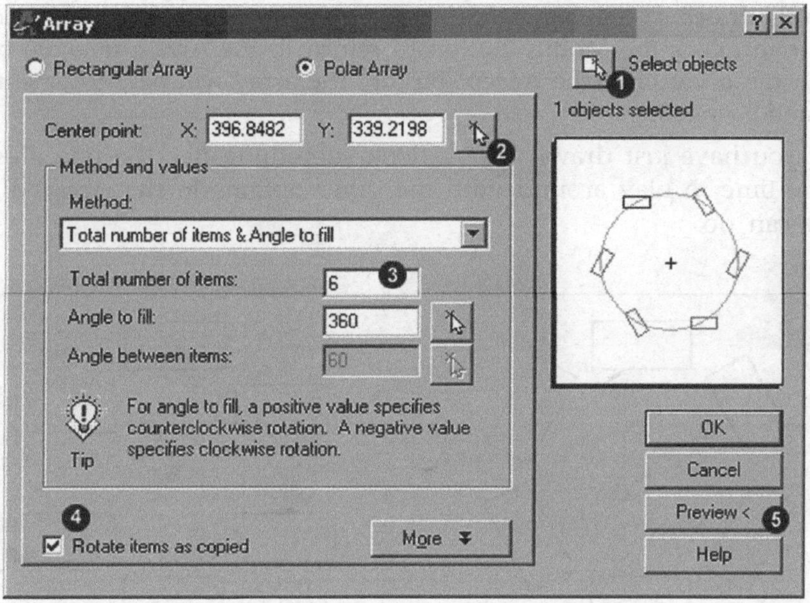


You can try this for yourself by drawing another rectangle as described above. This time, though, locate the rectangle in the centre top half of the drawing area. Now, start the Array command, click the Polar Array radio button and follow the steps below:

1. Click the Select objects button. The dialogue box will temporarily disappear enabling you to select the rectangle you just drew. Press the Return button on your keyboard to complete the selection. You are now returned to the dialogue box and the message immediately below the Select Objects button should read "1 object selected".
2. Specify the center point for the array. This is the point C in the illustration below. You can do this by entering x and y co-ordinates into the appropriate edit boxes if you know what these values should be. However, this is rarely the case and most often you will want to click the Pick Center Point button to pick a point from the drawing area. Pick a point somewhere below the rectangle you have just drawn.

3. Enter a value for the total number of items. For this example, enter the value "6". Notice that once again, the schematic preview updates to reflect the values you have entered.
4. Make sure that the rotate items as copied checkbox is checked.

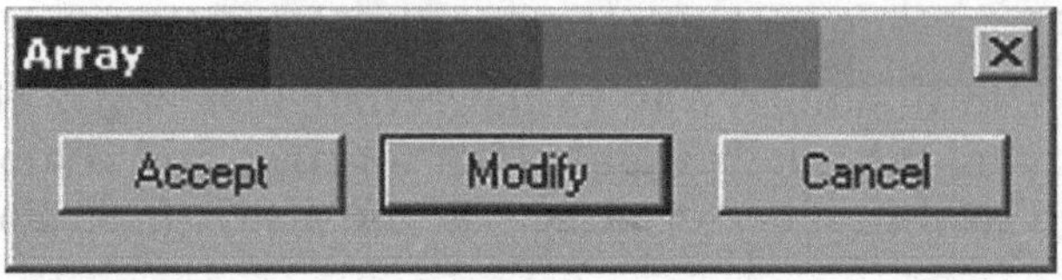


5. Click on the Preview button. Once again, the dialogue box disappears and the specified array is temporarily drawn so that we can preview it. We are now offered 3 choices. If the array isn't quite right, click the Modify button to return to the Array dialogue box. If you are happy with the array, click the Accept button, the array will be permanently drawn and the command is ended.

The array you have just drawn should look something like the one illustrated below, left. Take some time to play around with the other options in the Array dialogue box to see what they can do.

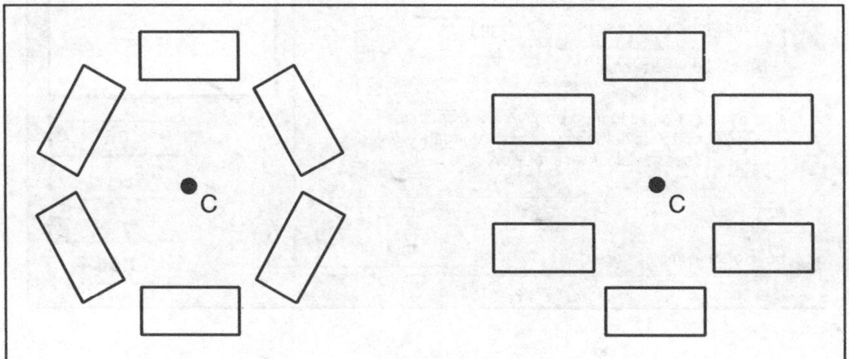


**Polar Array**

The illustration above shows the results of a polar array using an original rectangle (cyan) copied six times about a centre point C, through an angle of 360 degrees (full circle).

## 7. THE MOVE COMMAND

Toolbar Modify 

Pull-down **Modify ▸ Move**

Keyboard **MOVE** short-cut **M**

The Move command works in a similar way to the Copy command except that no copy is made, the selected object(s) is simply moved from one location to another.

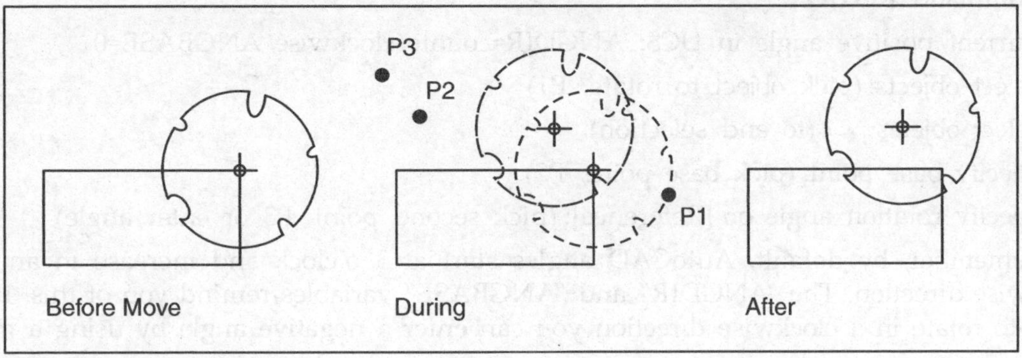


Command: **MOVE**

Select objects: (pick object to move, P1)

Select objects: ↵ (to end selection)

Specify base point or displacement: (pick P2)

Specify second point of displacement or <use first point as displacement>:(pick P3)

Note that as with the Copy command, the two pick points, P2 and P3 are used only to indicate the distance and direction of movement.

## 8. THE ROTATE COMMAND

Toolbar Modify

Pull-down **Modify ▸ Rotate**

Keyboard **ROTATE** short-cut **RO**

The Rotate command allows an object or objects to be rotated about a point selected by the user. AutoCAD prompts for a second rotation point or an angle which can be typed at the keyboard.

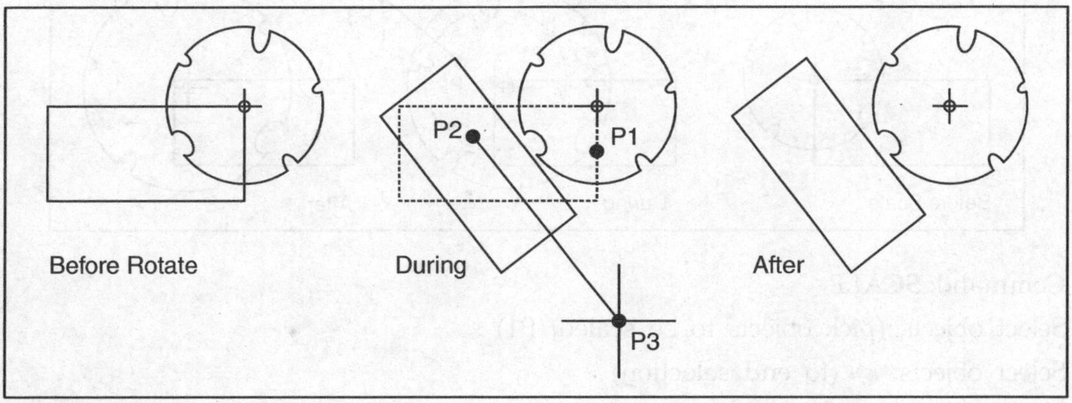

Command: **ROTATE**

Current positive angle in UCS: ANGDIR=counterclockwise ANGBASE=0

Select objects: (pick object to rotate, P1)

Select objects: ↵ (to end selection)

Specify base point: (pick base point, P2)

Specify rotation angle or [Reference]: (pick second point, P3 or enter angle)

Remember, by default, AutoCAD angles start at 3 o'clock and increase in an anti-clockwise direction. The "ANGDIR" and "ANGBASE" variables remind you of this. If you want to rotate in a clockwise direction you can enter a negative angle by using a minus sign.

**Note:** You can change the angle direction and the base angle using the Units command,**Format ▸ Units...** from the pull-down menu. Click the "Clockwise" check box to change the direction and click the "Direction..." button to set the base angle.

## 9. THE SCALE COMMAND

Toolbar Modify

Pull-down **Modify ▸ Scale**

Keyboard **SCALE** short-cut **SC**

The Scale command can be used to change the size of an object or group of objects. You are prompted for a pick point about which the selection set will be scaled. Scaling can then be completed by picking a second point (not always easy because it can sometimes be difficult to precisely control the scaling) or by entering a scale factor at the keyboard. For example a scale factor of 2 will double the size of the objects in the selection set and a factor of 0.5 will half them.

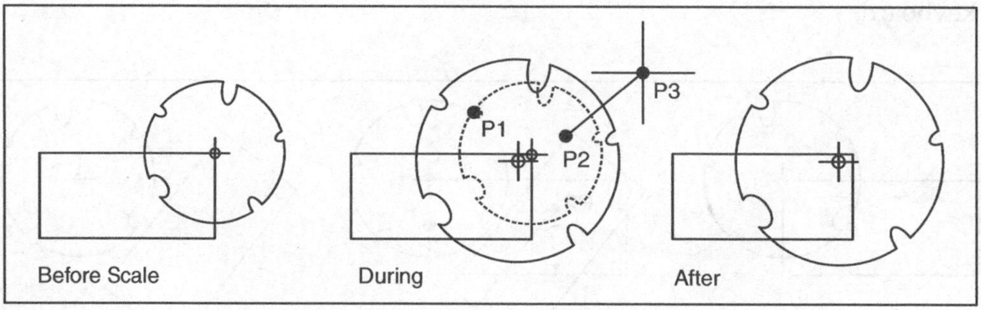


Command: **SCALE**

Select objects: (pick objects to be scaled, P1)

Select objects: ↵ (to end selection)

Specify base point: (pick base point, P2)

Specify scale factor or [Reference]: (pick second point, P3 or enter scale factor)

In the example shown above, the original tree symbol has been enlarged by dynamically scaling it using pick points to determine the change in scale. If you want to scale an object precisely, it is much easier to enter a scale factor using the keyboard.

Note that the position of the new sized tree symbol is determined by the location of the base point. The base point, P2 has been picked to the upper right of the centre of the tree which resulted in the centre of the tree shifting to a lower left position. If the base point had been picked in the centre of the tree symbol, the tree would have remained in the same position. In theory the base point can be any point in the drawing area but for ease of control it is best to choose a known point so that the results are obvious.

## 10. THE STRETCH COMMAND

Toolbar Modify

Pull-down **Modify ▸ Stretch**

Keyboard **STRETCH** short-cut **S**

The Stretch command can be used to move one or more vertices of an object whilst leaving the rest of the object unchanged. In the example below, a rectangle has been stretched by moving one vertex to create an irregular shape.

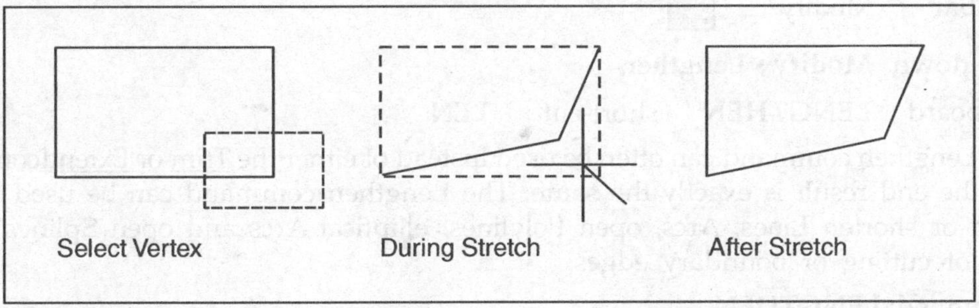


Command: **STRETCH**

Select objects to stretch by crossing-window or crossing-polygon...

Select objects: (pick first point of crossing window)

Specify opposite corner: (pick second point of window)

Select objects: ↵ (to end selection)

Specify base point or displacement: (pick base point)

Specify second point of displacement: (pick second point)

To select vertices to stretch, you must use a crossing window or polygon. See the "Object Selection" tutorial for details of these selection methods.

Stretching with Grips

Although the Stretch command can be very useful, it has largely been superseded by the use of "Grips" which allow this sort of modification to be made much more intuitively.

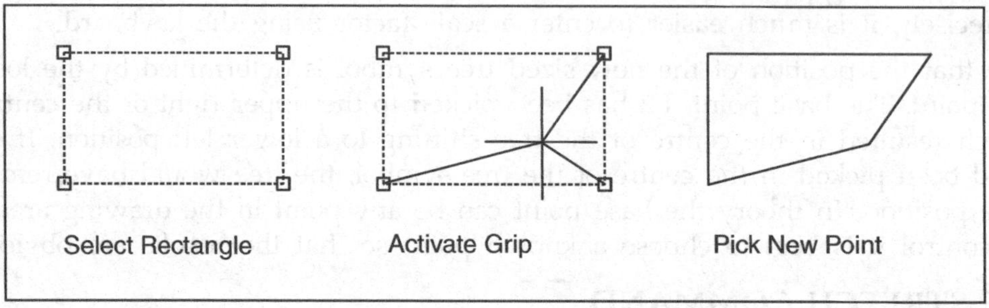


To stretch an object using grips, simply select the object by clicking on it (you can do this without starting a command). The object becomes highlighted and small square grips appear at each vertex and various snap points, depending upon the object type. Click a grip to activate it and click again to reposition it. When you have completed your modifications, use the Escape key (Esc) at the top left of your keyboard to deselect the object and release grips.

## 11. THE LENGTHEN COMMAND

Toolbar Modify 

Pull-down **Modify ▸ Lengthen**

Keyboard **LENGTHEN** short-cut **LEN**

The Lengthen command can often be used instead of either the Trim or Extendcommands. Indeed the end result is exactly the same. The Lengthen command can be used to either lengthen or shorten Lines, Arcs, open Polylines, elliptical Arcs and open Splines without the use of cutting or boundary edges.

Command: **LENGTHEN**

Select an object or [DElta/Percent/Total/DYnamic]: **DY**

Select an object to change or [Undo]: (select a line or arc)

Specify new end point: (pick new end point)

Select an object to change or [Undo]: ↵ (to end)

The command sequence above demonstrates the use of the Dynamic Lengthen option which is probably the most useful for general purpose drafting. However, the other options are worth getting to know because they can save lots of time and effort.

The Total option allows you to change the total length of a line to any value that you specify. The Percent option allows you to change a line length using a percentage. For example, a value of 50 will result in a line one half the length of the original and a value of 200 will result in a line twice the length of the original. The Delta option can be used to extend or reduce the endpoint of a line by a given distance. The endpoint affected by the change is the one closest to the pick point when the object selection is made.

## 12. THE TRIM COMMAND

Toolbar Modify

Pull-down **Modify ▸ Trim**

Keyboard **TRIM** short-cut **TR**

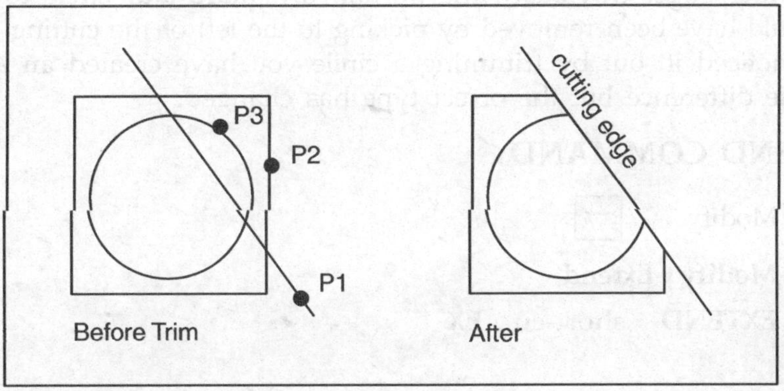


The Trim command can be used to trim a part of an object. In order to trim an object you must draw a second object which forms the "cutting edge". Cutting edges can be lines, xlines, rays, polylines, circles, arcs or ellipses. Blocks and text cannot be trimmed or used as cutting edges. The illustration on the right shows the Trim command in action. The red square and circle have been drawn using the Polygon and Circle commands respectively. In order to trim these objects, a line has been drawn (cyan in the illustration), this forms the cutting edge. The Trim command, unlike most other modify commands requires that two separate object selections are made. The cutting edges are selected first (there can be one or more) and then the objects to be trimmed are selected. In the example above, the line is selected first because it forms the cutting edge and then the square and circle are selected.

The Trim command is slightly more complicated than many other modify commands. To get a better understanding of how it works, draw a square, circle and line as illustrated above and then follow the command sequence below. Don't forget to watch the AutoCAD command line at each stage of the process.

Command: **TRIM**

Current settings: Projection=UCS Edge=None

Select cutting edges ...

Select objects: (select the cutting edge, P1)

Select objects: ↵ (to end cutting edge selection)

Select object to trim or shift-select to extend or [Project/Edge/Undo]:(pick the part of the square which you want to trim, P2)

Select object to trim or shift-select to extend or [Project/Edge/Undo]:(pick the circle, P3)

Select object to trim or shift-select to extend or [Project/Edge/Undo]: ↵ (to end)

Notice that at each trimming step you are given the option to undo the previous trim. This can be very useful if you inadvertently pick the wrong object.

In the above example, when the objects were trimmed, both pick points were made to the right of the cutting edge, resulting in the removal of that part of the objects to the right of the cutting edge. Obviously, the portion of square and circle to the left of the cutting edge could have been removed by picking to the left of the cutting edge. Also, you may not have noticed it, but by trimming a circle you have created an Arc object. This makes no visible difference but the object type has changed.

## 13. THE EXTEND COMMAND

Toolbar Modify 

Pull-down **Modify ▸ Extend**

Keyboard **EXTEND** short-cut **EX**

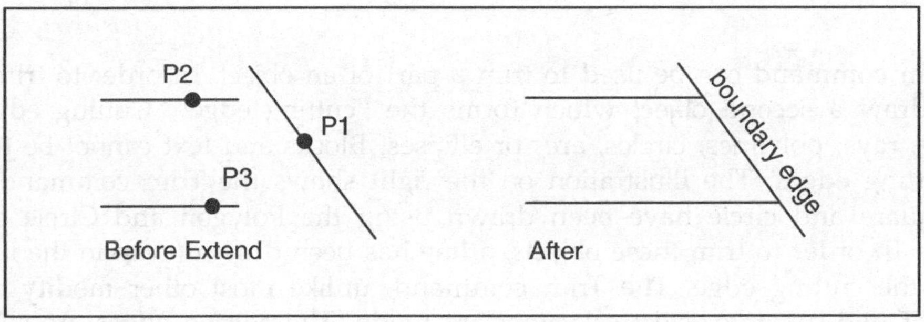


This command extends a line, polyline or arc to meet another drawing object (known as the boundary edge). In the illustration on the right, two lines (red) are extended to meet another line (cyan) which forms the boundary edge. This command works in a similar way to the Trim command, described above. Two selections are made, one for the boundary edge(s) and one for the object(s) to extend.

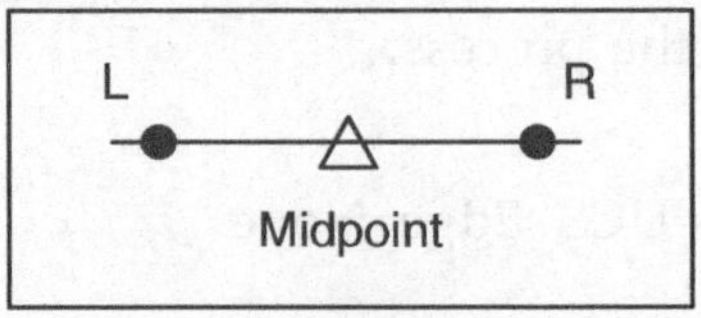


Lines and other objects can be extended in one of two directions. In the illustration on the right, the red line could be extended either to the right or to the left. You can tell AutoCAD in which direction to extend by picking a point to the right or left of the midpoint respectively. AutoCAD does not intuitively know where the boundary edge lies so you must explicitly indicate the direction of extension by picking either one side or other of the midpoint.

Draw the lines as shown in the illustration and follow the command sequence below.

Command: **EXTEND**

Current settings: Projection=UCS Edge=None

Select boundary edges ...

Select objects: (select the boundary edge, P1)

Select objects: ↵ (to end boundary edge selection)

Select object to extend or shift-select to trim or [Project/Edge/Undo]:(pick the object hich you want to be extended, P2)

Select object to extend or shift-select to trim or [Project/Edge/Undo]:(pick another object which you want to be extended, P3)

Select object to extend or shift-select to trim or [Project/Edge/Undo]: ↵ (to end)

Sometimes you may get the message "Object does not intersect an edge" or "No edge in that direction". If this happens it means that you are either picking the wrong end of the object or the object you are trying to extend will not meet the boundary edge. The solution is either to pick near the end you want to extend or to move the boundary edge so that the extended line will intersect with it.

## 13.1 Using Edge mode

If the line you are trying to extend does not intersect with the boundary line, you can use the "Edge" option to toggle *Edge mode* to "Extend" (the default is "No Extend"). When the Extend command is set to Extend Mode, the objects being extended will extend to an imaginary line through the boundary edge, irrespective of whether the extended object actually intersects with the boundary edge. This is particularly useful and can save lots of time.

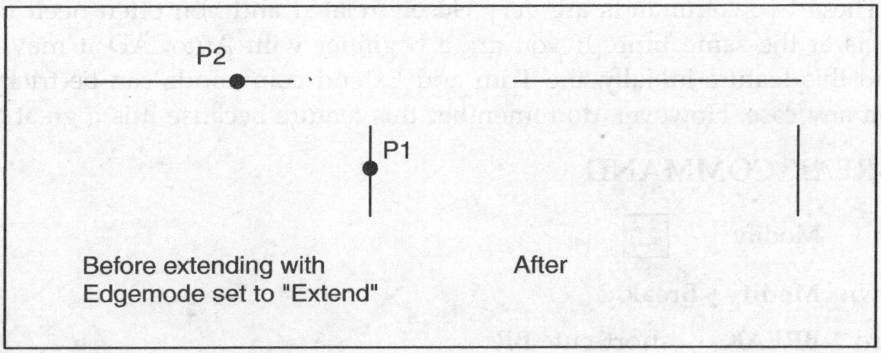


The illustration on the left shows the result of extending a line (red) to a boundary edge (cyan) with Edge mode set to "Extend". The same process would have resulted in an error message if Edge mode had been set to "No Extend". To get a better understanding of how this works, draw the two lines as shown in the illustration and try to extend them using the default settings. When you have done that, follow the command sequence below.

Edge mode

Command: **EXTEND**

Select boundary edges: (Projmode = UCS, Edgemode = No extend)

Select objects: (select the boundary edge, P1)

Select objects: ↵ (to end boundary edge selection)

Select object to extend or shift-select to trim or [Project/Edge/Undo]: E (to use the Edge option)

Enter an implied edge extension mode [Extend/No extend] <No extend>: E (to set Edgemode to Extend)

Select object to extend or shift-select to trim or [Project/Edge/Undo]:(pick the object to be extended, P2)

Select object to extend or shift-select to trim or [Project/Edge/Undo]: ↵ (to end)

Notice that the current value of Edgemode is always displayed on the command line when you start the Extend command. The Edge option can also be used with the Trim command to enable trimming to cutting edges which do not actually intersect the object to trim. Edgemode is a system variable, so any change to its value will affect both the Trim and Extend commands.

## 13.2 Shift Selection with Trim & Extend

You may have noticed during the command sequences for the Trim and Extend commands that you have the option to "shift-select". This feature is new to AutoCAD 2000i and it enables you to extend while using the Trim command and to trim while using the Extend command. These two commands are very closely related and you often need to trim and extend objects at the same time. If you are a beginner with AutoCAD it may be a good idea to avoid this feature initially, the Trim and Extend commands can be tricky to get to grips with in any case. However, do remember this feature because it is a great time saver.

# 14. THE BREAK COMMAND

Toolbar Modify 

Pull-down **Modify ▸ Break**

Keyboard **BREAK** short-cut **BR**

The Break command enables you to break (remove part of) an object by defining two break points. In the illustration below, a corner of a rectangle has been removed. The Break command can be used with lines, polylines, circles, arcs ellipses, splines, xlines and rays. When you break an object, you can either select the object using the first break point and then pick the second break point, or you can select the object and then pick the two break points.

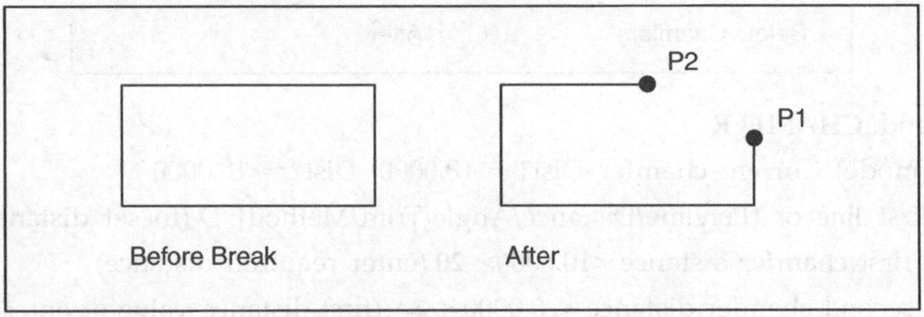


Command: **BREAK**

Select objects: (select the object using the first break point, P1)

Specify second break point or [First point]: (pick the second break point, P2)

The section of the object is removed and the command ends.

Sometimes you may want to select the object first and then specify the two break points. If this is the case, use the "First point" option to specify the first break point. By default, AutoCAD assumes that the point used to select the object is the first break point. This is often confusing for new users.

It may sometimes be necessary to break a line into two without removing any part of it. In this case, simply pick the first and second break points in the same position.

## 15. THE CHAMFER COMMAND

To

Toolbar Modify 

Pull-down **Modify ▸ Chamfer**

Keyboard **CHAMFER** short-cut **CHA**

The Chamfer command enables you to create a chamfer between any two non-parallel lines as in the illustration below or any two adjacent polyline segments. Usually, the Chamfer command is used to set the chamfer distances before drawing the chamfer. Follow the command sequence below where the chamfer distances are changed to 20 before the chamfer is made.

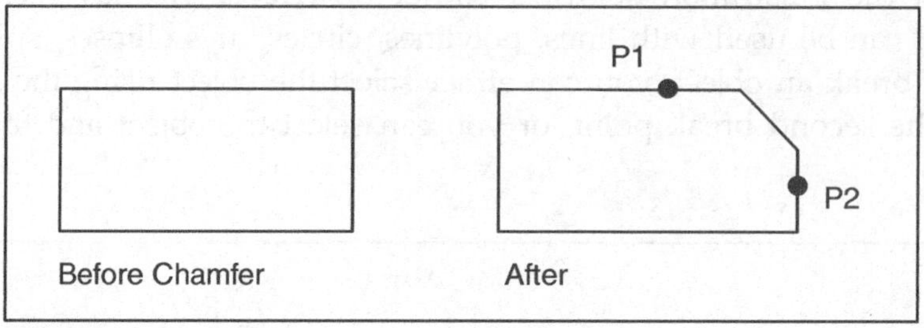


Command: **CHAMFER**

(TRIM mode) Current chamfer Dist1 = 10.0000, Dist2 = 10.0000

Select first line or [Polyline/Distance/Angle/Trim/Method]: **D** (to set distances)

Specify first chamfer distance <10.0000>: **20** (enter required distance)

Specify second chamfer distance <20.0000>: ↵ (first distance value or enter a different value)

Select first line or [Polyline/Distance/Angle/Trim/Method]: (pick P1)

Select second line: (pick P2)

The chamfer is made and the command ends.

Notice from the command sequence that there are a number of options which can be used to control the way the Chamfer command behaves. The Polyline option can be used to chamfer all vertexes of a polyline simultaneously. The Distance option allows you to specify the two chamfer distances. Angle allows the angle between the first line and the chamfer to be specified. Trim is used to control whether the original lines are trimmed to the chamfer or remain as they are. Finally, Method is used to toggle the command between Distance and Angle mode. When Angle mode is used, the chamfer is defined using one distance and an angle rather than two distances.

## 16. THE FILLET COMMAND

To

Toolbar Modify 

Pull-down **Modify ▸ Fillet**

Keyboard **FILLET** short-cut **F**

The Fillet command is a very useful tool which allows you to draw an arc between two intersecting lines or adjacent polyline segments. You first need to use the command to set the required radius and then a second time to select the two lines.

Command: **FILLET**

Current settings: Mode = TRIM, Radius = 10.0000

Select first object or [Polyline/Radius/Trim]: **R**

Specify fillet radius <10.000>: **25**

Select first object or [Polyline/Radius/Trim]: (pick P1)

Select second object : (pick P2)

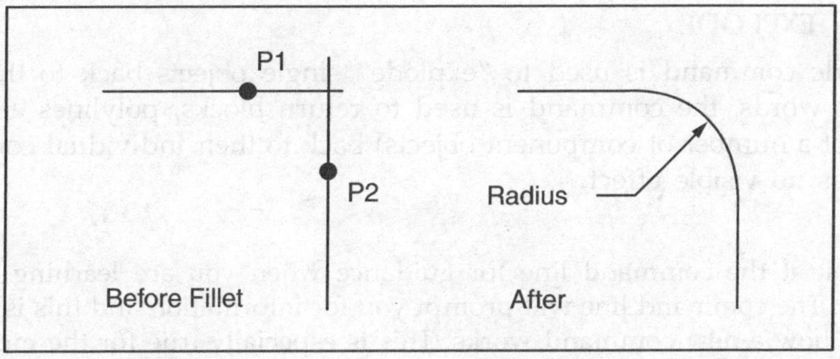


The Fillet command can also be used to fillet arcs and circles. The "Polyline" option also allows you to fillet all vertices of a polyline with a single command. It's worth experimenting with this command, it can save you lots of time and enables you to construct shapes which otherwise would be quite difficult.

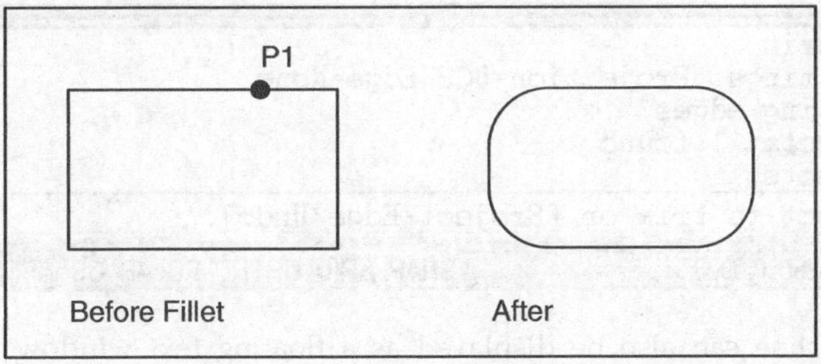


For example, you can easily create the lozenge shape shown on the right from a simple rectangle. Since AutoCAD rectangles are just closed polylines, you can use the Polyline option of the Fillet command to fillet all polyline vertexes simultaneously. Try this for yourself; draw a rectangle and then follow the command sequence below.

Command: **FILLET**

Current settings: Mode = TRIM, Radius = 10.0000

Select first object or [Polyline/Radius/Trim]: **P**

Select 2D polyline: (pick P1)

4 lines were filleted

**Tip:** Make sure that the radius you specify will fit the objects you select; otherwise the fillet command will not work.

## 17. THE EXPLODE COMMAND

Toolbar Modify 

Pull-down **Modify ▸ Explode**

Keyboard **EXPLODE**

The Explode command is used to "explode" single objects back to their constituent parts. In other words, the command is used to return blocks, polylines etc. (which may be composed of a number of component objects) back to their individual component parts. The change has no visible effect.

Tips & Tricks

- Always look at the command line for guidance when you are learning new AutoCAD commands. The command line will prompt you for information and this is the easiest way to find out how a new command works. This is especially true for the more complicated commands like Trim and Extend.
- The command line window displays 3 lines of text by default. You can change this by clicking and dragging the top of the window frame. When you are starting with AutoCAD you may like to see more than 3 lines. The illustration below shows the command line window increased in size to 6 lines.

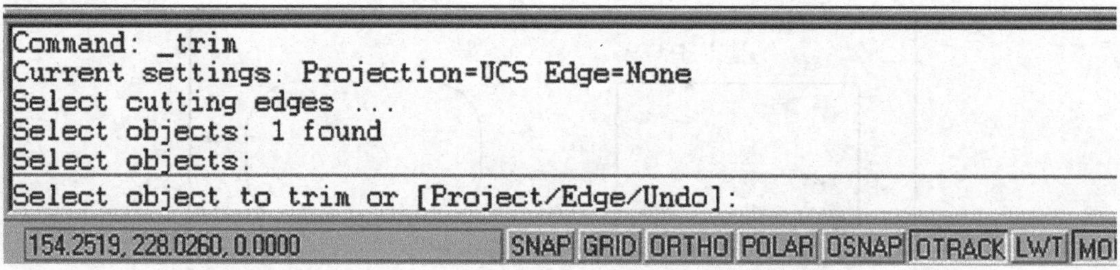


- The command line can also be displayed as a floating text window. The AutoCAD text window is displayed by pressing the **F2** key on the keyboard. See Function Keys on the Drawing Aids tutorial for more details.
- You can control the way text is mirrored using the MIRRTEXT variable.

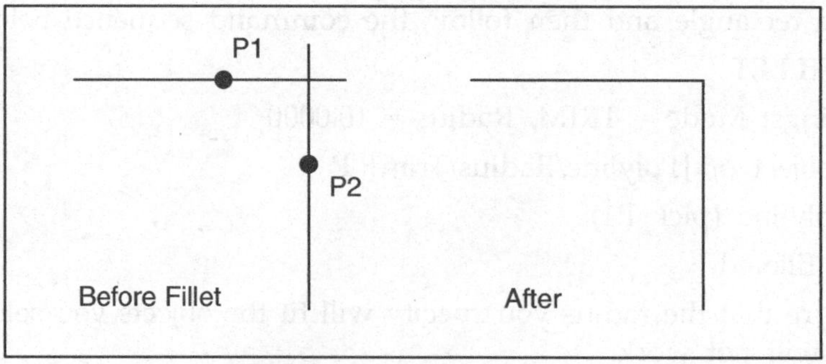

- You can use the Fillet command with a radius of zero to trim intersecting lines back to their intersection. Of course, you could also achieve this effect with the Trim command but if you have a number of operations to complete, the Fillet method is much quicker.
- When using the Trim and Extend commands, hitting ↵ when prompted to "Select cutting edges" and "Select boundary edges" respectively will automatically select all valid cutting or boundary edges on the screen. This can be a real time saver if you have a complicated set of edges to select.

CHAPTER 6

# Dimension Toolbar

# 1. INTRODUCTION

## 1.1 Dimensioning and annotation

New commands used in this section: **dimstyle**

We now have a simple layout drawing, showing the Sports Hall design using FRONT, LEFT SIDE, RIGHT SIDE & PLAN views created using 3rd angle orthographic projection. Now we will add more information to the drawing such as basic overall dimensions and positions of various features such as windows and doors, and descriptions of the views.

## 1.2 Creating dimensions

Create a new layer for the dimensions called **dimensions** and colour it **yellow**. Make this new layer the current layer. Bring up the dimension toolbar by right mouse button clicking in an empty area of the top toolbar and select **ADT > Dimension**.

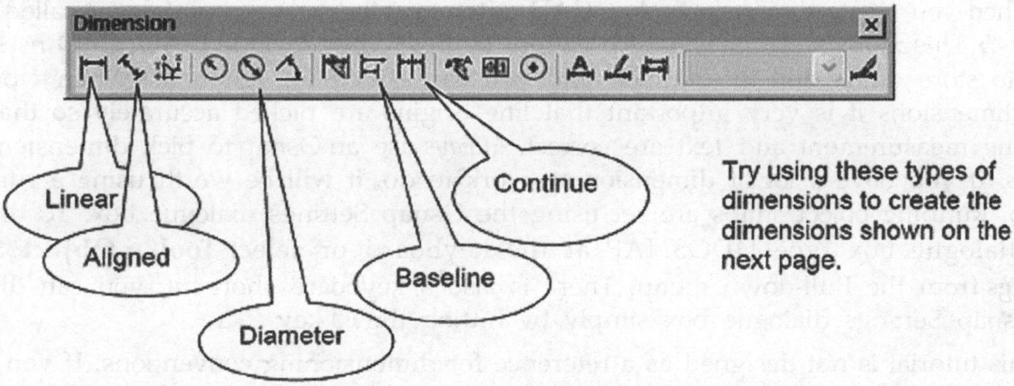


This tutorial describes the options and commands available for dimensioning drawings and how to use them. The correct use of AutoCAD's dimension tools is the key to producing clear and concise measured drawings. AutoCAD provides a whole range of dimensioning tools which can be used to quickly dimension any drawing without the need for measurement. Dimensioning in AutoCAD is automatic; lines, arrows and text are all taken care of by the dimension commands. AutoCAD dimensions are special blocks which can easily be edited or erased as necessary. AutoCAD provides lots of control over the way dimensions look. Using a system similar to text styles, dimension styles allow you to design dimensions so that they look just the way you want them to.

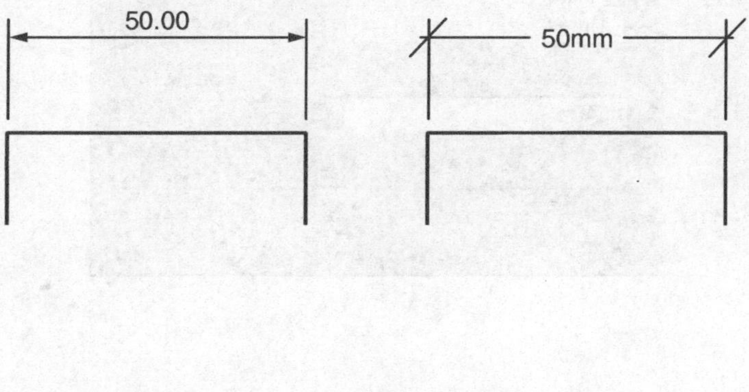

For example, the illustration above shows two different dimension styles. The one on the left is the default style known as STANDARD. If you do not create a style of your own or modify the standard style, all dimensions will look like this. The dimension line has arrow heads and the dimension text is positioned above the line and is drawn using the current text style. The dimension on the right has been drawn using a new style. The arrows have been changed to obliques, the vertical alignment of the text has been centered and the current text style has been changed. There are lots of dimension commands which include facilities for indicating tolerances and alternate units dimensioning. However, this tutorial aims to cover the most common commands for general use and constitutes an introduction to dimensioning with AutoCAD. If you would like to learn more about dimensions, refer to the AutoCAD user manual. AutoCAD divides dimensions into four main categories: Linear, Radial, Ordinate and Angular. For the purposes of this tutorial we will only consider some of the commands within the Linear, Radial and Angular categories.

When you create dimensions, AutoCAD automatically creates a new layer called "Defoliants". This is a special layer which cannot be deleted or renamed. AutoCAD uses this layer to store dimension information and you can effectively ignore it. When working with dimensions it is very important that line origins are picked accurately so that the resulting measurement and text are correct. *Always* use an Osnap to pick dimension line origins. If you have a lot of dimensioning work to do, it will be worth using a running Osnap. Running object snaps are set using the Osnap Settings dialogue box. To display this dialogue box type DDOSNAP at the keyboard or select **Tools ▸ Object Snap Settings** from the Pull-down menu. There is also a keyboard short-cut; you can display the Osnap Settings dialogue box simply by hitting the **F3** key.

This tutorial is not designed as a reference for dimensioning conventions. If you wish to learn more about dimensioning conventions, consult BS 308: Part 2.

Selecting Dimension Commands

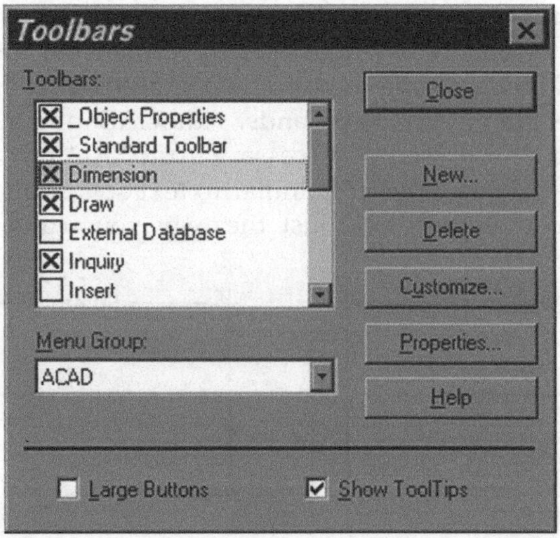

Selecting and working with the dimension commands in AutoCAD R14 is much easier than in previous versions. All commands can be accessed from the keyboard and now most commands are also available from the Dimension pull-down menu and the Dimension toolbar. The Dimension toolbar is particularly useful because it places all the dimension commands a single mouse click away. Since the Dimension toolbar is not displayed by default you will need to enable it from the Toolbars dialogue box. To display the Toolbar dialogue box, select **View ▸ Toolbars...**from the pull-down or type **TOOLBAR** at the keyboard. To display the Dimension toolbar, click in the checkbox against "Dimension" in the toolbar list.

## 2. THE LINEAR DIMENSION COMMANDS

As the name suggests the Linear dimension commands are used to dimension along straight lines. There are five linear dimension commands, namely: DIMLINEAR, DIMCONTINUE, DIMBASELINE, DIMALIGNED and DIMROTATED. The DIMLINEAR command is probably the most common dimension command you will use.

**The Linear Dimension Command**

Toolbar 

Pull-down **Dimension ▸ Linear**

Keyboard **DIMLINEAR**

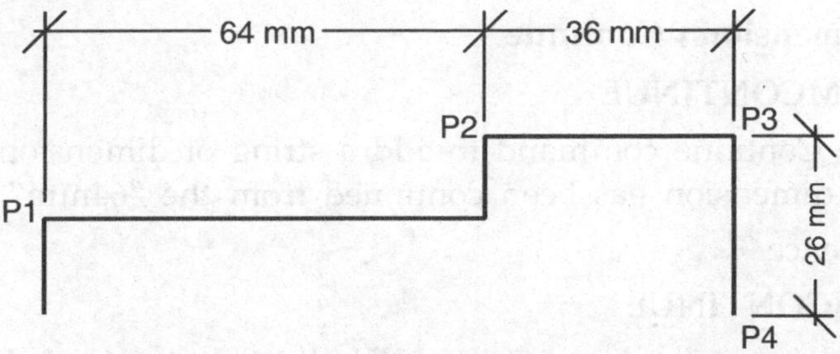


You can use this command to generate horizontal and vertical dimensions.

Creating a linear dimension is easy. All you have to do is start the command, specify the two points between which you want the dimension to be drawn and pick a point to fix the position of the dimension line. Consider the diagram (right) whilst working through the following examples.

Command: **DIMLINEAR**

First extension line origin or press ENTER to select: (pick P1)

Second extension line origin: (pick P2)

Dimension line location (Mtext/Text/Angle/Horizontal/Vertical/Rotated):(pick a point to position the dimension line, you will see the dimension rubber banding)

You may have noticed that the first prompt asks you to pick the first extension line origin or to press the ENTER key. Pressing the Enter/Return key results in the following prompt:

Select object to dimension:

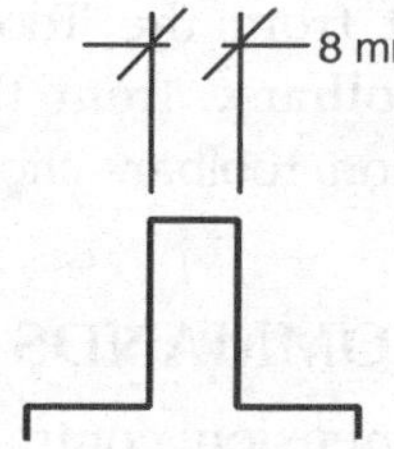


AutoCAD allows you to dimension an object simply by picking it. Try this out. Draw a line or a circle and use this option rather than the two point option to see what happens.

Dimensions will automatically adjust themselves to accommodate most situations. For example, the illustration on the right shows what happens to a dimension if the gap between the two extension lines is too small for the dimension text.

## 3. THE CONTINUE DIMENSION COMMAND

Toolbar 

Pull-down **Dimension ▸ Continue**

Keyboard **DIMCONTINUE**

You can use the Continue command to add a string of dimensions. In the illustration above the "36mm" dimension has been continued from the "64mm" dimension.

Command Sequence

Command: **DIMCONTINUE**

Specify a second extension line origin or (Undo/<Select>): (pick P3)

Specify a second extension line origin or (Undo/<Select>): (pick another or ↵ to end)

**Note:** There is no prompt for the first line origin, AutoCAD automatically selects the second line origin of the previous dimension to be the first of the new dimension. There is also no prompt for the dimension line position, AutoCAD automatically matches up with the previous dimension.

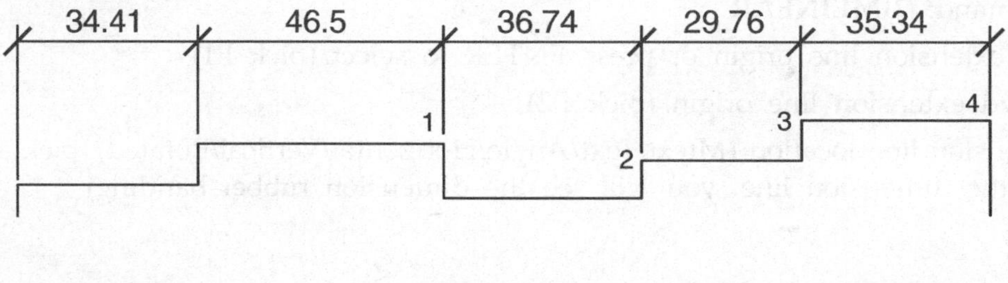

Using the Continue command you can very quickly generate a string of dimensions which align perfectly. In the example above, the "34.41" dimension was drawn with the DIMLINEAR command; all the other dimensions were drawn using the DIMCONTINUE command and simply picking the four points, one after the other. You can only continue a dimension in a single direction. To generate the "26mm" dimension in the previous illustration, you will need to use the DIMLINEAR command and pick P3 and P4 or enter ↵ at the first prompt and pick the line.

## 4. THE BASELINE DIMENSION COMMAND

Toolbar

Pull-down **Dimension ▸ Baseline**

Keyboard **DIMBASELINE**

You can use this command to generate a series of dimensions from a single base point. You must already have created the first dimension in the sequence using a command such as DIMLINEAR. The DIMBASELINE command then creates further dimensions in a similar way to the DIMCONTINUE command. All the user has to do is pick points.

Command Sequence

Command: **DIMBASELINE**

Specify a second extension line origin or (Undo/<Select>): (pick next point)

Specify a second extension line origin or (Undo/<Select>): (pick another or ↵ to end)

Select base dimension: (↵ again to end)

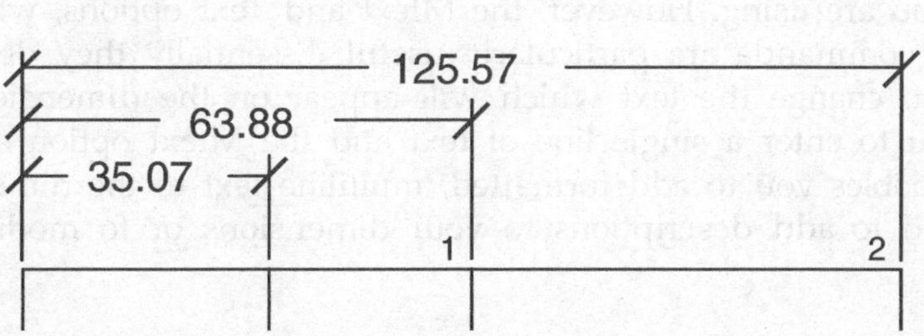


In the example above, the "35.07" dimension was created using the DIMLINEAR command. The others were created using DIMBASELINE and picking points 1 and 2.

## 5. THE ALIGNED DIMENSION COMMAND

Toolbar

Pull-down **Dimension ▸ Aligned**

Keyboard **DIMALIGNED**

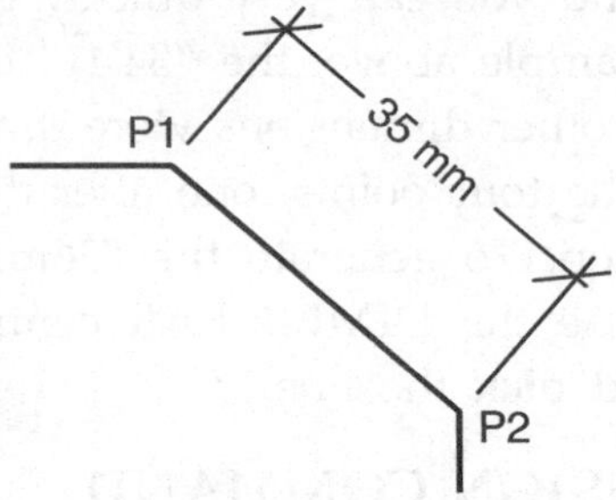


You can use this command to generate aligned dimensions. These are dimensions along inclined lines which cannot be dimensioned with the DIMLINEAR dimension command because that command will only give a measured dimension in either a horizontal or vertical direction. However, as you can see from the command sequence below, this command works in exactly the same way.

Command: **DIMALIGNED**

First extension line origin or press ENTER to select:(pick P1)

Second extension line origin: (pick P2)

Dimension line location (Mtext/Text/Angle): (pick a point)

The DIMCONTINUE and DIMBASELINE commands can both be used in conjunction with DIMALIGNED dimensions.

**Changing the Text**

You may have noticed that when you are prompted to pick the dimension line location you are also offered a number of options. The options vary depending upon the particular command that you are using. However, the Mtext and Text options, which are common to all dimension commands are particularly useful. Essentially they do the same thing, they allow you to change the text which will appear on the dimension line. The Text option allows you to enter a single line of text and the Mtext option starts the MTEXT command and enables you to add formatted, multiline text to the dimension. These options can be used to add descriptions to your dimensions or to modify the measured distance.

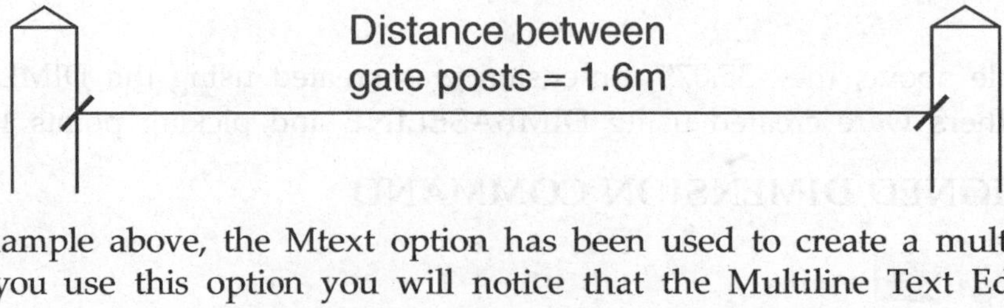


In the example above, the Mtext option has been used to create a multi-line annotation. When you use this option you will notice that the Multiline Text Editor dialogue already has some text in the text window. This is the measured dimension and is displayed as "<>". If you delete this marker the dimension measurement will not appear in the annotation.

If you need to edit dimension text after the dimension is drawn, you can use the DDEDIT command, **Modify/Object/Text...** from the pull-down. If you select a dimension, the Multiline Text Editor will appear and you can make any necessary changes to the annotation. The illustration on the right shows an extract from the Multiline Text Editor as it would appear if the dimension above were selected.

## 6. THE DIAMETER DIMENSION COMMAND

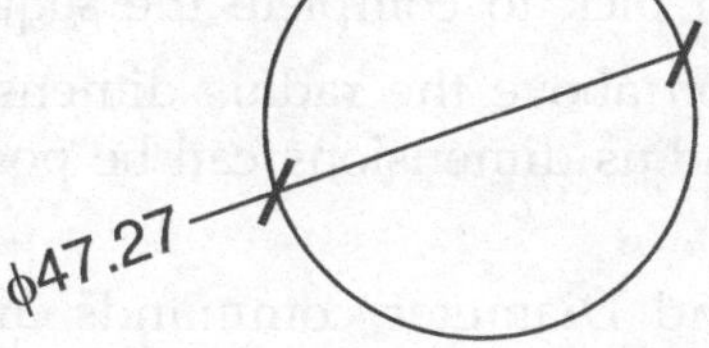


Toolbar 

Pull-down **Dimension ▸ Diameter**

Keyboard **DIMDIAMETER**

You can use the Diameter command to annotate a circle or an arc with a diameter dimension. To achieve this simply start the command, pick a point on the circumference of the circle, pick a second point to determine the length of the leader and then add the dimension text or Return to accept the default.

Command: **DIMDIAMETER**

Select arc or circle: (pick the circumference P1)

Dimension line location (Mtext/Text/Angle): (move the cursor until you are happy with the text position and then pick to complete the sequence)

## 7. THE RADIUS DIMENSION COMMAND

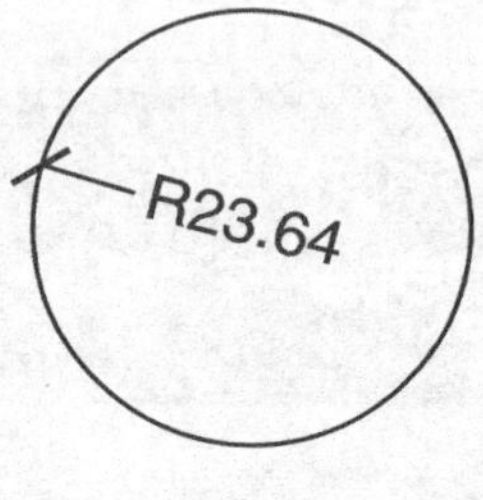


Toolbar 

Pull-down **Dimension ▸ Radius**

Keyboard **DIMRADIUS**

The Radius command is identical to the Diameter command except that the dimension measurement is a radius rather than a dimension and the resulting dimension text is prefixed with a "R" to indicate radius.

Command: **DIMRADIUS**

Select arc or circle: (pick the circumference P2)

Dimension line location (Mtext/Text/Angle): (move the cursor until you are happy with the text position and then pick to complete the sequence)

Notice that in the illustration above the radius dimension has been positioned inside the circle. Both diameter and radius dimensions can be positioned either inside or outside an arc or circle.

Practice with the Radial and Diameter commands until you understand how they work.

## 8. THE CENTER MARK COMMAND

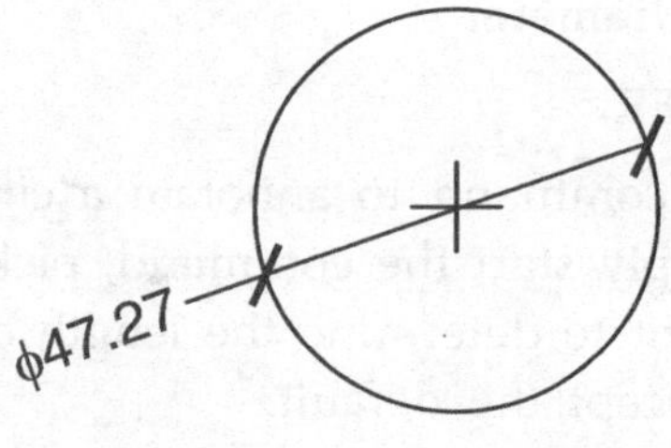


Toolbar 

Pull-down **Dimension ▸ Center Mark**

Keyboard **DIMCENTER**

You can use the Center Mark command to annotate a circle or an arc with a cross at the center. The illustration above shows a center mark added to a circle after a diameter has been drawn.

Command Sequence

Command: **DIMCENTER**

Select arc or circle: (Pick the circumference of a circle or arc)

A cross is drawn at the center point.

## 9. ANGULAR DIMENSIONS

There is only one command in this section and it is used to annotate angular measurements.

The Angular Dimension Command

Toolbar 

Pull-down **Dimension ▸ Angular**

Keyboard **DIMANGULAR**

The Angular command is amazingly flexible and can be used to indicate an angle in almost any situation. Just like the other dimension commands, all parts of the process are rubber banded so you can see the results of your actions before you make the final pick.

Command: **DIMANGULAR**

Select arc, circle, line, or press ENTER: (pick a line)

Second line: (pick another line)

Dimension arc line location (Mtext/Text/Angle): (pick point)

Move the cursor position until you are happy with the result. Notice that you can move the cursor to either side of the lines and the angular dimension will change accordingly.

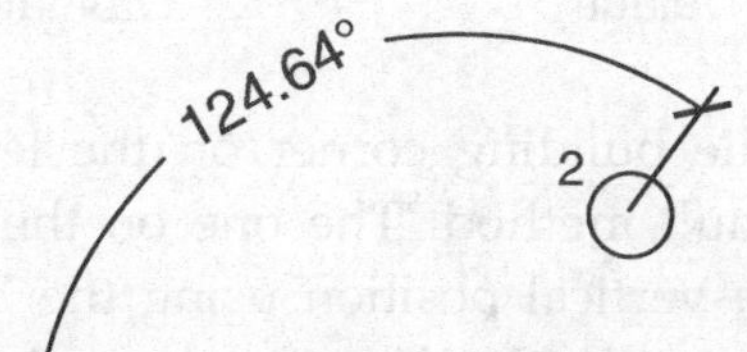


You may have noticed that at the first prompt you are given the option to press ENTER. If you use this option you will be prompted to pick the angle vertex and then the two angle endpoints. This is quite useful if the angle you need to dimension is not defined by physical lines on the drawing. The illustration on the right shows the result of this option. The centre point of circle 1 was picked as the angle vertex and the centre points of circles 2 and 3 were picked for the two angle endpoints.

## 10. ORDINATE DIMENSIONS

Ordinate dimensions are not really dimensions at all in that they do not indicate a measurement. Rather they annotate known co-ordinate points. The DIMORDINATE command is used to indicate the X and Y ordinate values at any point.

The Ordinate Dimension Command

Toolbar 

Pull-down **Dimension ▸ Ordinate**

Keyboard **DIMORDINATE**

The Ordinate command is used to annotate co-ordinate points with X or Y values. This may be useful for setting-out on site plans.

Command: **DIMORDINATE**

*Select feature: (pick the point to annotate)*

Leader endpoint (Xdatum/Ydatum/Mtext/Text): (pick endpoint or use one of the options)

By default a vertical leader will display the X ordinate and a horizontal one will display the Y ordinate. However, you can use the Xdatum and Ydatum options to override this default.

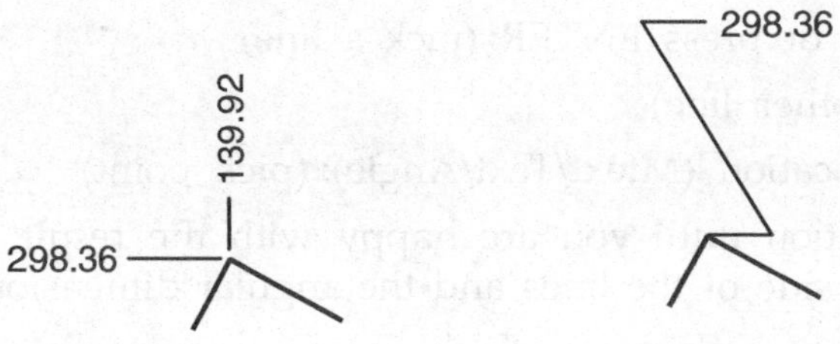


Ordinate Default Ordinate Ydatum

In the illustration above, the building corner on the left has been annotated with X and Y ordinates using the default method. The one on the right has a Y ordinate which has been forced to display in a vertical position using the Ydatum option. You could also use the Text or Mtext options to clearly describe the point you are annotating.

## 11. ANNOTATION WITH LEADERS

Ordinate dimensions are not really dimensions at all in that they do not indicate a measurement. Rather they annotate known co-ordinate points. The DIMORDINATE command is used to indicate the X and Y ordinate values at any point.

## The Leader Command

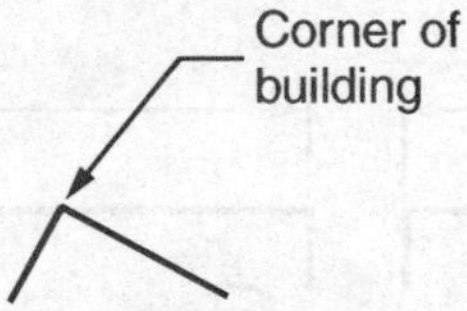


Toolbar

Pull-down **Dimension ▸ Leader**

Keyboard **LEADER**

The Leader command can be used to annotate any point on a drawing. The command sequence below was used to draw the leader shown in the illustration above.

Command Sequence

Command: **LEADER**

From point: (pick the point to annotate)

To point: (pick vertex point)

To point (Format/Annotation/Undo)<Annotation>: (pick end point)

To point (Format/Annotation/Undo)<Annotation>: ↵

Annotation (or press ENTER for options): Corner of ↵

MText: building ↵

MText: ↵ (to end)

Unlike other dimension commands the leader and annotation text are drawn as separate objects. So, if you need to move or edit the text, you can do so without affecting the leader line.

As you can see by the command line, there are a number of options with this command including "Format" options which include "Spline". Experiment with these options until you understand them.

## 12. EDITING DIMENSIONS

The dimension edit commands, DIMEDIT and DIMTEDIT are used primarily to adjust the position of the text part of a dimension. This is usually only necessary if the drawing is quite complex and the dimension would read more clearly if it were in a different position.

### 12.1 The Dimension Text Edit Command

Toolbar

Pull-down **Dimension ▸ Align Text ▸ *options***

Keyboard **DIMTEDIT**

The Dimension Text Edit command is used to modify the text position of any single dimension.

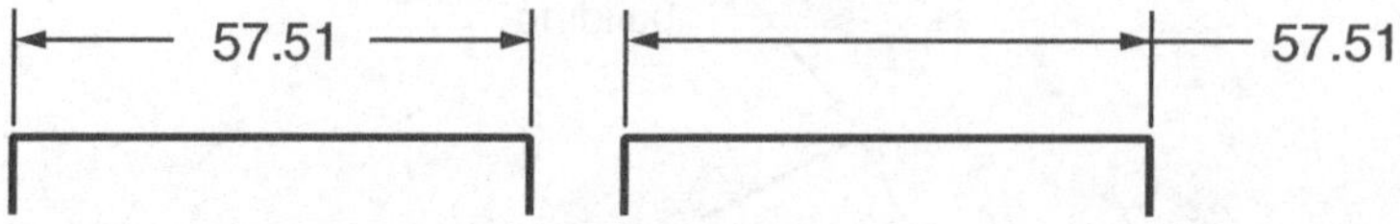


The command can be used to position the text dynamically (this is the default)or one of the options can be used for a specific type of movement. For example, the dimension shown on the right has been modified by dynamically moving the position of the text and then the text has been rotated using the Angle option.

Command: **DIMTEDIT**

Select dimension: (pick the dimension you want to edit)

Enter text location (Left/Right/Home/Angle): (pick a new position or use an option)

The results of the four available options are shown in the illustration below.

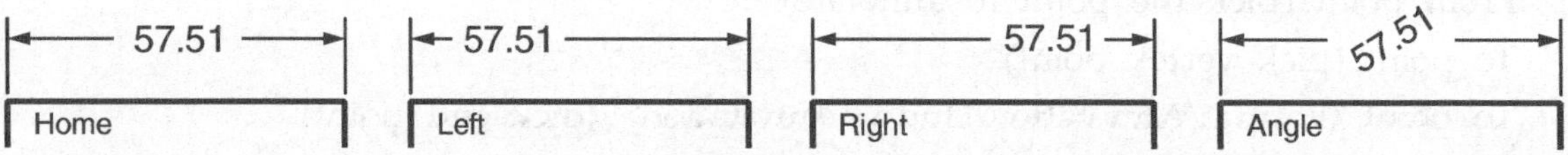


The **Left** option moves the text to a left justified position within the dimension.

The **Right** option moves the text to a right justified position within the dimension.

The **Home** option returns the text to the home position after it has been modified.

The **Angle** option enables the text to be rotated about its center.

## 12.2 The Dimension Edit Command

Toolbar 

Pull-down **Dimension ▸ Oblique** (other options are duplicated in DIMTEDIT so don't appear)

Keyboard **DIMEDIT**

The Dimension Edit command can be used to modify and change the text of any number of dimensions. The command could, for example, be used to add a standard prefix or suffix to a number of dimensions.

Command: **DIMEDIT**

Dimension Edit (Home/New/Rotate/Oblique) <Home>: (choose an option)

Select objects: (pick one or more dimensions)

Select objects: (pick more or ↵ end)

The command sequence will vary depending upon which option has been chosen but the results of the various options are illustrated below.

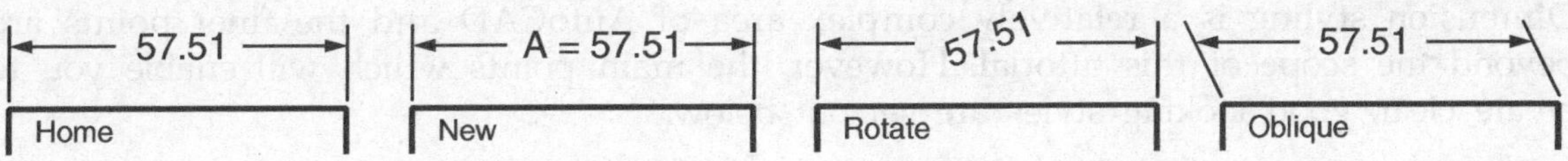


The **Home** option returns dimensions to their home position.

The **New** option displays the Multiline Text Editor. The changes you make to the text will be applied to all selected dimensions so it is important *not* to delete the "<>" marker from the text string. Deleting this marker will remove the values from all selected dimensions.

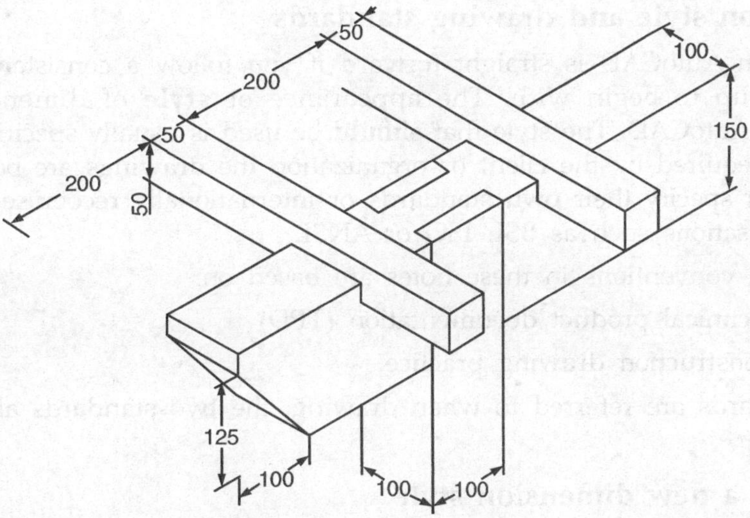


The **Rotate** option can be used to rotate dimension text about its center point. It works in exactly the same way as the Angle option of the DIMTEDIT command except that you can rotate any number of dimensions at once.

The **Oblique** option is used to set the dimension lines at an angle. This option can be very useful when you are dimensioning a drawing in isometric projection. In this case the drawing has been dimensioned using the Aligned command and then the oblique angle modified to suit the dimension position. This usually means setting an angle of 30, 330 or 90 degrees depending upon the dimension orientation. If you are creating details in isometric projection make sure you are using the isometric snap/grid option for greater efficiency. For more information on drawing in isometric projection and the use of the isometric snap grid, see the "Drawing Aids" tutorial.

## 13. DIMENSION STYLES

Dimension styles are the main method used to control the way dimensions look. Using styles you can change the text font, the arrow head style, the relative position of the text, the scale of dimensions and many other parameters. Styles are created using the DIMSTYLE command.

Dimension styling is a relatively complex area of AutoCAD and the finer points are beyond the scope of this tutorial. However, the main points which will enable you to create clear, good looking styles are set out below.

## 13.1 The Dimension Style Command

Toolbar 

Pull-down **Dimension ▸ Style...**

Keyboard **DDIM** short-cut **D**

## 13.2 Dimension style and drawing standards

Dimensioning in AutoCAD is straight forward if you follow a consistent procedure for setting things up to begin with. The appearance or **style** of dimensions is highly configurable in AutoCAD. The style that **should** be used is usually specified in the drawing standards required by the client or organization the drawings are being created for. They will either specify their own standards or internationally recognised standards defined by organisations such as BSI, ISO or ANSI.

All drawing conventions in these notes are based on:

**BS 8888** Technical product documentation (TPD)

**BS 1192** Construction drawing practice

If no standards are referred to when drawing, the two standards above are recommended.

## 13.3 Creating a new dimension style

We will use the default 'standard' style, modify it slightly and then save it so it can be used later on.

## 12.4 The features of dimensions

Standard dimensions have particular features which are all configurable in AutoCAD. Each has its own value which can be set in the **dimstyle** manager window, as you will be shown next. These are some of the features along with the system variable in bold.

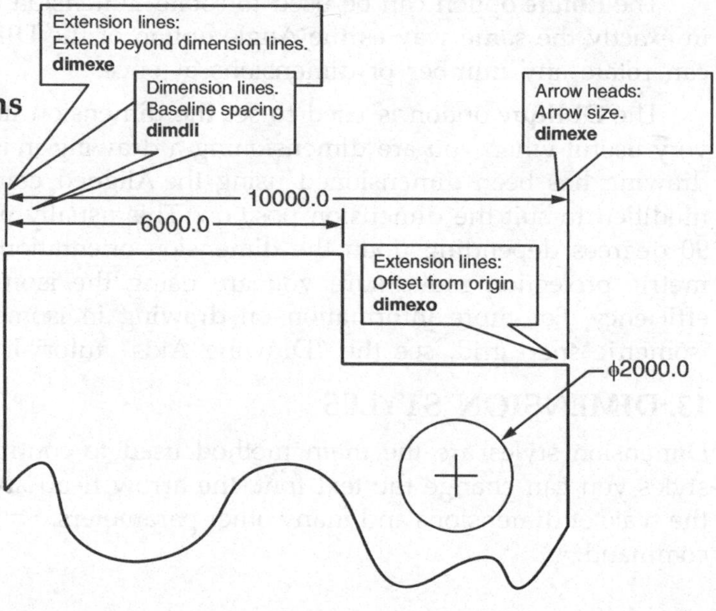

On the **Lines and Arrows** tab:

Change all of the settings to see what effects they have. Then set them as shown here. Note that the tabs in this window may be structured slightly differently on your version of the software, but the same parameters will be there somewhere, look for them.

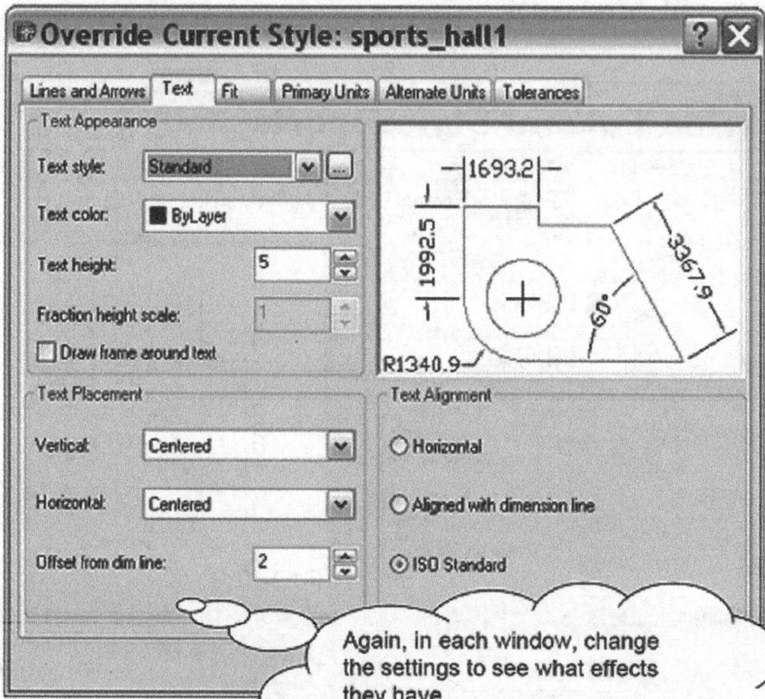


Again, in each window, change the settings to see what effects they have.

Then set them as shown here.

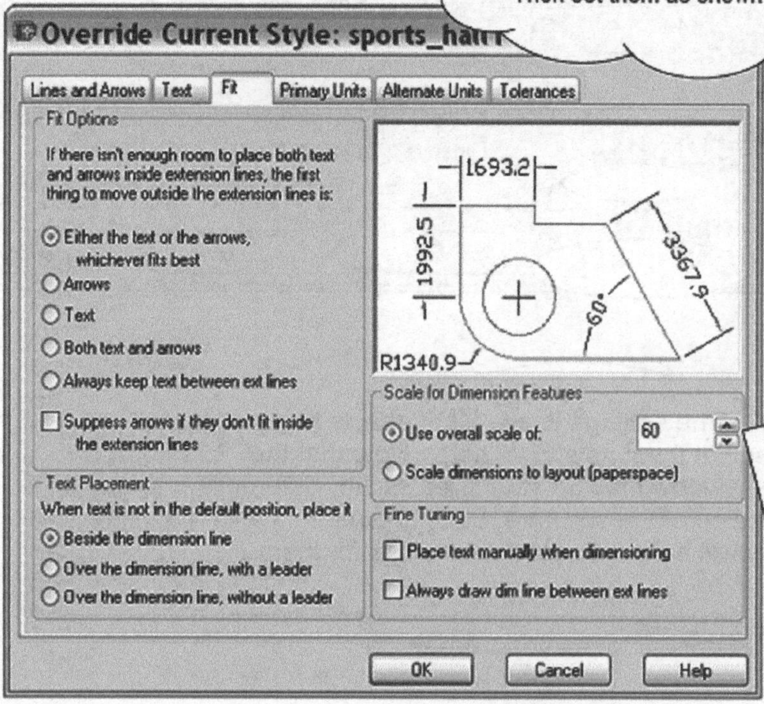


On the **Fit** tab:

Overall scale is important.

As we are dimensioning in model space, we will have to apply an overall scale to magnify the dimensions.

**Dimscale** command also sets this value.

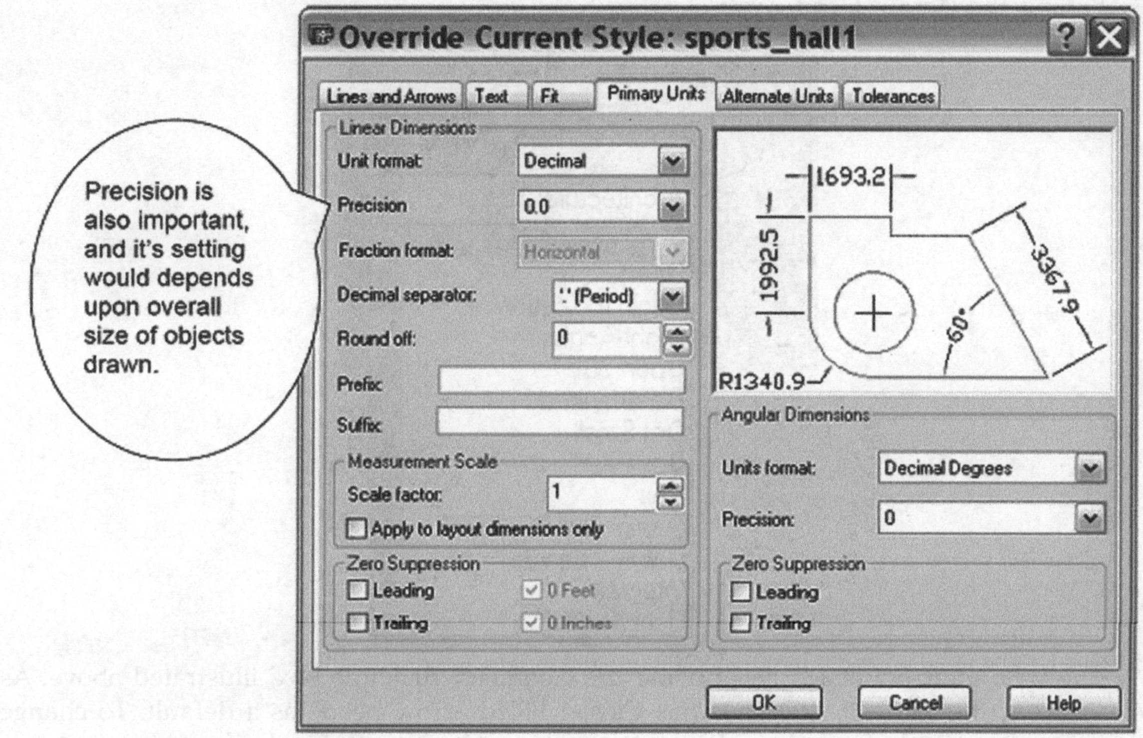


## 13.5 Creating dimensions

Create a new layer for the dimensions called **dimensions** and colour it **yellow**. Make this new layer the current layer.

Bring up the dimension toolbar by right mouse button clicking in an empty area of the top toolbar and select **ADT** > **Dimension**.

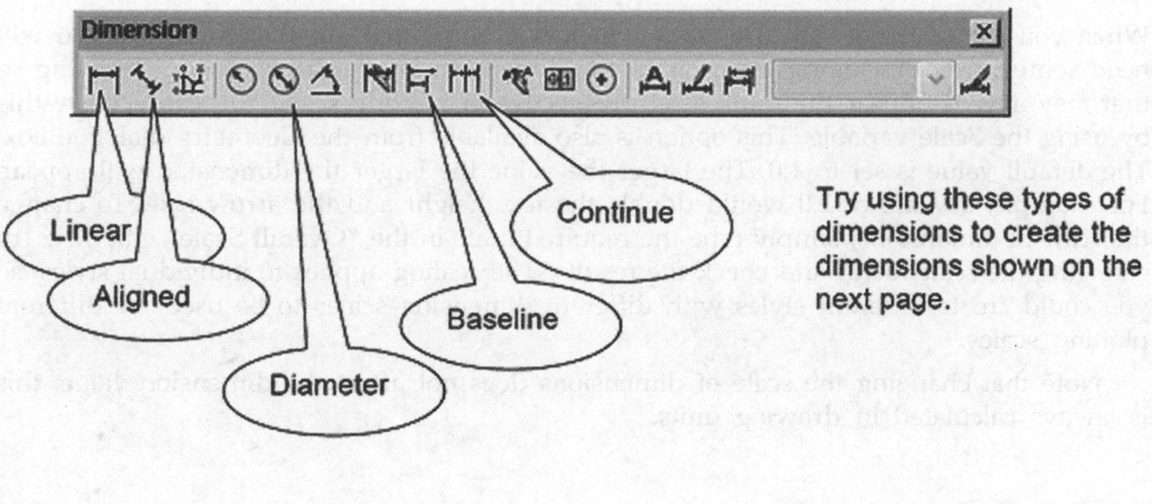

Setting the Arrow Head Type

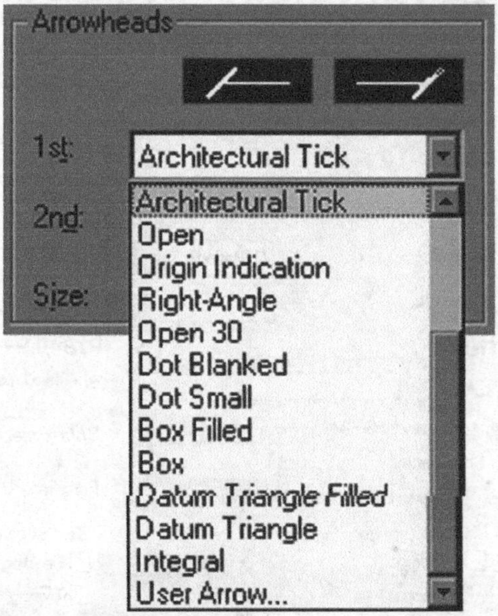


The style of arrow heads is set using the Geometry dialogue box, illustrated above. As you can see, the STANDARD style has Closed Filled arrow heads as a default. To change the arrow head style for a new dimension style, make sure the style is current and that the "Parent" radio button is selected (this assumes you are not modifying a child style), click on the "Geometry..." button and select a new arrow head type from the "1st" drop-down list.

Once selected the new arrow type is illustrated in the dialogue box. If you require different arrow heads at each end of your dimensions you can set the other type using the "2nd" drop-down list. Click on "OK" to return to the Dimension Styles dialogue box.

## 13.6 Dimension Scale

When you are working with drawings which will be plotted at different scales, you will need some way of changing the scale of the dimension lines relative to your drawing so that they always appear the same size, irrespective of plotting scale. You can achieve this by using the Scale variable. This option is also available from the Geometry dialogue box. The default value is set to 1.0. The larger the value the larger the dimension will appear. For example, a value of 2.0 would double the text height and the arrow size. To change the scale of dimensions, simply type the required scale in the "Overall Scale" edit box. Try changing the scale factor and check the results. The scaling applies to individual styles, so you could create different styles with different dimension scales to be used for different plotting scales.

Note that changing the scale of dimensions does not affect the dimension value; this is always calculated in drawing units.

Setting the Text Location

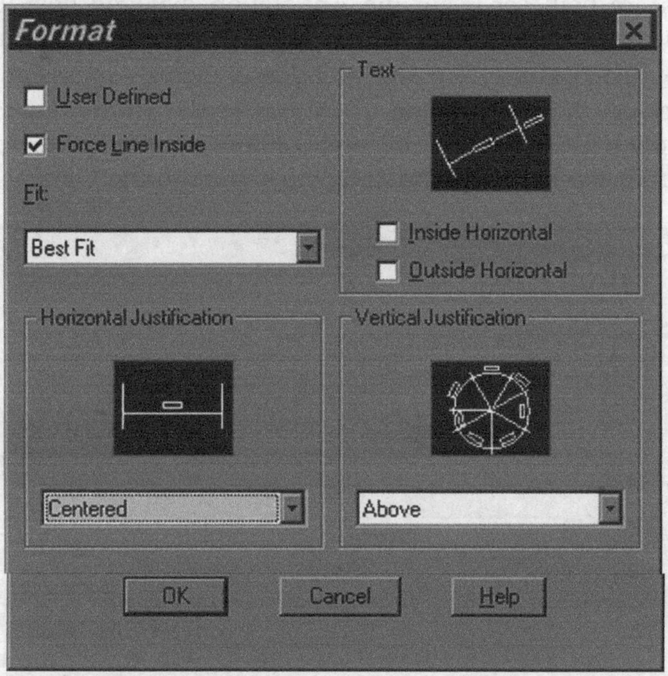


To change the text location click on the "Format..." button in the Dimension Styles dialogue box. The Format dialogue box is shown below. By default the horizontal justification is set to "Centered" and the vertical justification to "Above". This means that the dimension text will appear centered above a horizontal dimension line and centered left of a vertical dimension line. To have the text centered within the dimension line, click on the down arrow of the "Vertical Justification" pull-down list to reveal the options and click on "Centered". The illustration changes to reflect your choice. Click on "OK" to return to the Dimension Styles dialogue box. You can see the result of this action by looking at the illustration below. Experiment with the Horizontal Justification and Vertical Justification options to see what results they give.

You can also use Text the option in this dialogue box to change the text orientation in aligned dimensions. By default all dimension text is aligned with the dimension. This option allows you to force text to appear horizontal, irrespective of the orientation of the dimension. You have independent control over dimension text which appears inside and outside of the dimension lines.

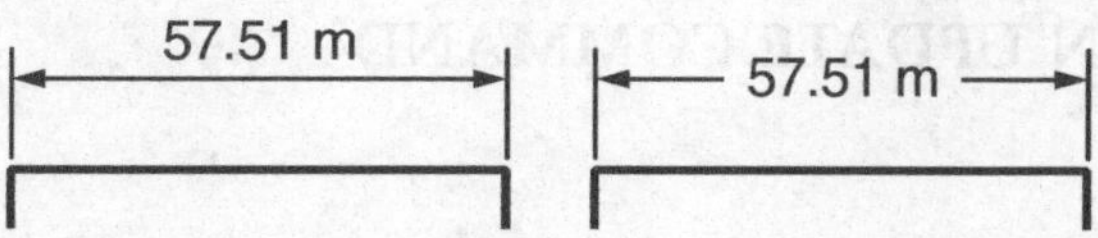


The illustration on the left shows a dimension with vertical justification set to "Above" (far left) and to "Centered" (near left).

## 13.7 Setting Text Style and Units

Text style and units are both set using the Annotation dialogue box, illustrated below. To set a text style to a dimension you must first have created the style using the Text Style command (**Format ▸ Text Style...** from the pull-down menu). To assign the text style to a dimension style, click on the "Annotation..." button in the Dimension Styles dialogue box, click on the drop-down list in the "Text" area of the Annotation dialogue and select the required text style from the list. Click on "OK" to return to the Dimension Styles dialogue.

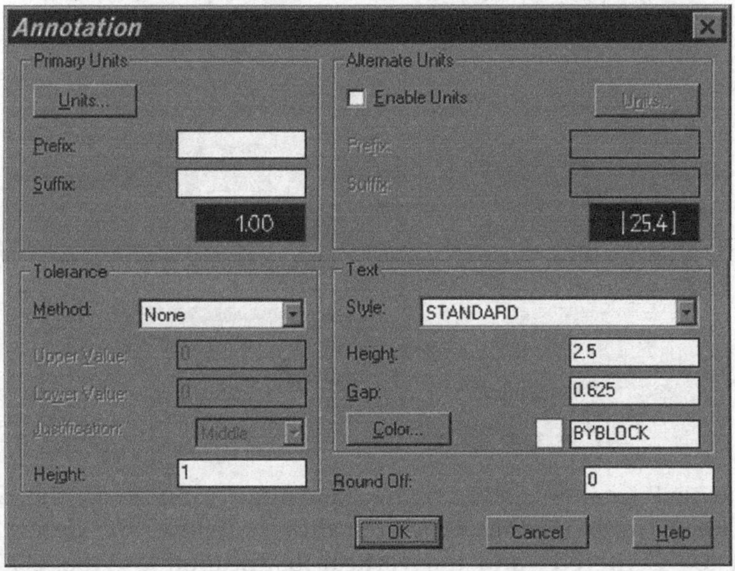


AutoCAD gives you the option to automatically include a unit prefix or suffix with the dimension text. For example, you could set the dimension style in such a way that it created dimensions with "m" to indicate meters after each dimension text. Most usually, dimensions are drawn without units displayed but with a note on the drawing indicating the units used, such as "All dimensions in meters". However, you may have a drawing where different units are being used for different elements of the drawing. In such a case it is a good idea to include units to avoid confusion. Remember that the main idea behind dimensioning is to give the maximum amount of information in the clearest and most concise way. To add units to a dimension style, click on the "Annotation..." button in the Dimension Styles dialogue box and enter the required unit character(s) in the "Prefix" and/or "Suffix" edit boxes of the "Primary Units" area of the dialogue box. For example, if you wanted to display meters, you would type "m" in the "Suffix" edit box.

## 14. THE DIMENSION UPDATE COMMAND

Toolbar 

Pull-down **Dimension ▸ Update**

Keyboard **DIM ↵ UPDATE**

The Dimension Update command is used to apply the current dimension style to existing dimensions. You can use this command to change the style of a dimension. Unlike text styles, dimension styles do not automatically update when the style is changed. The UPDATE command must be used to force dimensions to appear in the current text style.

Command Sequence

Command: DIM

Dim: **UPDATE**

Select objects: (pick dimension to update)

Select objects: (pick more dimensions or ↵ to end)

Dim: (press the escape key, **Esc** to return to the command prompt)

## Tips & Tricks

- Always attempt to use the least number of dimensions in order to provide the maximum amount of information.

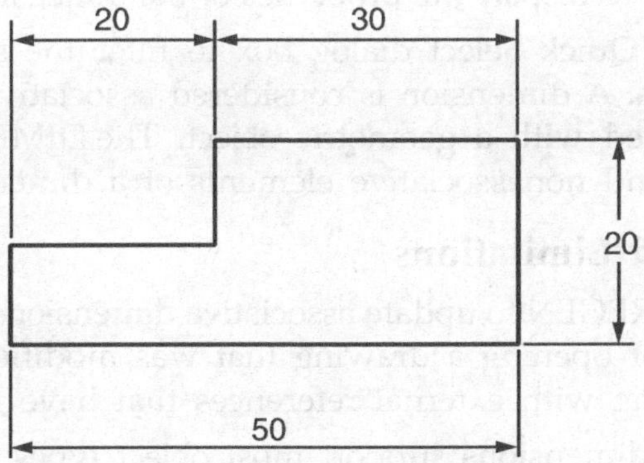


- Avoid giving duplicate information. For example, if you use a number of running dimensions along the length of an object, it is not necessary to include an additional dimension for the whole length. In the illustration on the right the "50" dimension is unnecessary because it gives no extra information and simply duplicates that which can be inferred from the "20" and "30" dimensions. This will also avoid any ambiguity which may arise from inaccurate dimensioning.
- Sometimes it may be more appropriate to add notes to your drawing which include dimension information rather than attempt to dimension small or complex items.
- If you do not include any units information with your dimensions you must always add a note to your drawing such as "All dimensions are in millimeter" to make it absolutely clear.

## Associative Dimensions

Dimensions can be associative, nonassociative, or exploded. Associative dimensions adjust to changes in the geometric objects that they measure.

Dimension associativity defines the relationship between geometric objects and the dimensions that give their distance and angles. There are three types of associativity between geometric objects and dimensions.

- **Associative dimensions.** Automatically adjust their locations, orientations, and measurement values when the geometric objects associated with them are modified. Dimensions in a layout may be associated to objects in model space. The DIMASSOC system variable is set to 2.
- **Nonassociative dimensions.** Selected and modified with the geometry they measure. Nonassociative dimensions do not change when the geometric objects they measure are modified. The dimension variable DIMASSOC is set to 1.
- **Exploded dimensions.** Contain a collection of separate objects rather than a single dimension object. The DIMASSOC system variable is set to 0.

You can determine whether a dimension is associative or nonassociative by selecting the dimension and doing one of the following:

- Use the Properties palette to display the properties of the dimension.
- Use the LIST command to display the properties of the dimension.

You can also use the Quick Select dialog box to filter the selection of associative or nonassociative dimensions. A dimension is considered associative even if only one end of the dimension is associated with a geometric object. The DIMREASSOCIATE command displays the associative and nonassociative elements of a dimension.

## Special Situations and Limitations

You may need to use DIMREGEN to update associative dimensions after panning or zooming with a wheel mouse, after opening a drawing that was modified with an earlier release, or after opening a drawing with external references that have been modified.

Although associative dimensions support most object types that you would expect to dimension, they do not support the following:

- Hatches
- Multiline objects
- 2D solids
- Objects with nonzero thickness
- Images
- DWF underlays

When selecting objects to dimension, make sure that the objects that you select don't include a directly overlapping object that does not support associative dimensioning such as a 2D solid.

Associativity is *not* maintained between a dimension and a block reference if the block is redefined.

Associativity is not maintained between a dimension and a 3D solid if the shape of the 3D solid is modified.

Dimensions created with QDIM are not associative but may be associated individually with DIMREASSOCIATE.

## Change Dimension Associatively

### To change the dimension associativity default

1. Click Tools menu ➤ Options.
2. In the Options dialog box, User Preferences tab, under Associative Dimensioning, select or clear Make New Dimensions Associative.
3. Do either or both of the following:
   - Click Apply to record the current Options settings in the system registry.
   - Click OK to record the current Options settings in the system registry and close the Options dialog box.

All subsequently created dimensions in the drawing use the new setting. Unlike most other option settings, dimension associativity is saved in the drawing file rather than in the system registry.

CHAPTER 7

# Layers

# OBJECT PROPERTIES

## INTRODUCTION

Every AutoCAD object, such as a line or a circle has properties. Some properties such as Colour, Linetype and Layer are common to all objects. Some objects have properties which are specific to themselves. Text, for example, is the only object type which has a Text Style property. In AutoCAD Release 14, the easiest way to control object properties is to use the Object Properties toolbar, illustrated below. This is one of AutoCAD's default toolbars and can usually be found directly below the Standard toolbar in the top left hand corner of the AutoCAD window.

Take time to work through this tutorial, it is particularly important to get to grips with object properties since it can make the difference between a really good AutoCAD drawing and a really terrible one. If you just need information quickly, use the Quick Find toolbar below to go straight to the information you need or select a topic from the contents list above.

## 1. LAYERS

Probably the most important object property to understand well is the layer property. Experienced AutoCAD users use layers all the time and that is why the Object Properties toolbar contains so many layer functions. Good use of layers is the most important aspect of good drawing practice.

The concept of layers is very important in AutoCAD and the correct use of layers can make your drawing much easier to work with. Basically, layers are the computer equivalent of tracing overlays on a drawing board. However, layers are much more powerful because you can have many layers in a single drawing and you can control the visibility, colour and linetype of layers independently. This makes working with very complicated drawings much more efficient. Layers are effectively a way of ordering your drawing. For example, you may need to create a number of construction lines in a drawing which will not form a part of the finished image. You could create a layer called "Construction" and use this for your construction lines. When the drawing is complete, you could simply turn this layer off so that it can't be seen. The beauty is that you could always turn this layer back on at some future time if modifications to the drawing are required. Experienced AutoCAD users will use layers to order their drawings by drawing components. For example, if you were creating a landscape master plan, you may have layers called "Trees", "Shrubs", "Path" etc. The main reason for this, apart from it being a simple way to control the drawing, is that the different drawing components may need to be printed in different colours, with different linetypes and with different line widths. Layers can be used to control the way objects are displayed on the computer monitor and how they appear when they are printed.

It is a common misapprehension amongst new users that layers can be used to control the visual hierarchy of objects. In other words, if two objects overlap, it seems reasonable to assume that you could cause one object to display "above" another with the use of layers. This layer model is common to illustration software such as Corel DRAW. However, AutoCAD uses a 3 dimensional drawing space where all objects coexist and are positioned in their correct co-ordinate locations. The concept of an object being displayed above or below another, therefore, is not consistent with this logic. In AutoCAD the display of one object in relation to another is determined by the objects place in the drawing database. Objects drawn more recently will display over another if the two objects occupy the same physical space. It is possible to override this effect using the Display Order tools found on the Tools pull-down, **Tools ▸ Display Order ▸** ***Options***. These options are particularly useful to control the display of overlapping solids and solid hatches that are coplanar. The layer of an object has no effect on its display order.

Although you can have many layers in a drawing, you can only draw on one layer at a time. The layer you are drawing on is said to be the *current* layer. The Object Properties toolbar displays the current layer information. In the illustration above, you can see that layer "0" is the current layer and that both the colour and linetype are set "ByLayer".

When you start a new drawing, AutoCAD has only one layer. This layer is special and is called layer "0" (zero). Layer 0 is special because you cannot change its name or delete it and it has certain properties which we do not need to consider just now. By default layer 0 is assigned the colour white (colour number 7) and the "Continuous" linetype. Layer 0 is always the current layer when you start a new drawing, however, it is bad drawing practice to use layer 0 for normal drawing. The first thing you should do, therefore, when you start a new AutoCAD drawing is to create some new layers.

## 2. THE LAYER COMMAND

Toolbar 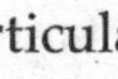

Pull-down **Format ▸ Layer...**

Keyboard **LAYER**

Although AutoCAD provides many shortcuts for working with layers, many of which will be covered later, the Layer command provides the most comprehensive control over layers and layer operations. This command uses a dialogue box. The dialogue box is a *tabbed*dialogue box and can be modified to show more or less details. This is quite nice because in its simplified form it looks much less intimidating to beginners. The following setions demonstrate how the Layer command can be used to perform many of the most common layer operations.

### 2.1 Creating a New Layer

To create a new layer, click on 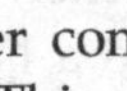 in the Object Properties toolbar, the Layer & Linetype Properties dialogue box, illustrated below, appears. This is a *tabbed* dialogue box and can be used to control either layer properties or linetype properties depending upon which tab is selected. The Layer tab is always selected by default. Now click on the "New" button. A new layer called "Layer1" is automatically created in the layer list below layer 0. As you can see from the illustration, the layer name is automatically highlighted for you so that you can give the layer a more meaningful name. When you have entered an appropriate name, press the ↵ key to complete the operation. You have now created a new layer and given it a name. Notice that by default it has been assigned the colour white and the linetype "Continuous".

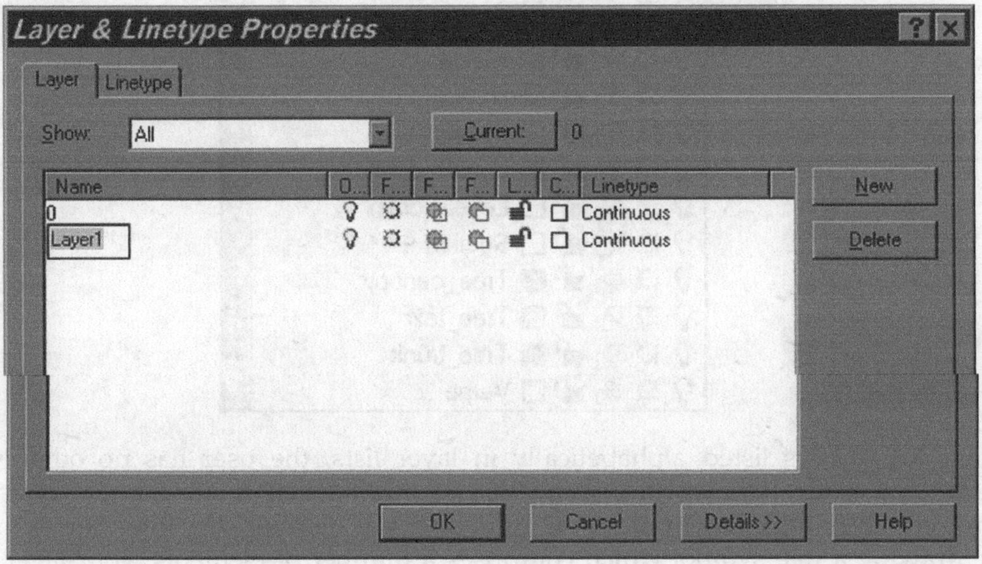


There are a few restrictions to consider when you are naming layers. The most annoying is that you cannot use spaces within layer names. So, for example, the layer name "Tree trunk" is illegal. However, it is common practice to replace the space with either a hyphen or an underscore, both of which are valid layer name characters. So, the layer names "Tree-trunk" and "Tree trunk" are both acceptable. Some other special characters are also not allowed. If you do use an illegal character, AutoCAD will alert you with the error message box illustrated above. Notice that it very helpfully tells you which characters are legal. Basically, if you stick with letters and numbers you won't experience any problems. In addition to the hyphen and underscore mentioned above, the dollar sign is the only other symbol allowed.

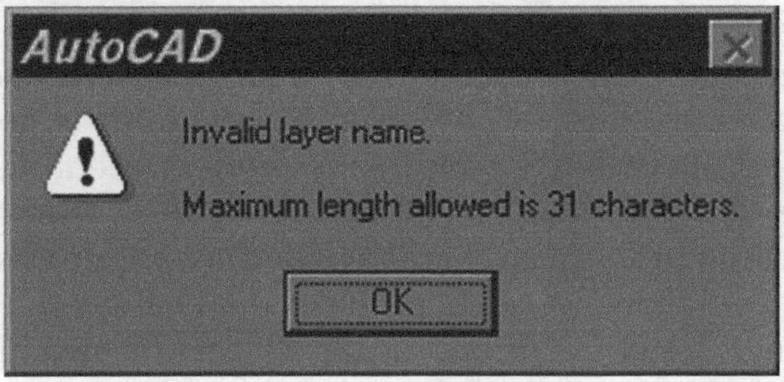

The only other restriction relating to layer names is the number of characters used. Layer names can be between one and thirty-one characters long. This should give you plenty of scope to devise understandable and descriptive names for your layers. It is good drawing practice to name your layers sensibly, bear in mind that other people may have to work with drawings which you create. If you enter a layer name longer that 31 characters, AutoCAD will display the error message box shown on the left.

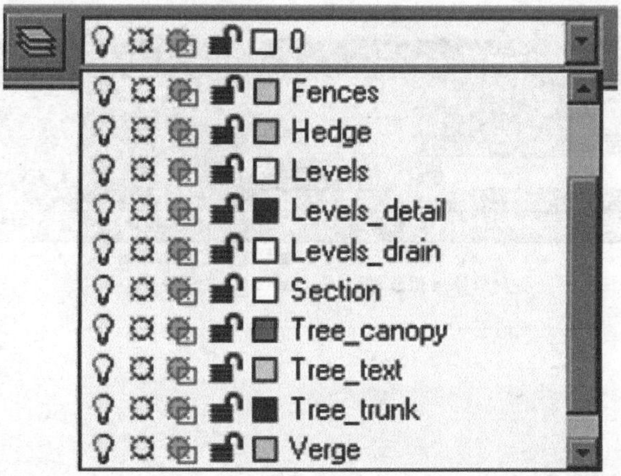


Layers are always listed alphabetically in layer lists, the user has no other way to control the list order. It is worth bearing this in mind when naming your layers. Keep similar object layers together by devising a hierarchical naming structure. For example, if you are drawing a tree symbol which comprises a number of elements, your layer names might be, "Tree_canopy", "Tree_text", "Tree_trunk" etc. This will cause all the Tree layers to be displayed together, see the illustration on the right. This is quite important because in complicated drawings there may be many layers and searching for the right group of layers can waste a lot of time.

## 2.2 Setting Colour and Linetype "ByLayer"

AutoCAD offers two methods of setting the colour and linetype of a drawing object. First of all, colour and linetype can be set *ByLayer*. In other words, an object will be displayed in the colour and linetype of its layer. For example, if you draw a circle on a layer which you have called "Detail" and you have also set the colour of Detail to blue and the linetype to dashed, then the circle will be displayed in a dashed blue line. When an object takes on the properties of its layer, the colour and linetype are said to be set "ByLayer".

The second method AutoCAD offers is to set the colour and linetype by object. Setting properties by object overrides those set ByLayer. In general it is good drawing practice to set colour and linetype properties ByLayer, this is more efficient and less confusing in the long-run. For example, imagine that you have drawn hundreds of objects on the same layer and have set their colour to green. Later in the drawing process you decide that these objects should, in fact, be yellow. In order to make the change you would have to use the Properties command and select every one of the objects by picking them. By contrast, if you had set the objects colour to ByLayer, you would only have to change the layer colour from green to yellow and all of the objects would change.

There are times, however, when in is useful to be able to set colour and linetype properties by object. Setting properties by object is covered later in this tutorial. The following sections cover the setting of colour and linetype ByLayer.

## 2.3 Setting the Colour of a Layer

It is often convenient to set the layer colour when the layer is created, although this can be done at any time. The layer colour can be changed as many times as you like. Each time it is changed, any objects on that layer will change to the new colour, providing their colour is set to "ByLayer".

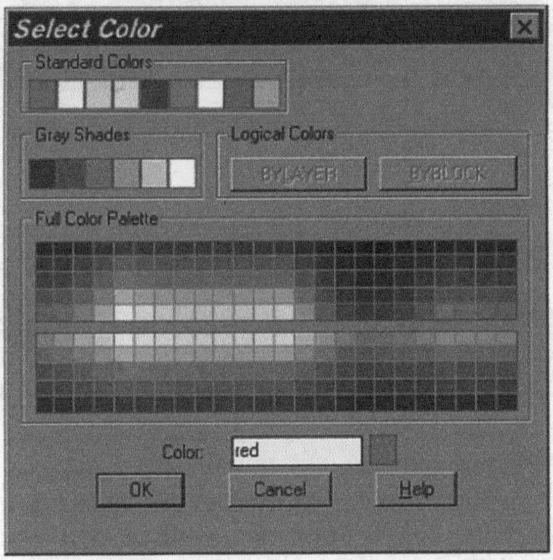


To set a layer colour, open the Layer & Linetype Properties dialogue box, click on and then click on the colour icon in the layer list associated with the layer you want. Notice that all layers have their own colour icon and that this changes to display the layer colour. Clicking on the icon brings up the Select Color dialogue box, shown on the right. You can select any of the 255 standard AutoCAD colours by picking on the colour palette or by entering the colour name or number in the text edit box. When you have selected the colour you want, click on the "OK" button to set the colour. AutoCAD uses only 255 colours plus the drawing background colour, irrespective of the capabilities of your video display.

Assigning different colours to your layers will make working with complex drawings much easier. You will be able to see at a glance what a particular line represents. For example, your construction lines may be on a layer called "Construction" and have the colour yellow. This will visually differentiate these lines from lines on other layers with different colours.

## 2.4 Setting the Linetype of a Layer

In the same way that you can assign a colour to a layer you can also assign a linetype to a layer. For example, you could have all the lines on a layer called "Construction" display in a yellow dashed line. To set a linetype to a layer, click on [icon] and then click on the current linetype name associated with your layer in the layer list. By default, layers have the "Continuous" linetype. Clicking on the linetype name brings up the Select Linetype dialogue box, shown on the right. You will notice that the "Continuous" linetype is the only one listed. That's because all linetypes, except "Continuous", are stored in an external file and have to be loaded before they can be used.

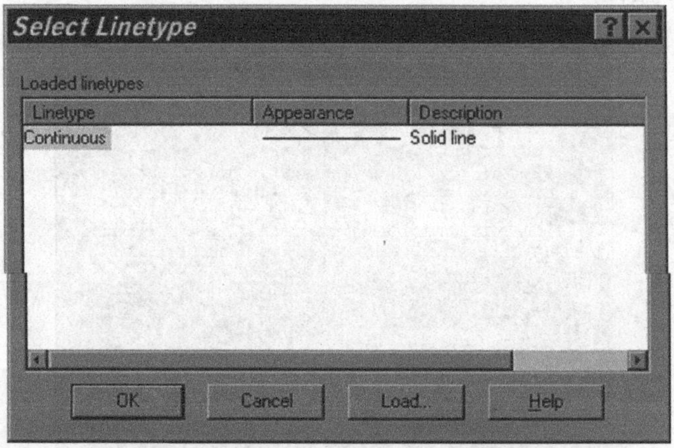


## 2.5 Loading Linetypes

To load a linetype, click on the "Load..." button in the Select Linetype dialogue box. The Load or Reload Linetypes dialogue box appears and displays a list of the available linetypes. Select as many of the listed linetypes as you wish and then click the OK button to return to the Select Linetype dialogue box.

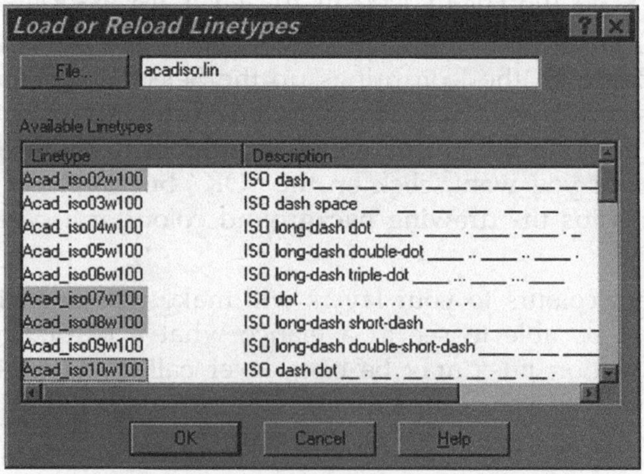

Selecting from list boxes works the same way in AutoCAD as it does in any other Windows application. For example, if you wish to select a block of linetypes from the list at one time, select the first linetype in the block, hold the Shift key down on the keyboard and select the last linetype in the block. All linetypes in the block will be highlighted and you can click the "OK" button to load them all in one go. You can also hold the Control (Ctrl) key down on the keyboard to make multiple selections which aren't adjacent in the list.

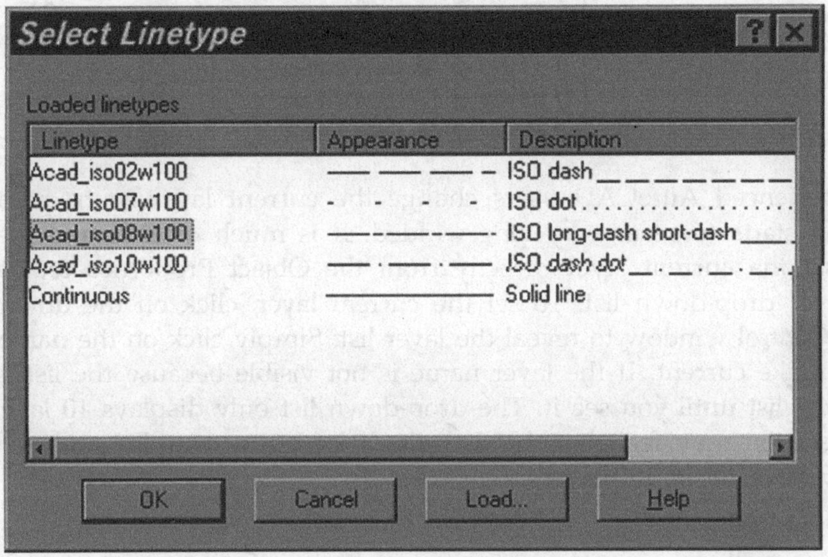


When you return to the Select Linetype dialogue box the loaded linetypes are displayed in the list. To assign a particular linetype to a layer, simply click on the name to highlight it and then click on the OK button. When you return to the Layer & Linetype Properties dialogue box, the new linetype name will be listed against your layer in the "Linetype" column. From now on, all objects drawn on this layer will be drawn with the chosen linetype. However, just like colours, you may change the linetype at any time and the objects drawn on that layer will automatically be updated to display the new linetype.

## 2.6 Making a Layer the Current Layer

Once you have created some layers you will want to start using them. As indicated above, you can only draw on one layer at a time. In order to draw on a particular layer you must first make it the *current* layer. As usual with AutoCAD there are a number of alternatives. You could, for example, use the Layer command, **Layer...** from the **Format** pull-down or  from the Object Properties toolbar. As you have seen previously, this command brings up the Layer & Linetype Properties dialogue box. To set the current layer, select a layer name from the list and then click on the "Current" button and then click the "OK" button to finish. The selected layer is now the current layer and it's properties are displayed on the Object Properties toolbar.

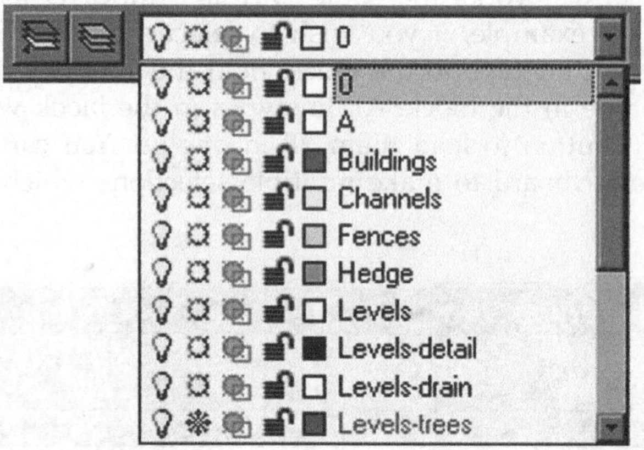


Most experienced AutoCAD users change the current layer so frequently that the above method starts to seem very long winded. It is much quicker and therefore more efficient to set the current layer directly from the Object Properties toolbar using the "Layer Control" drop-down list. To set the current layer, click on the down arrow next to the Layer Control window to reveal the layer list. Simply click on the name of the layer you wish to make current. If the layer name is not visible because the list is quite long, scroll down the list until you see it. The drop-down list only displays 10 layers at a time. As a beginner, you may feel that this is quite a lot but a complex and well structured drawing may have 50 or 100 layers.

Toolbar 

Pull-down not available

Keyboard **AI_MOLC**

There is an even quicker way to change the current layer providing you know which layer objects are on. You can use the Make Object's Layer Current command to set the current layer to the layer of any picked object.

Select Make Object's Layer Current from the Object Properties toolbar. 

When AutoCAD prompts

Select object whose layer will become current:

pick the object you know to be on the required layer. If you miss the object you are trying to select, the command is automatically canceled

AutoCAD confirms the action by writing to the command line

LAYER NAME is now the current layer.

You will also see the layer details change in the Object Properties toolbar. With a bit of practice and a good awareness of the layers you are using, this command can save lots of time.

## 2.7 Controlling Layer States

One of the best aspects of working with layers is the flexibility with which you can control their visibility. So far we have looked at the colour and linetype properties of layers. However, there are a number of other properties all of which relate to whether or not objects on a layer can be seen and/or modified. The current state of these properties are all indicated by icons in the various layer lists. You will already have seen them if you have been following this tutorial. The meaning of these icons is shown in the table below:

| Icon | Name | Description |
|---|---|---|
| | On | The layer is visible unless it is also frozen |
| | Off | The layer is invisible but objects are still regenerated unless it is also frozen |
| | Thaw in all viewports | The layer is not frozen |
| | Freeze in all viewports | The layer is invisible and objects are suspended from regeneration |
| | Thaw in current viewport | The layer is not frozen in the current viewport |
| | Freeze in current viewport | The layer is frozen and invisible in the current viewport but may be visible in other viewports. |
| | Thaw in new viewports | The layer is not frozen in new viewports when they are created |
| | Freeze in new viewports | The layer will be frozen in any new viewport |
| | Unlock | The layer is unlocked |
| | Lock | The layer is locked and objects cannot be selected or modified |

## 2.8 Turning Layers On and Off

You can turn layers off or on either by using the Layer command, from the Object Properties toolbar or you can more easily do it using the "Layer Control" list, directly from the Object Properties toolbar. In either case, all you have to do is click on the icon you wish to change. The icons all act as toggles, so if a layer is on, all you need to do is click on the icon and the icon will change to , turning the layer off. And conversely, clicking on changes the icon to and turns the layer back on.

Objects on a layer which is turned off aren't displayed in the drawing window and they won't be plotted. The objects still exist in the drawing; they are just invisible.

If a layer is turned off and you make it the current layer, AutoCAD turns it on. It's possible to turn off the current layer, but this is rarely desirable. To do so causes no harm, but it can be confusing if you don't realize what has happened; new objects you draw are added to the drawing but are not displayed until the layer is again turned on.

Each designated layer is turned on (made visible) using the colour number and linetype previously associated with it. If the layer is presently frozen, turning it on is not sufficient to make it display again; you must also thaw the layer (see Layers below).

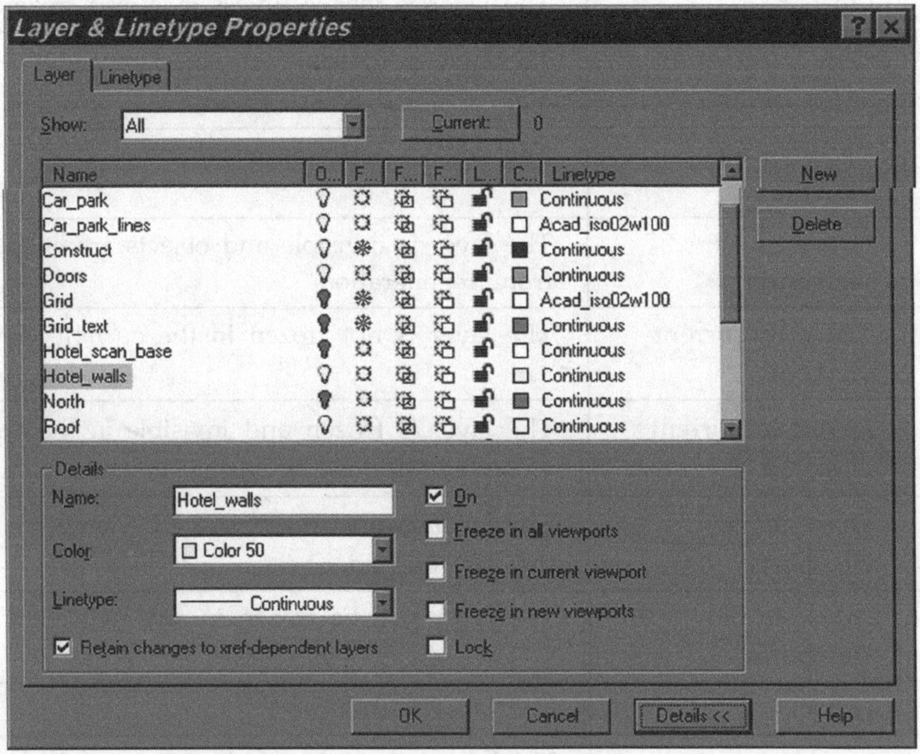


The illustration above shows the Layer & Linetype Properties dialogue box with a number of layers in different states of visibility. Notice also that the dialogue box has been enlarged to show more information. You can do this by clicking on the "Details>>" button.

## 2.9 Freezing and Thawing Layers

Freezing and thawing layers works in exactly the same way as turning them off or on. Simply click on the ☼ icon to freeze a layer or ❄ to thaw it.

By freezing a layer you are effectively instructing AutoCAD to ignore the objects on that layer when regenerating the drawing. Objects on frozen layers aren't displayed or plotted, and AutoCAD spends no time calculating where they go. Therefore, by freezing layers you can increase the ZOOM, PAN, VPOINT, REGEN, and object selection performance for complex drawings. It is always a good idea to freeze layers that aren't of immediate interest.

## 2.10 Turn Off or Freeze?

Since freezing a layer also makes it invisible, you may be confused about when to select Freeze as opposed to off. The main difference is a matter of efficiency. If you're frequently switching between layers and changing their visibility, doing a bit of editing on each of them, you should use Off when you want to make objects on a layer invisible. If, on the other hand, you're doing most of your editing on one layer (or a set of layers), and don't need to see the objects on another set of layers, you should freeze those layers. This will speed up your editing and make the drawing clearer to work with.

Objects on layers that are off are recalculated during regeneration, but simply not displayed. Therefore, when you turn a layer on that was previously off, it will display immediately. On the other hand, layers that are frozen are not recalculated during regeneration and therefore REGENs and object selection can be much faster because there is less work for AutoCAD to do. When a frozen layer is thawed, however, regeneration must be performed before objects on that layer can be displayed.

## 2.11 Locking and Unlocking Layers

Locking and unlocking layers work as for turning layers off and on and freezing and thawing them. Simply click on the unlocked-padlock icon to toggle an unlocked layer so that it becomes locked and click the locked-padlock icon to reverse the process.

You can't select or edit the objects on a locked layer; however, the objects are still visible if the layer is on and thawed. This is handy if you are working in detail, but don't want to inadvertently select certain objects. You can make a locked layer current, so you can draw on a locked layer. You can also use inquiry commands (such as LIST or ID) on locked layer objects. You can also use Object Snaps with objects on locked layers and you can even use them as Trim and Extend boundaries.

## 2.12 Layers in Viewports

AutoCAD beginners can operate quite effectively using the On/Off, Freeze/Thaw and Lock/Unlock layer states. However, when you start using Paper Space you will need to understand how to control the visibility of layers in different viewports. By default, all layers are visible in all viewports. However, you can use the "Freeze in current viewport" option to selectively freeze layers in different viewports. This is done by clicking the icon in a layer list when you are in Floating Model Space. This subject is covered in greater detail in the Paper Space tutorial. The viewport layer icons are greyed out when you are in Tiled Model Space.

## 2.13 Renaming a Layer

To rename a layer, start the Layer command by clicking on the  button on the Object Properties toolbar. When the Layer & Linetype Properties dialogue box appears click on the "Details>>" button to reveal the layer details. Pick the layer name you wish to change from the layer list. The name appears in the Name text edit box under "Details". Simply edit or retype the name in the edit box and you will see the name change simultaneously in the layer list. You cannot rename layer "0", the default layer, nor can you rename a layer called "Defpoints" which AutoCAD creates automatically when you use Dimensions. In theory you can also edit a layer name directly from the layer list but I have always found this to be a bit tricky. Notice that you can also change the layer colour and linetype using the "Details" section of the dialogue box.

## 2.14 Deleting a Layer

To delete a layer, start the Layer command,  from the Object Properties toolbar to open the Layer & Linetype Properties dialog box. Click the name of the layer to highlight it, click the "Delete" button and then click "OK".

You cannot delete any layer which has objects on it, you cannot, therefore, use this process to delete all of the objects on a particular layer. You cannot delete the current layer, layer "0", layer "Defpoints" or any layers from external references.

## 2.15 Purging Layers and Linetypes

Layer and linetype definitions add to the size of your drawing because they are kept in the drawing's database. It is, therefore, worthwhile purging layers and linetypes that you are not using. You can delete them, but it is often difficult to know which layers contain objects and therefore can't be deleted. The Purge command lets you delete many types of unused definitions, including blocks, dimension styles, layers and linetypes. You will find the Purge command on the pull-down menu at **File ▸ Drawing Utilities ▸ Purge ▸ Options**, there is no toolbar button for this command.

Command: **PURGE**

Purge unused Blocks/Dimstyles/LAyers/LTypes/SHapes/STyles/Mlinestyles/All:(select option)

Names to purge <*>: (type ↵ to delete all eligible definitions or specify particular names)

Verify each name to be purged? <Y> (Type N to automatically purge all eligible definitions)

The Purge command may not always remove all of the definitions you expect. This usually occurs if you have block definitions in a drawing which reference layers or linetypes etc. In such a case the Purge command will remove any unused block definitions but will not remove the other dependent definitions. All you have to do to get rid of these definitions is to run the Purge command a second time after the block definition has been removed.

## 2.16 Colours

In the same way that you can set a current layer, you can set a current colour so that every object you draw will be displayed in a particular colour irrespective of which layer it is on. As mentioned earlier, this method of assigning colour, by object, is recommended only in special circumstances.

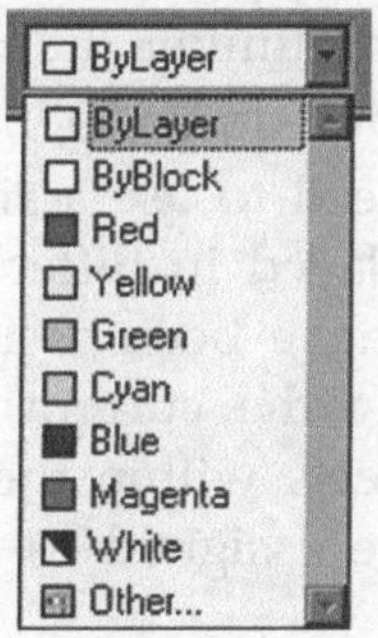


To set a current colour, simply click on the "Color Control" box on the Object Properties toolbar. The drop-down list contains the two logical colours ByLayer and ByBlock, the seven standard AutoCAD colours, Red, Yellow, Green, Cyan, Blue, Magenta and White (colour numbers 1 to 7 respectively) and the "Other..." option. Notice that the default colour for any new drawing is "ByLayer", this is because in most circumstances you will want to assign colours by this method. Select a colour directly from the drop-down list or click on the "Other..." option to bring up the Select Color dialogue box (illustrated below) where you can select any of the AutoCAD colours from the Full Color Palette. This dialogue box is the same as the one you see when setting colour by layer, except that the two logical colour buttons, ByLayer and ByBlock are no longer greyed-out.

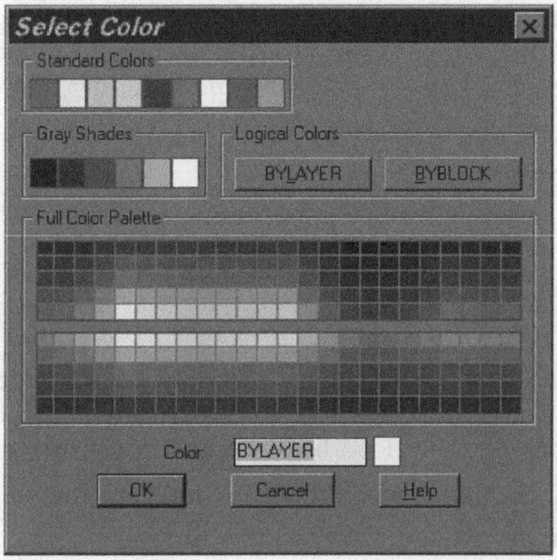

If you set a current colour, you can always return to assigning object colours by layer by setting the current colour to "ByLayer", either with the button in the Select Color dialogue box or directly from the "Color Control" drop-down list on the Object Properties toolbar. There are also a couple of methods for setting the current color from the keyboard. The DDCOLOR command simply launches the Select Color dialogue box from which you can select a colour, as before. The CECOLOR command allows you to change the CECOLOR system variable by entering a colour number, name or logical colour. The DDCOLOR command is also available from the pull-down menu, **Format ▸ Color....**The ByBlock logical colour can be very useful if you need to use a single block in a drawing but have the different insertions of that block displayed in different colours. When a block is inserted into a drawing, those objects which have been assigned the ByBlock colour will acquire the current drawing colour. Changing the current colour between block insertions will change the colour of the ByBlock objects within the block. Only objects which are to be included as part of a block should be assigned to this logical colour.

## 2.17. Linetypes

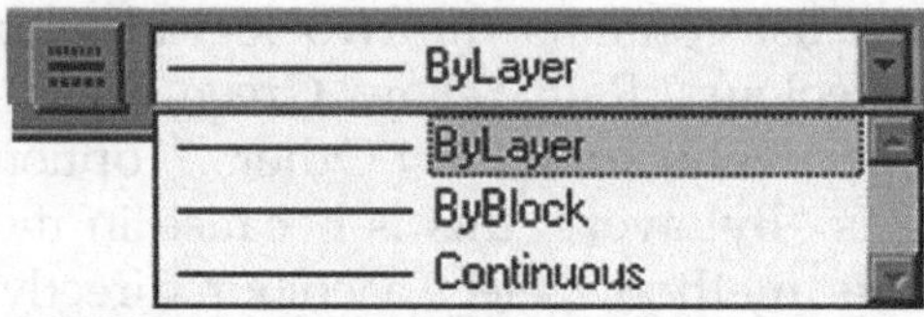


As with layers and colours, a current linetype can be set so that all objects drawn will be displayed with that linetype. However, the same warnings given above about assigning colour by object also apply to assigning linetypes by object, namely that linetypes should be set ByLayer wherever possible. That said, to set a current linetype, click on the "Linetype Control" box on the Object Properties toolbar, and select a linetype from the drop-down list. The list contains the two logical linetypes, ByLayer and ByBlock, these have the same function as the two logical colours of the same name and a list of the currently loaded linetypes.

## 5.1 The Linetype Command

Toolbar 

Pull-down **Format ▸ Linetype...**

Keyboard **LINETYPE**

If you have just started a new drawing the only true linetype available will be the "Continuous" linetype. Before you are able to assign any other linetype, you must first load the linetypes you may need. To load linetypes you must use the "Linetype" command. Click on the  button on the Object Properties toolbar. You will now see the familiar Layer & Linetype Properties dialogue box but this time the "Linetype" tab is automatically selected to display the linetype information,

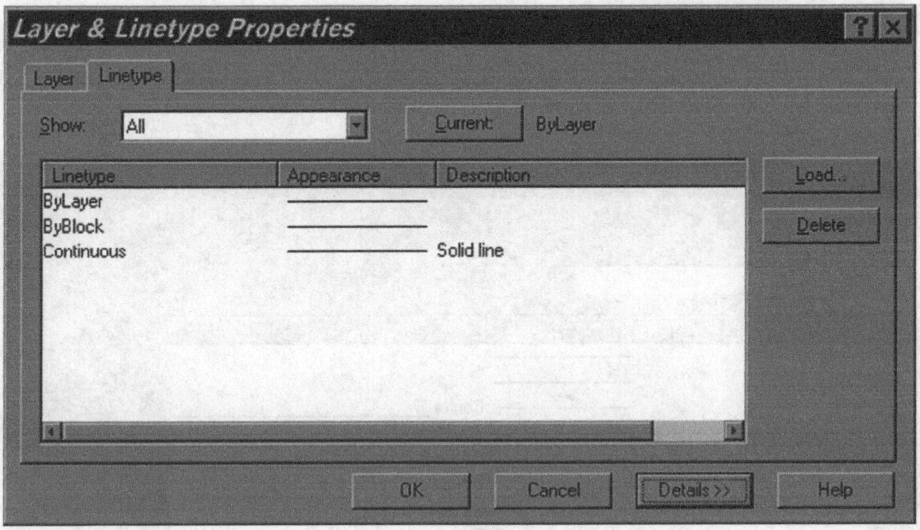


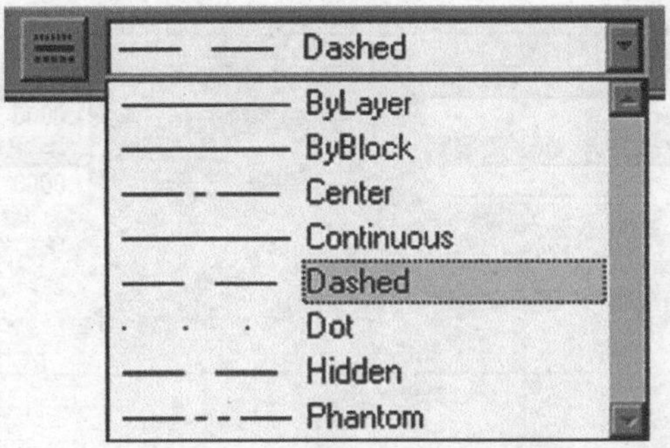


In the Layer & Linetype Properties dialogue box, click on the "Load..." button, this brings up the Load or Reload Linetypes dialogue box which you have seen previously in this tutorial. Select the required linetypes from this dialogue box and then click the "OK" button to return to the Layer & Linetype Properties dialogue box, where you will see the newly loaded linetypes in the Linetype list. This selection process is the same as that described in the "Loading Linetypes" section of this tutorial, above. Now that the required linetypes have been loaded you can set the current linetype either by highlighting it in the Linetype list and then clicking the "Current" button in the Layer & Linetype Properties dialogue box or you can simply select the linetype from the drop-down list in the Object Properties toolbar.

## 5.2 Setting the Linetype Scale

In many cases your linetypes will display just as you want them. However, it is inevitable that at some time you will need to change the scale at which your linetypes are displayed. By default the linetype scale is set to 1.0, this means that each linetype pattern will repeat every 1.0 drawing units. To make the pattern appear larger, change the scale to a larger number. Setting the linetype scale to 5.0 for example causes the linetype pattern to repeat every 5.0 drawing units so that the pattern will appear 5 times larger. Conversely, setting the scale to 0.2 causes a repetition every 0.2 drawing units which will make the pattern appear 5 times smaller. See the illustrations below.

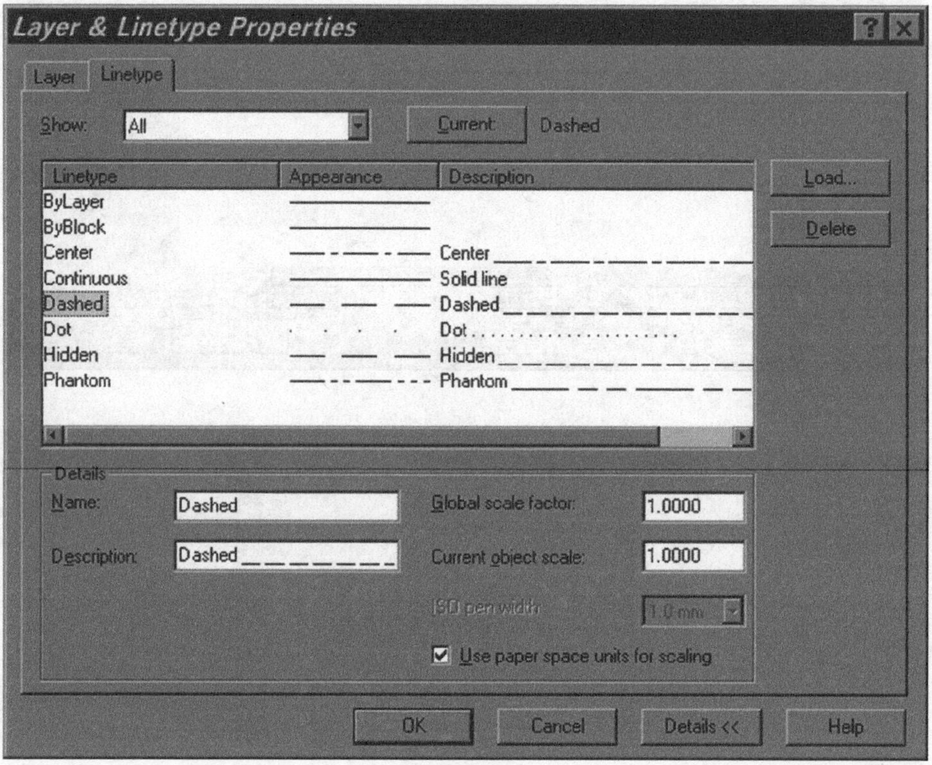


To change the linetype scale, click on the button to bring up the Layer & Linetype Properties dialogue box. If the "Details" section of the dialogue box is not visible, click on the "Details>>" button to reveal it. The dialogue box should now look similar to the one shown above. You set the linetype scale by changing the value in the "Global scale factor" edit box. Once you have changed the scale factor, click on the OK button to return to your drawing. AutoCAD automatically regenerates the drawing to display all linetypes with the new scale factor.

You may have noticed from the Layer & Linetype Properties dialogue box that you can also set the linetype scale by object, using the "Current object scale" edit box. Whilst this is perfectly easy to do, the results can sometimes be unexpected, since the linetype scale of any object is a function of both the Global and Current scales. For example, setting the Global scale to 2.0 and the Current scale of an object to 0.5 results in the same appearance as if both scales were set to 1.0, the default values. In short, unless you have a really compelling reason to change it, keep the Current object scale set to 1.0, this will avoid any confusion in the future.

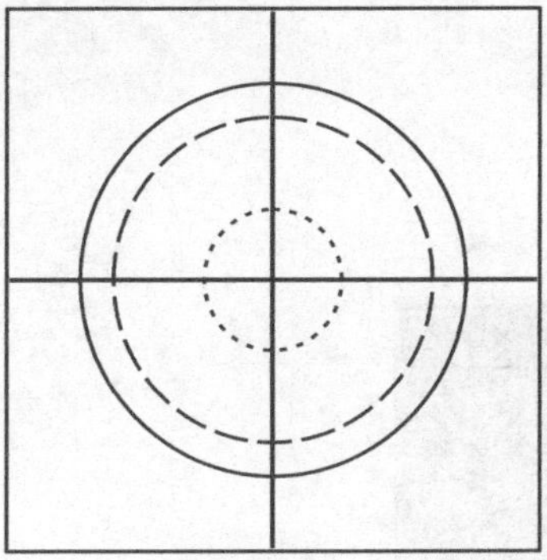

Linetype scale = 1.0

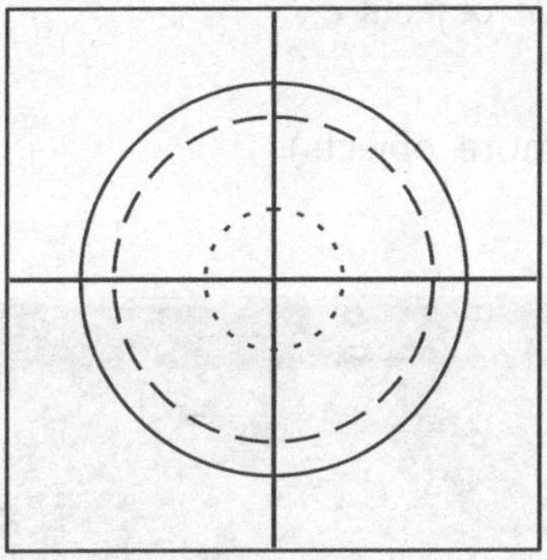

Linetype scale = 2.0

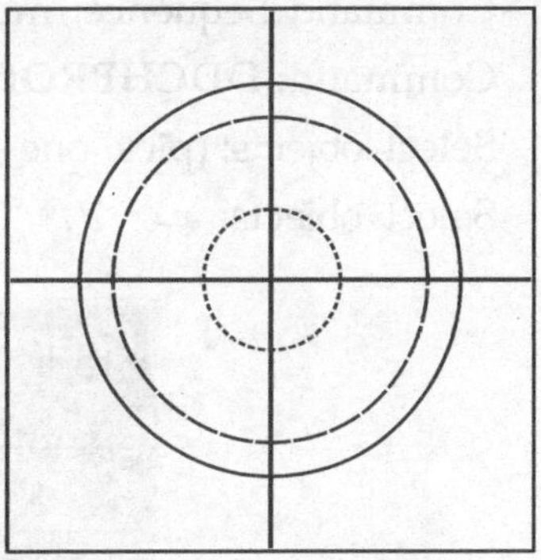

Linetype scale = 0.5

As with other settings, AutoCAD allows the user to set the Global and Current linetype scales using the keyboard. Use the LTSCALE command to change the Global scale and the CELTSCALE command to change the Current linetype scale. It is often quicker to use the LTSCALE command when you are experimenting with linetype scales; this avoids having to navigate the dialogue box each time.

## 3. CHANGING OBJECT PROPERTIES

So far we have concentrated on setting object properties so that we can simply draw objects with their required properties pre-set. However, there will be occasions when an objects properties will need to be changed. Say, for example, you have drawn on object on the wrong layer (a very common mistake). It's much simpler to change the layer for that object rather than to erase the object, set the current layer and then draw it again. There are a number of ways in which an objects properties can be changed but the most common method is to use the Properties command. Remember that you cannot change the properties of objects on locked layers.

### 3.1 The Properties Command

Toolbar 

Pull-down **Modify ▸ Properties...**

Keyboard **AI_PROPCHK** or **DDCHPROP** (multiple objects), **DDMODIFY** (single objects)

This command is unusual in that it is really two commands rolled into one. When you start the Properties command you are asked to "Select Objects:" If you select more than one object you will be able to change only those properties which are common to all objects, namely Colour, Layer, Linetype, Linetype Scale and Thickness. This is the equivalent of using the DDCHPROP command and object properties can be changed using the Change Properties dialogue box. If, however, you select only one object you will be able to modify all of the above properties and those properties which are specific to the selected object type. This is the equivalent of the DDMODIFY command and object properties can be modified using an object specific dialogue box.

Command Sequence, multiple objects

Command: **DDCHPROP**

Select objects: (pick one or more objects)

Select objects: ↵

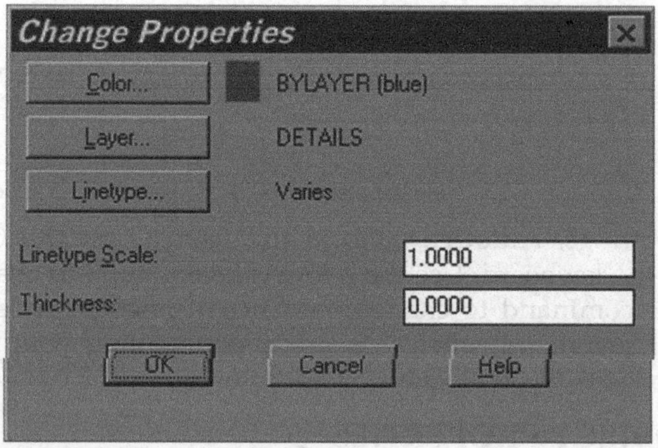


After you have created the selection set the Change Properties dialogue box appears. To change the layer of the selected objects, pick the "Layer..." button and you will see the Select Layer dialogue box which lists all the layers in the drawing. Simply pick the name of the layer you want and then pick "OK". On returning to the Change Properties dialogue box, you can either change other properties or return to the drawing by clicking the "OK" button. The selected objects are now on the chosen layer. If the new layer has a different colour, the objects will be redrawn in this colour. If the chosen layer is turned off or frozen, the entities will become invisible.

Changing the colour and linetype of a number of selected objects is very similar. Use the "Color..." and "Linetype..." buttons to invoke the Select Color and Select Linetype dialogue boxes from which you can make your choice of Colour and Linetype respectively. Notice in the dialogue box above that the current linetype is displayed as "Varies", this is because a number of objects have been selected with different linetypes. However, all the objects are on a layer called "Details", so the layer name appears against the "Layer..." button. Linetype scale and Thickness are set by entering a numeric value in the appropriate edit box. The "Thickness" option allows you to give an object a thickness in the Z direction. You can, for example create a cylinder by giving a circle thickness. Thickness should not be confused with Width. Width refers to a property of polylines which can be used to cause the polyline to display as a wide solid line. See the "Basic 3D" tutorial for more information on using object thickness.

Beware of using the Properties command to change the colour and linetype of drawing objects because this will override the settings that you have made in the Layer & Linetype Properties dialogue box. Once a colour or linetype property is changed using this command, any changes to the objects colour or linetype using layer settings will have no effect. To enable an objects colour and linetype to be controlled by layer, the object colour and linetype must be set to "ByLayer".

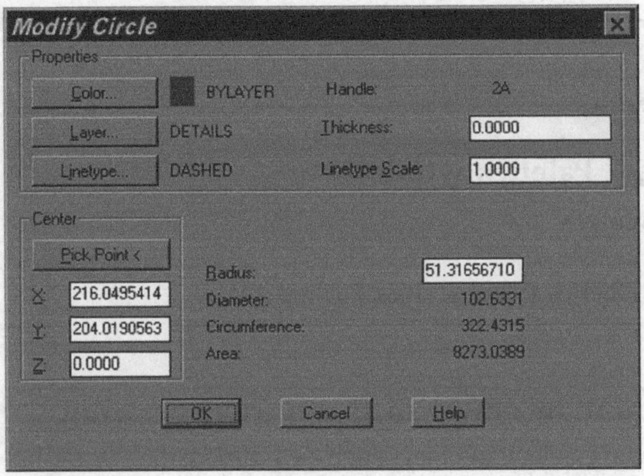


When you use the Properties command to edit a single object you get a dialogue box which contains options specific to the type of object you have selected. The illustration on the left shows the Modify Circle dialogue box. Notice that you can change two properties which are specific to circles, namely the Center Point and the Radius. Notice also that this dialogue box reports the circumference and area of the circle.

Command: **DDMODIFY**

Select objects: (pick an object)

When you pick a drawing object the Modify *Object* dialogue box appears. You can change any of the available properties. As you can see from the Modify MText dialogue box, below, the DDMODIFY version of the Properties command is extremely powerful, allowing you to change almost any property of an object.

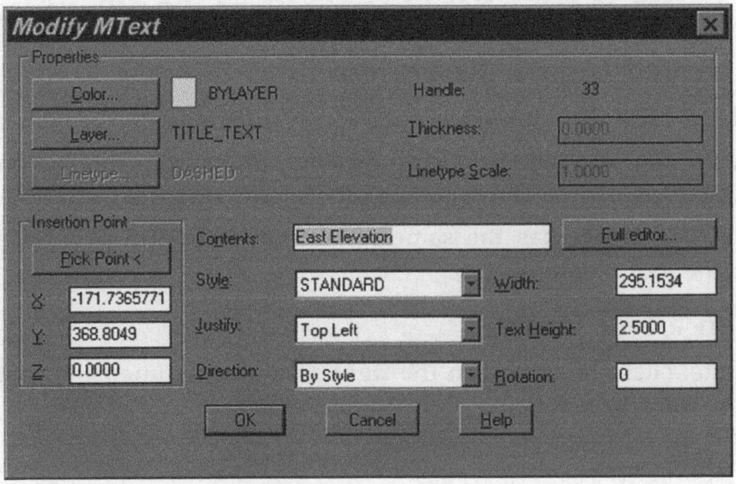

Experiment with the DDMODIFY command using different objects to see what properties can be changed. In many cases this command enables you to modify properties which are difficult or impossible to change in any other way. For example, the Modify Block Insertion dialogue box allows you to differentially scale the X, Y and Z scale factors of a block.

## 4. TOOL PALETTES

### To display the Tool Palettes window

Do one of the following:

- Click View tab ➤ Palettes panel ➤ Tool Palettes. 
- Press Ctrl+3.

### To create a tool from an object in the current drawing

1. In the current drawing, select an object such as a dimension, block, hatch, gradient fill, raster image, xref, or any geometric object.
2. Drag the object to a tool palette and, without releasing the mouse button, move the cursor to the place on the tool palette where you want the tool.

   You can switch to a different tab by hovering over the tab for a few seconds. The black line indicates where the tool is located.
3. Release the mouse button.

### To use a tool created from a geometric object

1. On a tool palette, click the geometric object tool you want to use.
2. Use the tool as if you selected the corresponding option from the Draw menu or the corresponding button on the Draw toolbar, following the Command prompts.

   The geometric object you create has the same properties as the tool you selected from the tool palette.

### To use a tool created from a dimension

1. On a tool palette, click the dimension tool you want to use.
2. Use the tool as if you selected the corresponding option from the Dimension menu or the corresponding button on the Dimension toolbar, following the Command prompts.

   The dimension you create has the same dimension style and properties as the tool you selected from the tool palette.

### To use a tool on a tool flyout

1. On a tool palette, click the arrow on the right side of the dimension tool or the geometric object tool you want to use.
2. On the flyout, select a tool.

3. Use the tool as if you selected the corresponding option from a menu or the corresponding button on a toolbar, following the Command prompts.

   The object you create has the same properties as the tool whose icon you selected on the tool flyout.

## To add or remove a tool flyout

1. On a tool palette, right-click the geometric object tool or the dimension tool whose flyout you want to add or remove. Click Properties.
2. In the Tool Properties dialog box, under Command, click in the Use Flyout box.
3. In the drop-down list, select Yes if you want to add a flyout, or select No if you want to remove one.
4. Click OK.

   **Note:** If you remove the flyout from a tool but then add the flyout back, the image, name, and description (the tooltip) that displays on the tool palette for each tool on the flyout will not be accurate. To correct this, return the image, name, and description of the flyout tool to the default settings.

## To customize a tool flyout

1. On a tool palette, right-click the geometric object tool or dimension tool whose flyout you want to customize. Click Properties.
2. In the Tool Properties dialog box, under Command, click in the Flyout Options box. Click the [...] button.
3. In the Flyout Options dialog box, select the tools that you want to show on the flyout. Click OK. (You must select at least one tool.)
4. In the Tool Properties dialog box, click OK.

## To use a tool created from a hatch

1. On a tool palette, click a hatch tool and drag it to an object in the drawing.
2. Release the mouse button to apply the hatch to the object.

   The hatch you create has the same hatch style and properties as the tool you selected from the tool palette.

## To use a tool created from a gradient fill

1. On a tool palette, click a gradient fill tool and drag it to an object in the drawing.
2. Release the mouse button to apply the gradient fill to the object.

   The gradient fill you create has the same style and properties as the tool you selected from the tool palette.

## To use a tool created from a block, xref, or raster image

1. On a tool palette, click the block, xref, or raster image you want to insert into your drawing.
2. Drag the block, xref, or raster image to the appropriate place in the drawing.

3. Release the mouse button to insert the block, xref, or raster image.

   The block, xref, or raster image you insert has the same properties as the tool you selected from the tool palette.

## To be prompted for a rotation angle when placing a block or xref from a tool palette

1. In a tool palette, right-click a block or xref tool. Click Properties.
2. In the Tool Properties dialog box, under Insert, click Prompt for Rotation.
3. In the drop-down list, select Yes.
4. Click OK.

## 5. TABLE

If you enter **-table** at the Command prompt, the following prompts are displayed.

Current table style: "Standard" Cell width: 2.5000 Cell height: 1 line(s)

Enter number of columns or [Auto/ from Style/ data Link] <5>:

Number of Columns

Specifies the number of columns

Enter number of rows or [ Auto] <1>:

### Number of Rows

Specifies the number of rows

Specify insertion point or [Style/ Width/ Height]:

### Insertion Point

Specifies the location of the upper-left corner of the table. You can use the pointing device or enter coordinate values at the Command prompt. If the table style sets the direction of the table to read from the bottom up, the insertion point is the lower-left corner of the table.

### Width

Specifies a width for the table columns

Enter cell width <2.50000>:

Specify insertion point or [Style/Width/Height]:

### Height

Specifies a height for the table rows

Enter minimum cell height <1 line>:

Specify insertion point or [Style/Width/Height]:

## Style

Specifies a table style for the table the specified table style must contain a starting table. To learn more about startingtables, see Work with Table Styles.

Enter table style name <*current*>

Specify insertion point or [Style/Width/Height]:

## Auto

Specifies a size and a location for the table. You can use the pointing device or enter coordinate values at the Command prompt. When this option is selected, you can set the number of columns or the column width, but not both. The number of rows and the row height depend on the size of the window you specify.

Specify first corner or [Height]:

## First Corner

*Specifies the location of the upper-left corner of the table. If the table style sets the direction* of the table to read from the bottom up, the insertion point is the lower-left corner of the table.

Specify second corner:

## Height

Specifies a height for the table rows

Enter minimum cell height <1 line>:

Specify first corner or [Height]:

## Auto

Specifies a size and a location for the table you can use the pointing device or enter coordinate values at the Command prompt. When this option is selected, you can set the number of columns or the column width, but not both. The number of rows and the row height depend on the size of the window you specify.

Enter number of rows or [ Auto] <1>:

## Number of Rows

Specifies the number of rows

Specify first corner or [Width]:

Specify second corner:

## Auto

Specifies a size and a location for the table

Specify first corner or [Width]:

Specify second corner:

### From Style

Specifies a table style for creating the table you can use the pointing device or enter coordinate values at the Command prompt. The specified table style must contain a starting table. For more information about starting tables, see Work with Table Styles.

Specify insertion point or [Style/ Rows/ Columns/ Options]:

### Insertion Point

Specifies the location of the upper-left corner of the table. You can use the pointing device or enter coordinate values at the Command prompt. If the table style sets the direction of the table to read from the bottom up, the insertion point is the lower-left corner of the table.

Specify insertion point or [Style/Rows/Columns/Options]:

### Style

Specifies a table style for the table

Enter the name of a table style or [?] <Standard>:

You are prompted if the table style you chose does not contain a starting table.

Table style does not contain a table.

Entering [?] displays a list of table styles available in your drawing.

### Rows

Specifies the number of rows you want to add to the table stored in the specified table style. The rows are added to the rows already in the specified table.

Enter number of additional rows <0>:

### Columns

Specifies the number of columns you want to add to the table stored in the specified table style. The columns are added to the columns already in the specified table.

Enter number of additional columns <0>:

### Options

Specifies special formatting options that can be inserted in the table

Enter an insert option [Label text/ Data text/ Formulas/ fIelds/ data liNks/ Blocks/cell style Overrides] <exit>:

### Label Text

Retains rows with a cell type of Label found in the table style's starting table the cell type is set in the Properties palette. The Header and Title cell styles use the Label cell type by default.

### Data Text

Retains rows with a cell type of Data found in the table style's starting table the cell type is set in the Properties palette. The Data cell style uses the Data cell type property by default.

### Formulas

Retains formulas found in the specified table style's starting table.

### Fields

Retains fields found in the specified table style's starting table. For more information about fields

### Data Links

Retains data links found in the specified table style's starting table. For more information about data links

### Blocks

Retains blocks found in the specified table style's starting table.

### Cell Style Overrides

Retains cell style overrides found in the specified table style's starting table.

## 6. OVERVIEW OF HATCH PATTERNS AND FILLS

You can hatch an area using a predefined hatch pattern, define a simple line pattern using the current linetype, or create more complex hatch patterns. One type of pattern is called solid, which fills an area with a solid color.

You can also create a gradient fill, which uses a transition between shades of one color or between two colors. Gradient fills can be used to enhance presentation drawings, giving the appearance of light reflecting on an object.

### Define the Boundaries of a Hatch

You can choose from several methods to specify the boundaries of a hatch.

- Specify a point in an area that is enclosed by objects.
- Select objects that enclose an area.
- Drag a hatch pattern into an enclosed area from a tool palette or DesignCenter.

When you hatch a drawing, whole or partial objects that are not part of the object boundary are ignored.

If a hatch line encounters an object such as text, an attribute, or a solid-fill object, and if the object is selected as part of the boundary set, HATCH hatches around the object.

## Add Hatch Patterns and Solid Fills

You can use several methods to add hatch patterns to your drawing.

- The HATCH command provides the most options.
- You can drag hatches from a tool palette. Use tool palettes when you need additional speed and convenience.

With the Tool Palettes window open, you can right-click a pattern tool to access the Tool Properties dialog box from the shortcut menu. This dialog box contains several hatch pattern options that are also available through HATCH.

## Control the Hatch Origin

By default, hatch patterns always "line up" with each other. However, sometimes you might need to move the starting point, called the origin point, of the hatch. For example, if you create a brick pattern, you might want to start with a complete brick in the lower-left corner of the hatched area. In that case, use the Hatch Origin options in the Hatch and Gradient dialog box.

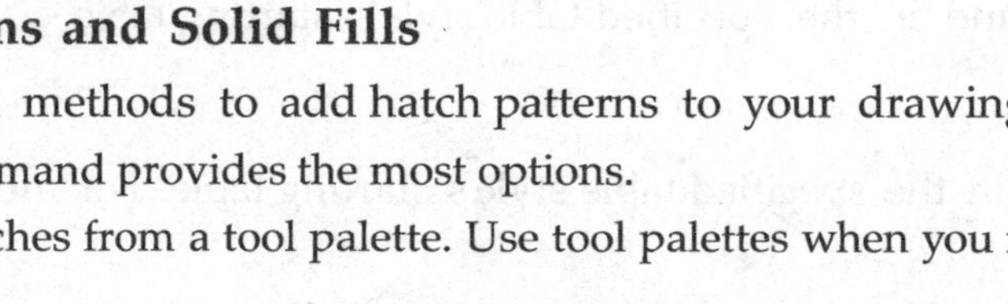


The location and behavior of a hatch pattern depends on the HPORIGIN, HPORIGINMODE, and HPINHERIT system variables, and the location and orientation of the user coordinate system.

## Choose a Hatch Pattern

The program supplies a solid fill and more than 50 industry-standard hatch patterns that you can use to differentiate the components of objects or represent object materials. The program also comes with 14 hatch patterns that conform to the ISO (International Standards Organization) standards. When you select an ISO pattern, you can specify a pen width, which determines the lineweight in the pattern.

On the Hatch of the Hatch and Gradient dialog box, the Type and Pattern area displays the names of all the hatch patterns defined in the acad.pat text file.

## Create Associative Hatches

An *associative* hatch is updated when you change the boundary. Hatched areas created with HATCH are associative by default. This setting is stored in the system variable HPASSOC. Hatches created by dragging hatch patterns from tool palettes or DesignCenter use the setting in HPASSOC. You can remove hatch associativity at any time or use HATCH to create a no associative hatch. When the HPGAPTOL system variable is set to 0 (the default), associativity is automatically removed if editing creates an open boundary.

You can use HATCH to create nonassociative hatches, which are independent of their boundaries.

hatched object — result of editing boundary with nonassociative hatch — result of editing boundary with associative hatch

## Create an Annotative Hatch

An annotative hatch is defined at a paper size. You can create individual annotative hatch objects as well as annotative hatchpatterns.

Use an annotative hatch to symbolically represent material such as sand, concrete, steel, earth, etc.

## Assign a Draw Order to a Hatch

You can assign a draw order to a hatch so that it is drawn either behind or in front of the hatch boundary, or behind or in front of all other objects.

When you create a hatch, by default the hatch is drawn behind the hatch boundary. This makes it easier to view and select the hatch boundary. You can change the draw order of the hatch so that the hatch is drawn in front of the hatch boundary instead, or either behind or in front of all other objects. This setting is stored in the HPDRAWORDER system variable. Hatches created by dragging hatch patterns from tool palettes or DesignCenter use the draw order setting in HPDRAWORDER.

## Limit Hatch Pattern Density

If you create a very dense hatch, the program may reject the hatch and display a message indicating that the hatch scale is too small or its dash length too short. You can change the maximum number of hatch lines by setting the HPMAXLINES system variable. You can set values between 100 and 10000000 (ten million). The default value for HPMAXLINES is 1000000.

## Edit Hatch Boundaries

Because there are so many combinations of objects that can be hatched, editing hatched geometry can produce unexpected results. If you create a hatch that you don't want, you can undo it, trim the hatch, or delete the hatch and rehatch the area.

## Create Custom Hatch Patterns

You can also define your own hatch pattern using the current linetype with the User Defined Pattern option of the Hatch and Gradient dialog box, or you can create more complex hatch patterns.

### To drag hatch patterns into your drawing

1. Click Insert tab > Content panel > Design Center.
2. On the Folders , click the Search button.
3. In the Search dialog box, make the following entries:
    - In Look For, select Hatch Pattern Files.
    - In the In box, select the drive where the program is installed.
    - Select the Search Subfolders option.
    - On the Hatch Pattern Files , in Search for the Name, enter * (asterisk).
4. Click Search Now.

    The default hatch pattern file is **acad.pat** *or* **acadiso.pat**. The search results may display the same file in different locations.
5. In the search results, double-click the file to load the hatch patterns into the content area of DesignCenter.
6. (Optional) Right-click a pattern to display a shortcut menu with the following options:
    - **HATCH**. Opens the Hatch and Gradient dialog box.
    - **Copy**. Stores the hatch pattern to the Clipboard.
    - **Create Tool Palette**. Creates a new tool palette with the selected pattern displayed.
7. From the content area, drag a hatch pattern onto a closed object in your drawing or onto a tool palette.

### To hatch areas

1. Click Home tab > Draw panel > Hatch. 
2. In the Hatch and Gradient dialog box, click Add: Pick points.
3. In your drawing, specify a point inside each area that you want hatched, and then press ENTER.

    This point is known as the internal point.
4. In the Hatch and Gradient dialog box, Hatch in the swatch box, verify that the sample pattern is the pattern you want to use. To change patterns, select another pattern from the Pattern list.

5. In the Hatch and Gradient dialog box, make adjustments, if necessary.
6. Under Draw Order, click one of the options.

   You can change the draw order of the hatch so that the hatch is drawn either behind or in front of the hatch boundary, or behind or in front of all other objects.
7. Click OK.

## To hatch selected objects

1. Click Home tab ▸ Draw panel ▸ Hatch. 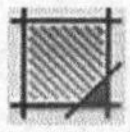
2. In the Hatch and Gradient dialog box, click Add: Select objects.
3. Specify the object or objects you want to hatch.

   The objects need not form a closed boundary. You can also specify any islands that should remain unhatched. Also, you can set the HPGAPTOL system variable to treat a set of objects that almost enclose an area as a closed hatch boundary.
4. Under Draw Order, click one of the options.

   You can change the draw order of the hatch so that the hatch is drawn either behind or in front of the hatch boundary, or behind or in front of all other objects.
5. Click OK.

## Properties

Specifies new hatch pattern properties to apply.

Enter a pattern name or [? /Solid/User defined] <current>: Enter a predefined or custom pattern name, enter **s**, enter **u**, enter? Or press ENTER

## Pattern Name—Predefined or Custom

Specifies a predefined pattern in the **acad.pat *or* acadiso.pat** file or a custom pattern in its own PAT file

Enter the pattern name followed by an optional hatch style code. Precede the pattern name with an asterisk (*) to fill the area with individual lines instead of a hatch object.

Specify a scale for the pattern <current>: Specify a scale or press ENTER

Specify an angle for the pattern <current>: Specify an angle or press ENTER

## ?—List Pattern Names

Lists and describes the hatch patterns defined in the *acad.pat* file.

Pattern(s) to list <*>: Enter a name list or press ENTER

## Solid

Specifies a solid fill and redisplays the first HATCH Command prompt, where you can define a boundary.

## User Defined

Specifies a user-defined pattern Enter ***u***, followed by an optional hatch style code. Precede the ***u*** with an asterisk (*) to fill the area with individual lines instead of a hatch block.

Specify angle for crosshatch lines <current>: Specify an angle for the pattern or press ENTER

Specify spacing between the lines <current>: Specify the distance between pattern lines or press ENTER

Double hatch area? [Yes/No] <Current>: Enter **y** to specify a second set of lines to be drawn at 90 degrees to the original lines, or press ENTER

## Select Objects

Determines a boundary from selected objects that form an enclosed area. Adds objects to the boundary definition.

Select objects: Use an object selection method

## Draw Boundary

Uses specified points to define the boundary of a hatch or fill.

Retain polyline boundary? [Yes/No] <current>: Entery to retain the polyline *hatch* boundary object or **n** to discard it after the area is hatch*ed*

Specify start point: Specify the start point of the polyline boundary

Specify next point or [Arc/Close/Length/Undo]: Specify a point, enter an option, or press ENTER

These options are also available in the PLINE command. When you complete the polyline boundary, press ENTER. You can then create additional polyline boundaries, or press ENTER to twice to apply the hatch.

Specify start point for new boundary or <apply hatch>: Specify a point or press ENTER twice to apply the hatch

## Remove Boundaries

Removes from the boundary definition any of the objects that were added previously

Select Objects or [Add boundaries]: Select objects to be removed from the boundary definition, enter an option, or press ENTER to return to the previous prompt

## Select Objects

Removes objects from the boundary definition.

## Add Boundaries

Adds objects to the boundary definition.

## Advanced

Sets the method used to create the hatch boundary.

Enter an option [Boundary set/Retain boundary/Island detection/Style/Associativity/Gap tolerance/separate Hatches]: Enter an option or press *ENTER* to return to the previous prompt

## Boundary Set

Defines the set of objects to be analyzed when defining a boundary from a specified internal point.

Specify candidate set for boundary [New/Everything] <*current*>: Enter an option or press ENTER

## New

*Creates a boundary set from a selection set you define.*

Select objects: Use an object selection method

## Everything

Creates a boundary set from everything visible in the current viewport. Selecting this option discards any current boundary set and uses everything visible in the drawing or in the current viewport.

## Retain Boundary

Specifies whether to add the temporary boundary objects to the drawing after hatching is completed.

Retain derived boundaries? [Yes/No] <*Current*>: Enter y or n, or press ENTER

## Island Detection

Specifies whether to use objects within the outermost boundary as boundary objects.

Do you want island detection? [Yes/No] <Current>: Enter **y** or **n**, or press ENTER

Specifying no island detection prompts for the ray casting method.

Enter type of ray casting [Nearest/+X/-X/+Y/-Y/Angle] <current>: Enter an option or press ENTER

## Nearest

Runs a line from the point you specify to the nearest object and then traces the boundary in a counterclockwise direction.

**+X**

Runs a line in the positive *X* direction from the point you specify to the first object encountered and then traces the boundary in a counterclockwise direction.

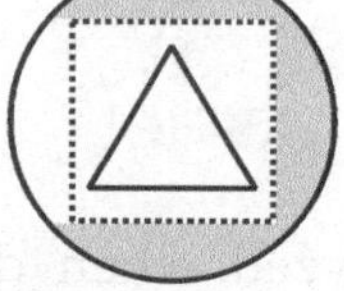

ray casting direction (+X)

**-X**

Runs a line in the negative *X* direction from the point you specify to the first object encountered and then traces the boundary in a counterclockwise direction.

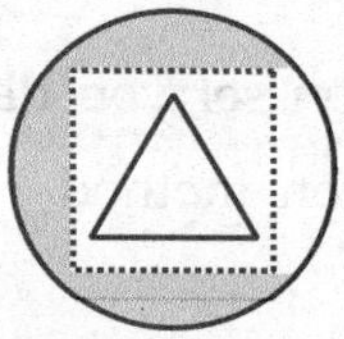

ray casting direction (–X)

**+Y**

Runs a line in the positive *Y* direction from the point you specify to the first object encountered and then traces the boundary in a counterclockwise direction.

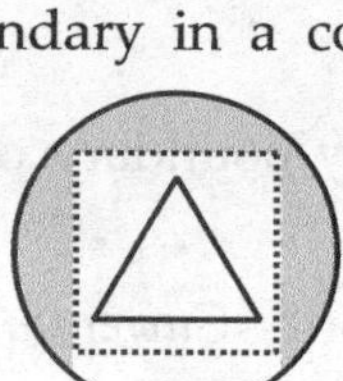

ray casting direction (+Y)

**-Y**

Runs a line in the negative *Y* direction from the point you specify to the first object encountered and then traces the boundary in a counterclockwise direction.

ray casting direction (–Y)

## Angle

Runs a line at the specified angle from the point you specify to the first object encountered and then traces the boundary in a counterclockwise direction.

Specify ray casting angle: Specify an angle

## Style

Specifies the method used to hatch objects within the outermost hatch boundary. If you have selected no internal objects, a hatching style has no effect. Because you can define a precise set of boundaries, it's often best to use the Normal style.

Enter hatching style [Ignore/Outer/Normal] <current>: Enter an option or press ENTER

## Ignore

Ignores all internal objects and hatches or fills through them. You can also set the Ignore style by adding, I to the pattern name in the HPNAME system variable.

## Outer

Hatches or fills inward from the outer boundary. HATCH turns hatching or filling off if it encounters an internal island. This option hatches or fills only the outermost level of the structure and leaves the internal structure blank. You can also set the Outer style by adding, O to the pattern name in the HPNAME system variable.

## Normal

Hatches or fills inward from the outer boundary. If HATCH encounters an internal island, it turns off hatching or filling until it encounters another island within the island. You can also set the Normal style by adding, N to the pattern name in the HPNAME system variable.

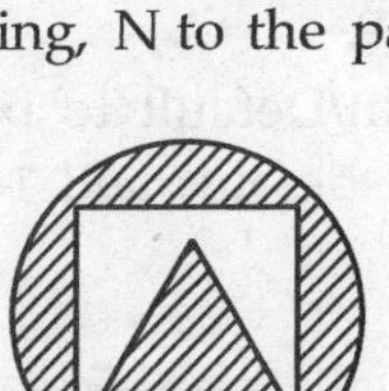

## Associativity

Specifies that the new hatch pattern is updated when its boundaries are modified a new hatch pattern's associativity is set by the HPASSOC system variable. Changing the associativity setting here also changes the setting in the HPASSOC system variable.

Do you want associativity? [Yes/No] <Current>: Enter **y** or **n**, or press ENTER

## Gap Tolerance

Sets the maximum size of gaps that can be ignored when objects are used as a hatch boundary. The default value, 0, specifies that the objects must enclose the area with no gaps.

Specify a boundary gap tolerance value <0>: Enter a value, in drawing units, from 0 to 5000

Any gaps equal to or smaller than the value you specify in the gap tolerance are *ignored, and the boundary is treated as closed.*

## Separate Hatches

Controls whether the command creates a single hatch object or multiple hatch objects when several separate closed boundaries are specified.

Create separate hatches? [Yes/No] <Current>: Enter **y** or **n**, or press ENTER

## Draw Order

Assigns the draw order to a hatch or fill. You can place a hatch or fill behind all other objects, in front of all other objects, behind the hatch boundary, or in front of the hatch boundary.

Enter draw order [do Not assign/send to Back/bring to Front/send beHind boundary/ bring in front of bounDary] <send beHind boundary>: Enter an option, or press ENTER to accept the default and return to the previous prompt

## Origin

Controls the starting location of hatch pattern generation. Some hatches, such as brick patterns, need to be aligned with a point on the hatch boundary. By default, all hatch origins correspond to the current UCS origin.

[Use current origin/Set new origin/Default to boundary extents] <current>: Enter an option, or press ENTER to accept the default and return to the previous prompt

## Use current origin

Sets the value of the HPORIGINMODE system variable. The last 5 options listed below correspond to the values 1-5.

[Use current origin/Set new origin/bottom Left/bottom Right/top rIght/top lEft/Center] <current>: Enter an option, or press ENTER to accept the default and return to the previous prompt

## Set new origin

Specifies the new hatch origin point directly

## Default to boundary extents

Calculates a new origin based on the rectangular extents of the hatch. Choices include each of the four corners of the extents and its center. You can also store the value of the new hatch origin in the HPORIGIN system variable.

## Annotative

Specifies that the hatch is annotative

Create annotative hatch [Yes/No] <current>: Enter **y** or **n**, or press ENTER

Gradient Tab

Defines the appearance of the gradient fill to be applied

# COLOR

## One Color

Specifies a fill that uses a smooth transition between darker shades and lighter tints of one color. When One Color is selected, HATCH displays a color swatch with Browse button and a Shade and Tint slider.

## Two Color

Specifies a fill that uses a smooth transition between two colors. When Two Color is selected, HATCH displays a color swatch with a Browse button for color 1 and for color 2.

## Color Swatch

Specifies the color for the gradient fill. Click the Browse button [...] to display the Select Color dialog box, where you can select an AutoCAD Color Index (ACI) color, true color, or color book color. The default color displayed is the current color in the drawing.

## Shade and Tint Slider

Specifies the tint (the selected color mixed with white) or shade (the selected color mixed with black) of a color to be used for a gradient fill of one color.

### Gradient Patterns

Displays nine fixed patterns for gradient fills These patterns include linear sweep, spherical, and parabolic.

### Orientation

Specifies the angle of the gradient and whether it is symmetrical.

### Centered

Specifies a gradient configuration that is symmetrical If this option is not selected, the gradient fill is shifted up and to the left, creating the illusion of a light source to the left of the object.

### Angle

Specifies the angle of the gradient fill the specified angle is relative to the current UCS. This option is independent of the angle specified for hatch patterns.

CHAPTER

8

# Productivity Tool

## 1. ATTACH EXTERNAL REFERENCE DIALOG BOX

Attaches drawings as an external reference (xref)

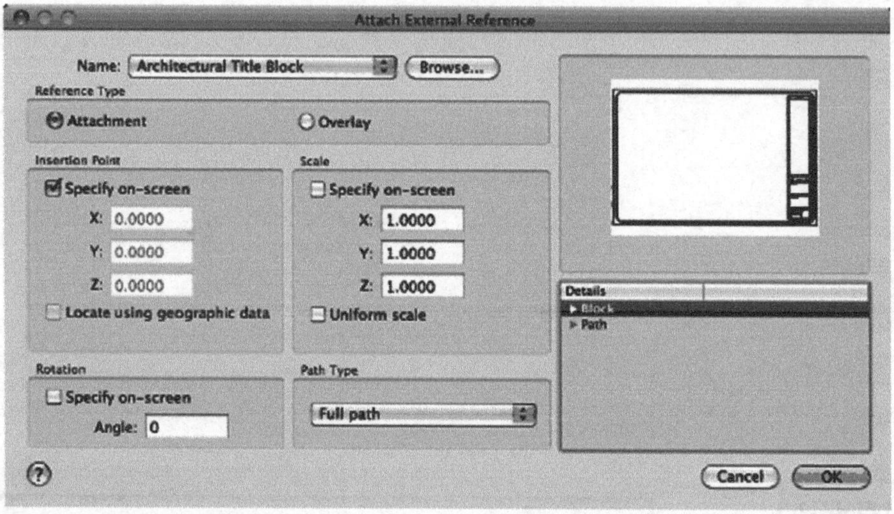


### To attach an xref

1. Click Blocks & References tab ➤ Reference panel ➤ DWG. 
2. In the Select Reference File dialog box, select the file you want to attach and then click Open.
3. In the External Reference dialog box, under Reference Type, select Attachment.
4. Specify the insertion point, scale, and rotation angle. Click Specify On-Screen to use the pointing device.

   Attachment includes all nested xrefs.
5. Click OK.

### To attach or overlay an xref using DesignCenter

1. Click View tab ➤ Palettes panel ➤ DesignCenter. 
2. In the content area or in the Search dialog box, locate the DWG reference you want to attach or overlay.
3. Right-click. Drag the DWG reference into the open drawing.
4. Release the right-pointing device button. Click Attach as Xref.
5. In the External Reference dialog box, under Reference Type, select Attachment or Overlay.
6. Enter values for Insertion Point, Scale, and Rotation, or select Specify On-Screen to use the pointing device.
7. Click OK.

You can also attach an xref by dragging or by clicking Attach as Xref on the shortcut menu.

8. Click OK.

## To view referenced files by type in the External References palette

1. Click Insert tab ➤ Reference panel ➤ Dialog box launcher. ↘
2. In the External References palette, in the File References pane, click the List View button.
3. Click the Icon column.

   The attached referenced files are sorted by type in the list view.

## To adjust the fade display of the DWG xref

1. Click Insert tab ➤ Reference panel ➤ Xref Fading.
2. Drag the slider to adjust the fade display of the DWG xref.

   The DWG xref fades as you drag the slider.

### *List of Options*

The following options are displayed.

### Name

Identifies the DWG you have selected to attach.

### Browse

Displays the Select Reference File dialog box in which you can select a new external reference for the current drawing.

### Reference Type

Specifies whether the external reference is an attachment or an overlay. Unlike an xref that is an attachment, an overlay is ignored when the drawing to which it is attached is then attached as an xref to another drawing.

See Attach Drawing References (Xrefs) and Nest and Overlay Referenced Drawings.

### Preview

Displays the DWG you have selected to attach.

### Insertion Point

Specify On-Screen Allows you to input at the Command prompt or the pointing device.

X Sets the *X* coordinate value.

Y Sets the *Y* coordinate value.

Z Sets the *Z* coordinate value.

### Scale

Specify On-screen Allows you to input at the Command prompt or the pointing device.

X Sets the *X* scale factor.

Y Sets the *Y* scale factor.

Z Sets the *Z* scale factor.

Uniform Scale Sets the *Y* and *X* scale factors as the same as *Z*.

## Rotation

Specify on-screen If Specify On-Screen is selected, you may wait until you exit the dialog box to rotate the object with your pointing device or at the Command prompt.

Angle If Specify On-Screen is cleared, enter the rotation angle value in the dialog box.

## Path Type

Select the full (absolute) path, the relative path to the external reference file, or No Path, the name of the external reference

## Details

Displays block and path information about the external reference being attached. Block Displays information about the block in the drawing.

**Unit.** Displays the specified INSUNITS value for the inserted block.

**Factor.** Displays the unit scale factor, which is calculated based on the INSUNITS (page 913) value of the block and the drawing units. Path Displays the external reference file paths.

**Found In.** Displays the path where the external reference file is located.

**Saved Path.** Displays the path that is saved with the drawing when the external reference is attached. The path is dependent upon the Path Type setting.

## 2. MATCHPROP

Applies the properties of a selected object to other objects.

**Access Methods**

**Menu: Modify □ Match Properties**

**Command entry: painter** (or **'matchprop** for transparent use)

## Summary

The types of properties that can be applied include color, layer, linetype, linetype scale, line weight, plot style, transparency, and other specified properties.

## List of Prompts

The following prompts are displayed.

Current active settings: Currently selected matchprop settings

Select destination object(s) or [Settings]: **Enter s or select one or more objects to copy properties to**

Destination Object(s) Specifies the objects to which you want to copy the properties of the source object.

Settings Displays the Match Properties Settings dialog box (page 425), in which you can control which object properties to copy to the destination objects. By default, all object properties are selected for copying.

## Match Properties Settings Dialog Box

Specifies the properties that are copied from the select source object to the destination objects.

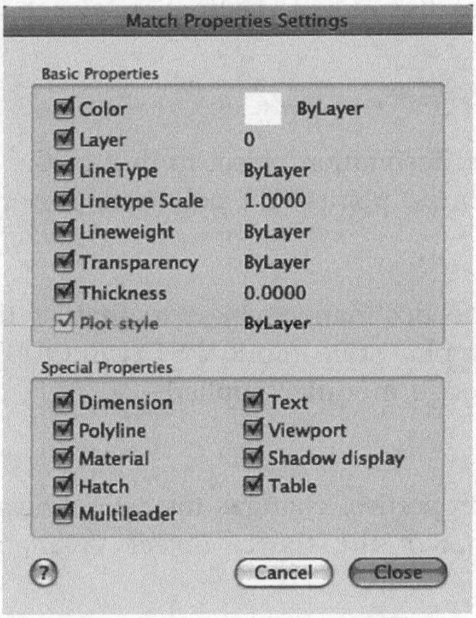


## List of Options

The following options are displayed.

## Basic Properties

Color

Changes the color of the destination object to that of the source object. Available for all objects.

## Layer

Changes the layer of the destination object to that of the source object. Available for all objects.

## Linetype

Changes the linetype of the destination object to that of the source object. Available for all objects except attributes, hatches, multiline text, points, and viewports.

### Linetype Scale

Changes the linetype scale factor of the destination object to that of the source object. Available for all objects except attributes, hatches, multiline text, points, and viewports.

### Lineweight

Changes the line weight of the destination object to that of the source object. Available for all objects.

### Transparency

Changes the transparency of the of the destination object to that of the source object. Available for all objects.

### Thickness

Changes the thickness of the destination object to that of the source object. Available only for arcs, attributes, circles, lines, points, 2D polylines, regions, and text.

### Plot Style

Changes the plot style of the destination object to that of the source object. If you are working in color-dependent plot style mode PSTYLEPOLICY Available for all objects, except those with the Jitter edge modifier applied.

### Text

In addition to basic object properties, changes the text style and annotative properties of the destination object to that of the source object. Available only for single-line and multiline text objects.

### Viewport

In addition to basic object properties, changes the following properties of the destination paper space viewport to match those of the source viewport: on/off, display locking, standard or custom scale, shade plot, snap, grid, and UCS icon visibility and location. The settings for clipping and the freeze/thaw state of the layers are not transferred to the destination object.

### Shadow Display

In addition to basic object properties, changes the shadow display. The object can cast shadows, receive shadows, or both, or it can ignore shadows.

### Hatch

In addition to basic object properties, changes the hatch properties (including its annotative properties) of the destination object to that of the source object. To match the hatch origin, use Inherit Properties in HATCH or HATCHEDIT. Available only for hatch objects.

## Table

In addition to basic object properties, changes the table style of the destination object to that of the source object. Available only for table objects.

## Multileader

In addition to basic object properties, changes the multileader style and annotative properties of the destination object to that of the source object. Available only for multileader objects.

### Tips & Tricks

- Make sure you always start a new drawing by creating some new layers. Two or three will do initially, you can add more lately and you can rename the initial layers if necessary. This is much easier than drawing entities on layer 0 and then having to change them later.
- Avoid drawing on layer 0, its bad practice!
- When you are trying to select objects in a complicated drawing it may be easier to turn some layers off first so that you don't inadvertently select entities you don't want.
- Always stratify your drawing using different layers for different sorts of objects. For example, use separate layers for trees and shrubs, even if they are the same colour and have the same linetype.
- Make your layer names understandable. Use common names such as "TREE" or "PATH" rather than simply using numbers or codes unless you must in order to conform to the British Standard or a project specific naming scheme.
- If you are working on any AutoCAD drawing project which involves others, make sure you devise a layer naming strategy **before** drawing begins. This will avoid many headaches later on.
- If you turn off a layer containing 3D Faces, the 3D Faces become invisible. However, the 3D Faces still hide objects when you use a command such as HIDE. To prevent 3D faces hiding other objects you must freeze them. This is particularly annoying when you are plotting with hidden lines removed. I always considered this an AutoCAD bug but since it has been around for such a long time it must be considered a feature.
- If your linetypes do not display correctly along polylines, use the PEDIT command and set "Ltype gen" on. This will force the linetype to display correctly. You can also do this using the DDMODIFY command (**Modify ▸ Object ▸ Polyline** from the pull-down menu) by checking the "LT Gen" box in the "Modify Polyline" dialogue box.

Learning to work with object properties is a very important aspect of AutoCAD. Layers are particularly important and you need to work with them all the time. If you're not, then you're doing something wrong. Make sure you understand all of the topics covered in this tutorial.

## 3. MEASURE

Creates point objects or blocks at measured intervals along the length or perimeter of an object.

**Access Methods**

**Menu: Draw □ Point □ Measure**

The resulting points or blocks are always located on the selected object and their orientation is parallel to the XY plane of the UCS.

Use DDPTYPE to set the style and size of all point objects in a drawing.

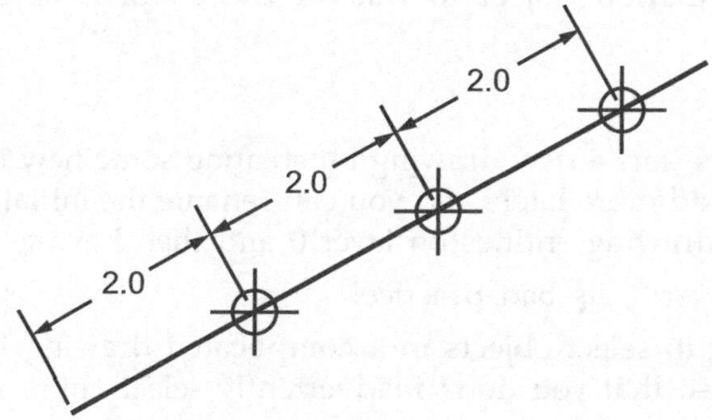


The points or blocks are placed in the previous selection set, so you can select them all by entering **p** at the next Select Objects prompt. You can use the Node object snap to draw an object by snapping to the point objects. You can then remove the points by entering **erase previous.**

## 4. DIVIDE

Creates evenly spaced point objects or blocks along the length or perimeter of an object.

### Access Methods



**Button**

**Ribbon:** Home tab ➤ Draw panel ➤ Divide

**Menu:** Draw ➤ Point ➤ Divide

**Command entry: divide**

Select object to divide: Use an object selection method

Enter number of segments or [Block]: Enter a value from 2 through 32,767, or enter **b**

### Number of Segments

Places point objects at equal intervals along the selected objects.

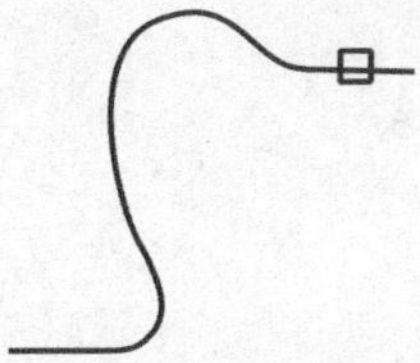
select polyline

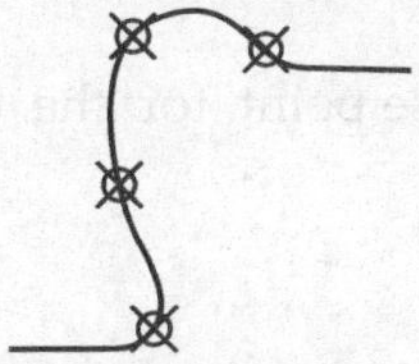
divide into five parts

Use DDPTYPE to set the style and size of all point objects in a drawing.

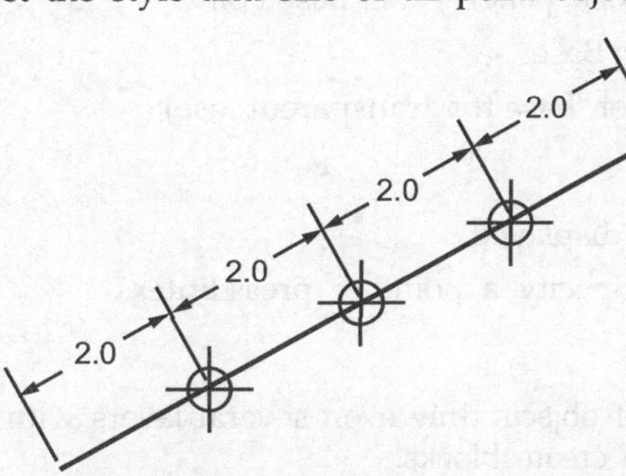


## Block

Places blocks at equal intervals along the selected object. If the block has variable attributes, these attributes are not included.

Enter name of block to insert: Enter the name of a block currently defined in the drawing

Align block with object? [Yes/No] <Y>: Enter y or n or press ENTER

## Yes

Specifies that the X axes of the inserted blocks be tangent to, or collinear with, the divided object at the dividing points.

## No

Aligns the blocks according to their normal orientation.

Enter number of segments: *Enter a value from 2 through 32,767*

The illustration shows an arc divided into five equal parts using a block consisting of a vertically oriented ellipse.

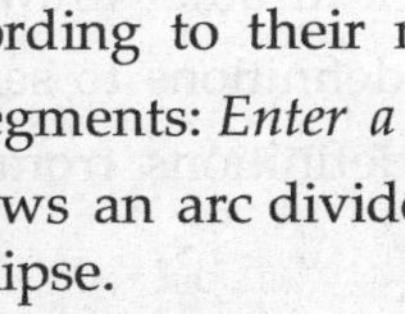
block not aligned

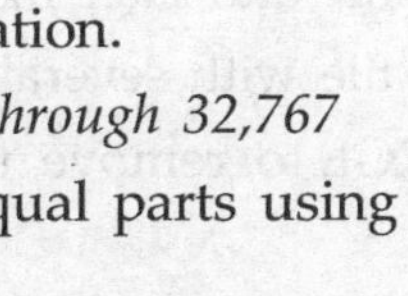
block aligned

## BASE

Sets the insertion base point for the current drawing

### Access Methods

**Button**

**Ribbon:** Insert tab ➤ Block panel ➤ Set Base Point

**Menu:** Draw ➤ Block ➤ Base

**Command entry: base** (or **'base** for transparent use)

### List of Prompts

The following prompts are displayed.

Enter base point <current>: Specify a point or press Enter

## 5. BLOCK

A block can be composed of objects drawn on several layers with various properties. You can use several methods to create blocks.

A block can be composed of objects drawn on several layers with various colors, linetypes, and lineweight properties. Although a block is always inserted on the current layer, the block reference preserves information about the original layer, color, and linetype properties of the objects that are contained in the block. You can control whether objects in a block retain their original properties or inherit their properties from the current layer, color, linetype, or lineweight settings.

### Create Blocks

You can use several methods to create blocks:

- Combine objects to create a block definition in your current drawing.
- Use the Block Editor contextual tab (when the ribbon is active) or Block Editor (when the ribbon is not active) to add dynamic behavior to a block definition in your current drawing.
- Create a drawing file and later insert it as a block in other drawings.
- Create a drawing file with several related block definitions to serve as a block library.

You can use PURGE to remove unused block definitions from a drawing.

### Dynamic Blocks

A block definition can contain elements that add dynamic behavior to a block, which adds flexibility and intelligence to the geometry. When you insert a block reference with dynamic behavior in a drawing, you can manipulate the geometry of the block reference through custom grips or custom properties, depending on how the block was defined. You can also constrain block geometry.

## Annotative Blocks

You can also create **annotative** blocks. For more information about creating and working with an annotative blocks, see Create Annotative Blocks and Attributes.

## How block are stored and reference

Every drawing file has an invisible data area called the block definition table. The block definition table stores all block definitions, which consist of all information associated with the block. It is these block definitions that are referenced when you insert blocks in your drawing.

The following illustrations are conceptual representations of three drawing files. Each rectangle represents a separate drawing file and is divided into two parts: the smaller part represents the block definition table, and the larger part represents the objects in a drawing.

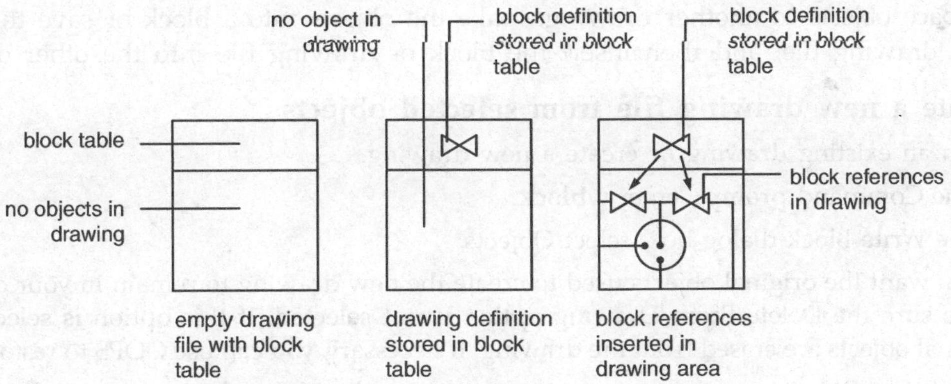


When you insert a block, you are inserting a block reference. The information is not simply copied from the block definition to the drawing area. Instead, a link is established between the block reference and the block definition. Therefore, if the block definition is changed, all references are updated automatically.

To reduce the size of a drawing, you can purge unused block definitions.

## To define a block for the current drawing

1. Create the objects you want to use in the block definition.
2. Click Insert tab ➤ Block panel ➤ Create.
3. In the Block Definition dialog box, enter a block name in the Name box.
4. Under Objects, select Convert to Block.

   If you want the original objects used to create the block definition to remain in your drawing, make sure the Delete option is not selected. If this option is selected, the original objects are erased from the drawing. If necessary, you can use OOPS to restore them.
5. Click Select Objects.

6. Use your pointing device to select the objects to be included in the block definition. Press Enter to complete object selection.
7. In the Block Definition dialog box under Base Point, specify the block insertion point using one of these methods.
   - Click Pick Point to specify a point using the pointing device.
   - Enter the *X,Y,Z* coordinate values of the point.
8. In the Description box, enter a description for the block definition. This description is displayed in DesignCenter (ADCENTER).
9. Click OK.

   The block is defined in the current drawing and can be inserted at any time.

## Use Paper Space Objects in Blocks

Objects in paper space are not included when you insert a drawing as a block. To transfer paper space objects to another drawing, make the objects into a block or save them in a separate drawing file, and then insert the block or drawing file into the other drawing.

### To create a new drawing file from selected objects

1. Open an existing drawing or create a new drawing.
2. At the Command prompt, enter **wblock**.
3. In the Write Block dialog box, select Objects.

   If you want the original objects used to create the new drawing to remain in your drawing, make sure the Delete From Drawing option is not selected. If this option is selected, the original objects are erased from the drawing. If necessary, you can use OOPS to restore them.
4. Click Select Objects.
5. Use your pointing device to select the objects to be included in the new drawing. Press Enter to complete object selection.
6. In the Write Block dialog box under Base Point, specify the point to be the origin point (0,0,0) for the new drawing using one of these methods:
   - Click Specify Point to specify a point using the pointing device.
   - Enter the *X, Y, Z* coordinate values of the point.
7. Under Destination, enter a file name and path for the new drawing, or click the [...] button to display a standard file selection dialog box.
8. Click OK.

   A new drawing is created with the selected objects.

### To create a new drawing file from an existing block definition

1. Click Insert tab ▸ Block panel ▸ Create. 
2. In the Block Definition dialog box, in the Name box, select the block to modify.

3. In the Name box, enter a new name.
4. In the Description box, enter or modify the description for the new drawing file. Click OK

## To set the color for all new objects

1. Click Home tab ➤ Properties panel ➤ Object Color.
2. Either click a color to draw all new objects in that color, or click Select Color to display the Select Color dialog box and do one of the following:
   - On the Index tab, click a color or enter the ACI color number (1-255) or name in the Color box, and then click OK.
   - On the True Color tab, select the HSL color model in the Color Model option and specify a color by entering a color value in the Color box or by specifying values in the Hue, Saturation, and Luminance boxes, and then click OK.
   - On the Color Books tab, select a color book from the Color Book box, select a color by navigating the color book (using the up and down arrows) and clicking on a color chip, and then click OK.
   - Click BYLAYER to draw new objects in the color assigned to the current layer.
   - Click BYBLOCK to draw new objects in the current color until they are grouped into a block. When the block is inserted into the drawing, the objects in the block acquire the current color setting.
3. Click OK.

   The Color control displays the current color.

## To set the linetype for all new objects

a. Click Home tab ➤ Properties panel ➤ Linetypes.

b. If you need to load additional linetypes, click Load, select one or more linetypes, and click OK.

c. You can hold down Ctrl to select several linetypes or Shift to select a range of linetypes.

d. In the Linetype Manager, do one of the following:

   a. Select a linetype and select Current to draw all new objects with that linetype.

   b. Select BYLAYER to draw new objects in the linetype assigned to the current layer.

   c. Select BYBLOCK to draw new objects in the current linetype until they are grouped into a block. When the block is inserted in a drawing, the objects in the block acquire the current linetype setting.

e. Click OK.

f. The Linetype control displays the current linetype. If the linetype you want to use is already loaded, you can click the Linetype control and click the linetype to make it current.

## 6. ATTRIBUTE

**Ribbon:** Home tab ➤ Block panel ➤ Define Attributes.

**Menu:** Draw ➤ Block ➤ Define Attributes

**Command entry: attdef**

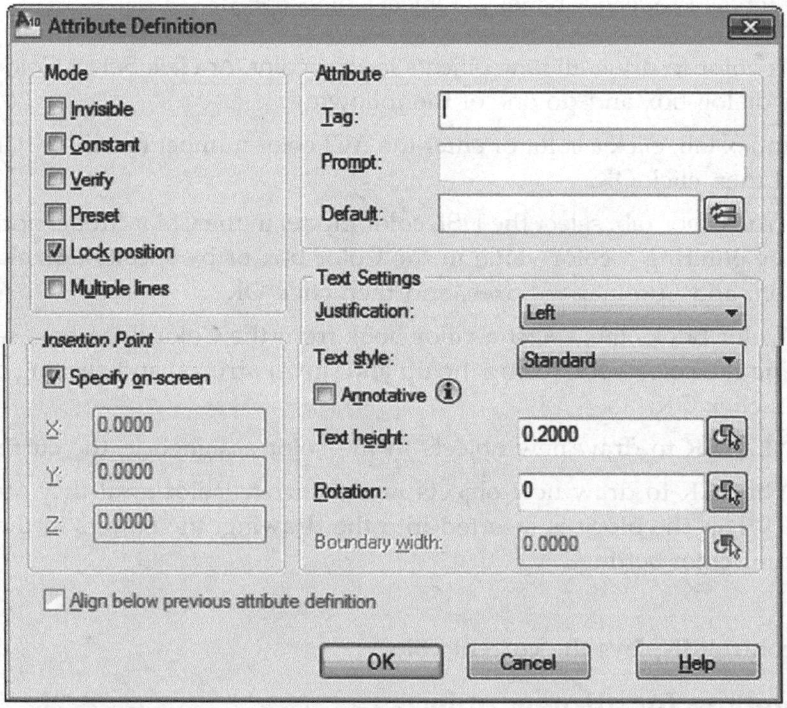


### Mode

Sets options for attribute values associated with a block when you insert the block in a drawing.

The default values are stored in the AFLAGS system variable. Changing the AFLAGS setting affects the default mode for new attribute definitions and does not affect existing attribute definitions.

### Invisible

Specifies that attribute values are not displayed or printed when you insert the block. ATTDISP overrides Invisible mode.

### Constant

Gives attributes a fixed value for block insertions.

### Verify

Prompts you to verify that the attribute value is correct when you insert the block.

## Preset

Sets the attribute to its default value when you insert a block containing a preset attribute.

## Lock Position

Locks the location of the attribute within the block reference. When unlocked, the attribute can be moved relative to the rest of the block using grip editing, and multiline attributes can be resized.

## Multiple Lines

Specifies that the attribute value can contain multiple lines of text. When this option is selected, you can specify a boundary width for the attribute.

**Note:** In a dynamic block, an attribute's position must be locked for it to be included in an action's selection set.

## Attribute

Sets attribute data.

## Tag

Identifies each occurrence of an attribute in the drawing. Enter the attribute tag using any combination of characters except spaces. Lowercase letters are automatically changed to uppercase.

## Prompt

Specifies the prompt that is displayed when you insert a block containing this attribute definition. If you do not enter a prompt, the attribute tag is used as a prompt. If you select Constant in the Mode area, the Prompt option is not available.

## Default

Specifies the default attribute value.

## Insert Field Button

Displays the Field dialog box. You can insert a field as all or part of the value for an attribute.

## Multiline Editor Button

When Multiple Line mode is selected, displays an in-place text editor with a text formatting toolbar and ruler. Depending on the setting of the ATTIPE system variable, the Text Formatting toolbar displayed is either the abbreviated version, or the full version.

For more information, see the In-Place Text Editor.

**Note:** Several options in the full In-Place Text Editor are grayed out to preserve compatibility with single-line attributes.

## Insertion Point

Specifies the location for the attribute. Enter coordinate values or select Specify On-screen and use the pointing device to specify the placement of the attribute in relation to the objects that it will be associated with.

## Specify On-Screen

Displays a Start Point prompt when the dialog box closes. Use the pointing device to specify the placement of the attribute in relation to the objects that it will be associated with.

**X:** Specifies the *X* coordinate of the attribute's insertion point.

**Y:** Specifies the *Y* coordinate of the attribute's insertion point.

**Z:** Specifies the *Z* coordinate of the attribute's insertion point.

## Text Settings

Sets the justification, style, height, and rotation of the attribute text.

## Justification

Specifies the justification of the attribute text. See TEXT for a description of the justification options.

## Text Style

Specifies a predefined text style for the attribute text. Currently loaded text styles are displayed. To load or create a text style, see STYLE.

## Annotative

Specifies that the attribute is annotative. If the block is annotative, the attribute will match the orientation of the block. Click the information icon to learn more about annotative objects.

## Text Height

Specifies the height of the attribute text. Enter a value, or choose Height to specify a height with your pointing device. The height is measured from the origin to the location you specify. If you select a text style that has fixed height (anything other than 0.0), or if you select Align in the Justification list, the Height option is not available.

## Rotation

Specifies the rotation angle of the attribute text. Enter a value, or choose Rotation to specify a rotation angle with your pointing device. The rotation angle is measured from the origin to the location you specify. If you select Align or Fit in the Justification list, the Rotation option is not available.

## Boundary Width

Specifies the maximum length of the lines of text in a multiple-line attribute before wrapping to the next line. A value of 0.000 means that there is no restriction on the length of a line of text.

## Align Below Previous Attribute Definition

Places the attribute tag directly below the previously defined attribute. If you have not previously created an attribute definition, this option is not available.

## 7. BATTMAN

**Ribbon:** Insert tab ➤ Attributes panel ➤ Manage

**Menu:** Modify ➤ Object ➤ Attribute ➤ Block Attribute Manager

**Toolbar:** Modify II 

**Command entry: battman**

## Summary

Manages the attribute definitions for blocks in the current drawing. You can edit the attribute definitions in blocks, remove attributes from blocks, and change the order in which you are prompted for attribute values when inserting a block.

Attributes of the selected block are displayed in the attribute list. By default, Tag, Prompt, Default, Mode, and Annotative attribute properties are displayed in the attribute list. You can specify which attribute properties you want displayed in the list by choosing Settings.

For each selected block, a description below the attribute list identifies the number of its instances in the current drawing and in the current layout.

## Select Block

Allows you to use your pointing device to select a block from the drawing area. When you choose Select Block, the dialog box closes until you select a block from the drawing or cancel by pressing ESC.

If you modify attributes of a block and then select a new block before you save the attribute changes you made, you are prompted to save the changes before selecting another block.

## Block

Lists all block definitions in the current drawing that have attributes. Select the block whose attributes you want to modify.

## List of Attributes

Displays the properties of each attribute in the selected block.

### Blocks Found in Drawing

The number of instances of the selected block in the current drawing.

### Blocks Found in Current Space

The number of instances of the selected block in the current model space or layout.

### Sync

Updates all instances of the selected block with the attribute properties currently defined. This does not affect any values assigned to attributes in each block.

### Move Up

Moves the selected attribute tag earlier in the prompt sequence. The Move Up button is not available when a constant attribute is selected.

### Move Down

Moves the selected attribute tag later in the prompt sequence. The Move Down button is not available when a constant attribute is selected.

### Edit

Opens the Edit Attribute dialog box, where you can modify attribute properties.

### Remove

Removes the selected attribute from the block definition. If Apply Changes to Existing References is selected in the Settings dialog box before you choose Remove, the attribute is removed from all instances of the block in the current drawing. The Remove button is not available for blocks with only one attribute.

### Settings

Opens the Block Attribute Settings dialog box, where you can customize how attribute information is listed in the Block Attribute Manager.

### Apply

Applies the changes you made, but leaves the dialog box open.

### Define Block Attributes

To create an attribute, you first create an attribute definition, which stores the characteristics of the attribute.

The characteristics include the tag, which is a name that identifies the attribute, the prompt displayed when you insert the block, value information, text formatting, location within the block, and any optional modes (Invisible, Constant, Verify, Preset, Lock Position, and Multiple Lines).

If you plan to extract the attribute information for use in a parts list, you may want to keep a list of the attribute tags you have created. You will need this tag information later when you create the attribute template file.

## Choose Attribute Modes

Attribute modes control the behavior of attributes in blocks. For example, you can control

- Whether an attribute is visible or invisible in the drawing
- Whether an attribute has a constant value, such as a part number
- Whether the attribute can be moved relative to the rest of the block
- Whether the attribute is a single-line attribute or a multiple-line attribute

If an attribute has a constant value, you will not be prompted for its value when you insert the block. If an attribute has a variable value, such as the asset number of a computer, you will be prompted when you insert the block.

## Understand Single-Line and Multiple-Line Attributes

There are several differences between single-line and multiple-line attributes.

- Single-line attributes are limited to 255 characters from the user interface.
- Multiple-line attributes provide more formatting options than single-line attributes.
- When editing single-line and multiple line attributes, different editors are displayed.
- Multiple line attributes display four grips similar to MTEXT objects, while single-line attributes display only one grip.
- When a drawing is saved to AutoCAD 2007 or earlier, a multiple-line attribute is converted to several single-line attributes, one for every line of text in the original multiple-line attribute. If the drawing file is opened in the current release, these single line attributes are automatically merged back into a multiple-line attribute.

## 8. Attach Attributes to Blocks

After you create one or more attribute definitions, you attach the attributes to a block when you define or redefine that block. When you are prompted to select the objects to include in the block definition, include in the selection set any attributes you want to attach to the block.

Usually, the order of the attribute prompts is the same as the order in which you selected the attributes when you created the block. However, if you used crossing or window selection to select the attributes, the order of the prompts is the reverse of the order in which you created attributes. You can use the Block Attribute Manager to change the order in which you are prompted for attribute information when you insert the block reference.

When you open a block definition in the Block Editor, you can use the Attribute Order dialog box to change the order in which you are prompted for attribute information when you insert the block reference.

## Use Attributes With-out attaching them to Blocks

Stand-alone attributes can also be created. Once attributes have been defined, and the drawing is saved, this drawing file can be inserted into another drawing. When the drawing is inserted, you are prompted for the attribute values.

## To create an attribute definition

1. Click Home tab ➤ Block panel ➤ Define Attributes.
2. In the Attribute Definition dialog box, set the attribute modes and enter tag information, location, and text options.
3. Click OK.

   After creating the attribute definition, you can select it as an object while creating a block definition. If the attribute definition is incorporated into a block, whenever you insert the block, you are prompted with the text string you specified for the attribute. Each subsequent instance of the block can have a different value specified for the attribute.

## To create a multiline attributes definition

1. Click Home tab ➤ Block panel ➤ Define Attributes.
2. In the Attribute Definition dialog box, under Mode, select Multiple Lines.
3. Enter tag information, location, and text options.
4. (Optional) Under Text Settings, Boundary Width, specify a value.
5. (Optional) Click the Multiline In-Place Text Editor button to use the in-place text editor to format the attribute in the drawing.
6. Click OK.

   After creating the attribute definition, you can select it as an object while creating a block definition. If the attribute definition is incorporated into a block, whenever you insert the block, you are prompted with the text string you specified for the attribute. Each subsequent instance of the block can have a different value specified for the attribute.

## To edit an attribute definition before it is associated with a block

1. Click Modify menu ➤ Object ➤ Text.
2. Select the attribute to edit.
3. In the Edit Attribute Definition dialog box, specify the attribute tag, prompt, and default value. Then click OK.

## To change the prompt order of attribute definitions

1. Click Insert tab ➤ Block panel ➤ Block Editor.
2. In the Block Editor, select a block attribute.
3. Right-click in the Block Editor drawing area.
4. Click Attribute Order.
5. In the Attribute Order dialog box, select an attribute definition.
6. Click Move Up or Move Down to change the prompt order of the attribute definitions.
7. Repeat steps 2 and 3 until the attribute definition list is in the desired order.
8. Click OK.

CHAPTER

9

# Miscellaneous Command

## 1. FILTER COMMAND

The filter command has 3 advantages:

- You can create very complex filtering parameters, using relational operators
- You can group multiple filters
- You can save filters

Create a single filter

To create a single filter, follow these steps:

1. Type filter on the command line. If you're in the middle of a command, type 'filter to start the command transparently. The Object Selection Filters dialog box opens.
2. Click the drop-down list in the Select Filter section of the dialog box to display the available objects, properties, object snaps (such as Line End and Line Start), and logical operators. You use the logical operators to combine filters.

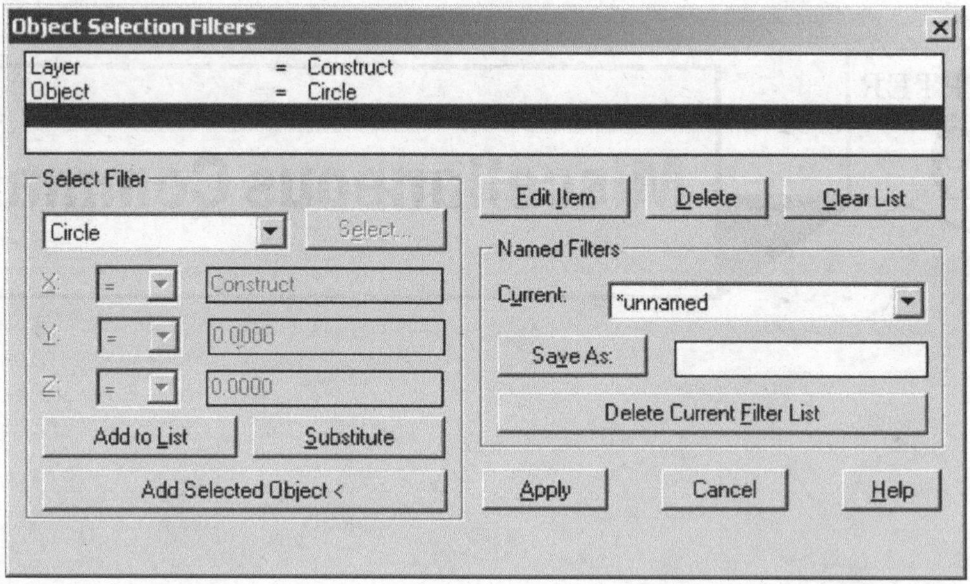


- Choose the item that want from the drop-down list and click Add to List. You now see the item in the top pane. This filter you see here selects all polylines.

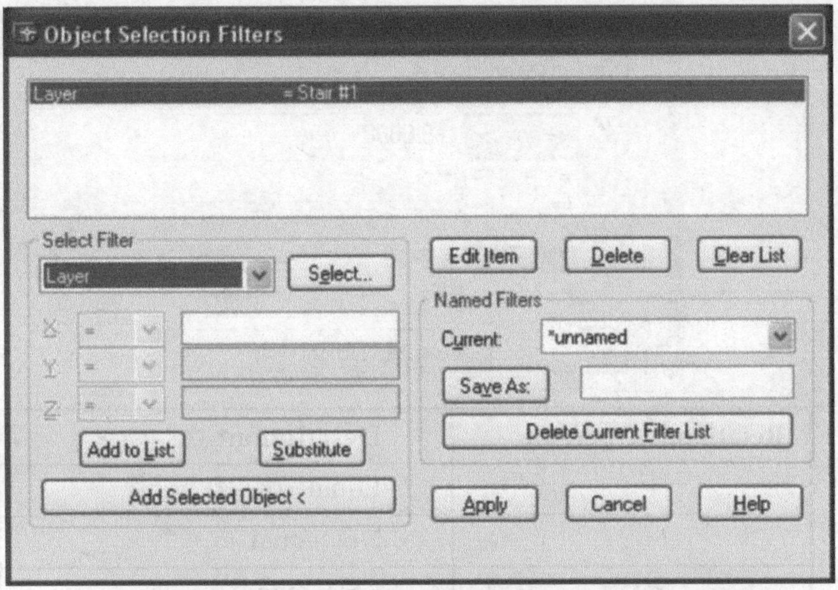


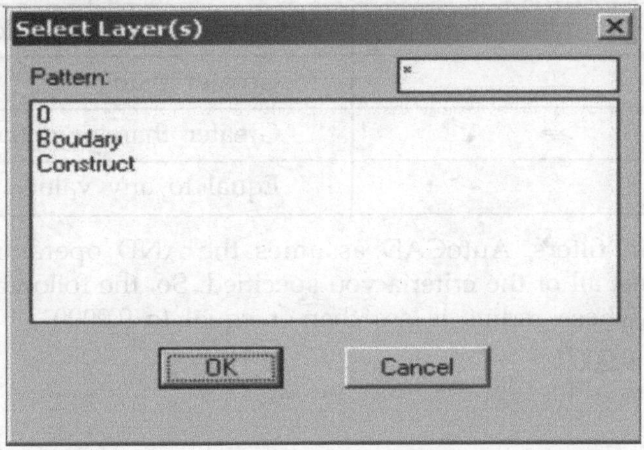


- Repeat to add other criteria, clicking Add to List each time. Some filters need a value, which you can supply in 2 ways:
- You can choose from a list. For example, you can choose Layer. Then click the Select button to open the Select Layer(s) dialog box, where you can choose from the layers that exist in the drawing.
- You can enter a value. For example, you can choose Circle Radius. Depending on which item you choose, one or more of the X, Y, and Z boxes become available. When you need only one value, use the X box. Then choose one of the relational operators from the drop-down list, as shown in the table. Here, I set the Circle Radius item to be less than or equal to 9.0000.

Here are your choices for operators that you can use when you need to specify a value.

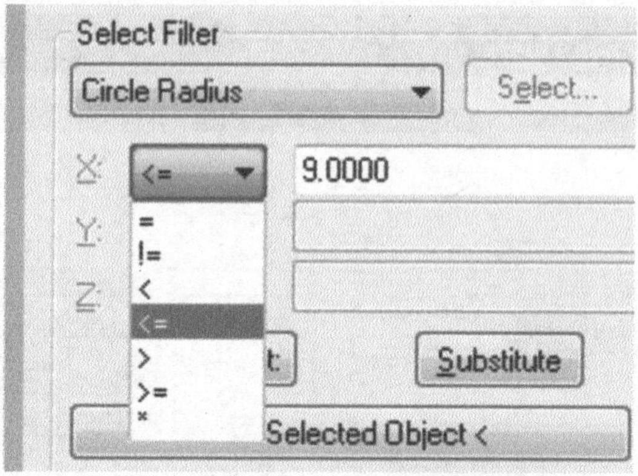


| Relational Operator | Description |
|---|---|
| = | Equal to |
| != | Not equal to |
| < | Less than |
| <= | Less than or equal to |
| > | Greater than |
| >= | Greater than or equal to |
| * | Equal to any value |

**Note:** As you add filters, AutoCAD assumes the AND operator, meaning that the selection needs to meet all of the criteria you specified. So, the following filter finds circles on the WALL layer whose radius is less than or equal to 9.0000.

Circle Radius <= 9.0000

Layer = WALL

Object = Circle

1. Save your filter, in case you didn't get it right or may need it again. Enter a name in the Save As text box and click the Save As button.
2. To correct a filter item, click it in the top pane and click Delete, or Edit Item. You can also click Clear List to start over.
3. When you're done, click the Apply button.
4. The dialog box closes and you see the *Select objects:* prompt. This allows you to specify the objects that you want to filter. You can type all and press Enter, or specify a window. AutoCAD selects the objects you specified in the filter.

If you didn't start a command, you can start one now and use the Previous option to select the objects defined by the filter. Here you see the circles on the WALL layer with radius less than or equal to 9.0000 selected.

Create multiple filters

The previous example uses multiple filters with the default AND logical operator. However, you can combine filter criteria using the following logical operators:

| Operator | Description | Example |
|---|---|---|
| AND | Objects that meet all criteria | Circles on the WALL layer |
| OR | Objects that meet any of the criteria | All circles and all objects on the WALL layer |
| XOR | Objects that meet one or the other criteria, but not both | Circles not on the WALL layer and non-circles on the WALL layer |
| NOT | Objects that don't meet the criteria | If applied to the Object=Circle criterion, objects on the WALL layer that are not circles |

For example, to find objects that are not circles on the WALL layer and circles not on the WALL layer, follow these steps:

1. From the Select Filter drop-down list, choose BEGIN XOR and click Add to List.
2. From the Select Filter drop-down list, choose Circle and click Add to List.
3. From the Select Filter drop-down list, choose Layer. Click the Select button and choose the WALL layer. Click OK. Click Add to List.
4. From the Select Filter drop-down list, choose END XOR and click Add to List.

The result is shown here.

```
** Begin XOR
Object            • Circle
Layer             • WALL
**End   XOR
```

**Note:** The XOR logical operator must enclose 2 criteria. The NOT logical operator must enclose only 1 criterion, the one that you don't want to include in the selection.

1. Continue to add criteria as described.
2. Save the filter as previously described.
3. Click Apply.
4. The dialog box closes and you see the *Select objects:* prompt. This allows you to specify the objects that you want to filter. You can type all and press Enter, or specify a window.

## 2. 'CAL

```
Command: ._CIRCLE
Specify center point for circle or [3P/2P/Ttr (tan tan radius)]: 'CAL
>>>> Expression: plt(end,end,2/9)
>>>> Select entity for END snap:
>>>> Select entity for END snap:
Resuming CIRCLE command.
Specify center point for circle or [3P/2P/Ttr (tan tan radius)]:
3018809.0299135,1320280.6000424,0
Specify radius of circle or [Diameter] <766.991>:
Command:
```

**Example:** Except we are going to get one of the distances from the drawing itself. This time the circle radius is specified by two points in the drawing + 12.5.

Start the ._CIRCLE command, pick the center point. Again, you are prompted for the radius, so enter 'CAL, then the equation. The result is calculated and the circle is constructed. In this example "cur" is part of the equation used to tell AutoCAD that you are going to pick a point on the screen.

```
Command: ._CIRCLE
Specify center point for circle or [3P/2P/Ttr (tan tan radius)]:
Specify radius of circle or [Diameter] <242.440>: 'CAL
>>>> Expression: dist(cur, cur)+12.5
>>>> Enter a point:
>>>> Enter a point:
Resuming CIRCLE command.
Specify radius of circle or [Diameter] <242.440>: 21.1804714
Command:
```

## 3. VIEWING SLIDE FILES, THE VSLIDE COMMAND

Toolbar None

Pull-down none

Keyboard - VSLIDE

The VSLIDE command can be used to view any slide file created with the MSLIDE command. The VSLIDE command also uses the familiar file dialogue box. To view a slide, highlight the file you wish to view and click the "OK" button. The slide is displayed on the monitor screen in the AutoCAD drawing area. The slide is just a two dimensional image, like a photograph, and cannot be modified in any way. To return to your drawing, use the REDRAW command, the slide will disappear and the normal drawing view will be displayed.

## Script Files

Script files can be used to automate any AutoCAD command sequence. Scripts are text files which list a sequence of AutoCAD commands, one on each line. When the script is run, AutoCAD executes each command just as if you typed them from the keyboard. Scripts provide an ideal method for automating the process of displaying a number of slide files in a predetermined sequence.

To create a script file you need to use a text editor such as Notepad. It doesn't matter which text editor you use provided that the file format is plain ASCII text and that the saved file has a ".SCR" extension. To start Notepad, click on the "Start" button at the bottom left of your screen, select "Programs" then "Accessories" and click on the Notepad icon.

Below is an example of a script file which displays three slides, one after the other and then returns to the normal drawing view by issuing the REDRAW command:

```
VSLIDE VIEW-01
VSLIDE VIEW-02
VSLIDE VIEW-03
REDRAW
```

As you can see, each command is on a new line and the command parameter, in this case the slide file name is separated from the command string by a single space. There is no need to add the ".SLD" extension since the VSLIDE command assumes that you will want to view a slide file. The DELAY command if you ran the script above just as it is shown, each slide would be displayed on the screen and then immediately replaced with the next slide. This doesn't give enough time for us to view the slide properly. We need some method of pausing before moving on to the next slide. The DELAY command can be used to insert a pause between each VSLIDE command. If we add DELAY to the script above, the script file would look like the one below:

```
VSLIDE VIEW-01
DELAY 6000
VSLIDE VIEW-02
DELAY 6000
VSLIDE VIEW-03
DELAY 6000
REDRAW
```

The syntax for the DELAY command is:

DELAY Time in milliseconds

There are 1000 milliseconds in a second, so there is a pause of 6 seconds between each slide in the script above. You can use any number between 1 and 32767 with the DELAY command. This means that you can pause between any two commands from one millisecond to just fewer than 33 seconds. Of course, if you need to pause for more than 33 seconds, you could use two DELAY commands, one after the other. The RSCRIPT command the script above displays each slide, pauses for 6 seconds, views the next slide and then uses the REDRAW command to return to normal viewing. However, sometimes we may want to have the script loop, so that when it gets to the end of the script it will start again at the top. We can do this using the RSCRIPT command and create a rolling slide show which will continue to repeat itself until we stop it. To change the script above into a loop, just replace the REDRAW command with the RSCRIPT command.

The final script would look like the one below:

VSLIDE VIEW-01

DELAY 6000

VSLIDE VIEW-02

DELAY 6000

VSLIDE VIEW-03

DELAY 6000

RSCRIPT

You must always end a script file with a carriage return, otherwise the script will pause indefinitely and the last command will never be issued. In the above example a carriage return must be added after the "T" of "RSCRIPT". This is a common mistake and is difficult to spot because the script file doesn't look any different. The RESUME commands you can suspend the operation of a script at any time by hitting the Backspace key. You may, for example want to pause a little longer at a particular slide in order to talk about it if you are giving a presentation. Once the Backspace key is pressed the script stops. To continue the script where you left off, use the RESUME command. Just type "RESUME" at the command prompt and the script will restart from the point at which Backspace was pressed.

Running a script file, the SCRIPT command

Toolbar None

Pull-down Tools/Run Script...

Keyboard SCRIPT

The SCRIPT command is used to start the operation of a script file.

The SCRIPT command uses the familiar file dialogue box, but only displays ".SCR" files. To start running a script, highlight the script file you want and then click the "OK" button at the bottom of the "Select Script File" dialogue box.

## 4. GROUP

In addition to choosing the objects that will become the members of a group, you can give the group a name and description.

When you create a group, you can give the group a name and description. If you copy a group, the copy is given the default name Ax and is considered unnamed. Unnamed groups are not listed in the Object Grouping dialog box unless you select Include Unnamed.

If you choose a member of a group that can be selected for inclusion in a new group, all members of the former group are included in the new group.

The objects in your drawing can be members of more than one group, and groups themselves can be nested in other groups. You can ungroup a nested group to restore the original group configuration.

Named groups are not maintained when you use a drawing as an external reference or insert it as a block. However, you can bind and then explode the external reference or explode the block to make the group available as an unnamed group.

## To create a group

1. At the Command prompt, enter **group**.
2. In the Object Grouping dialog box, under Group Identification, enter a group name and a description.
3. In the Create Group area, click New.

**The dialog box closes temporarily.**

4. Select objects and press ENTER.
5. Click OK.

If you enter **-group** at the command prompt, the following GROUP command prompts are displayed.

Enter a group option

[?/Order/Add/Remove/Explode/REName/Selectable/Create] <Create>: *Enter an option or press* ENTER

?—List Groups

Lists names and descriptions of groups defined in the drawing.

Enter group name(s) to list <*>: *Enter a name list or press* ENTER *to list all groups*

**Order**

Changes the numerical order of objects within a group. Reordering is useful when creating tool paths. For example, you can change the cut order for the horizontal and vertical lines of a tool path pattern.

Enter a group name or [?]: *Enter a name list or enter* **?** *to list all groups*

Enter position number of the object to reorder (0-*n*) or [Reverse order]: *Enter a position number or enter* **r**

**Position Number**

Specifies the position number of the object to reorder. To reorder a range of objects, specify the first object's position number.

Replace at position <0-*n*>: *Enter the position number to which you want the object to move*

Number of objects to re-order <0-*n*>: *Enter the number of objects to reorder*

**Reverse Order**

Reverses the order of all members in a group.

Add

Adds objects to a group.

Enter a group name or [?]: *Enter a name or enter* **?** *to list all groups*

Select objects to add to group...

Select objects:

**Remove**

Removes objects from a group.

Enter a group name or [?]: *Enter a name or enter* **?** *to list all groups*

Select objects to remove from group...

Remove objects:

*If you remove all the group's objects, the group remains defined. You can remove the* group definition from the drawing by using the Explode option.

**Explode**

Deletes a group definition by exploding the group into its component objects.

Enter a group name or [?]: *Enter a name or enter* **?** *to list all groups*

**Ungroup**

Removes the group name and the association of objects in the group.

**Rename**

Assigns a new name to an existing group.

Enter a group name to rename or [?]: *Enter an existing group name or enter* **?** *to list all groups*

Enter a new name for group or [?]: *Enter a new name or enter* **?** *to list all groups*

**Selectable**

Specifies whether a group is selectable. When a group is selectable, selecting one object in the group selects the whole group. Objects on locked or frozen layers are not selected.

Enter a group name or [?]: *Enter a name or enter* **?** *to list all groups*

This group is *current*, do you want to change it [Yes/No]? <Y>: *Enter* **y** *or* **n**, *or press* ENTER

**Create**

Creates a group.

Enter a group name or [?]: *Enter a name or enter* **?**

Group names can be up to 31 characters long and can include letters, numbers, and special characters dollar sign ($), hyphen (-), and underscore (_) but not spaces. The name is converted to uppercase characters.

Enter a group description: *Enter up to 64 text characters or press* ENTER

Select objects:

CHAPTER 10

# Constraints

## GEOMETRIC CONSTRAINTS

Geometric constraints associate geometric objects together, or specify a fixed location or angle.

For example, you can specify that a line should always be perpendicular to another one, that an arc and a circle should always remain concentric, or that a line should always be tangent to an arc.

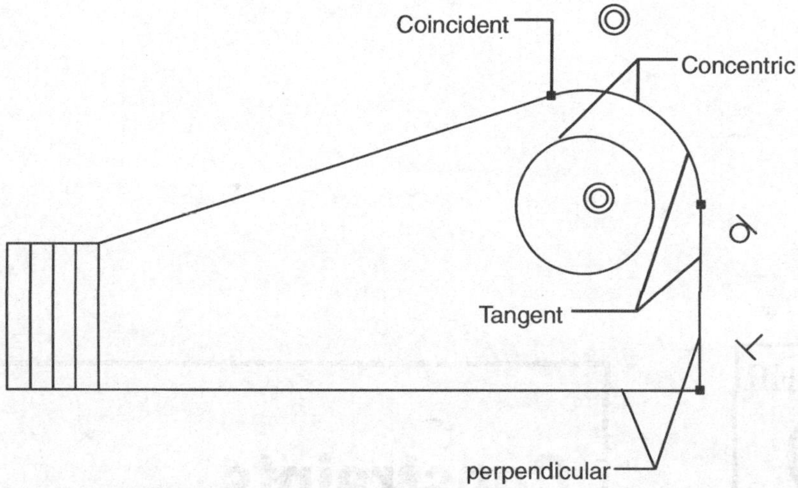


When you apply a constraint, two things occur:

- The object that you select adjusts automatically to conform to the specified constraint
- By default, a gray constraint icon displays near the constrained object as shown in the previous illustration, and a small, blue glyph displays with your cursor when you move it over a constrained object

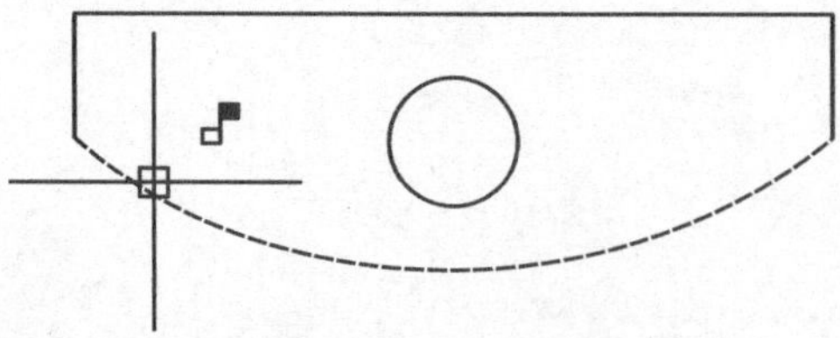

Once applied, constraints permit only those changes to the geometry that do not violate the constraints. This provides a method for exploring design options or making design changes while maintaining the requirements and specifications of the design.

**Note:** The order in which you select two objects when you apply a constraint is important in some cases. Normally, the second object you select adjusts to the first object. For example, when you apply a Perpendicular constraint, the second object you select will adjust to become perpendicular to the first.

You can apply geometric constraints to 2D geometric objects only. Objects cannot be constrained between model space and paper space.

## 1. SPECIFY CONSTRAINT POINTS

With some constraints, you specify constraint points on objects instead of selecting the objects. This behavior is similar to that of object snaps, but the locations are limited to endpoints, midpoints, center points, and insertion points.

For example, the Coincident constraint can restrict the location of the endpoint of one line to the endpoint of another line.

The following glyph is displayed on the object as you roll over the object.

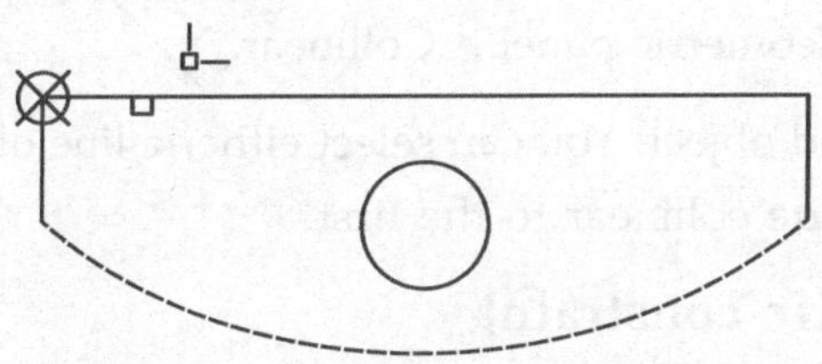

You use this glyph to confirm whether you are specifying the intended point to constrain.

## 2. USE FIX CONSTRAINTS

A Fix constraint associates a constraint point on an object, or the object itself with a fixed location with respect to the World Coordinate System.

It is often advisable to specify a Fix constraint at an important geometric feature. This locks the location of that point or object, and prevents geometry from relocating when you make changes to the design.

When you fix an *object*, the angle of a line, or the center of an arc or circle is also fixed.

## 3. APPLY MULTIPLE GEOMETRIC CONSTRAINTS

You can apply multiple geometric constraints to objects either manually or automatically.

When you want to apply all essential geometric constraints to a design automatically, you can use AUTOCONSTRAIN with the objects that you select in your drawing. This helps constrain the geometric shape of the design—depending on your design, there might be cases where you need to apply additional geometric constraints.

AUTOCONSTRAIN also provides settings in which you can specify the following options:

- What geometric constraints to apply
- What order to apply geometric constraints
- What tolerances are used to determine whether objects are horizontal, vertical, or touching

**Note:** Equal or Fix constraints are not applied with AUTOCONSTRAIN. You must apply these constraints individually.

To fully constrain the size and proportions of a design, you will later need to apply dimensional constraints.

## a. To apply a coincident constraint

1. Click Parametric tab ➤ Geometric panel ➤ Coincident. 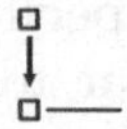
2. Select the first and second points on two different objects.
   The second point is made coincident to the first.

## b. To apply a collinear constraint

1. Click Parametric tab ➤ Geometric panel ➤ Collinear. 
2. Select the first and second object. You can select either a line object or a polyline sub object.
   The second object is made collinear to the first.

## c. To apply a concentric constraint

1. Click Parametric tab ➤ Geometric panel ➤ Concentric. 
2. Select the first and second arc or circle object.
   The second arc or circle moves to have the same center point as the first object.

## d. To apply a fix constraint

1. Click Parametric tab ➤ Geometric panel ➤ Fix. 
2. Select a point on an object.
   Applying the Fix constraint to a point on the object locks the node in place. You can still move the object.

## e. To apply a parallel constraint

1. Click Parametric tab ➤ Geometric panel ➤ Parallel. 
2. Select the two objects to be made parallel. You can select either a line object or a polyline subobject.
   The second object is made parallel with the first object.

## f. To apply a perpendicular constraint

1. Click Parametric tab ➤ Geometric panel ➤ Perpendicular. 
2. Select the two objects to be made perpendicular. You can select either a line object or a polyline subobject.
   The second object is made perpendicular to the first object.

## g. To apply a horizontal constraint

1. Click Parametric tab ➤ Geometric panel ➤ Horizontal.
2. Select the line object or polyline subobject to be made horizontal.

## h. To apply a vertical constraint

1. Click Parametric tab ➤ Geometric panel ➤ Vertical.
2. Select the line object or polyline subobject to be made vertical.

## i. To apply a tangent constraint

1. Click Parametric tab ➤ Geometric panel ➤ Tangent.
2. Select the two objects to be made tangential.

   The second object maintains a point of tangency with the first object.

## j. To apply a smooth constraint

1. Click Parametric tab ➤ Geometric panel ➤ Smooth.
2. Select the first spline curve.
3. Select the second spline, line, polyline (subobject), or arc object.

   The two objects are updated to be contiguous with one another.

## k. To apply a symmetric constraint

1. Click Parametric tab ➤ Geometric panel ➤ Symmetric.
2. Select the first and second object.
3. Select the symmetry line.

   The selected objects become symmetrically constrained about the selected line.

## l. To apply an equal constraint

1. Click Parametric tab ➤ Geometric panel ➤ Equal.
2. Select the first and second object.

   The second object is made equal to the first object.

## m. To apply multiple geometric constraints to an object

1. Click Parametric tab ➤ Geometric panel ➤ AutoConstrain.
2. Select the objects that you want to constrain.

3. Press Enter when you select the objects to be automatically constrained.

   The Command prompt displays the number of constraints applied.

### n. To set the order for applying multiple geometric constraints to an object

1. Click Parametric tab † Geometric panel † AutoConstrain.
2. At the Command prompt, enter **s** (Settings).
3. In the Constraint Settings dialog box, on the AutoConstrain tab, select a Constraint Type.
4. Click Move Up or Move Down. This changes the priority for a constraint when you use the AUTOCONSTRAIN command on an object.
5. Click OK.

## 4. DIMENSIONAL CONSTRAINTS

Dimensional constraints control the size and proportions of a design. They can constrain the following:

- Distances between objects, or between points on objects
- Angles between objects, or between points on objects
- Sizes of arcs and circles

For example, the following illustration includes linear, aligned, angular, and diameter constraints.

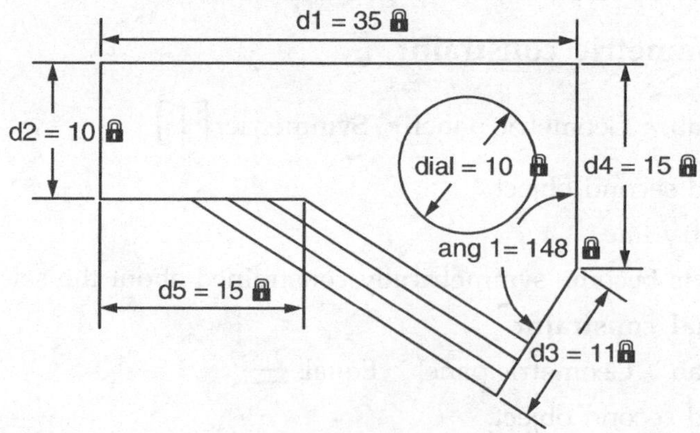


If you change the value of a dimensional constraint, all the constraints on the object are evaluated, and the objects that are affected are updated automatically.

Also, constraints can be added directly to segments within a polyline as if they were separate objects.

**Note:** The number of decimal places displayed in dimensional constraints is controlled by the LUPREC and AUPREC system variables.

## Compare Dimensional Constraints with Dimension Objects

Dimensional *constraints* are different from dimension *objects* in the following ways:

- Dimensional constraints are used in the design phase of a drawing, but dimensions are typically created in the documentation phase
- Dimensional constraints drive the size or angle of objects, but dimensions *are driven* by objects
- By default, dimensional constraints are not objects, display with only a single dimension style, maintain the same size during zoom operations, and are not plotted

If you need to plot dimensional constraints or use dimension styles, you can change the form of a dimensional constraint from dynamic to annotational.

## Define Variables and Equations

With the Parameters Manager, you can define custom *user variables* that you can reference from within dimensional constraints and other user variables. The expressions that you define can include a variety of predefined functions and constants.

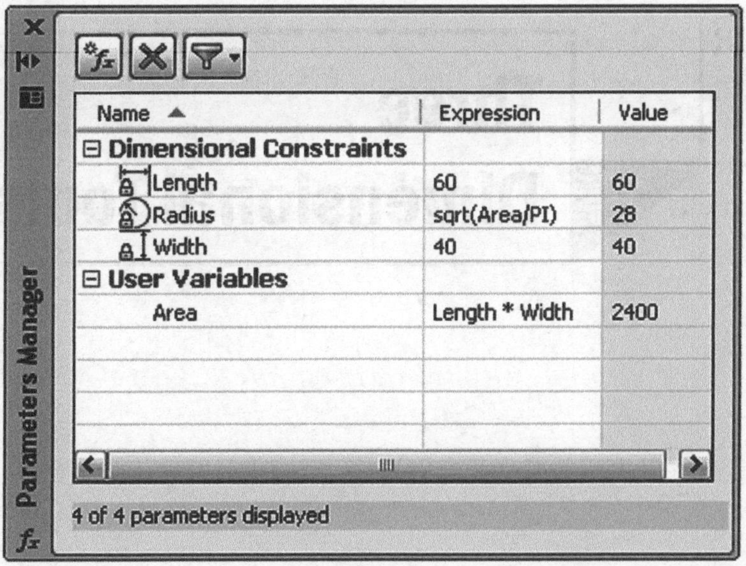

CHAPTER 11

# Three Dimensional Tools

## 1. 3D

Creates 3D polygon mesh objects in common geometric shapes that can be hidden, shaded, or rendered.

**Access Methods**

**Command entry: 3d**

Enter an option
[ Box/ Cone/ DIsh/ DOme/ Mesh/ Pyramid/ Sphere/ Torus/ Wedge]:

### Box

Creates a 3D box polygon mesh

Specify corner point of box:

Specify length of box: *Specify a distance*

Specify width of box or [Cube]: *Specify a distance or enter* **c**

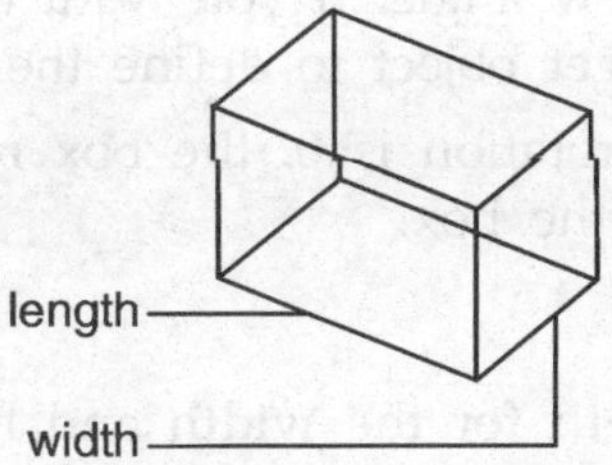


### Width

Specifies the width of the box. Enter a distance or specify a point relative to the corner point of the box.

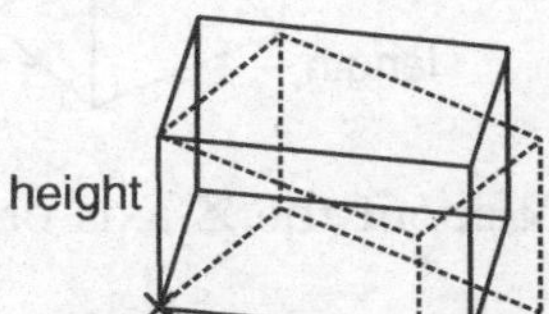


Specify height of box: *Specify a distance*

Specify rotation angle of box about the Z axis or [Reference]: *Specify an angle or enter* **r**

### Rotation Angle

Rotates the box about the first corner specified. If you enter **0**, the box remains orthogonal to the current *X* and *Y* axes.

### Reference

Aligns the box with other objects in the drawing or relative to an angle you specify. The base point for the rotation is the first corner of the box.

Specify the reference angle <0>: *Specify a point, enter an angle, or press Enter*

You can define a reference angle by specifying two points or an angle from the X axis on the *XY* plane. For example, you can rotate the box to align two specified points on the box with a point on another object. After defining a reference angle, specify a point for the reference angle to align with. The box then rotates around the first corner relative to the angle of rotation specified for the reference angle.

If you enter **0** as a reference angle, the new angle alone determines the rotation of the box.

Specify the new angle: *Specify a point or enter an angle*

To specify the new angle of rotation, specify a point relative to the base point. The base point for the rotation is the first corner of the box. The box rotates by the angle between the reference angle and the new angle. If you want to align the box with another object, specify two points on the target object to define the new angle of rotation for the box.

If the reference angle of rotation is 0, the box rotates the angular distance entered relative to the first corner of the box.

### Cube

Creates a cube using the length for the width and height of the box

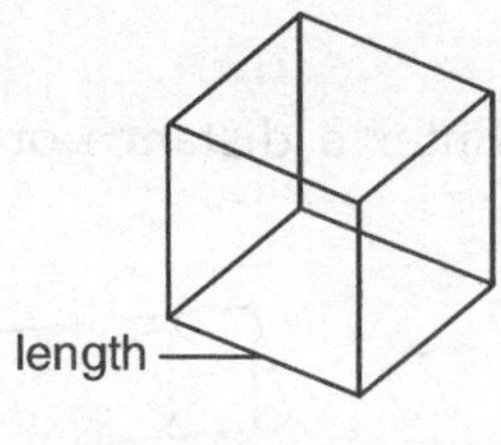


Specify rotation angle of box about the Z axis or [Reference]: *Specify an angle or enter* **r**

### Rotation Angle

Rotates the cube about the first corner of the box. If you enter **0**, the box remains orthogonal to the current X and Yaxes.

### Reference

Aligns the box with other objects in the drawing or relative to an angle you specify. The base point for the rotation is the first corner of the box.

Specify the reference angle <0>: *Specify a point, enter an angle, or press Enter*

You can define a reference angle by specifying two points or an angle from the *X* axis on the *XY* plane. For example, you can rotate the box to align two specified points on the box with a point on another object. After defining a reference angle, specify a point for the reference angle to align with. The box then rotates around the first corner relative to the angle of rotation specified for the reference angle.

If you enter **0** as a reference angle, the new angle alone determines the rotation of the box.

Specify the new angle: *Specify a point or enter an angle*

To specify the new angle of rotation, specify a point relative to the base point. The base point for the rotation is the first corner of the box. The box rotates the angular distance between the reference angle and the new angle. If you want to align the box with another object, specify two points on the target object to define the new angle of rotation for the box.

If the reference angle of rotation is 0, the box rotates the angular distance entered relative to the first corner point of the box.

## Cone

Creates a cone-shaped polygon mesh

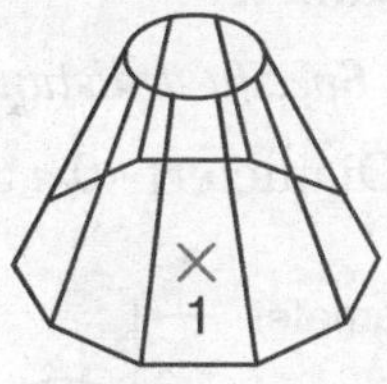


Specify center point for base of cone: *Specify a point (1)*

Specify radius for base of cone or [Diameter]: *Specify a distance or enter* **d**

## Radius for Base

Defines the base of the cone by its radius

Specify radius for top of cone or [Diameter] <0>: *Specify a distance, enter* **d**, *or press Enter*

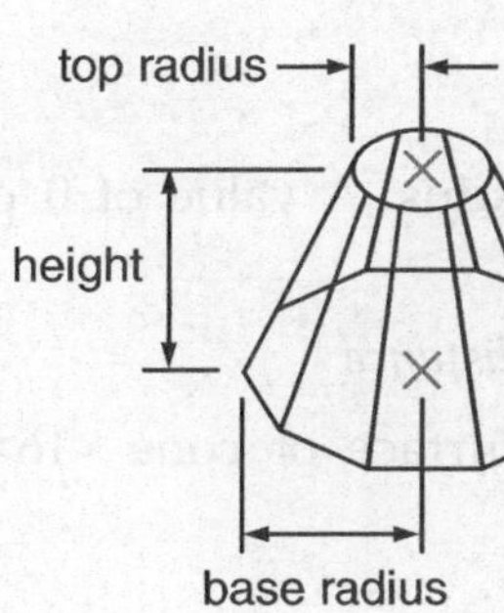

### Radius for Top

Defines the top of the cone by its radius. A value of 0 produces a cone. A value greater than 0 produces a truncated cone

Specify height of cone: *Specify a distance*

Enter number of segments for surface of cone <16>: *Enter a value greater than 1 or press Enter*

### Diameter for Top

Defines the top of the cone by its diameter. A value of 0 produces a cone. A value greater than 0 produces a truncated cone

Specify diameter for top of cone <0>: *Specify a distance or press* Enter

Specify height of cone: *Specify a distance*

Enter number of segments for surface of cone <16>: *Enter a value greater than 1 or press* Enter

### Diameter for Base

Defines the base of the cone by its diameter

Specify diameter for base of cone: *Specify a distance*

Specify radius for top of cone or [Diameter] <0>: *Specify a distance, enter* **d**, *or press* Enter

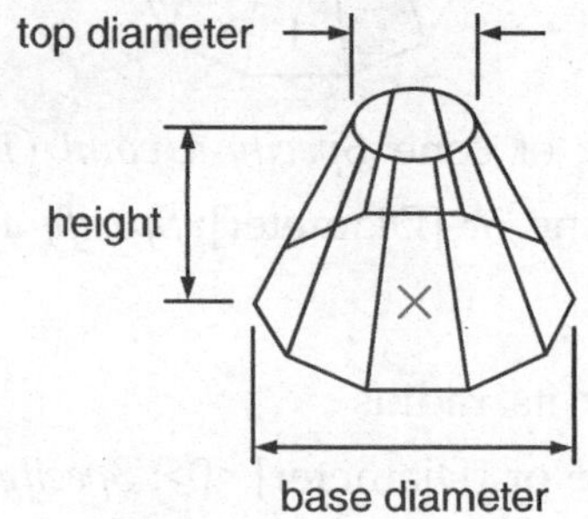


### Radius for Top

Defines the top of the cone by its radius. A value of 0 produces a cone. A value greater than 0 produces a truncated cone

Specify height of cone: *Specify a distance*

Enter number of segments for surface of cone <16>: *Enter a value greater than 1 or press* Enter

## Diameter for Top

Defines the top of the cone by its diameter. A value of 0 produces a cone. A value greater than 0 produces a truncated cone.

Specify diameter for top of cone <0>: *Specify a distance*

Specify height of cone: *Specify a distance*

Enter number of segments for surface of cone <16>: *Enter a value greater than 1 or press* Enter

## Dish

Creates the lower half of a spherical polygon mesh.

Specify center point of dish: *Specify a point (1)*

Specify radius of dish or [Diameter]: *Specify a distance or enter* **d**

## Radius

Defines the dish by its radius

Enter number of longitudinal segments for surface of dish <16>: *Enter a value greater than 1 or press* Enter

Enter number of latitudinal segments for surface of dish <8>: *Enter a value greater than 1 or press* Enter

## Diameter

Defines the dish by its diameter.

Specify diameter of dish: *Specify a distance*

Enter number of longitudinal segments for surface of dish <16>: *Enter a value greater than 1 or press* Enter

Enter number of latitudinal segments for surface of dish <8>: *Enter a value greater than 1 or press* Enter

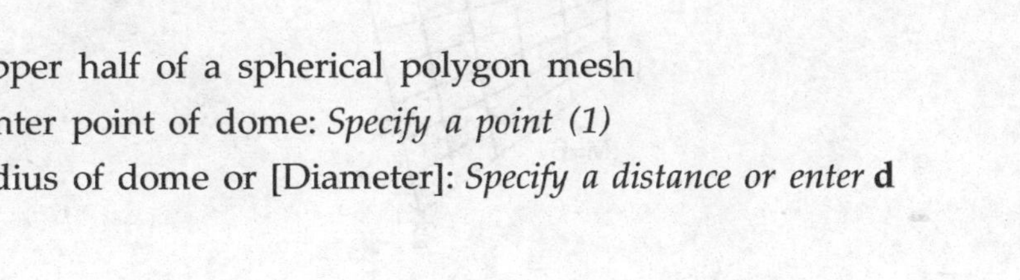


## Dome

Creates the upper half of a spherical polygon mesh

Specify center point of dome: *Specify a point (1)*

Specify radius of dome or [Diameter]: *Specify a distance or enter* **d**

## Radius

Defines the dome by its radius.

Enter number of longitudinal segments for surface of dome: *Enter a value greater than 1 or press* Enter

Enter number of latitudinal segments for surface of dome <8>: *Enter a value greater than 1 or press* Enter

## Diameter

Defines the dome by its diameter.

Specify diameter of dome: *Specify a distance*

Enter number of longitudinal segments for surface of dome <16>: *Enter a value greater than 1 or press* Enter

Enter number of latitudinal segments for surface of dome <8>: *Enter a value greater than 1 or press* Enter

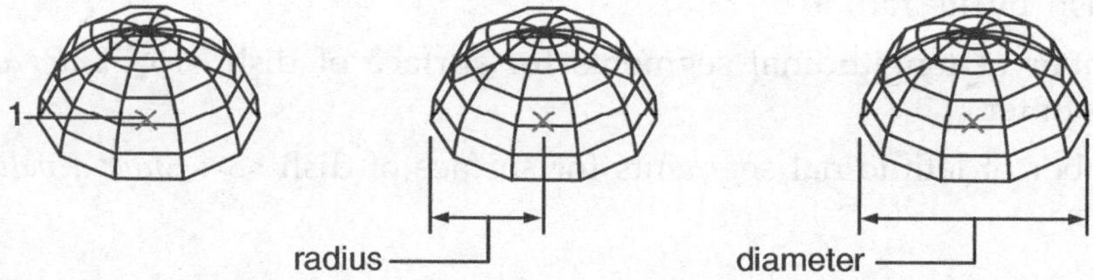


## Mesh

Creates a planar mesh whose *M* and *N* sizes determine the number of lines drawn in each direction along the mesh. The *M* and *N* directions are similar to the *X* and *Y* axes of an *XY* plane.

Specify first corner point of mesh: *Specify a point (1)*

Specify second corner point of mesh: *Specify a point (2)*

Specify third corner point of mesh: *Specify a point (3)*

Specify fourth corner point of mesh: *Specify a point (4)*

Enter mesh size in the M direction: *Enter a value between 2 and 256*

Enter mesh size in the N direction: *Enter a value between 2 and 256*

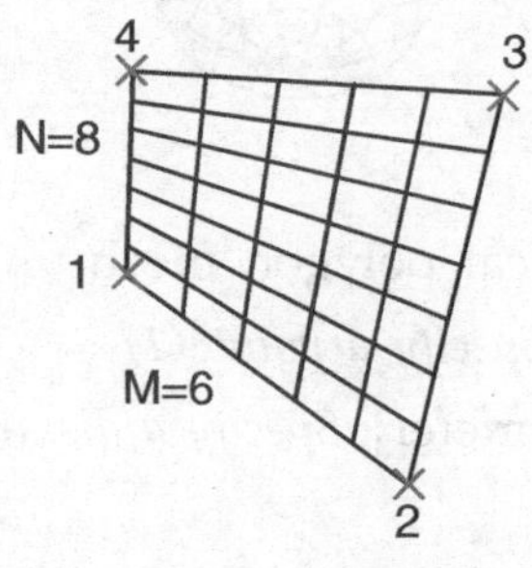

## Pyramid

Creates a pyramid or a tetrahedron.

Specify first corner point for base of pyramid: *Specify a point (1)*

Specify second corner point for base of pyramid: *Specify a point (2)*

Specify third corner point for base of pyramid: *Specify a point (3)*

Specify fourth corner point for base of pyramid or [Tetrahedron]: *Specify a point (4) or enter* **t**

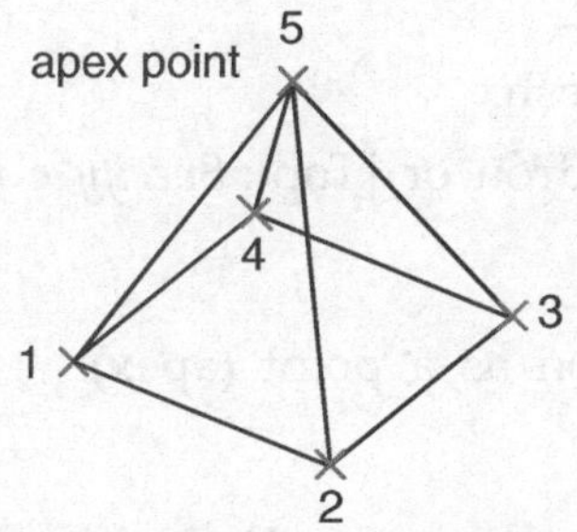


## Fourth Corner Point

Defines the fourth corner point of the base of a pyramid.

Specify apex point of pyramid or [Ridge/Top]: *Specify a point (5) or enter an option*

The *Z* value of the point specified determines the height for the pyramid's apex, top, or ridge line.

## Apex Point

Defines the top of the pyramid as a point (apex).

## Ridge

Defines the top of the pyramid as a ridge line. The two endpoints must lie in the same direction as the base points to prevent a self-intersecting wireframe.

Specify first ridge end point of pyramid: *Specify a point (1)*

Specify second ridge end point of pyramid: *Specify a point (2)*

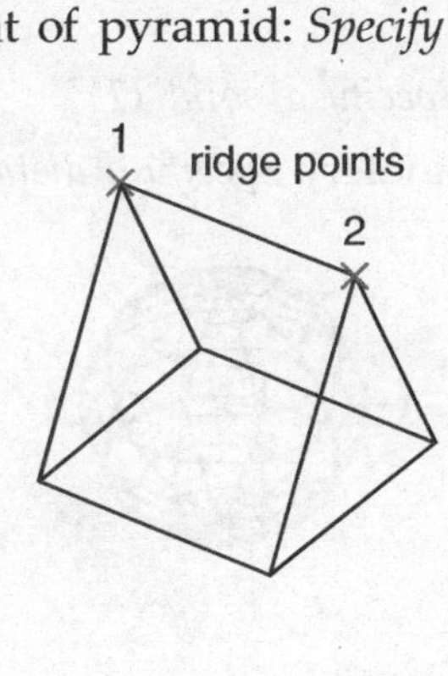

## Top

Defines the top of the pyramid as a rectangle. If the top points cross, they create a self-intersecting polygon mesh.

Specify first corner point for top of pyramid: *Specify a point*

Specify second corner point for top of pyramid: *Specify a point*

Specify third corner point for top of pyramid: *Specify a point*

Specify fourth corner point for top of pyramid: *Specify a point*

## Tetrahedron

Creates a tetrahedral polygon mesh.

Specify apex point of tetrahedron or [Top]: *Specify a point or enter* **t**

## Apex Point

Defines the top of the tetrahedron as a point (apex)

### Top

Defines the top of the tetrahedron as a triangle. If the top points cross, they create a self-intersecting polygon mesh.

Specify first corner point for top of tetrahedron: *Specify a point (1)*

Specify second corner point for top of tetrahedron: *Specify a point (2)*

Specify third corner point for top of tetrahedron: *Specify a point (3)*

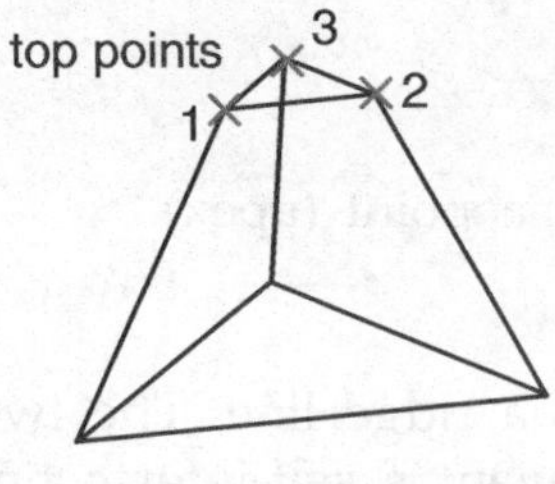


## Sphere

Creates a spherical polygon mesh.

Specify center point of sphere: *Specify a point (1)*

Specify radius of sphere or [Diameter]: *Specify a distance or enter* **d**

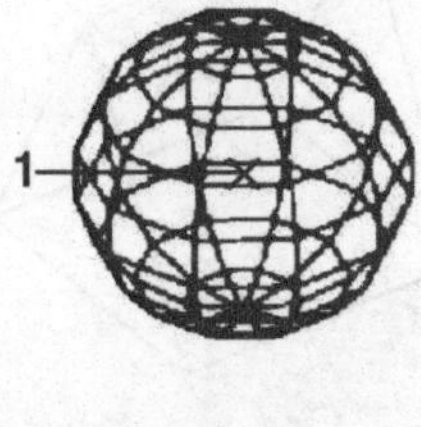

## Radius

Defines the sphere by its radius

Enter number of longitudinal segments for surface of sphere <16>: *Enter a value greater than 1 or press* Enter

Enter number of latitudinal segments for surface of sphere <16>: *Enter a value greater than 1 or press* Enter

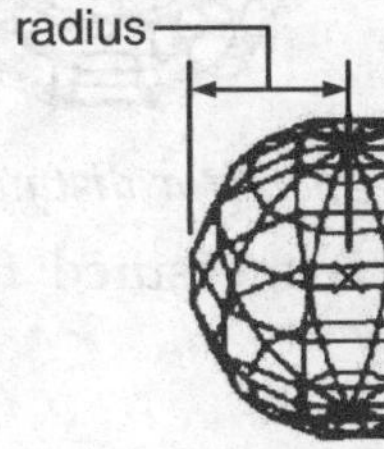


## Diameter

Defines the sphere by its diameter

Specify diameter of sphere: *Specify a distance*

Enter number of longitudinal segments for surface of sphere <16>: *Enter a value greater than 1 or press* Enter

Enter number of latitudinal segments for surface of sphere <16>: *Enter a value greater than 1 or press* Enter

## Torus

Creates a toroidal polygon mesh that is parallel to the *XY* plane of the current UCS.

Specify center point of torus: *Specify a point (1)*

Specify radius of torus or [Diameter]: *Specify a distance or enter* **d**

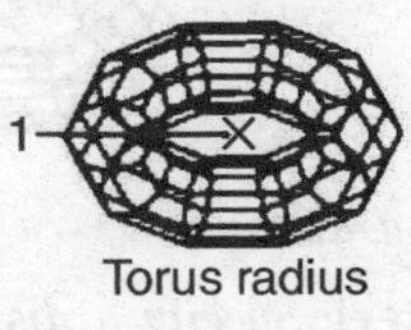


The radius of the torus is measured from its center point to its outside edge, not to the center of the tube.

## Radius

Defines the torus by its radius

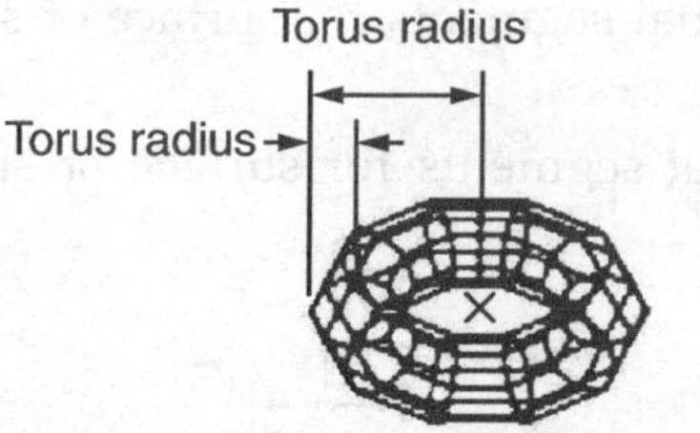


Specify radius of tube or [Diameter]: *Specify a distance or enter* **d**

The radius of the tube of the torus is measured from the center of the tube to the outside edge of the tube.

## Radius

Defines the tube by its radius.

Enter number of segments around tube circumference <16>: *Enter a value greater than 1 or press* Enter

Enter number of segments around torus circumference <16>: *Enter a value greater than 1 or press* Enter

## Diameter

Defines the tube by its diameter.

Specify diameter of tube: *Specify a distance*

Enter number of segments around tube circumference <16>: *Enter a value greater than 1 or press* Enter

Enter number of segments around torus circumference <16>: *Enter a value greater than 1 or press* Enter

## Diameter

Defines the torus by its diameter

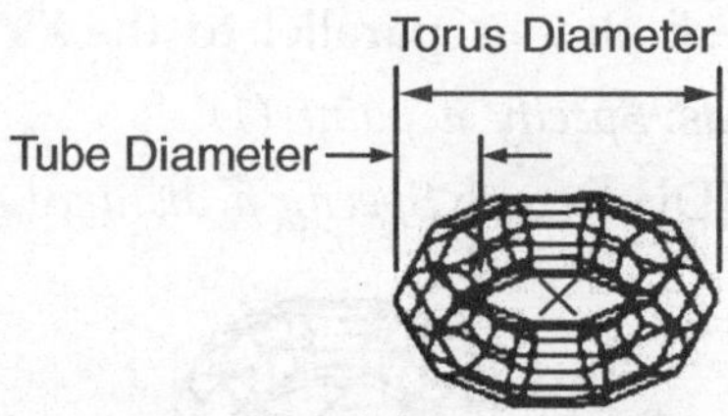


Specify diameter of torus: *Specify a distance*

Specify radius of tube or [Diameter]: *Specify a distance or enter* **d**

The radius of the tube of the torus is measured from the center of the tube to the outside edge of the tube.

### Radius

Defines the tube by its radius.

Enter number of segments around tube circumference <16>: *Enter a value greater than 1 or press* Enter

Enter number of segments around torus circumference <16>: *Enter a value greater than 1 or press* Enter

### Diameter

Defines the tube by its diameter

Specify diameter of tube: *Specify a distance*

Enter number of segments around tube circumference <16>: *Enter a value greater than 1 or press* Enter

Enter number of segments around torus circumference <16>: *Enter a value greater than 1 or press* Enter

### Wedge

Creates a right-angle, wedge-shaped polygon mesh with a sloped face tapering along the X axis.

Specify corner point of wedge: *Specify a point (1)*

Specify length of wedge: *Specify a distance*

Specify width of wedge: *Specify a distance*

Specify height of wedge: *Specify a distance*

Specify rotation angle of wedge about the Z axis: *Specify an angle*

The base point for the rotation is the corner point of the wedge. If you enter **0**, the wedge remains orthogonal to the current UCS plane.

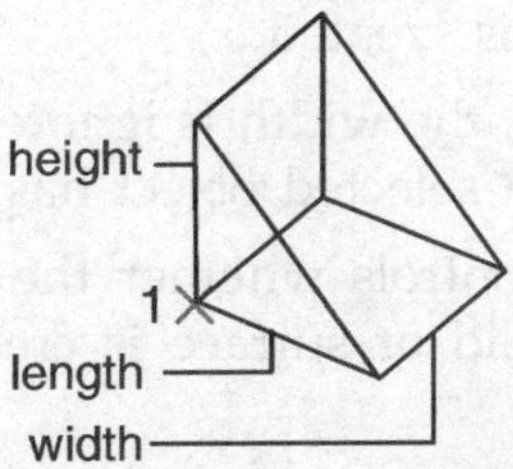

## 2. EXTRUDE

Extends the dimensions of a 2D object or 3D face into 3D space

**Access Methods**

**Button**

**Ribbon:** Home tab ➤ Modeling panel ➤ Extrude

**Menu:** Draw ➤ Modeling ➤ Extrude

**Toolbar:** Modeling

**Command entry: extrude**

### Summary

In most cases, if you extrude a closed object, the result is a new 3D solid. If you extrude an open object, the result is a surface.

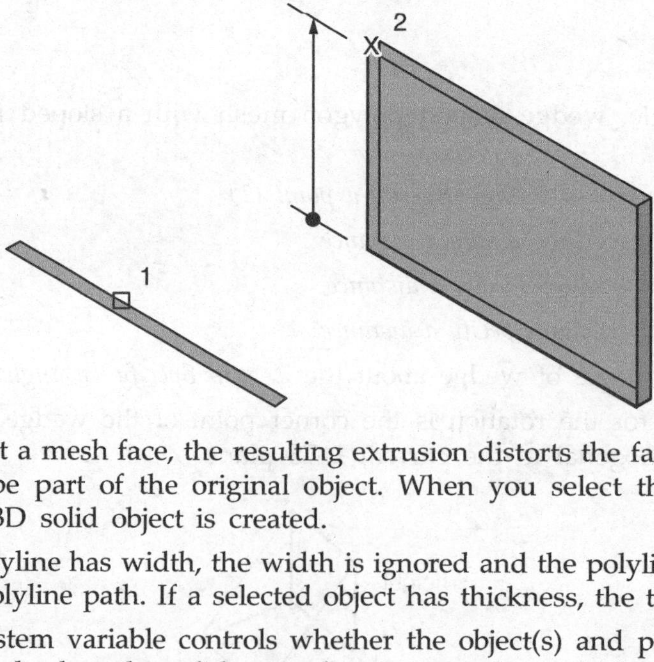


When you select a mesh face, the resulting extrusion distorts the face, but the extruded face continues to be part of the original object. When you select the face of 3D solid to extrude, a new 3D solid object is created.

If a selected polyline has width, the width is ignored and the polyline is extruded from the center of the polyline path. If a selected object has thickness, the thickness is ignored.

The DELOBJ system variable controls whether the object(s) and path (if selected) are automatically deleted when the solid or surface is created or whether you are prompted to delete the object(s) and path.

You can extrude the following objects and subobjects:

## Objects That Can Be Extruded or Used as Paths

| Object type | Can be extruded? | Can be extrusion path? | Comments |
|---|---|---|---|
| 3D faces | X | | |
| Arcs | X | X | |
| Blocks | | | |
| Circles | X | X | |
| Ellipses | X | X | |
| Elliptical arcs | X | X | |
| Helixes | | X | |
| Lines | X | X | |
| Mesh faces | X | | |
| Polylines: 2D | X | X | Cannot be extruded: polylines with crossing segments. Ignored: Thickness Ignored: Width (extends extrusion from centerline) |
| Polylines: 3D | | X | |
| Regions | X | | |
| Solids: 2D | X | | |
| Solids: edges | | X | |
| Solids: planar faces | X | | |
| Splines: 2D | X | X | |
| Splines: 3D | | X | |
| Surfaces: edges | | X | |
| Surfaces: planar | X | | |
| Traces | X | | |

## List of Prompts

The following prompts are displayed

## Objects to Extrude

Specifies the objects to extrude

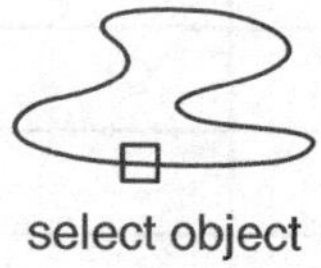


**Note:** You can select faces on solids and meshes by pressing and holding Ctrl, and then selecting the subobjects.

- Height of extrusion
- Direction
- Path
- Taper angle

## Height of extrusion

Extrudes objects along the positive Z axis of the object's coordinate system if you enter a positive value. If you enter a negative value, the objects are extruded along the negative Z axis. Objects do not have to be parallel to the same plane. If all the objects are on a common plane, the objects are extruded in the direction of the normal of the plane.

By default, planar objects are extruded in the direction of the object's normal.

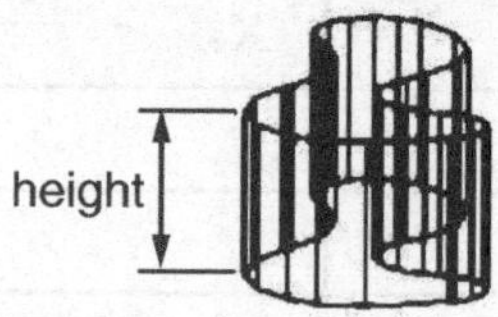


## Direction

Specifies the length and direction of the extrusion with two points you specify. (The direction cannot be parallel to the plane of the sweep curve created by the extrusion.)

- **Start point of direction.** Specifies the first point in the direction vector.
- **End point of direction.** Specifies the second point in the direction vector.

## Path

Specifies the extrusion path based on an object that you select. The path is moved to the centroid of the profile. Then the profile of the selected object is extruded along the chosen path to create solids or surfaces.

**Note:** Press Ctrl+click to select faces and edges on 3D objects.

The path should not lie on the same plane as the object, nor should the path have areas of high curvature.

The extrusion starts from the plane of the object and maintains its orientation relative to the path.

If the path contains segments that are not tangent, the program extrudes the object along each segment and then miters the joint along the plane bisecting the angle formed by the segments. If the path is closed, the object should lie on the miter plane. This allows the start and end sections of the solid to match up. If the object is not on the miter plane, the object is rotated until it is on the miter plane.

Objects with multiple loops are extruded so that all the loops appear on the same plane at the end section of the extruded solid.

## Taper angle

Sets an angle of taper for an extrusion

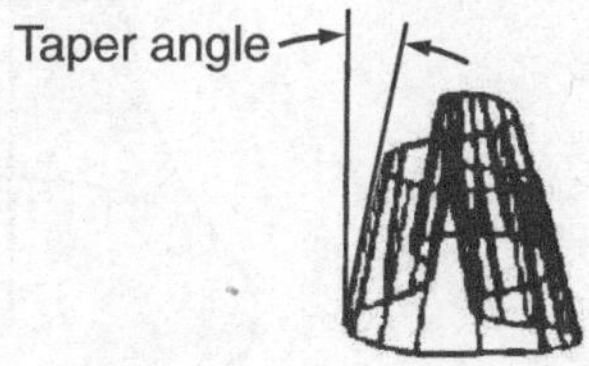


Positive angles taper in from the base object. Negative angles taper out. The default angle, 0, extrudes a 2D object perpendicular to its 2D plane. All selected objects and loops are tapered to the same value.

Specifying a large taper angle or a long extrusion height can cause the object or portions of the object to taper to a point before reaching the extrusion height.

Individual loops of a region are always extruded to the same height.

When an arc is part of a tapered extrusion, the angle of the arc remains constant, and the radius of the arc changes.

- **Angle of taper.** Sets an angle between -90 and +90 degrees.
- **Specify two points.** Sets the taper angle based on two points you specify in the drawing area. The taper angle applied to the extrusion is the distance between the two specified points.

## 3. REVOLVE

Creates a 3D solid or surface by sweeping a 2D object around an axis.

**Access Methods**

**Button**

- **Ribbon:** Home tab ➤ Modeling panel ➤ Revolve
- **Menu:** Draw ➤ Modeling ➤ Revolve
- **Toolbar:** Modeling
- **Command entry: revolve**

## Summary

*You can revolve closed objects to create 3D solids and open objects to create surfaces.* Objects can be revolved 360 degrees or another specified angle.

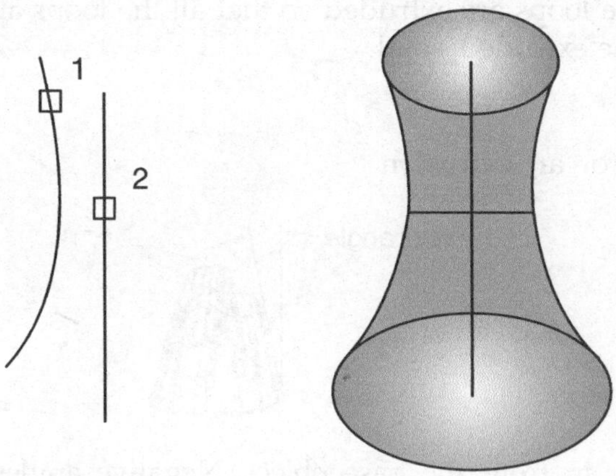


With the REVOLVE command, you can create a new solid or surface by revolving an open or closed planar curve about an axis. You can revolve more than one object.

The DELOBJ system variable controls whether revolved objects are automatically deleted when the solid or surface is created or whether you are prompted to delete the objects.

You can select the objects to revolve before you start the command.

You can revolve the following objects:

## Objects that Can Be Revolved

| Object types |
|---|
| 2D solids |
| 3D faces - planar |
| Arcs |
| Circles |
| Ellipses |
| Elliptical arcs |
| Lines |
| Polylines - 2D |
| Regions |
| Solids - planar faces |
| Splines - 2D |
| Surfaces - planar faces |
| Traces |

You cannot revolve objects contained within a block. Polylines that have crossing or self-intersecting segments cannot be revolved. REVOLVE ignores the width of a polyline and revolves from the center of the path of the polyline.

The right-hand rule determines the positive direction of rotation. See Control the User Coordinate System in 3Din the *User's Guide.*

## List of Prompts

## Object to Revolve

Specifies the objects to be revolved about an axis

## Axis Start Point

Specifies the first and second points of the axis of revolution. The positive axis direction is from the first to the second point.

**Axis endpoint.** Sets the endpoint for the axis of revolution

- Start angle
- Angle of revolution

### Start angle

Specifies an offset for the revolution from the plane of the object being revolved.

- Angle of revolution

### Angle of revolution

Specifies how far the selected object revolves about the axis.

A positive angle revolves the objects in a counterclockwise direction. A negative angle revolves the objects in a clockwise direction.

The objects are revolved to the specified angle.

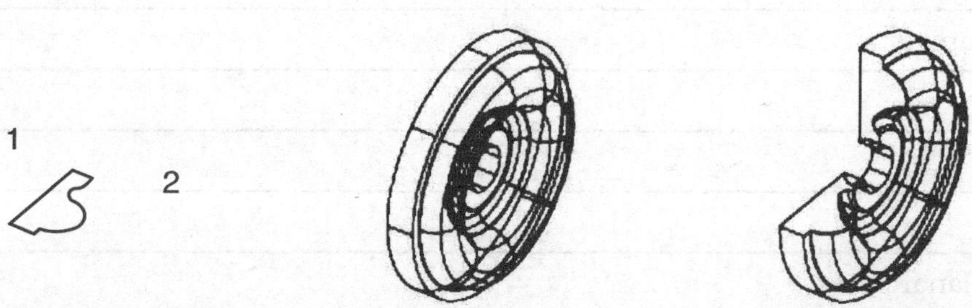


selected axis points full circle specified angle

### Object

Specifies an existing object to be used as an axis. The positive axis direction is from the closest to the farthest endpoint of this object.

selected axis full circle specified angle

You can use lines, linear polyline segments, and linear edges of solids or surfaces as an axis:

**Note:** You can select an edge on a solid by pressing and holding CTRL, and then selecting an edge.

- Start angle
- Angle of revolution

### X (Axis)

Sets the positive X axis of the current UCS as the positive axis direction

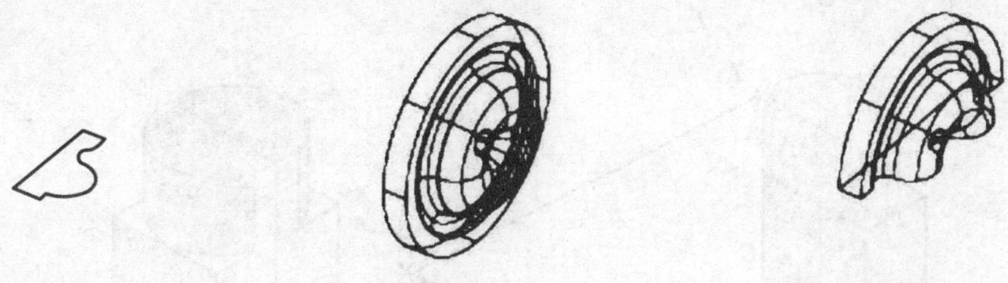

X axis full circle specified angle

- Start angle
- Angle of revolution

**Y (Axis)**

Sets the positive *Y* axis of the current UCS as the positive axis direction

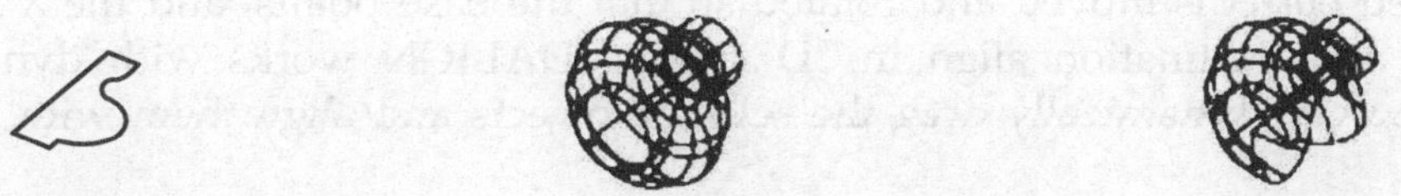

Y axis full circle specified angle

- Start angle
- Angle of revolution

## Z (Axis)

Sets the positive *Z* axis of the current UCS as the positive axis direction

- Start angle
- Angle of revolution

## 4. 3 DALIGN

Aligns objects with other objects in 2D and 3D.

**Access Methods**

**Button**

**Ribbon:** Home tab ➤ Modify panel ➤ 3D Align

**Menu:** Modify ➤ 3D Operations ➤ 3D Align

**Toolbar:** Modeling

**Command entry: 3dalign**

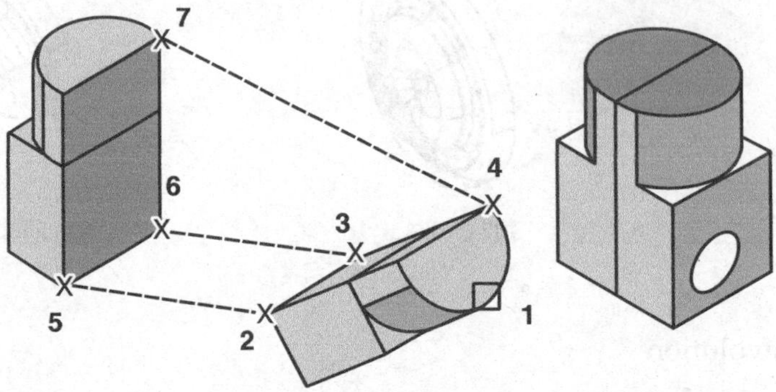


Select objects: *Select the objects to align and press* Enter

Specify source plane and orientation . . .

The selected object is moved and rotated so that the base points, and the *X* and *Y* axes of the source and destination align in 3D space. 3DALIGN works with dynamic UCS (DUCS), so you can dynamically drag the selected objects and align them with the face of a solid object.

Specify base point or [Copy]: *Specify a point or enter* **c** *to create a copy*

The base point of the source object will be moved to the base point of the destination.

Specify second point or [Continue] <C>: *Specify a point on the object's X axis, or press Enter to skip forward to specifying destination points*

The second point specifies a new *X* axis direction within a plane parallel to the *XY* plane of the current UCS. If you press Enter instead of specifying a second point, the *X* and *Y* axes are assumed to be parallel with the *X* and *Y* axes of the current UCS.

Specify third point or [Continue] <C>: *Specify a point on the object's positive XY plane, or press Enter to skip forward to specifying destination points*

The third point fully specifies the orientation of the *X* and *Y* axes of the source object that will be aligned with the destination plane.

Specify destination plane and orientation . . .

Specify first destination point: *Specify a point*

This point defines the destination of the base point of the source object.

Specify second source point or [eXit] <X>: *Specify a point for the X axis of the destination or press* Enter

The second point specifies a new *X* axis direction for the destination within a plane parallel to the *XY* plane of the current UCS. If you press Enter instead of specifying a second point, the *X* and *Y* axes of the destination are assumed to be parallel with the*X* and *Y* axes of the current UCS.

Specify third destination point or [eXit] <X>: *Specify a point for the destination's positive XY plane, or press* Enter

The third point fully specifies the orientation of the *X* and *Y* axes of the destination plane.

**Note:** If the destination is a plane on an existing solid object, you can define the destination plane with a single point by turning on dynamic UCS.

## 5. 3DARRAY

Creates a 3D matrix of objects in a rectangular or polar arrangement

**Access Methods**

**Button**

**Ribbon:** Home tab ➤ Modify panel ➤ 3D Array.

**Menu:** Modify ➤ 3D Operations ➤ 3D Array

**Toolbar:** Modeling

**Command entry: 3darray**

## Summary

For 3D rectangular arrays, in addition to columns and rows, you also specify the number of levels in the Z direction. For 3D polar arrays, you specify the axis of rotation with any two points in space.

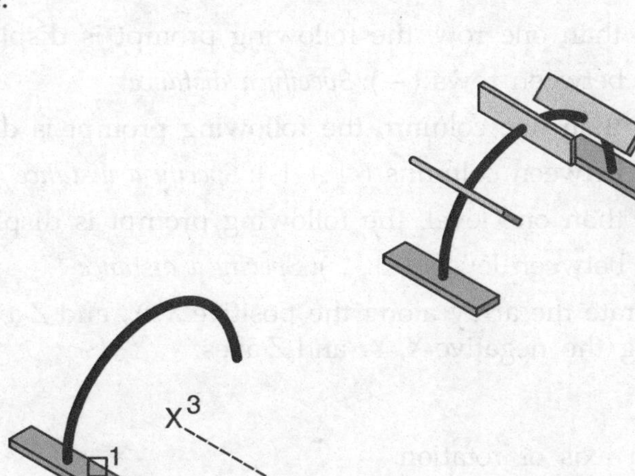


Select objects: *Use an object selection method*

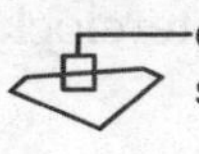

The entire selection set is treated as a single element in the array.

Enter type of array [ Rectangular/ Polar] <R>: *Enter an option or press Enter*

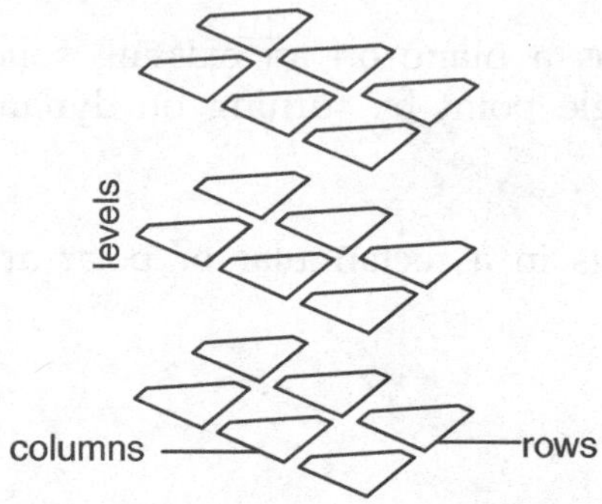


## Rectangular Array

Copies objects in a matrix of rows (*X* axis), columns (*Y* axis), and levels (*Z* axis). An array must have at least two rows or two columns or two levels.

Enter the number of rows (—) <1>: *Enter a positive value or press* Enter

Enter the number of columns ( | | | ) <1>: *Enter a positive value or press* Enter

Enter the number of levels ( . . . ) <1>: *Enter a positive value or press* Enter

Specifying one row requires that more than one column be specified, and vice versa. Specifying one level creates a two-dimensional array.

If you specify more than one row, the following prompt is displayed:

Specify the distance between rows (—): *Specify a distance*

If you specify more than one column, the following prompt is displayed:

Specify the distance between columns ( | | | ): *Specify a distance*

If you specify more than one level, the following prompt is displayed:

Specify the distance between levels ( . . . ): *Specify a distance*

Positive values generate the array along the positive *X*, *Y*, and *Z* axes. Negative values generate the array along the negative *X*, *Y*, and *Z* axes.

## Polar Array

Copies objects about an axis of rotation.

Enter the number of items in the array: *Enter a positive value*

Specify the angle to fill (+=ccw, –=cw) <360>: *Specify an angle or press* Enter

The specified angle determines how far the objects are arrayed about the axis of rotation. A positive number produces a counterclockwise array rotation. A negative number produces a clockwise array rotation.

Rotate arrayed objects? [Yes/No] <Y>: *Enter* **y** *or* **n**, *or press* Enter

Entering **y** or pressing Enter rotates each array element.

Specify center point of array: *Specify a point (1)*

Specify second point on axis of rotation: *Specify a point (2)*

## 6. 3DCORBIT

Rotates the view in 3D space with continuous motion

**Access Methods**

**Button**

**Ribbon:** View tab ➤ Navigate panel ➤ Continuous Orbit.

**Menu:** View ➤ Orbit ➤ Continuous Orbit

**Toolbar:** 3D Navigation

**Shortcut menu:** Start any 3D navigation command, right-click in the drawing area, and click Other Navigation Modes ➤ Continuous Orbit (3).

**Command entry: 3dcorbit**

Click in a drawing area and drag the pointing device in any direction to start the objects moving in the direction that you're dragging. Release the button on the pointing device and the objects continue their orbit in the direction that you specified. The speed set for the cursor movement determines the speed at which the objects spin.

You can change the direction of the continuous orbit by clicking and dragging again. You can also change the display of the continuous orbit by right-clicking in the drawing area and choosing an option from the shortcut menu. For example, you can choose Visual Aids ➤ Grid to add a grid to the view without exiting Continuous Orbit.

## 7. 3DMOVE

In a 3D view, displays the 3D Move gizmo to aid in moving 3D objects a specified distance in a specified direction.

**Access Methods**

**Button**

**Ribbon:** Home tab ➤ Modify panel ➤ 3D Move

**Menu:** Modify ➤ 3D Operations ➤ 3D Move

**Toolbar:** Modeling

**Command entry: 3dmove**

## Summary

With the 3D Move gizmo, you can move selected objects and subobjects freely or constrain the movement to an axis or plane.

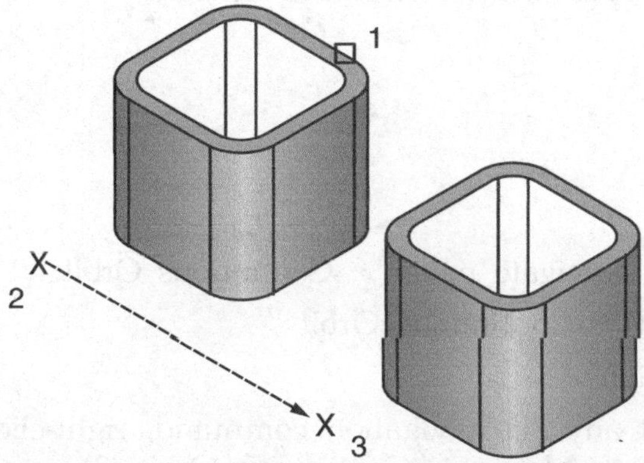


If the default gizmo ( DEFAULTGIZMO) is 3D Move, the 3D Move gizmo is displayed whenever you select an object in a view with a 3D visual style. If you are working in a viewport with 2D Wireframe set as the visual style, 3DMOVE temporarily changes the visual style to 3D Wireframe for the duration of the command.

The 3D Move gizmo is displayed at the center of the selected 3D object or objects by default. You can use the shortcut menu to change its location.

You can also align the 3D Move gizmo with the plane of a face or object by using the Align Gizmo With ➤ Face option on the shortcut menu. The direction of the move operation is then constrained relative to this workplane.

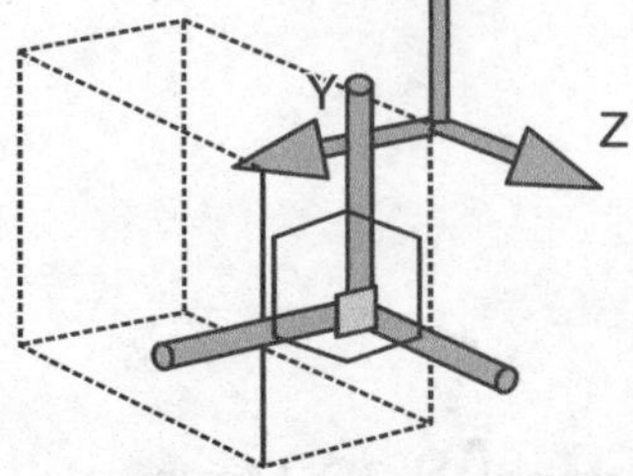


When the 3D Move gizmo is displayed, the 3D Move Gizmo shortcut menu offers options for aligning, moving, or changing to another gizmo.

## List of Prompts

The following prompts are displayed.

## Select objects

Selects the 3D objects you want to move. When you have selected the objects, press Enter.

When you have selected an object, the gizmo is displayed. You can constrain the movement by clicking one of the following locations on the gizmo:

- **Move along an axis.** Click an axis to constrain the movement to that axis.

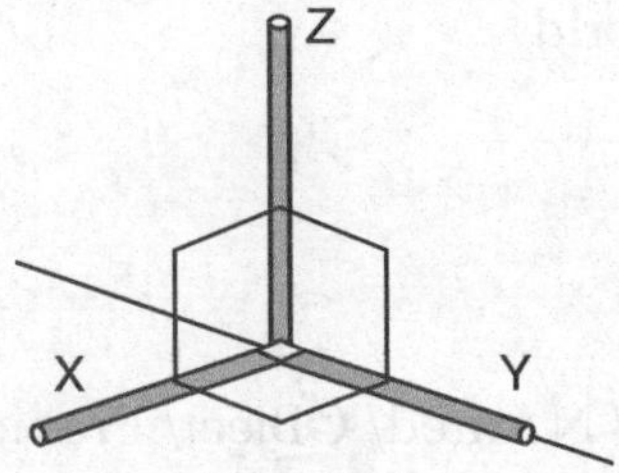


- **Move along a plane.** Click the area between the axes to constrain the movement to that plane.

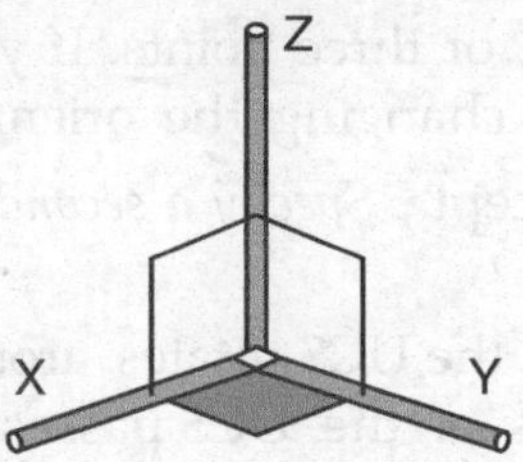


## Stretch point

When you are specifying the move using the gizmo, sets the new location of the selected objects. Drag and click to move the objects dynamically.

## Copy

When you are specifying the move using the gizmo, creates a copy of the selected objects instead of moving them. You can make multiple copies by continuing to specify locations.

## Base point

Specifies the base point of the 3D objects you want to move.

- **Second point.** Specifies where the 3D object or objects will be dragged. You can also move the cursor to indicate a direction and then enter a distance.

## Displacement

Specifies a relative distance and direction for the placement of the selected 3D objects using coordinate values that you enter at the command prompt.

## UCS

Manages user coordinate systems

**Access Methods**

**Button**

**Ribbon:** View tab ▸ Coordinates panel ▸ World

**Menu:** Tools ▸ New UCS ▸ World

**Toolbar:** UCS 

## Command entry: ucs

Specify Origin of UCS or [ Face/ NAmed/ OBject/ Previous/ View/ World/ X/Y/Z/ ZAxis] <World>:

## Specify Origin of UCS

Defines a new UCS using one, two, or three points. If you specify a single point, the origin of the current UCS shifts without changing the orientation of the X, Y, and Z axes.

Specify point on X-axis or <Accept>: *Specify a second point or press Enter to limit input to a single point*

If you specify a second point, the UCS rotates around the previously specified origin point such that the positive X axis of the UCS passes through the point.

Specify point on XY plane or <Accept>: *Specify a third point or press Enter to limit input to two points*

If you specify a third point, the UCS rotates around the X axis such that the positive *Y* half of the *XY* plane of the UCS contains the point.

The three points specify an origin point, a point on the positive X axis, and a point on the positive *XY* plane.

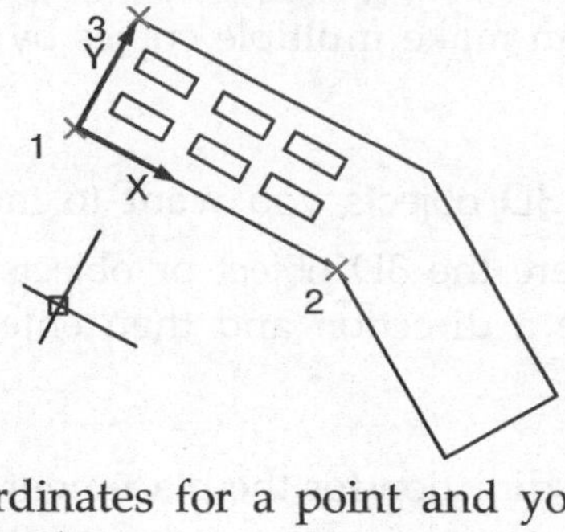


**Note:** If you enter the coordinates for a point and you do not specify a Z coordinate value, the current Z value is used.

## Face

Aligns the user coordinate system to a face on a 3D solid.

Select a face by clicking within the boundary or on an edge of the face. The UCS X axis is aligned with the closest edge of the original face selected.

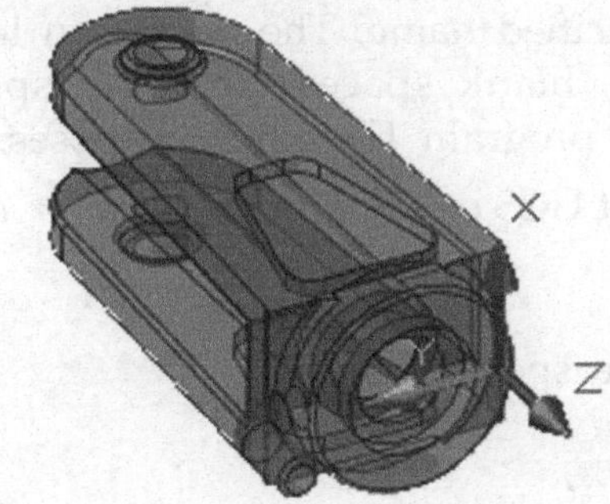


Select face of solid object:

Enter an option [Next/Xflip/Yflip] <accept>:

## Next

Locates the UCS on either the adjacent face or the back face of the selected edge

## Xflip

Rotates the UCS 180 degrees around the *X* axis

## Yflip

Rotates the UCS 180 degrees around the *Y* axis

## Accept

If you press Enter, accepts the location. The prompt repeats until you accept a location.

## Named

Save and restore commonly used UCS orientations by name.

Enter an option [Restore/Save/Delete/?]: *Specify an option*

## Restore

Restores a saved UCS so that it becomes the current UCS

Enter name of UCS to restore or [?]: *Enter a name or enter* **?**

## Name

Specifies a named UCS

## ?—List UCSs

Lists the names of currently defined UCSs.

Enter UCS name(s) to list <*>: *Enter a name list or press* Enter *to list all UCSs*

## Save

Saves the current UCS to a specified name. The name can have up to 255 characters and can include letters, numbers, blank spaces, and any special character not used by Microsoft® Windows® and this program for other purposes.

Enter name to save current UCS or [?]: *Enter a name or enter* ?

## Name

Saves the current UCS with the specified name.

## ?—List UCSs

Lists the names of currently defined UCSs

UCS name(s) to list <*>: *Enter a name list or press* Enter *to list all UCSs*

## Delete

Removes the specified UCS from the list of saved user coordinate systems.

Enter UCS name(s) to delete <none>: *Enter a name list or press* Enter

If you delete a named UCS that is current, the current UCS is renamed UNNAMED.

## ?—List UCSs

Lists names of user coordinate systems and provides the origin and *X*, *Y*, and *Z* axes for each saved UCS relative to the currentUCS. If the current UCS is unnamed, it is listed as WORLD or UNNAMED, depending on whether it's the same as the WCS.

UCS name(s) to list <*>: *Enter a name list*

## Object

Aligns the user coordinate system to a selected object.

The positive Z axis of the UCS is aligned perpendicular to the plane in which the object was originally created.

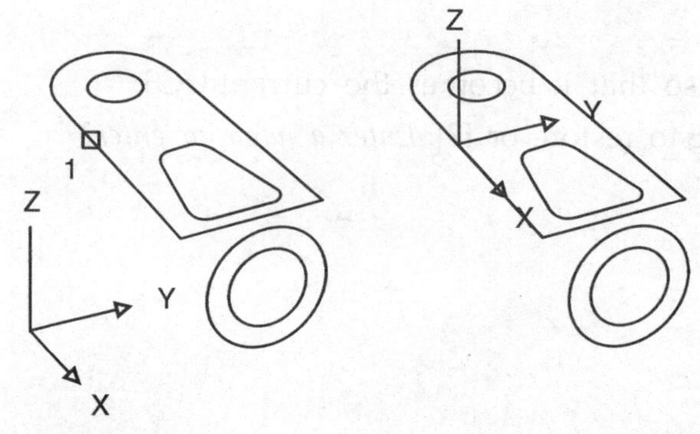

Select object to align UCS: *Select an object*

The following objects cannot be used with this option: 3D polylines, 3D meshes, and xlines.

For most objects, the origin of the new UCS is located at the nearest vertex to where you select the object, and the X axis is aligned with an edge or is tangent to an edge. For planar objects, the XY plane of the UCS is aligned with the plane in which the object is located. For complex objects, the origin is relocated, but the current orientation of the axes is maintained.

The new UCS is defined as shown in the following table.

| **Define a UCS by selecting an object** | |
|---|---|
| **Object** | **Method of determining UCS** |
| Arc | The center of the arc becomes the new UCS origin. The *X* axis passes through the arc endpoint that is closest to the selection point. |
| Circle | The center of the circle becomes the new UCS origin. The *X* axis passes through the selection point. |
| Dimension | The midpoint of the dimension text becomes the new UCS origin. The direction of the new Xaxis is parallel to the *X* axis of the UCS in effect when the dimension was drawn. |
| Line | The endpoint nearest the selection point becomes the new UCS origin. The new *X* axis is set so that the line lies in the *XZ* plane of the new UCS. The line's second endpoint has a *Y*coordinate of zero in the new UCS. |
| Point | The point becomes the new UCS origin. |
| 2D polyline | The start point of the polyline is the new UCS origin. The *X* axis extends along the line segment from the start point to the next vertex. |
| Solid | The first point of the solid determines the new UCS origin. The new *X* axis lies along the line between the first two points. |
| Trace | The "from" point of the trace becomes the UCS origin, with the *X* axis lying along its centerline. |
| 3D face | The new UCS origin is taken from the first point, the *X* axis from the first two points, and the*Y* positive side from the first and fourth points. The *Z* axis follows by application of the right-hand rule. |
| Shape, text, block reference, attribute definition | The insertion point of the object becomes the new UCS origin, and the new *X* axis is defined by the rotation of the object about its extrusion attribute definitiondirection. The object you select to establish a new UCS has a rotation angle of zero in the new UCS. |

### Previous

Restores the previous UCS

The last 10 user coordinate systems created in model space and the last 10 created in paper space layouts are retained. Repeating this option steps back through one set or the other, depending on which space is current.

If you have saved different UCS settings in individual viewports and you switch between viewports, the different UCSs are not retained in the Previous list. However, if you change a UCS setting within a viewport, the last UCS setting is retained in the Previous list. For example, changing the UCS from World to UCS1 would retain World at the top of the Previous list. If you then switch viewports with Front as the current UCS, and then change the UCS to Right, the Front UCS is retained at the top of the Previous list. If you then choose the UCS Previous option twice in this viewport, the UCS setting changes to Front, and then back to World. See the UCSVP system variable.

### View

Aligns the *XY* plane of the user coordinate system to a plane perpendicular to your viewing direction. The origin point remains unchanged, but the *X* and *Y* axes become horizontal and vertical.

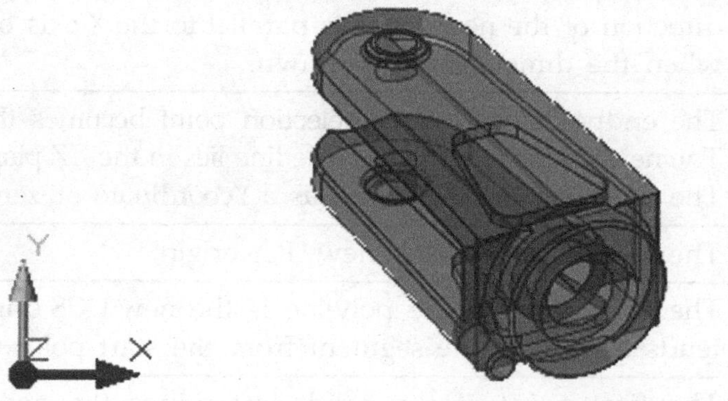


### World

Sets the current user coordinate system to the world coordinate system (WCS).

The WCS is the basis for all user coordinate systems and cannot be redefined.

### X, Y, Z

Rotates the current UCS about a specified axis.

Specify rotation angle about *n* axis <0>: *Specify an angle*

In the prompt, *n* is *X*, *Y*, or *Z*. Enter a positive or negative angle to rotate the UCS.

Point your right thumb in the positive direction of the axis and curl your fingers. Your fingers indicate the positive rotation direction about the axis.

Point your right thumb in the positive direction of the *X* axis and curl your fingers. Your fingers indicate the positive rotation direction about the axis.

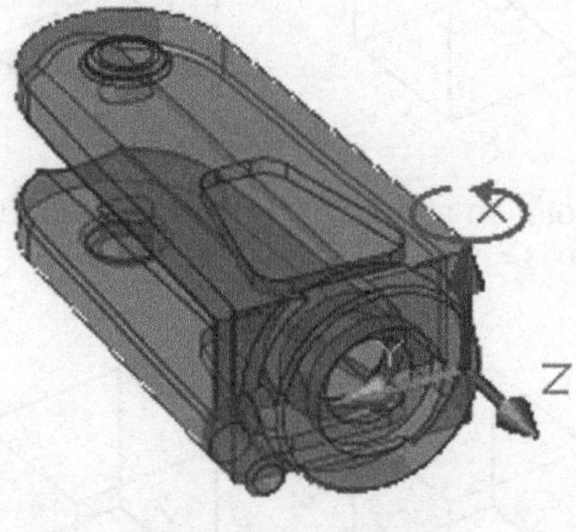


Point your right thumb in the positive direction of the *Y* axis and curl your fingers. Your fingers indicate the positive rotation direction about the axis.

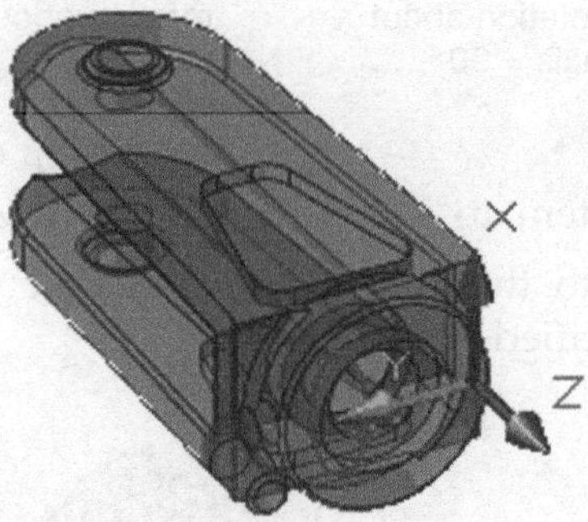


Point your right thumb in the positive direction of the *Z* axis and curl your fingers. Your fingers indicate the positive rotation direction about the axis.

You can define any UCS by specifying an origin and one or more rotations around the *X*, *Y*, or *Z* axis.

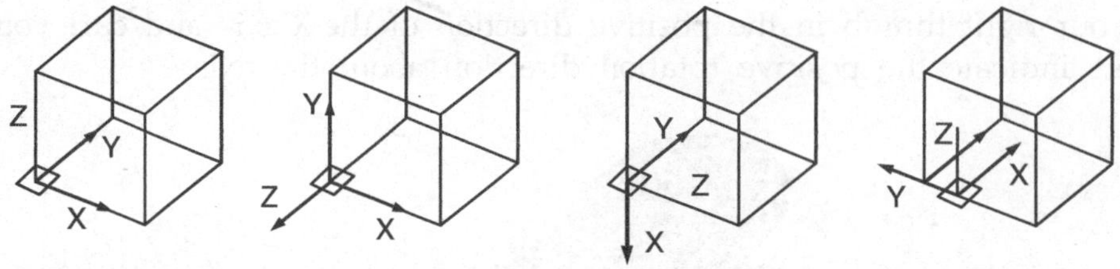


world coordinate system | rotation about X axis = 90 | rotation about Y axis = 90 | rotation about Z axis = 90

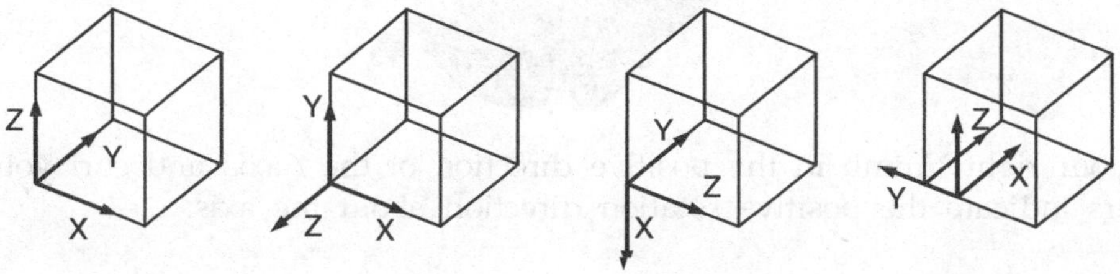


world coordinate system | rotation about X axis = 90 | rotation about Y axis = 90 | rotation about Z axis = 90

## Z Axis

Aligns the user coordinate system to a specified positive Z axis

The UCS origin is moved to the first point specified and its positive Z axis passes through the second point specified.

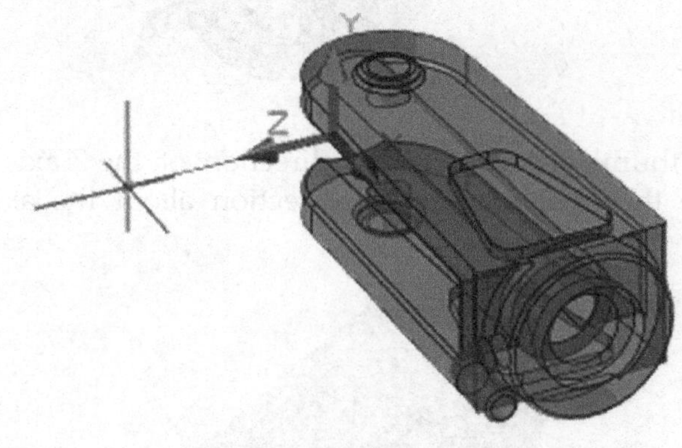


Specify new origin point or [Object] <0,0,0>: *Specify a point or enter* **o**

Specify point on positive portion of Z-axis <*current*>: *Specify a point*

## Object

Aligns the Z axis in the direction tangent to the endpoint nearest to where the object was selected. The positive Z axis points away from the object.

Select object: *Select an open-ended object*

## Apply

Applies the current UCS setting to a specified viewport or all active viewports when other viewports have a different UCS saved in the viewport. The UCSVP system variable determines whether a UCS is saved with a viewport.

Pick viewport to apply current UCS or [All] *<current>: Specify a viewport by clicking inside it, enter* **a**, *or press* Enter

## Viewport

Applies the current UCS to the specified viewport and ends the UCS command.

## All

Applies the current UCS to all active viewports

## To define a new UCS origin in 3D

1. Click View tab ➤ UCS panel ➤ Origin. 
2. Specify a point for the new origin.
   The UCS origin (0,0,0) is redefined at the point you specify.

## To define a new UCS with a specified Z axis

1. Click View tab ➤ UCS panel ➤ Z. 
2. Specify a point for the new origin.
   The UCS origin (0,0,0) is redefined at the point you specify.
3. Specify a point that lies on the positive *Z* axis.

## To define a new UCS with particular *X* and *Y* axes

1. Click View tab ➤ UCS panel ➤ 3 Point. 
2. Specify a point for the new origin.
   The UCS origin (0,0,0) is redefined at the point you specify.
3. Specify a point that lies on the positive *X* axis.
4. Specify a point that lies on the positive *Y* axis.

## To shift the *XY* plane

1. Click View tab ➤ UCS panel ➤ 3 Point. 
2. Specify an origin point for the new UCS (1).
   For example, in a large drawing, you might specify an origin point near the area in which you want to work.

3. Specify a point to indicate the horizontal orientation of the new UCS (2). This point should be on the positive portion of the new *X* axis.
4. Specify a point to indicate the vertical orientation of the new UCS (3). This point should be on the positive portion of the new *Y* axis.

   The UCS, including grid, shifts to represent the *X* and *Y* axes you have specified.

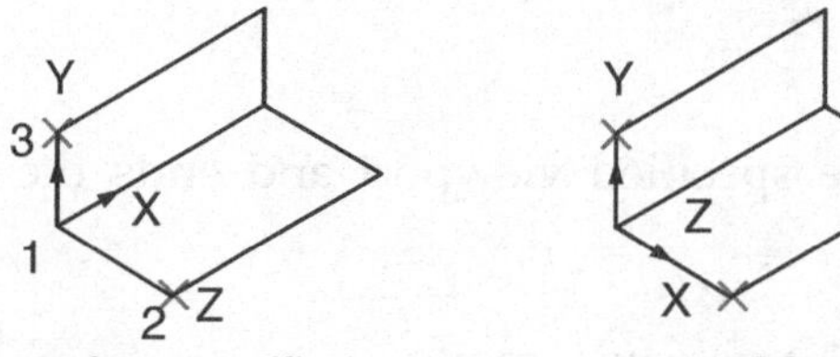

points specified    new UCS

## To select a UCS preset

1. Click View tab ➤ UCS panel ➤ Named UCS. 
2. In the UCS dialog box, Orthographic UCSs tab, select a UCS orientation from the list.
3. Click Set Current.
4. Click OK.

   The UCS changes to the selected option.

## To restore the location and orientation of the previous UCS

- Click View tab ➤ UCS panel ➤ Previous. 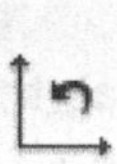

  The previous UCS is restored.

CHAPTER

12

# Page Setup & Plot Manager

## OVERVIEW OF PAGE SETUP SETTINGS

A page setup is a collection of plot device and other settings that affect the appearance and format of your final output. These settings can be modified and applied to other layouts.

After you complete a drawing on the Model tab, you can begin creating a layout to plot by clicking a layout tab. When you click a layout tab for the first time, a single viewport is displayed on the page. A dashed line indicates the printable area of the paper for the currently configured paper size and plotter.

Once you have your layout set up, you specify the settings for the layout's page setup, which includes the plot device settings and other settings that affect the appearance and format of the output. The settings you specify in the page setup are stored in the drawing file with the layout. You can modify the settings of a page setup at any time.

By default, every initialized layout has a page setup associated with it. You can initialize a layout by clicking on its tab to activate the previously unused layout. A layout does not contain any plot settings before initialization. A layout must be initialized (its paper size can be defined in the page setup to any size other than 0 x 0) before it can be published. Once initialized, layouts can be drawn upon, published, and added to sheet sets as sheets (after the drawing has been saved). You can apply a named page setup saved with one layout to another layout. This creates a new page setup with the same settings as the first one.

If you want the Page Setup Manager to be displayed each time you begin a new drawing layout, select the Show Page Setup Manager for New Layouts option on the Display tab in the Options dialog box. If you don't want a viewport to be automatically created for each new layout, clear the Create Viewport in New Layouts option on the Display tab in the Options dialog box.

### To modify the settings of a layout's page setup

1. Click the layout tab for which you want to modify the page setup settings.
2. Click Output tab ➤ Plot panel ➤ Page Setup Manager. 
3. In the Page Setup Manager, Page Setups area, select the page setup that you want to modify.
4. Click Modify.
5. In the Page Setup dialog box, modify the required settings. Click OK.
6. In the Page Setup Manager, click Close.

### To apply a layout's named page setup to another layout

1. Click the layout tab to which you want to apply another layout's page setup settings.
2. Click Output tab ➤ Plot panel ➤ Page Setup Manager. 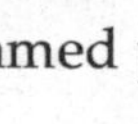
3. In the Page Setup Manager, Page Setups area, select a named page setup that you want to apply to the layout selected in the drawing area.

4. Click Set Current.
5. Click Close.

Select a Printer or Plotter for a Layout

When you create a layout, you must select a printing or plotting device in the Page Setup dialog box in order for the layout to be printed or plotted. Once you've selected a device, you can view details about the name and location of the device, and you can change the device's configuration.

The printer or plotter you select in the Page Setup dialog box determines the printable area of the layout. This printable area is indicated by the dashed line in the layout. If you change the paper size or the printing or plotting device, it may change the printable area of your drawing page.

## To select a printer or plotter for a layout

1. Click the layout tab for which you want to specify a printer or plotter.
2. Click Output tab ➤ Plot panel ➤ Page Setup Manager. 
3. In the Page Setup Manager, Page Setups area, select the page setup that you want to modify.
4. Click Modify.
5. In the Page Setup dialog box, under Printer/Plotter, select a printer or plotter from the list. Click OK.
6. In the Page Setup Manager, click Close.

## To change the configuration of a printer or plotter specified in a page setup

1. Click the layout tab for which you want to specify a printer or plotter.
2. Click Output tab ➤ Plot panel ➤ Page Setup Manager. 
3. In the Page Setup Manager, Page Setups area, select the page setup that you want to modify.
4. Click Modify.
5. In the Page Setup dialog box, under Printer/Plotter, click Properties.
6. In the Plotter Configuration Editor, change the required settings. Click OK.
7. In the Page Setup dialog box, click OK.
8. In the Page Setup Manager, click Close.

Select a Paper Size for a Layout

You can select a paper size from a standard list, or you can add custom paper sizes using the Plotter Configuration Editor.

You can select a paper size from a standard list. The paper sizes available in the list are determined by the plot device that is currently selected for the layout. If your plotter is configured for raster output, you must specify the output size in pixels. You can add custom paper sizes, which are stored in the plotter configuration (PC3) file, using the Plotter Configuration Editor.

If you are using a system printer, the paper size is determined by the document defaults that are set in the Windows Control Panel. The default paper size is displayed in the Page Setup dialog box when you create a new layout for that configured device. If you change the paper size in the Page Setup dialog box, the new paper size is saved with the layout and overrides the size saved in the plotter configuration (PC3) file.

### To set the paper size for a layout

1. Click the layout tab for which you want to set the paper size.
2. Click Output tab ➤ Plot panel ➤ Page Setup Manager. 
3. In the Page Setup Manager, Page Setups area, select the page setup that you want to modify.
4. Click Modify.
5. In the Page Setup dialog box, under Paper Size, select a paper size from the list. Click OK.
6. In the Page Setup Manager, click Close.

### To start the Plotter Configuration Editor

1. Click Output tab ➤ Plot panel ➤ Plotter Manager. 
2. In the Plotter Manager, double-click the plotter configuration (PC3) file you want to edit.

   The Plotter Configuration Editor is displayed.

### To add a custom paper size from scratch

1. Click Output tab ➤ Plot panel ➤ Plotter Manager. 
2. In the Plotter Manager, double-click the plotter configuration (PC3) file you want to edit.
3. In the Plotter Configuration Editor, Device and Document Settings tab, double-click User-Defined Paper Sizes & Calibration to display the calibration and paper size options.
4. Select Custom Paper Sizes.

5. Under Custom Paper Sizes, click Add.
6. In the Custom Paper Size wizard, Begin page, select Start from Scratch. Click Next.
7. On the Media Bounds page, in the Units list, select either Inches or Millimeters for paper size.

   When a nondimensional raster image, such as BMP or TIFF, is plotted, the size of the plot is specified in pixels, not inches or millimeters.
8. In the Width and Length lists, specify the paper width and length. Click Next.
9. On the Printable Area page, use Top, Bottom, Left, and Right to specify the printable area. Click Next.
10. On the Paper Size Name page, enter a name for the paper size. Click Next.
11. On the File Name page, enter a name for the PMP file.
12. On the Finish page, specify whether the paper source is Sheet-Fed or Roll-Fed.
13. Click Print Test Page to verify the custom size.

    A cross is printed that defines the paper size and a rectangle that defines the printable area. If all four sides of the rectangle are not printed, increase the printable area.
14. Click Finish to exit the Custom Paper Size wizard.

## To add a new custom paper size starting from an existing paper size

1. Click Output tab ➤ Plot panel ➤ Plotter Manager. 
2. In the Plotter Manager, double-click the plotter configuration (PC3) file you want to edit.
3. In the Plotter Configuration Editor, Device and Document Settings tab, double-click User-Defined Paper Sizes & Calibration to display the calibration and paper size settings.
4. Select Custom Paper Sizes.
5. Under Custom Paper Sizes, click Add.
6. In the Custom Paper Size wizard, Begin page, select Use Existing.
7. In the list of existing standard paper sizes, select a paper size on which to base the custom paper size you are creating.
8. Follow the instructions in To add a custom paper size from scratch to continue through the Custom Paper Size wizard.

   The new paper size is a user-defined size, not a standard size.
9. Click Finish to exit the Custom Paper Size wizard.

## To edit a custom paper size

1. Click Output tab ➤ Plot panel ➤ Plotter Manager. 
2. In the Plotter Manager, double-click the plotter configuration (PC3) file you want to edit.
3. In the Plotter Configuration Editor, Device and Document Settings tab, double-click User-Defined Paper Sizes & Calibration to display the calibration and paper size settings.
4. Select Custom Paper Sizes.
5. Under Custom Paper Sizes, select a paper size from the list. Click Edit.
6. In the Custom Paper Size wizard, make changes to the paper size, printable area, custom paper size name, and source.
7. Click Finish to exit the Custom Paper Size wizard.

## To delete a custom paper size

1. Click Output tab ➤ Plot panel ➤ Plotter Manager. 
2. In the Plotter Manager, double-click the plotter configuration (PC3) file you want to edit.
3. In the Plotter Configuration Editor, Device and Document Settings tab, double-click User-Defined Paper Sizes & Calibration to display the calibration and paper size settings.
4. Click Custom Paper Sizes.
5. Under Custom Paper Sizes, select a paper size from the list.
6. Click Delete.

## To modify a standard paper size

1. Click Output tab ➤ Plot panel ➤ Plotter Manager. 
2. In the Plotter Manager, double-click the Plotter Configuration (PC3) file you want to edit.
3. In the Plotter Configuration Editor, Device and Document Settings tab, double-click User-Defined Paper Sizes & Calibration to display the calibration and paper size settings.
4. Select Modify Standard Paper Sizes.
5. Under Modify Standard Paper Sizes, select the paper size you want to adjust. Click Modify.

6. In the Custom Paper Size wizard, adjust the printable area as necessary. Click Finish to exit the Custom Paper Size wizard.

   Set the Plot Area of a Layout

   You can specify the plot area to determine what will be included in the plot.

When you prepare to plot from the Model tab or a layout tab, you can specify the plot area to determine what will be included in the plot. When you create a new layout, the default Plot Area option is Layout. Layout plots all objects within the printable area of the specified paper size.

The Display Plot Area option plots all the objects displayed in the drawing. The Extents Plot Area option plots all the visible objects in the drawing. The View Plot Area option plots a saved view. You can use the Window Plot Area option to define an area to be plotted.

### To set the plot area and adjust the display

1. Click the layout tab for which you want to set the plot area and adjust the display.
2. Click Output tab ➤ Plot panel ➤ Page Setup Manager. 
3. In the Page Setup Manager, Page Setups area, select the page setup that you want to modify.
4. Click Modify.
5. In the Page Setup dialog box, under Plot Area, select one of the following options:
   - **Layout.** Prints all objects within the printable area of the paper. This option is only available from a layout tab.
   - **Limits.** Prints or plots the current grid limits. This option is only available from the Model tab.
   - **Extents.** Plots all objects in the drawing.
   - **Display.** Plots all objects displayed in the drawing area.
   - **View.** Prints or plots a saved view. Select a named view from the list provided.
   - **Window.** Plots objects in the area you define. Select the Window option, and then respond to the prompts to define the area. Click the Window button to edit the defined area.
6. Click OK.
7. In the Page Setup Manager, click Close.

   Set the Plot Scale for a Layout

   When you plot a drawing layout, you can either specify a precise scale for the layout or fit the image to the paper.

Normally, you plot a layout at a 1:1 scale. To specify a different scale for the layout, set the plot scale for the layout in the Page Setup or the Plot dialog box. In those dialog boxes, you can select a scale from a list or enter a scale.

## To set the plot scale in a layout

1. Click the layout tab for which you want to set the plot scale.
2. Click Output tab ➤ Plot panel ➤ Page Setup Manager. 
3. In the Page Setup Manager, Page Setups area, select the page setup that you want to modify.
4. Click Modify.
5. In the Page Setup dialog box, under Plot Scale, select a scale from the Scale list.

   The default scale when plotting a layout is 1:1. To set a custom plot scale, enter values in the Inches or Millimeters box and the Units box. The type of unit is determined by the paper size, but you can change it in the list box.
6. Click OK.
7. In the Page Setup Manager, click Close.

## To set the Fit to Paper option when plotting

1. Click the layout tab for which you want to set the plot scale to Fit to Paper.
2. Click Output tab ➤ Plot panel ➤ Page Setup Manager. 
3. In the Page Setup Manager, Page Setups area, select the page setup that you want to modify.
4. Click Modify.
5. In the Page Setup dialog box, Under Plot Scale, select Fit to Paper.

   **Note:** If the Plot Area is set to Layout, you cannot select the Fit to Paper option.
6. Click OK.
7. In the Page Setup Manager, click Close.

   Determine the Drawing Orientation of a Layout

You can specify the orientation of the drawing on the paper using the Landscape and Portrait settings. Landscape orients the drawing on the paper so that the long edge of the paper is horizontal, and Portrait orients the paper so that the short edge is horizontal. Changing the orientation creates the effect of rotating the paper underneath the drawing.

In either landscape or portrait orientation, you can select Plot Upside-Down to control whether the top or bottom of the drawing is plotted first.

Although you can specify the drawing orientation in both the Page Setup dialog box and the Plot dialog box, the Page Setup settings are always saved and reflected in the layout. In the Plot dialog box, you can override the page setup settings for a single plot; however, the settings you apply are not saved in the layout. To save the settings you apply using the Plot dialog box, click the Apply to Layout button in the Plot dialog box.

If you change the drawing orientation, the layout origin remains in the lower-left corner of the rotated page.

### To set the orientation of the plotted drawing

1. Click the layout tab for which you want to set the drawing orientation.
2. Click Output tab ➤ Plot panel ➤ Page Setup Manager.
3. In the Page Setup Manager, Page Setups area, select the page setup that you want to modify.
4. Click Modify.
5. In the Page Setup dialog box, under Drawing Orientation, do one of the following:
   - If your drawing is horizontal, select Landscape.
   - If your drawing is vertical, select Portrait.
   - To rotate 180 degrees, select either Portrait or Landscape, and then select Plot Upside-Down.
6. Click OK.
7. In the Page Setup Manager, click Close.

## Preview a Plot

It is good practice to generate a preview of the plotted drawing before sending the drawing to the printer or plotter. Generating a preview saves time and material.

You can preview the drawing from the Plot dialog box. The preview shows exactly how the drawing will look when plotted, including lineweights, fill patterns, and other plot style options.

When you preview your drawing, the active toolbars and tool palettes are hidden and a temporary Preview toolbar is displayed that provides buttons to plot, pan, and zoom the drawing.

In the Plot and Page Setup dialog boxes, a thumbnail preview is also displayed, which shows the printable area and the position of the drawing on the page.

### To preview a plot

1. Click Output tab ➤ Plot panel ➤ Plot.
2. In the Plot dialog box, click Preview.

   A preview window opens, and the cursor changes to the real-time zoom cursor.
3. Right-click to display a shortcut menu with the following options: Plot, Pan, Zoom, Zoom Window, or Zoom Original (to zoom to the original preview magnification).
4. Press ESC to exit the preview and return to the Plot dialog box.

5. If necessary, make additional adjustments to the plot settings and preview the plotted drawing again.
6. Once the settings are correct, click OK to plot the drawing.

## Overview of Plotting

Understanding terms and concepts that relate to plotting makes your first plotting experience in the program easier.

### Plotter Manager

The Plotter Manager is a window that lists plotter configuration (PC3) files for every non-system printer that you install. Plotter configuration files can also be created for Windows® system printers if you want to use default properties different from those used by Windows. Plotter configuration settings specify port information, raster and vector graphics quality, paper sizes, and custom properties that depend on the plotter type.

The Plotter Manager contains the Add-a-Plotter wizard, which is the primary tool for creating plotter configurations. The Add-a-Plotter wizard prompts you for information about the plotter you want to set up.

### Layouts

A layout represents a plotted page. You can create as many layouts as you need. Each layout is saved on its own layout tab and can be associated with a different page setup.

Elements that appear only on a plotted page, such as title blocks and notes, are drawn in paper space in a layout. The objects in the drawing are created in model space on the Model tab. To view these objects in the layout, you create layout viewports.

### Layout Initialization

Layout initialization is a process in which a previously unused layout is made active, by clicking on its tab.

A layout does not contain any plot settings before initialization. Once initialized, layouts can be drawn upon, published, and added to sheet sets as sheets (after the drawing has been saved).

### Page Setups

When you create a layout, you specify a plotter and settings such as page size and plot orientation. These settings are saved in a page setup. You can control these settings for layouts and for the Model tab using the Page Setup Manager. You can name and save page setups for use with other layouts.

If you don't specify all the settings in the Page Setup dialog box when you create a layout, you can set up the page just before you plot. Or you can override a page setup at plot time. You can use the new page setup temporarily for the current plot, or you can save the new page setup.

## Plot Styles

A plot style controls how an object or layer is plotted by determining plotted properties such as lineweight, color, and fill style. Plot style tables collect groups of plot styles. The Plot Style Manager is a window that shows all the plot style tables available.

There are two plot style types: color-dependent and named. A drawing can use only one type of plot style table. You can convert a plot style table from one type to the other. You can also change the type of plot style table a drawing uses once it has been set.

For *color-dependent plot style tables*, an object's color determines how it is plotted. These plot style table files have *.ctb*extensions. You cannot assign color-dependent plot styles directly to objects. Instead, to control how an object is plotted, you change its color. For example, all objects assigned the color red in a drawing are plotted the same way.

*Named plot style tables* use plot styles that are assigned directly to objects and layers. These plot style table files have *.stb*extensions. Using them enables each object in a drawing to be plotted differently, independent of its color.

## Plot Stamps

A plot stamp is a line of text that is added to your plot. You can specify where this text is located on the plot in the Plot Stamp dialog box. Turn this option on to add specified plot stamp information—including drawing name, layout name, date and time, and so on—to a drawing that is plotted to any device. You can choose to record the plot stamp information to a log file instead of plotting it, or in addition to plotting it.

## To plot a drawing

1. Click Output tab ➤ Plot panel ➤ Plot.
2. In the Plot dialog box, under Printer/Plotter, select a plotter from the Name list.
3. Under Paper Size, select a paper size from the Paper Size box.
4. (Optional) Under Number of Copies, enter the number of copies to plot.
5. Under Plot Area, specify the portion of your drawing to plot.
6. Under Plot Scale, select a scale from the Scale box.
7. For more options, click the More Options button.
8. (Optional) Under Plot Style Table (Pen Assignments), select a plot style table from the Name box.
9. (Optional) Under Shaded Viewport Options and Plot Options, select any appropriate settings.

   **Note:** Plot stamping happens at plot time and is not saved with the drawing.
10. Under Drawing Orientation, select an orientation.
11. Click OK.

    To plot at the command prompt instead of in a dialog box, use -PLOT.

### To turn background plotting on or off

1. Click Tools menu ➤ Options.
2. In the Options dialog box, Plot and Publish tab, under Background Processing Options, select or clear the Enable Background Plot When Plotting option.
3. Click OK.

   **Note:** When you plot in the background, you can return immediately to your drawing. While a plot job is being processed in the background, you can check the status of your job by placing your cursor over the plotter icon in the status tray. You can also view details about all completed jobs from the current program session.

### To check the status of a plot job currently processing in the background

- In the status tray, place your mouse over the plotter icon. The tooltip displays the status of the plot job.

### To cancel part or all of a plot job that is processing in the background

- In the status tray, right-click the plotter icon. Click Cancel Sheet <*sheetname*> or Cancel Entire Job.

### To view details about jobs you have plotted

1. Do one of the following:
   - Click Output tab ➤ Plot panel ➤ View Details. 
   - In the status tray, click the plotter icon.
2. In the Plot and Publish Details dialog box, view details about plotted jobs.

## Create and Modify a Drawing Set for Publishing

You can assemble a collection of drawing sheets to publish to a plotter, plot files, DWF, DWFx, or PDF file. You can save the drawing set and modify it.

You can assemble a collection of drawing sheets to publish to a plotter, plot files, DWF, DWFx, or PDF file. You can customize your drawing set for a specific user, and you can add, remove, reorder, copy, and rename sheets in a drawing set as a project evolves.

You can publish the drawing set directly to paper and single or multiple DWF, DWFx, or PDF files. DWF, DWFx, and PDF files can be distributed using e-mail, FTP sites, project websites, or CD. You can save a description of a drawing set that has been assembled to publish in a Drawing Set Descriptions (DSD) file.

### To create a drawing set for publishing

1. Open a drawing. Click Output tab ➤ Publish panel ➤ Publish. 

   The Publish dialog box is displayed. If the Include Layouts When Adding Sheets option is selected, either in the shortcut menu or in the Publish dialog box, all the layouts in the current drawing are listed in the sheetlist.

2. In the Publish dialog box, you can modify the list of sheets by doing any of the following as needed:

 - **Add sheets.** To add sheets from other drawings, click the Add Sheets button (or drag drawings from the desktop). In the Select Drawings dialog box, select drawings. Click Select to add them to the list of sheets in the Publish dialog box. All of the layouts in a drawing become individual sheets in the list of drawing sheets. You can remove the individual sheets if you do not want them to become part of the drawing set. A layout must be initialized (its paper size must be defined in the page setup to any size other than 0 x 0) before it can be published.

**Note:** To include all layouts when you add sheets to a drawing set, ensure the Include Layouts When Adding Sheets option is selected either in the shortcut menu or in the Publish dialog box.

 - **Include model layouts.** If you include an uninitialized (the paper size is not defined in the page setup or is set to 0 x 0) model layout, it will be marked as Uninitialized in the Status column on the sheet list. It can be plotted if you select an override page setup for it in the Publish dialog box from the page setup drop-down list under Page Setups in the sheet list.

**Note:** To include the model when you add sheets to a drawing set, ensure the Include Model When Adding Sheets option is selected either in the shortcut menu or in the Publish dialog box.

 - **Remove sheets.** To remove sheets from the list, select one or more sheets in the list. Click the Remove Sheets button. To remove all sheets, right-click the selection. Click Remove All.
 - **Reorder sheets.** To reorder the sheets up or down one position in the list, select a sheet. Click either the Move Sheet Up or Move Sheet Down button. Sheets in the drawing set are viewed or plotted in the order shown in the list.
 - **Rename sheets.** To rename a sheet, select it in the list and right-click. Click Rename Sheet. Enter the new sheet name.
 - **Change page setups.** To change the page setup for a layout, select the sheet, and in the Page Setup list select a named page setup from the list; or select one or more sheets and right-click. Click Change Page Setup. In the Page Setup list, select a page setup, or select Import to import page setups from another drawing or template. In the Import Page Setups dialog box, select a drawing with one or more page setups. Click Import. In the Page Setup list, select a named page setup.

**Note:** Change the page setup for each layout depending on your desired output. Model space page setups can only be applied to model space sheets; paper space page setups can only be applied to paper space sheets.

 - **Copy sheets.** To copy one or more drawing sheets, select the sheets in the list and right-click. Click Copy Selected Sheets. The copied drawing sheets are added and highlighted at the end of the sheet list. When a sheet is copied, its name is created by the addition of *-Copy(n)* at the end of the original sheet name. For example, if you create one copy of a sheet called *Plumbing*, the copied sheet is called *Plumbing-Copy(1)*. Each time you copy the same sheet, the *n* is incremented by 1. By creating copies of a sheet, you can have different page setups and other settings for the same sheet.

3. When your list of drawing sheets is assembled and configured the way you want for your drawing set, click the Save List button.
4. In the Save List As dialog box, in the File Name box, enter a name for the list. Click Save.

   The drawing set list is saved as a DSD (Drawing Set Descriptions) file.

## To add sheets from a drawing to a drawing set for publishing

1. Click Output tab ➤ Publish panel ➤ Publish. 
2. In the Publish dialog box, click the Add Sheets button.
3. In the Select Drawings dialog box, select drawings. Click Select to add them to the list of sheets in the Publish dialog box.

   **Note:** You can also drag drawings from the desktop into the Publish dialog box to add sheets to the list.

   All of the layouts in a drawing become individual sheets in the list of drawing sheets. You must remove the drawing sheets that you don't want to become a part of the drawing set. Layouts must be initialized before they can be published. (A layout is initialized if its paper size is defined in the page setup to any size other than 0 x 0.)

## To add sheets from a DSD file to a drawing set for publishing

1. Click Output tab ➤ Publish panel ➤ Publish. 
2. In the Publish dialog box, click the Load Sheet List button.
3. In the Load List of Sheets dialog box, select a DSD file. Click Load.
4. In the Replace or Append dialog box, click Replace to replace the current sheets with the sheets in the DSD file, or click Append to add the sheets in the DSD file to the list of sheets in the Publish dialog box.

## To remove a sheet from a drawing set for publishing

1. Click Output tab ➤ Publish panel ➤ Publish. 
2. In the Publish dialog box, ensure the sheets that you want to remove are listed.
3. Under Sheets, select one or more sheets to remove. Click the Remove Sheets button.

## To remove all sheets from a drawing set for publishing

1. Click Output tab ➤ Publish panel ➤ Publish.
2. In the Publish dialog box, ensure the sheets that you want to remove are listed.
3. Right-click the selection. Click Remove All.

   **Note:** Removing all sheets cannot be undone.

## To reorder sheets in a drawing set for publishing

1. Click Output tab ➤ Publish panel ➤ Publish.
2. In the Publish dialog box, ensure the sheets that you want to reorder are listed.
3. Select a sheet. Click the Move Sheet Up or Move Sheet Down button.

   **Note:** Sheets in the drawing set are viewed or plotted in the order shown in the Publish dialog box.

## To copy sheets in a drawing set for publishing

1. Click Output tab ➤ Publish panel ➤ Publish.
2. In the Publish dialog box, ensure the sheets that you want to copy are listed.
3. Right-click the selection. Click Copy Selected Sheets.

   The copied drawing sheets are added and highlighted at the end of the sheet list. When a sheet is copied, its name is created by the addition of *-copy(n)* at the end of the original sheet name.

   For example, if you create one copy of a sheet called *Plumbing*, the copied sheet is called *Plumbing-Copy(1)*.

   Each time you copy the same sheet, the *n* is incremented by 1. By creating copies of a sheet, you can have different page setups and other settings for the same sheet.

## To rename sheets in a drawing set for publishing

1. Click Output tab ➤ Publish panel ➤ Publish.
2. In the Publish dialog box, ensure the sheets that you want to rename are listed.
3. Select a sheet in the Sheet list, and then do one of the following:
   - Right-click the selection. Click Rename Sheet.
   - Press F2.
4. Enter the new sheet name.

## To change the page setup of one sheet in a drawing set for publishing

1. Click Output tab ➤ Publish panel ➤ Publish. 
2. In the Publish dialog box, ensure the sheet for which you want to change the page setup is listed.
3. Select a sheet in the Sheet list.
4. Under Page Setup, select a page setup to apply to the drawing sheet.

## To change the page setup of one or more sheets in a drawing set for publishing

1. Click Output tab ➤ Publish panel ➤ Publish. 
2. In the Publish dialog box, ensure the sheets for which you want to change the page setups are listed.
3. Select one or more sheets in the list.
4. Right-click the selection. Click Change Page Setup.
5. In the Page Setup list, select a page setup to apply to the drawing sheets.

   **Note:** Change the page setup for each layout depending on your desired output. Model space page setups can only be applied to model space sheets; paper space page setups can only be applied to paper space sheets.

## To import a page setup from another drawing to apply to a drawing sheet for publishing

1. Click Output tab➤ Publish panel➤ Publish. 
2. In the Publish dialog box, ensure the sheet for which you want to change the page setup is listed.
3. Select a sheet in the Sheet list.
4. Under Page Setup, select Import from the list.
5. In the Import Page Setups dialog box, select the drawing whose page setups you want to import. Click Import.

## To publish multiple layouts in a drawing

1. In the drawing area, click a layout tab that you want to publish.
2. Press and hold the CTRL key, and then click the other layout tabs that you want to publish.
3. Right-click one of the selected layout tabs. Click Publish Selected Layouts.
4. In the Publish dialog box, change any settings for the selected layouts.
5. Click Publish.

# OBJECTIVE QUESTION

**1.** What is the alias for the construction line:

(a) CL (b) CLINE

(c) XLINE (d) CONLINE

**2.** What symbol used for relative co-ordinate system in AutoCAD

(a) @ (b) <

(c) > (d) #

**3.** The BISECT command comes under the

(a) Angle (b) Construction Line

(c) Polyline (d) Offset

**4.** What is the size of A4 size paper

(a) 210 mm X 297 mm (b) 210 mm X 148 mm

(c) 420 mm x 297 mm (d) None of these

**5.** Which of the following key combinations issues the ISOPLANE command?

(a) CONTROL and T or F4 (b) CONTROL and E or F5

(c) CONTROL and D or F6 (d) CONTROL and I or F7

**6.** The effect of QTEXT being ON is to?

(a) Place text directly in the drawing as defined

(b) Speed up drawing regeneration by replacing text with rectangles

(c) Use simplified text font to replace complex text font

(d) Allow automatic line spacing of textual input

**7.** Which one of the following key combinations will toggle COORDS?

(a) Either F7 or CONTROL and G (b) Either F6 or CONTROL and D

(c) Either F9 or CONTROL and B (d) Either F8 or CONTROL and O

**8.** To reverse the UNDO command the correct entry is?

(a) REDO (b) REDRAW

(c) Esc (d) U

**9.** Which one of the following is an AutoCAD relative polar co-ordinate

(a) @81,30 (b) 30<81

(c) @81<30 (d) None of these

**10.** How many entity colours does AutoCAD support?

(a) 255 (b) 16

(c) Unlimited (d) 64

**11.** Which one of the following BEST defines a "prototype" or "template" drawing?

(a) The drawing which is currently being edited by AutoCAD

(b) A drawing used to store a library of standard symbols

(c) A means of setting the initial drawing environment for new drawings

(d) A file which holds details of the display, digitizer, and plotters that AutoCAD is currently configured for

**12.** Which one of the following options of the UNDO command allows the undo facility to be disabled?

(a) AUTO (b) CONTROL

(c) END (d) GROUP

**13.** Which one of the following commands allows simultaneous pan and zoom?

(a) ZOOM DYNAMIC (b) ZOOM EXTENTS

(c) ZOOM CENTER (d) ZOOM PAN

**14.** Which of the following shapes CANNOT be drawn by the polygon command?

(a) Square (b) Hexagon

(c) Rectangle (d) Equilateral triangle

**15.** When is a space NOT interpreted as the enter key?

(a) When entering text.

(b) When using the PEDIT command.

(c) When selecting objects.

(d) The space is always an alternative to the enter key.

**16.** Which one of the following commands can be used to change the value of a system variable?

(a) CHANGE (b) DIMVAR

(c) SELECT (d) SETVAR

**17.** Which one of the following statements is False?

(a) Plines can be filled but not outlined.

(b) Plines can have either a consistent width or varying widths.

(c) Plines can be made from lines and arcs.

(d) Plines can be smoothed.

**18.** Which one of the following key combinations will toggle SNAP?

(a) Either F7 or CONTROL and G (b) Either F6 or CONTROL and D

(c) Either F9 or CONTROL and B (d) Either F8 or CONTROL and O

**19.** The following two commands used one after the other BOUNDARY then pick inside an area ERASE ALL R LAST produces which of these results

(a) Changes layer to the Boundary layer then erases all items on the last layer

(b) Calculates the area of the boundary and erases all the construction lines

(c) Draws a polyline that touches the extremes of the area then erases all the recently drawn lines

(d) Draws a polyline that touches the extremes of the area then erases all but that polyline

**20.** The effect of the EXPLODE command when applied to a block is to?

(a) Reduce a block to its constituent entities to allow editing.

(b) Return a block to its created scale and rotation.
(c) Allow the editing of a block with different X,Y factors.
(d) Place constituent entities all onto the current layer

**21.** Which of the following statements is true for AutoCAD?
(a) ZOOM ALL will reach beyond the drawing limits if an object is there.
(b) ZOOM ALL only reaches out to the drawing limits.
(c) There is not real difference between ZOOM ALL and ZOOM E.
(d) ZOOM ALL makes all objects visible irrespective of the layer visibility state.

**22.** Which one of the following is the AutoCAD filename extension used to indicate a compiled text font?
(a) HDX (b) SHP
(c) SHX (d) TXT

**23.** If the system variable MIRRTEXT is set to 1, text is
(a) Mirrored
(b) Not mirrored
(c) Not reproduced in the mirror image
(d) Mirrored and reversed

**24.** The shortcuts or command alias that allows us to key in L and AutoCAD responds with LINE are stored in a file named
(a) SHORT-CUT.TXT (b) ACAD.COM
(c) ACAD.PGP (d) ACAD.EXE

**25.** Which one of the following commands forces AutoCAD to revise the entire drawing taking into account the effect of changes within the system?
(a) CHANGE (b) REDO
(c) REDRAW (d) REGEN

**26.** Which one of the following system variables disables the prompt which asks for attribute values, and causes attributes to be set to their defaults?
(a) ATTDIA (b) ATTDISP
(c) ATTPROMPT (d) ATTREQ

**27.** Which one of the following is a correct statement regarding AutoCAD blocks?
(a) Blocks can only be inserted into a drawing if they already exist in that drawing.
(b) A block can have no more than ten attributes.
(c) The insert command looks first within the drawing for blocks and then to the disk.
(d) Every block has to have at least one attribute.

**28.** The command to scale a paper space viewport to half the drawn size is?
(a) Zoom 0.5x (b) Zoom 1/2x
(c) Zoom 2xp (d) zoom 0.5xp

**29.** One effect of setting the value of MIRRTEXT=0 is that?
(a) Text is displayed but not mirrored
(b) Text is displayed as a mirror
(c) Text is not displayed
(d) Only text can be mirrored

**30.** The MAXIMUM number of commands whose effect can be undone by the UNDO command is?
(a) 256
(b) 1000
(c) All the command issued since the drawing was first created
(d) All commands issued since the drawing was last loaded into the drawing editor

**31.** Which one of the following could be an AutoCAD drawing file?
(a) DWG.PLAN (b) PLAN.DWG
(c) DRAW.FLE (d) FILE.TXT

**32.** What snap mode is used to snap to a point located on an object that is the closest to the current location of the cursor?
(a) NODE (b) POINT
(c) NEAREST (d) CLOSEST
(e) ON

**33.** When AutoCAD finds the dimension or measures the object in a dimensioning command, it does not display the actual number. What characters does it display to represent the default measurement?
(a) < > (b) “ “
(c) { } (d) [ ]
(e) # #

**34.** When associative and non-associative dimensions are inserted, they insert points at the dimensions location. What are these points called?
(a) Definition Points (b) Dimension Points
(c) Extension Points (d) Insert Points
(e) Assoc Points

**35.** On what layer are the points in question 3 inserted on?
(a) The current layer (b) Layer Dimpoints
(c) Layer 0 (d) Layer Defpoints
(d) Layer Dimension

**36.** Which one of the following best describes one difference between an associative and an exploded dimension?
(a) Exploded Dimensions are inserted as blocks.
(b) Associative Dimensions are inserted as xrefs.
(c) Exploded Dimensions are inserted as xrefs.

(d) Associative Dimensions are inserted as blocks.
(e) Associative dimensions are inserted as individual objects.

**37.** What command is used to totally remove a block definition from the current drawing?

(a) WBLOCK (b) PURGE
(c) ERASE (d) REMOVE
(e) BLOCK

**38.** What command is used to change the name of a block definition in the current drawing?

(a) BLOCK (b) NAME
(c) WBLOCK (d) RENAME
(e) PURGE

**39.** What do you have to do to completely remove a reference file from the current drawing?

(a) Detach it using the XREF command.
(b) Detach it using the XBIND command.
(c) Erase it.
(d) Detach it using the BLOCK command.
(e) Detach it using the BIND command.

**40.** If a block has another block as one of its objects, what is the internal block called?

(a) Nested object (b) Block object
(c) Xref object (d) Bound object
(e) Wblock object

**41.** When the command XREF is used to bind an xref into the drawing, what object type(s) is the xref converted into?

(a) Individual objects (b) Lines
(c) A block (d) Plines
(e) Bound

**42.** What is the main advantage of an XREF object over a BLOCK?

(a) More accurate information.
(b) More reliable.
(c) Always kept up to date from a single source file.
(d) Faster to Plot.
(e) Less time to load the drawing.

**43.** What is the significance of using the command WBLOCK

(a) WBLOCK only works on blocks
(b) The block is written to disk and can be used later in other drawings.
(c) The block is written to the current drawing file only, saving disk space.
(d) The block can have attributes written to it later.

**44.** The effect of the EXPLODE command when applied to a block is to

(a) Reduce a block to its constituent entities to allow editing.

(b) Return a block to its created scale and rotation.

(c) Allow the editing of a block with different X, Y factors.

(d) Place constituent entities all onto the current layer.

**45.** The use of blocks allows libraries of standard parts to be developed and saved for later use. Blocks maybe stored

(a) On disk. (b) On disk, CDROM and the Internet.

(c) On disk and CDROM. (d) On disk and the Internet.

**46.** Which one of the following methods should be used to repeat a complex part in a drawing in order to

minimize file size

(a) use the COPY command (b) use the MIRROR command

(c) use the ARRAY command (d) create a BLOCK then use INSERT

**47.** Which one of the following is a correct statement regarding AutoCAD blocks

(a) Blocks can only be inserted into a drawing if they already exist in that drawing.

(b) A block can have no more than ten attributes.

(c) The insert command looks first within the drawing for blocks and then to the disk.

(d) Every block has to have at least one attribute.

**48.** When using the move command to move a single object by a given distance, which is the best of the following methods?

(a) Set Osnap to END, pick the object, pick a base point then pick on the end of another object

(b) Pick the object then key in the relative distance that it is to be moved

(c) Pick the object then key in the absolute distance that it is to be moved

(d) Pick the object, key in 'END' key in 'END' again then pick on the end of another object

**49.** When the breaking a circle the break will in the

(a) Anti clockwise direction (b) Clockwise direction

(c) Horizontal direction (d) Shortest direction

**50.** The effect of freezing a layer is to

(a) Make it invisible and prevent regeneration

(b) Make it invisible but allow regeneration

(c) Allow visibility and generation

(d) Display the layer but prevent editing of it.

**51.** Which of the following key combination does not invoke an I/O command

(a) Ctrl + P (b) Ctrl + F

(c) Ctrl + S (d) Ctrl +O

**52.** The purge command use for

(a) Deleting the layers and blocks (b) Deleting the object

(c) Moving the object (d) Copy the object

**53.** The attributes are use for

(a) Tagging the object (b) Define the object

(c) Assembly the object (d) Moving the object

**54.** The script is save as the file

(a) .scr (b) .dwg

(c) .xrf (d) .doc

**55.** The alias come under the which menu bar

(a) Tool (b) Draw

(c) Modify (d) Express

**56.** The slide format in AutoCAD

(a) .sld (b) .docx

(c) .scr (d) .text

**57.** The CP window are which colour

(a) Green (b) Blue

(c) Red (d) Yellow

**58.** Which type of selection window used in the stretch command

(a) CP (b) WP

(c) EP (d) CW

**59.** To convert the rectangle into the area by using command

(a) Region (b) Convert

(c) Polyline (d) Block

**60.** The ORTHO command use for

(a) Draw only Horizontal and Vertical line

(b) Draw the angular line

(c) Draw the vertical and angular line

(d) Draw the horizontal and angular line

**61.** Which is the reducing scale

(a) 1:2 (b) 2:1

(c) 3:1 (d) 1:1

**62.** Command prompt use for the

(a) Command input

(b) Command list view

(c) Command setting

(d) Command input detail and command input

**63.** The multiline use to draw
(a) The only two parallel lines (b) The vertical line
(c) The more than two parallel lines (d) The rectangle

**64.** The tool pallet use for the
(a) Import pre define drawing (b) Draw and save the new drawing
(c) Create the templates (d) Creating of block

**65.** The hatching line are always at
(a) $45^0$ (b) $60^0$
(c) $30^0$ (d) $90^0$

**66.** How many snap points does a circle have?
(a) 2 (b) 3
(c) 4 (d) 5

**67.** What is the meaning of TTR is circle command
(a) Tangent Tangent Radius (b) Trim Trim Radius
(c) Tool Tool Remove (d) None of these

**68.** How many way to draw the circle
(a) 3 (b) 4
(c) 5 (d) 6

**69.** DIMASSOC used for
(a) Change the dimensions settings (b) Change the Dimension text
(c) Change the valve of dimension (d) Change the dimension style

**70.** Leader are used for
(a) Define the dimension with some text
(b) Define the radius
(c) Define the diameter (d) Define the text

**71.** AutoCAD LT stand for
(a) AutoCAD Light (b) AutoCAD solid
(c) AutoCAD Little (d) AutoCAD 3D

**72.** Fill command used in
(a) To fill the Area (b) To fill the Donut
(c) To fill the Polyline (d) None of these

**73.** What is the short command used for the Match Properties
(a) MA (b) MP
(c) MR (d) MT

**74.** How many way to draw the Ellipse
(a) 2 (b) 3
(c) 4 (d) 5

**75.** By using which command create the concentric circle

(a) Offset (b) Circle

(c) Bisect (d) Copy

**76. What is first version of AutoCAD**

(a) R-1 (b) 200i

(c) 2000 (d) R-12

**77.** You can extrude the rectangle after

(a) Visibility (b) Region

(c) Regen (d) Redraw

**78.** To insert the external image into the drawing

(a) By using Xref

(b) By using Raster image References

(c) By using OLE object

(d) By using Image

**79.** Filter is

(a) Selection option (b) Copy option

(c) Use to Filter the line (d) None of these

**80.** Which command use to draw the isometric circle

(a) Ellipse (b) Circle

(c) Arc (d) None of these

**81.** The isometric view have the angle of

(a) $45^0$ (b) $60^0$

(c) $30^0$ (d) $90^0$

**82.** Logic gate used in

(a) Filter (b) Attributes

(c) Block (d) Script

**83.** Continues an interrupted script by using

(a) Resume command (b) SCR command

(c) SLD command (d) RS command

**84.** MVSETUP use for

(a) Sets up the specifications of a drawing

(b) Set up layout

(c) Unit setup

(d) Dimension setup

**85.** LIMITS use for

(a) Sets and controls the limits of the grid display in the current Model or layout tab

(b) Sets the global linetype scale factor

(c) Sets the current line weight, line weight display options, and line weight units
(d) None of these

**86.** How to writes objects or a block to a new drawing file
(a) WBLOCK (b) BLOCK
(c) BLOCK EDITOR (d) INSERT BLOCK

**87.** Oops command used to
(a) Restores erased objects (b) Erase the object
(c) Select the object (d) Move the object

**88.** Displays the coordinate of a location by
(a) ID command (b) UCS command
(c) WCS command (d) LIST command

**89.** Group is define as
(a) Creates and manages saved sets of objects called groups
(b) Create the object
(c) Manage the object
(d) Define name of object

**90.** CAL command used to
(a) Evaluates mathematical and geometric expressions
(b) Changes the properties of existing objects
(c) Closes the current drawing
(d) Converts objects to surfaces

**91.** Controls coordinate and angle display formats and precision by
(a) UNITS (b) CONTROL
(c) UCS (d) WCS

**92.** Which one is not in AutoCAD Unit system
(a) Millimeter (b) Decimal
(c) Engineering (d) Scientific

**93.** What is the use of REGEN Command
(a) Regenerates the entire drawing from the current viewport
(b) Regenerates the entire drawing into the block
(c) Regenerates the entire into the X-ref
(d) Regenerates the entire on the layout

**94.** RENDER used for
(a) Creates a photorealistic or realistically shaded image of a three-dimensional wireframe or solid model
(b) Colour the object
(c) Displays the Render Window without invoking a render task
(d) Provides visual cues for the apparent distance of objects

**95.** Changes the length of objects and the included angle of arcs by

(a) LENGTHEN (b) EXTEND

(c) JOIN (d) None of these

**96.** Calculates the area and perimeter of objects or of defined areas by

(a) AREA (b) INQUIRY

(c) LIST (d) ID

**97.** Displays an image slide file in the current viewport by using

(a) VSLIDE command (b) MSLIDE command

(c) SRCIPT command (d) RUN SCRIPT command

**98.** XCLIP command use

(a) Defines an x-ref or block clipping boundary and sets the front and back clipping planes

(b) Attaches an external reference to the current drawing

(c) Opens a selected drawing reference (x-ref) in a new window

(d) Breaks a compound object into its component objects

**99.** Exports a body object, solid, or region to an ACIS file name of command is

(a) ACISIN (b) ACISOUT

(c) INSTALL (d) DFXIN

**100.** ADCENTER is use for

(a) Manages and inserts content such as blocks, xrefs, and hatch patterns

(b) Closes Design Center

(c) Changes attribute information in a block

(d) Changes attribute information in a block

**101.** BASSOCIATE is used for

(a) Associates an action with a parameter in a dynamic block definition

(b) Adds an action to a dynamic block definition

(c) Obsolete. BACKGROUND functionality has been merged into the VIEW command

(d) Opens the Edit Block Definition dialog box and then the Block Editor

**102.** Edits attribute properties of a block definition by using

(a) BATTMAN (b) BEDIT

(c) BLIPMODE (d) BASE

**103.** For Bevels the edges of objects using by command

(a) CHAMFER (b) FILLET

(c) CIRCLE (d) CLOSE

**104.** For Provides a timed pause within a script by command

(a) DELAY (b) SCRIPT

(c) DBLIST (d) SLIDE

**105.** DIMEDIT command use for
(a) Edits dimension text and extension lines on dimension objects
(b) Removes associatively from selected dimensions
(c) Create or remove inspection dimensions
(d) Creates ordinate point dimensions

**106.** DIVIDE command use for
(a) Places evenly spaced point objects or blocks along the length or perimeter of an object
(b) Creates a distant light
(c) Changes the draw order of images and other objects
(d) Allows adjustment of a DWF underlay at the command prompt

**107.** For Changes the visibility of three-dimensional face edges by using command
(a) EDGE (b) ELEV
(c) EDGESURF (d) EXPLODE

**108.** FLATSHOT command use for
(a) Creates a 2D representation of all 3D objects in the current view
(b) Rounds and fillets the edges of objects
(c) Lists database information for each object in the drawing
(d) Sets the three-dimensional viewing direction

**109.** HYPERLINK command for
(a) Attaches a hyperlink to an object or modifies an existing hyperlink
(b) Controls the display of the hyperlink cursor, tooltips, and shortcut menu
(c) Fills an enclosed area or selected objects with a hatch pattern, solid fill, or gradient fill
(d) Controls the display properties of models

**110.** Which command used for Saves selected objects to a file in JPEG file format
(a) JPGOUT (b) .JPG
(c) SAVEJPG (d) JPEG

**111.** LSEDIT used for
(a) Has no effect except to preserve the integrity of scripts
(b) Sets the global linetype scale factor
(c) Closes the text window log file opened by LOGFILEON
(d) Turns on live sectioning for a selected section object.

**112.** Which command used for Sets the global linetype scale factor
(a) LTSCALE
(b) LTGLOB
(c) LTVIEW
(d) LSGV

**113.** Which command used for Calculates the mass properties of regions or 3D solids

(a) MASSPROP (b) MATCHPROP

(c) MASSCAL (d) MASSVIEW

**114.** Inscribed the circle define as

(a) The edge of polygon should lie on the circle

(b) The sides of polygon tangent to the circle

(c) Any object inside the circle

(d) Rectangle inside the circle

**115.** The arrowhead ratio should be

(a) 1:3 (b) 1:6

(c) 2:3 (d) 1:1

**116.** The text on the drawing sheet should be

(a) CAPITAL LETTER (b) Small letter

(c) Arial (d) Times new roman

**117.** PEDIT command also used to

(a) Convert line to polyline

(b) Edit line properties

(c) Convert the polyline properties

(d) None of these

**118.** How many method of orthographic projection

(a) 2 (b) 3

(c) 4 (d) 5

## ANSWERS

| 1 | 2 | 3 | 4 | 5 | 6 | 7 | 8 | 9 | 10 |
|---|---|---|---|---|---|---|---|---|---|
| (c) | (a) | (b) | (a) | (b) | (b) | (b) | (a) | (c) | (a) |
| **11** | **12** | **13** | **14** | **15** | **16** | **17** | **18** | **19** | **20** |
| (c) | (b) | (a) | (c) | (d) | (d) | (d) | (c) | (c) | (a) |
| **21** | **22** | **23** | **24** | **25** | **26** | **27** | **28** | **29** | **30** |
| (d) | (d) | (a) | (c) | (d) | (a) | (a) | (a) | (a) | (d) |
| **31** | **32** | **33** | **34** | **35** | **36** | **37** | **38** | **39** | **40** |
| (b) | (a) | (a) | (c) | (c) | (d) | (b) | (c) | (a) | (c) |
| **41** | **42** | **43** | **44** | **45** | **46** | **47** | **48** | **49** | **50** |
| (c) | (e) | (b) | (b) | (a) | (a) | (d) | (a) | (b) | (a) |
| **51** | **52** | **53** | **54** | **55** | **56** | **57** | **58** | **59** | **60** |
| (b) | (a) | (a) | (a) | (a) | (d) | (a) | (a) | (a) | (a) |
| **61** | **62** | **63** | **64** | **65** | **66** | **67** | **68** | **69** | **70** |
| (a) | (a) | (a) | (c) | (a) | (a) | (d) | (a) | (d) | (a) |
| **71** | **72** | **73** | **74** | **75** | **76** | **77** | **78** | **79** | **80** |
| (a) | (a) | (b) | (a) | (a) | (a) | (a) | (b) | (b) | (a) |
| **81** | **82** | **83** | **84** | **85** | **86** | **87** | **88** | **89** | **90** |
| (a) | (a) | (a) | (a) | (a) | (a) | (a) | (a) | (a) | (a) |
| **91** | **92** | **93** | **94** | **95** | **96** | **97** | **98** | **99** | **100** |
| (a) | (a) | (a) | (a) | (a) | (a) | (a) | (a) | (a) | (b) |
| **101** | **102** | **103** | **104** | **105** | **106** | **107** | **108** | **109** | **110** |
| (a) | (a) | (a) | (a) | (a) | (a) | (a) | (a) | (a) | (a) |
| **111** | **112** | **113** | **114** | **115** | **116** | **117** | **118** | | |
| (a) | (a) | (a) | (a) | (a) | (a) | (a) | (a) | | |

## EXERCISES

This **exercise is** to help you test out your basic **AutoCAD** skills.

### *Exercise* 1

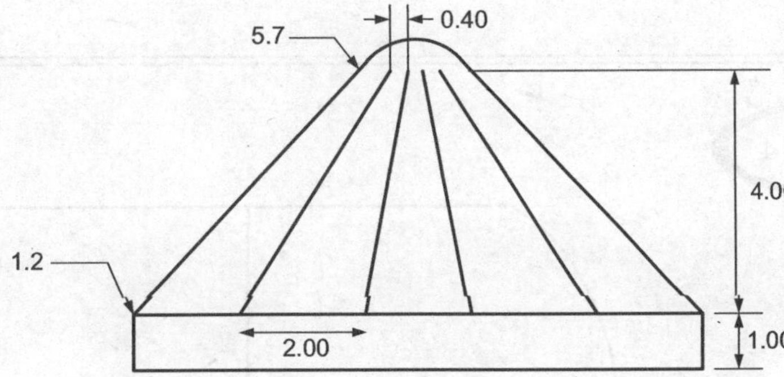


### *Exercise* 2

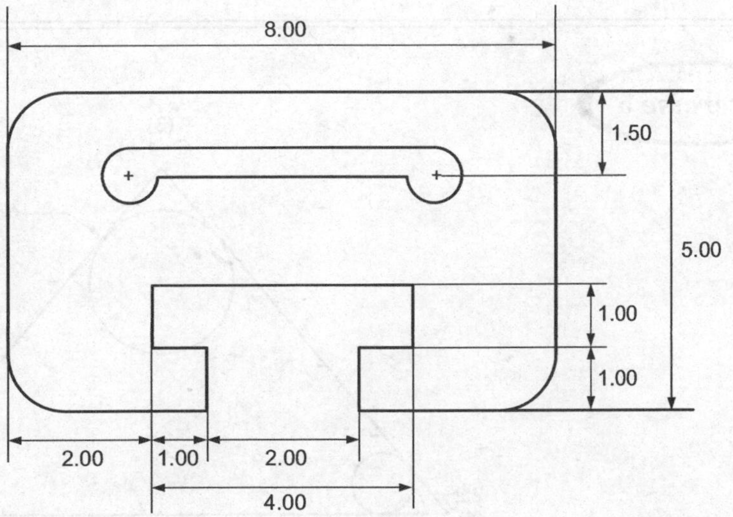

## Exercise 3

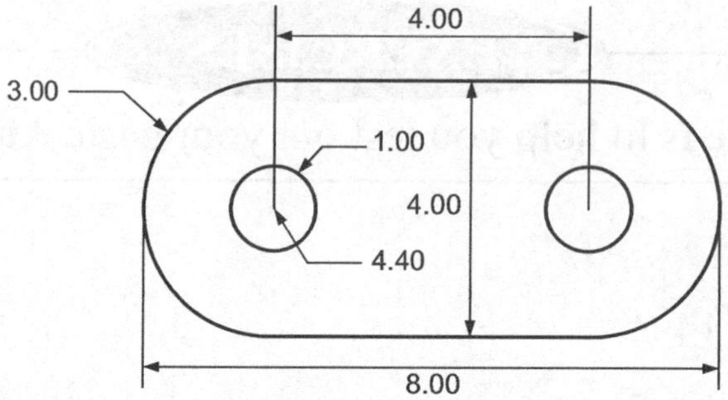


## Exercise 4

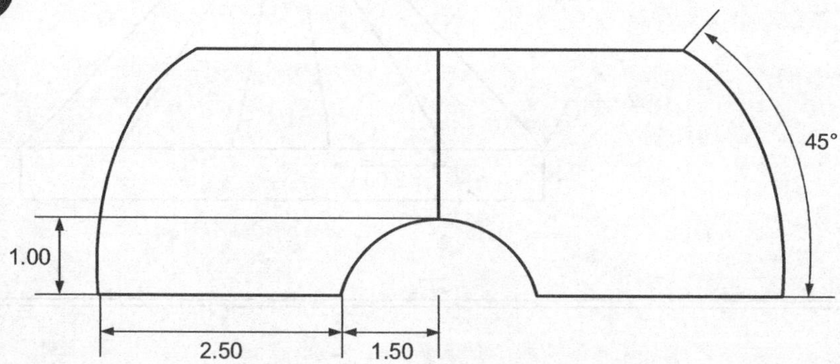


## Exercise 5

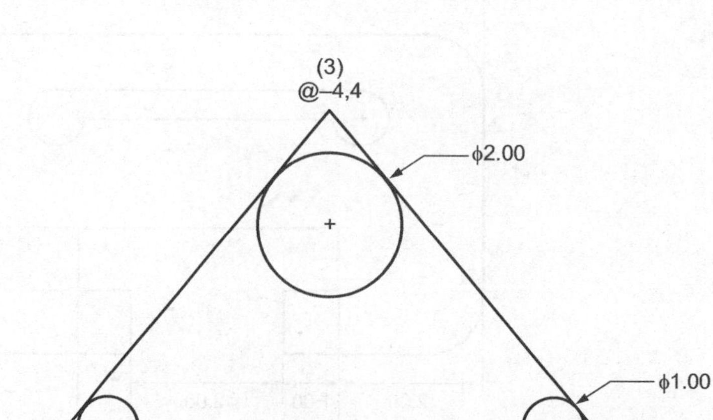

## Exercise 6

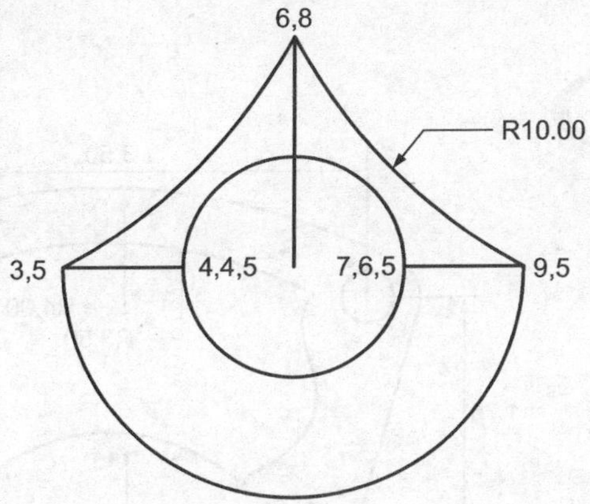


## Exercise 7

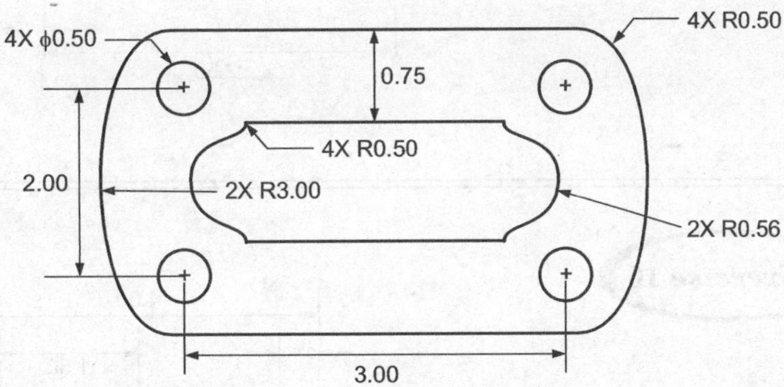


## Exercise 8

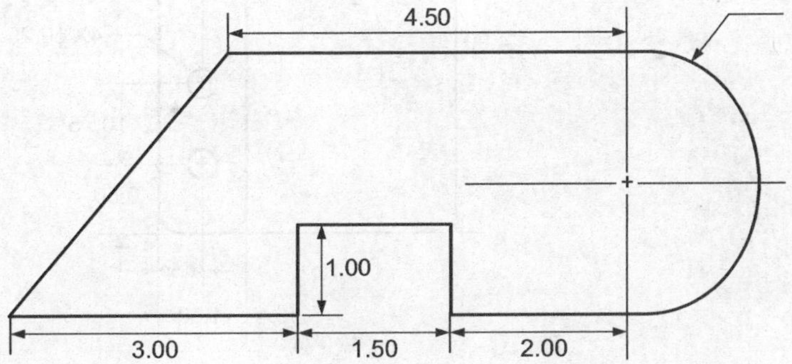

## Exercise 9

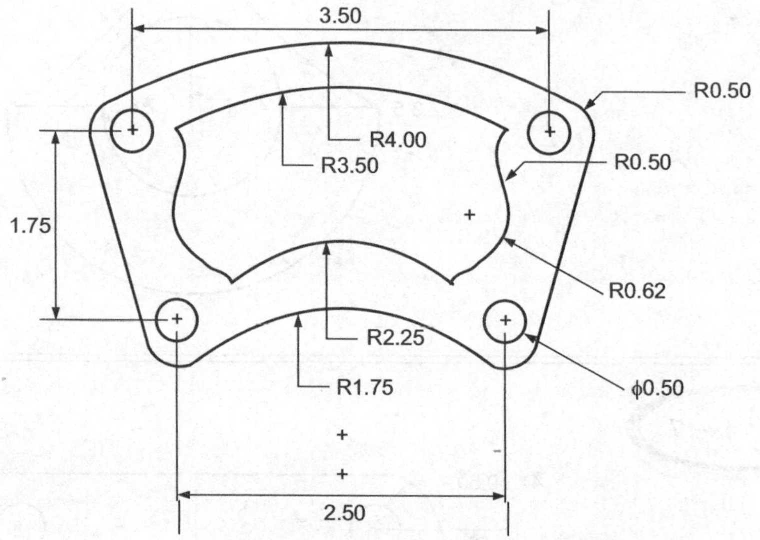


## Exercise 10

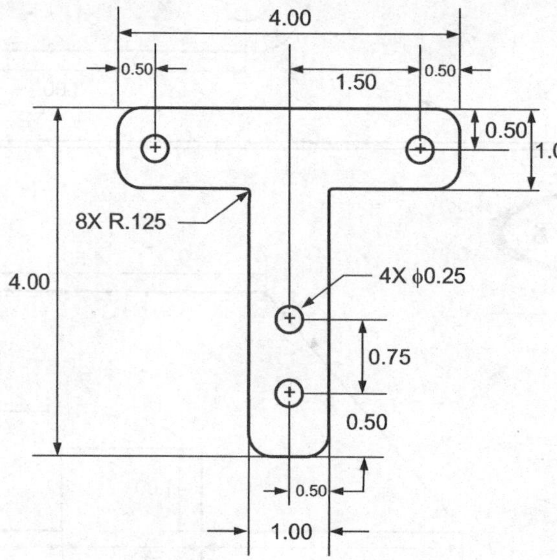

## Exercise 11

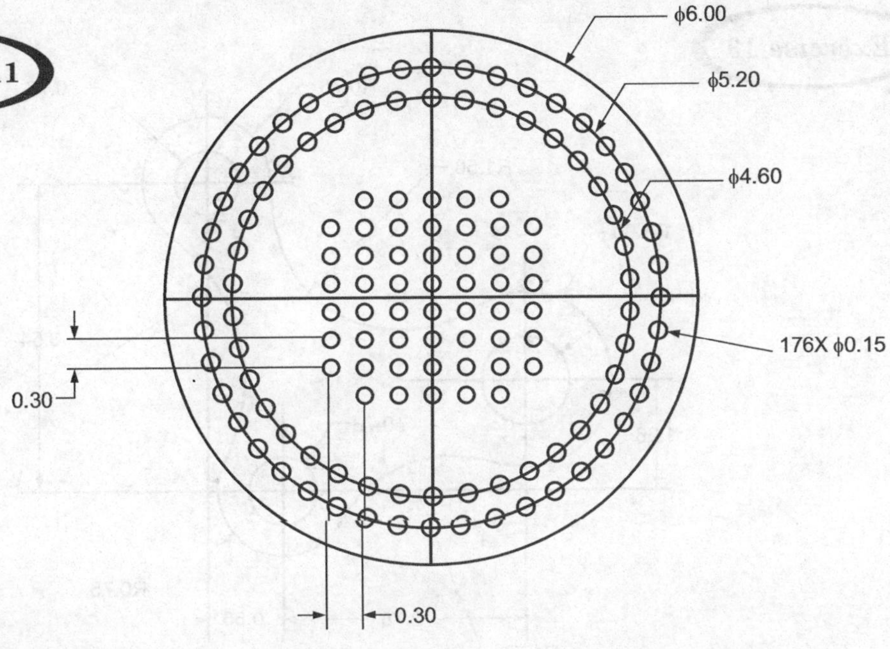


## Exercise 12

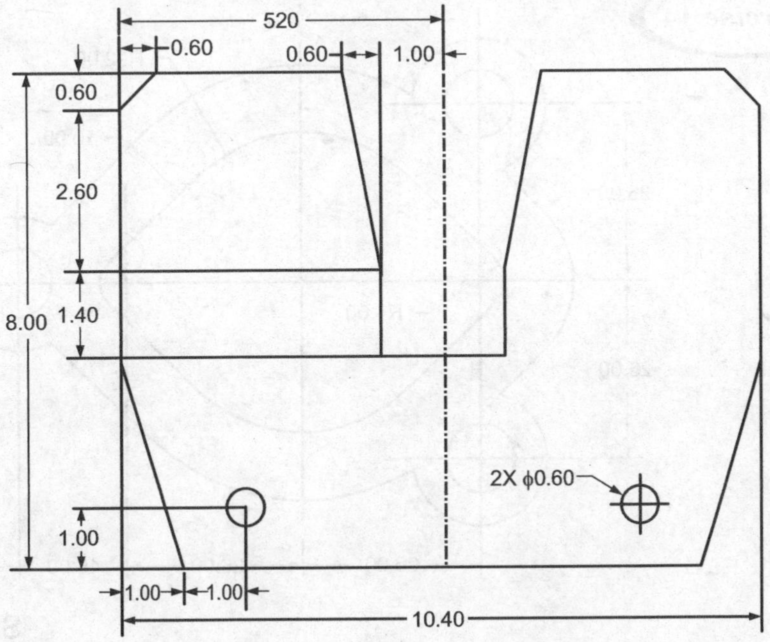

## *Exercise* 13

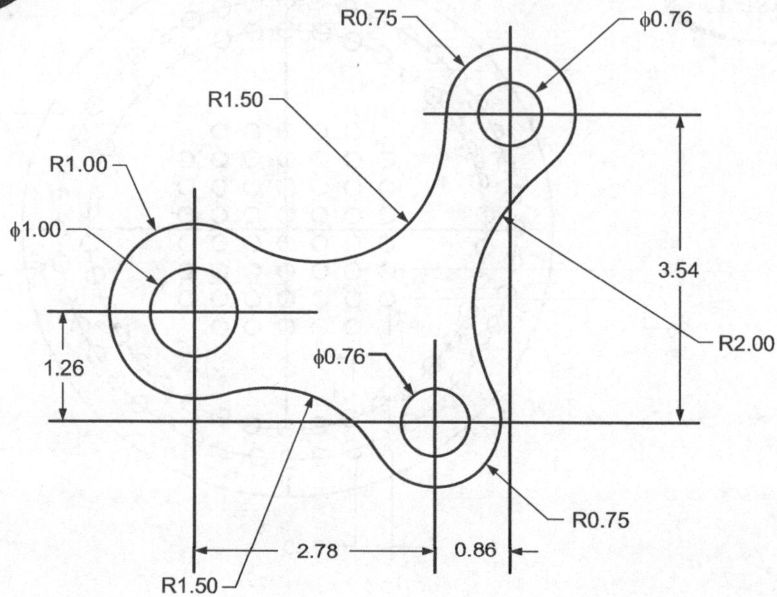


## *Exercise* 14

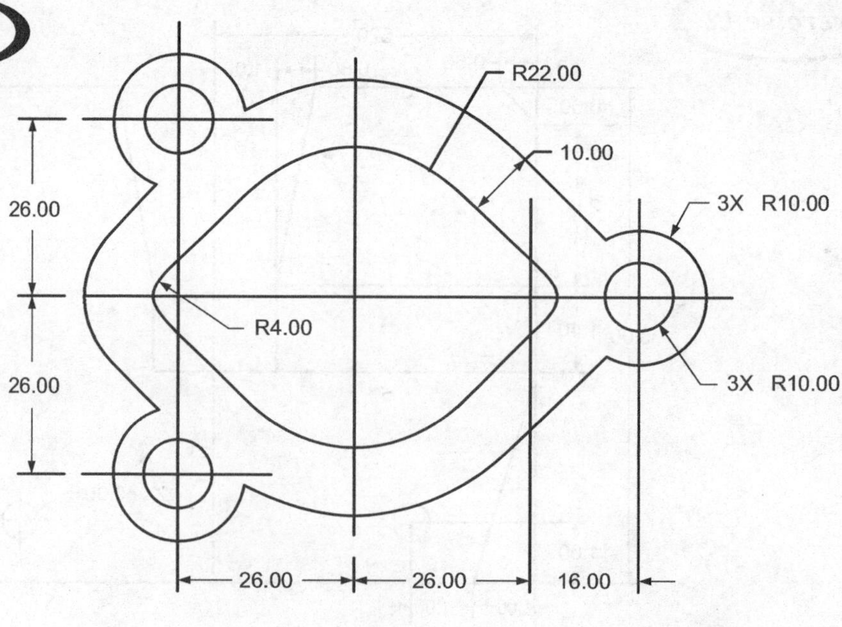

## *Exercise 15*

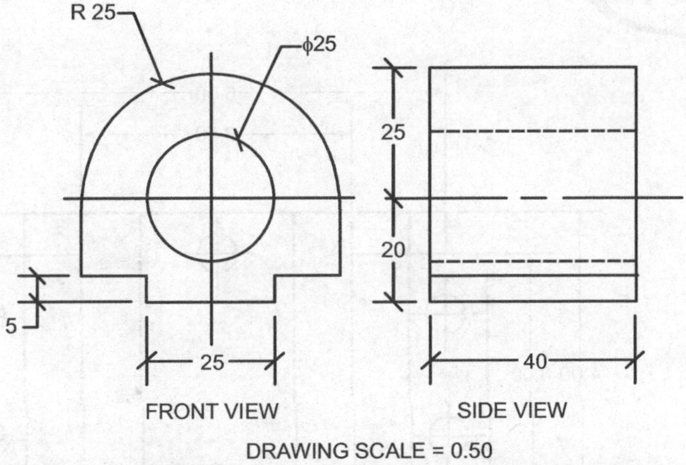


## *Exercise 16*

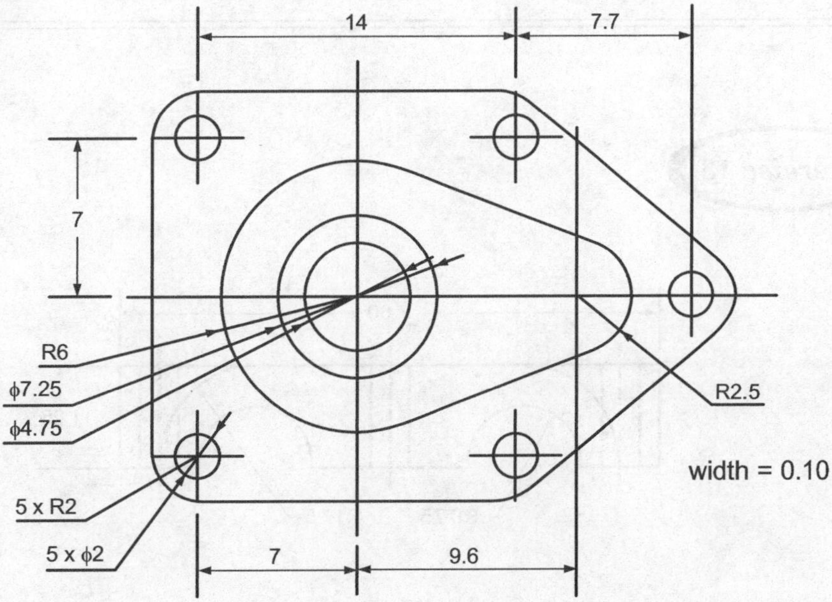

## Exercise 17

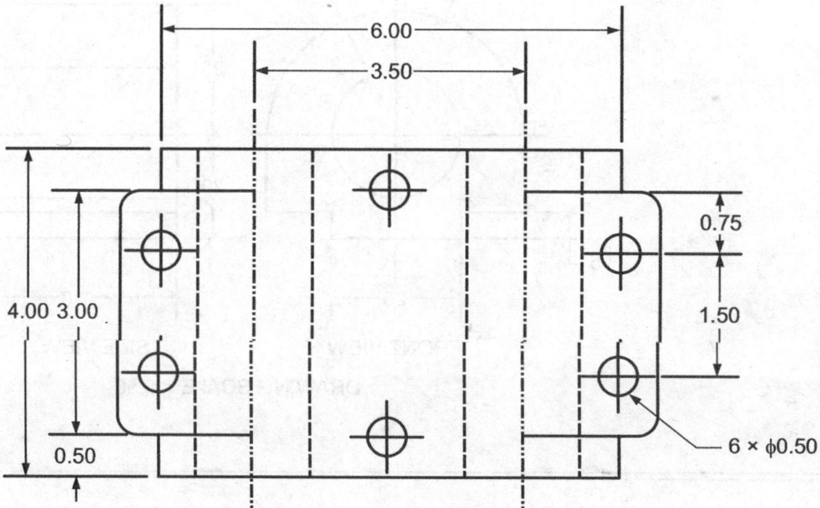


## Exercise 18

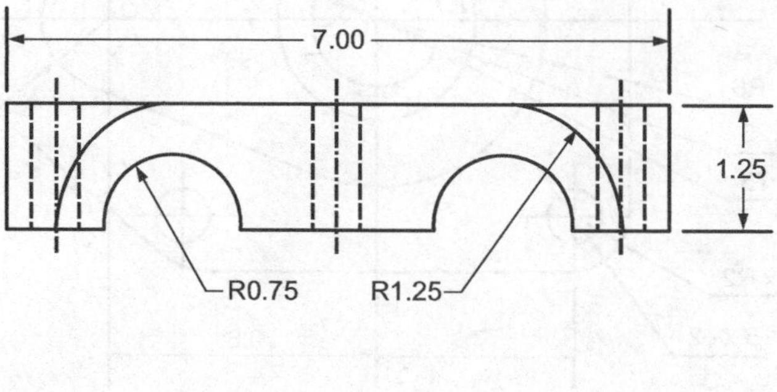

## *Exercise* 19

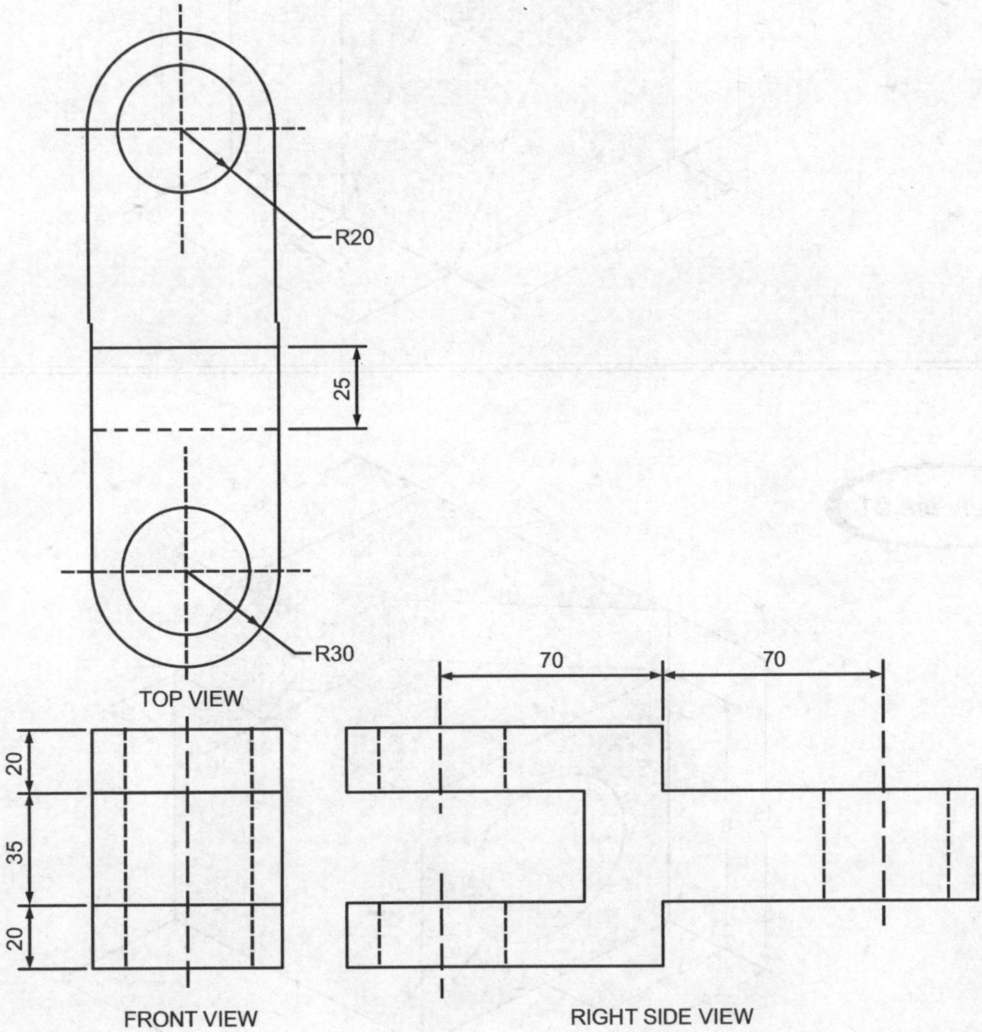

## Exercise 20

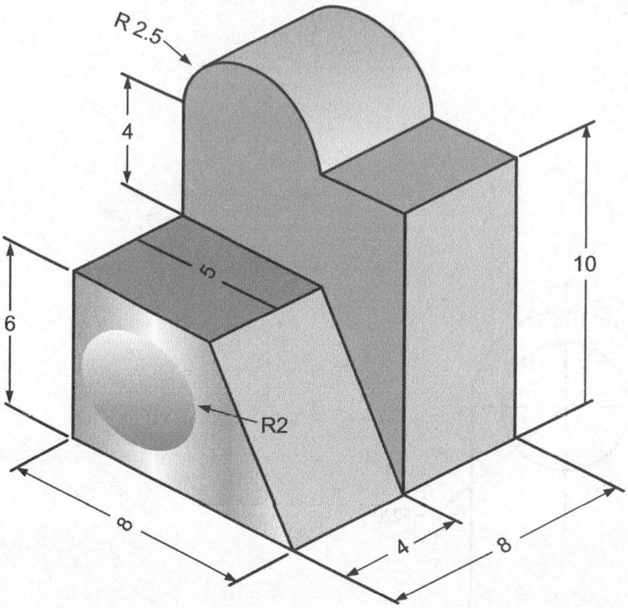


## Exercise 21

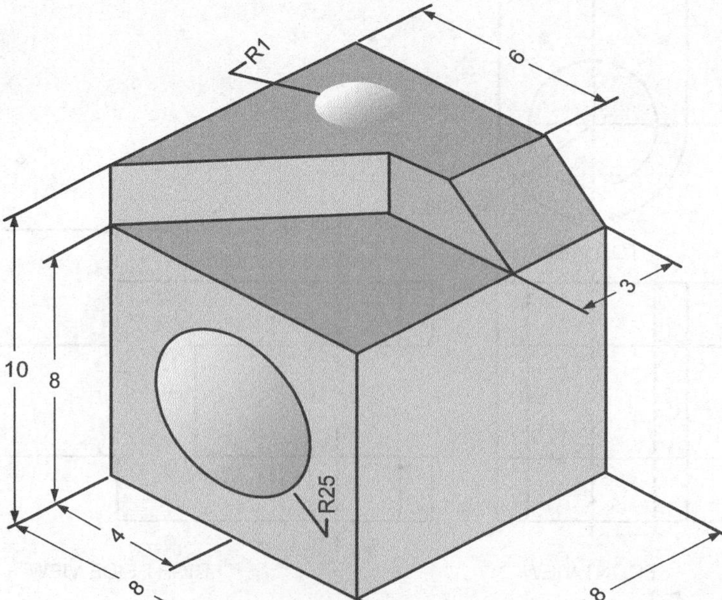

# Index

## M



## O



## P



## R



## S



## T